OECD Development Pathways

Multi-dimensional Review of Paraguay

VOLUME 1. INITIAL ASSESSMENT

OECD

DEVELOPMENT CENTRE

Please cite this publication as:
OECD (2018), *Multi-dimensional Review of Paraguay: Volume 1. Initial Assessment*, OECD Development Pathways, OECD Publishing, Paris.
http://dx.doi.org/10.1787/9789264301900-en

ISBN 978-92-64-30189-4 (print)
ISBN 978-92-64-30190-0 (PDF)
ISBN 978-92-64-30257-0 (ePub)

Series: OECD Development Pathways
ISSN 2308-734X (print)
ISSN 2308-7358 (online)

Photo credits: Cover © design by the OECD Development Centre.

Corrigenda to OECD publications may be found on line at: *www.oecd.org/about/publishing/corrigenda.htm*

Foreword

Economic growth matters, but is just one facet of development. Policy makers need to reconcile economic, social, and environmental objectives to ensure that their country's development path is sustainable and leads to durable improvements in citizens' well-being.

OECD Development Pathways *is a series that looks at development from the perspective of the multiple objectives it involves, beyond an exclusive focus on growth. It recognises well-being as part and parcel of development and helps governments identify the main constraints to more equitable and sustainable development by undertaking a multi-dimensional country review (MDCR). To meet their development ambition, governments need to understand the constraints they face and development comprehensive and well-sequenced strategies that take into account complementarities and trade-offs across policies. The MDCR methodology combines quantitative economic analysis, qualitative approaches including foresight, and participatory workshops that involve actors from the private and public sectors, civil society and academia.*

MDCRs are carried out in three distinct phases: initial assessment, in-depth analysis and recommendations, and from analysis to action. This approach allows for progressively deeper interaction between the OECD and the country and a mutual learning process about the country's specific challenges and opportunities. The Mutual Learning Group for Multi-dimensional Country Reviews gathers policy makers in development strategy from countries undertaking MDCRs and members of the OECD Development Centre to support the exchange of experience on shared development challenges.

Paraguay has embarked in a process to strengthen its ties with the OECD. This contributes to one of the three axes of its national development plan, which aims to enhance the inclusion of Paraguay in the global economy. Paraguay became a member of the OECD Development Centre in March 2016 and the Global Forum on Transparency and Exchange of Information for Tax Purposes in June 2016. As part of this whole-of-government effort, Paraguay is also implementing two OECD reviews – a Multi-dimensional Country Review and a Public Governance Review – and examining its national legislation and practices in light of OECD standards.

This report is the first volume of the MDCR of Paraguay. It delivers an overarching assessment of development in Paraguay and identifies the main constraints to sustainable and equitable development. The report is organised around the five pillars of the Sustainable Development Goals (Prosperity, People, Planet, Peace and Institutions and Partnerships). This reflects the ongoing effort to align OECD tools to the SDGs. It is also a reflection of the relevance of the SDGs for Paraguay. Paraguay's own National Development Plan is largely in line with the SDGs.

This report was approved for publication in November 2017 and uses the latest available data at the time of writing.

Acknowledgements

Multi-dimensional Country Reviews are the result of a collaborative effort of the OECD and the country under review. Work on the first phase of the MDCR of Paraguay was carried out jointly by the OECD Development Centre, the OECD Economics Department and the OECD Statistics Directorate, with support from the Technical Secretariat for Economic and Social Development Planning of Paraguay (*Secretaría Técnica de Planificación del Desarrollo Económico y Social*, STP).

Mario Pezzini, Director of the OECD Development and Special Counsellor to the Secretary-General on Development, guided the review, with contributions from Martine Durand, OECD Chief Statistician and Catherine Mann, OECD Chief Economist. The Multi-dimensional Country Review process is led by Jan Rieländer, Head of the MDCR Unit. Marco Mira d'Ercole, Head of Household Statistics and Progress Measurement in the OECD Statistics Directorate, and Patrick Lenain, Assistant Director at the OECD Economics Department, provided supervision.

The review was co-ordinated by Juan Ramón de Laiglesia (OECD Development Centre) and drafted by Rolando Avendaño (OECD Development Centre), Tim Bulman (OECD Development Centre), Mabel Gabriel (OECD Economics Department), Santiago González (OECD Statistics Directorate), and Juan R. de Laiglesia (OECD Development Centre). Deirdre Culley (OECD Development Centre) managed the workshop "Paraguay: Future, challenges and global environment" held in Asunción on 23 March 2017 and provided significant inputs to the report. The review also benefited from contributions made by Juan Carlos Benítez (Inter-American Development Bank), Céline Colin (OECD Development Centre), Adrien Moutel (OECD Economics Department), Carine Viac (OECD Development Centre), and Koffi Zougbede (PARIS21, OECD Statistics Directorate). William Herrera (OECD Development Centre), Toma Savitki (OECD Development Centre) and Astrid Pineda (OECD Development Centre) provided excellent research assistance.

The team is grateful for insightful comments provided by Martha Baxter (OECD Development Centre), Jorge Carbonell (OECD Global Relations Secretariat), David Goessmann (OECD Governance Directorate), José Rene Orozco (OECD Development Centre) and Katherine Scrivens (OECD Statistics Directorate) as well as by participants in the revision sessions held on 4 and 5 July in Asunción. The report incorporates remarks made during the review of the report by the Mutual Learning Group for Multi-dimensional Country Reviews on its meeting held 24 October 2017. The review was led by Marcelo Scaglione (Undersecretary of State and representative to the OECD, Argentina) and Paulo Areosa Feio (Counsellor, Portuguese delegation to the OECD). The team is also grateful for boxes and contributions from OECD colleagues, including Catalina Covacevich (Education and Skills Directorate).

The Multi-dimensional Country Review of Paraguay is made possible by the financial contribution of the European Union. The team extends its gratitude to the Delegation of the European Union to Paraguay for its support throughout the process and the insights of its staff into the development of Paraguay.

The Review benefited greatly from the support of Minister José Molinas Vega, Executive Secretary of the Technical Secretariat for Economic and Social Development Planning (STP) of Paraguay, and his staff. Emiliano Fernández (Deputy Minister of the STP) and his team have been valuable counterparts throughout the process. The contributions of Claudia Martínez, Marcos Martínez, and Federico Sosa were particularly valuable for ensuring the pertinence of the report and continuous interaction between the OECD team and Paraguayan authorities. The team is also grateful to Florencia Villalba, Director for Territorial Development, for her efforts to acquaint them with the regions of Paraguay, and to Carlos Alberto Giménez, mayor of Carayaó, and Carlos Giménez, mayor of Choré, for their hospitality. The team extends its gratitude to the Directorate-General for Surveys, Censuses and Statistics (DGEEC), and to Elizabeth Barrios, Director-general of DGEEC and her staff for providing primary data used in this report and completing the questionnaire used for the assessment of statistical capacity, and to the Central Bank of Paraguay for providing data and information on their statistical practices. Other ministries and institutions provided useful inputs and contributions to the review throughout the production of this report, namely the Ministry of Finance, its State Secretariat for Tax Administration, its Under-Secretariat for Economy and their staff, the Ministry of Agriculture, the Ministry of Education and Culture, the Ministry of Foreign Affairs, the Ministry for Health and Social Well-Being (MSPBS), the Ministry of Industry and Commerce, the Ministry of Justice, the Ministry of Labour, Employment and Social Security (MTESS), the Ministry of Public Works (MOPC), the Ministry for Women, the National Anti-Corruption Secretariat (SENAC), the National Council for Science and Technology (CONACYT), the National Competition Council (CNC), the National Development Bank (BNF), the National Directorate for Public Procurement (DNCP), the National Electrical Administration (ANDE), the National Land and Rural Development Institute (INDERT), the National Secretariat for Tourism (SENATUR), the National Secretariat for Youth and Adolescence (SNNA), the National Securities Commission (CNV), the Secretariat for the Environment (SEAM), the Secretariat for Housing (SENAVITAT), the Secretariat for Public Administration (SFP), the Secretariat for Social Action (SAS), and the Social Security Institute (IPS).

Other institutions, agencies, international organisations and members of civil society and academia also provided support though inputs and discussion on the review. The National Country Strategy Team (ENEP), its co-ordinator, Jacinto Santa María, and its members are thanked for their inputs and participation in the participatory process of the review. The review also received valuable insights from the Association of Paraguayan Banks (ASOBAN), the Association of Small and Medium Enterprises (AMPYME), the Chamber of Paraguayan Exporters (CAPEX), the Center for Analysis and Diffusion of the Paraguayan Economy (CADEP), Continental, Gladys Banegas, Investor, Itaú Bank, Martha La Fuente, the National Chamber of Commerce and Services (CNCSP), the National Workers Confederation (CNT), Oxfam, the Paraguayan Centre for Information and Resources (CIRD) and the Paraguayan Industrial Union (UIP), the Corporación Andina de Fomento (CAF), the Inter-American Development Bank, the International Monetary Fund, the United Nations Development Programme, USAID, and the World Bank.

The team is grateful for Stephen Jessel for editing the manuscript and to the OECD Development Centre's Communications and Publications Unit, especially Delphine Grandrieux, Aida Buendía, Elizabeth Nash and Vanda Lintott, for their support in editing, laying out and producing the report.

* *This publication was produced with the financial support of the European Union. Its contents are the sole responsibility of the OECD Development Centre and do not necessarily reflect the views of the European Union.*

Table of contents

Tables

Figures

Boxes

Abbreviations and acronyms

AEC	Asociación de Estados del Caribe (*Association of Caribbean States*)
AFD	Agencia Financiera de Desarrollo (*Financial Development Agency*)
AIDIS	Asociación Interamericana de Ingeniería Sanitaria y Ambiental (*Inter-American Association of Sanitary and Environmental Engineering*)
AIP	Agencia de Información Paraguaya (*Paraguayan Information Agency*)
ALIDE	Asociación Latinoamericana de Instituciones Financieras para el Desarrollo (*Latin American Association of Financial Institutions for Development*)
ANDE	Administración Nacional de Electricidad (*National Electricity Administration*)
ANNP	Administración Nacional de Navegación y Puertos (*National Administration of Navigation and Ports*)
BCP	Banco Central del Paraguay (*Central Bank of Paraguay*)
BECAL	Programa Nacional de Becas de Postgados en el Exterior Don Carlos Antonio López (*National Program of Postgraduate Scholarships Abroad Don Carlos Antonio López*)
BEPS	Base Erosion and Profit Shifting
BIRF	Banco Internacional de Reconstrucción y Fomento (*International Bank for Reconstruction and Development*)
BNF	Banco Nacional de Fomento (*National Development Bank*)
CADEP	Centro de Análisis y Difusión de la Economía Paraguya (*Center for Analysis and Dissemination of the Paraguayan Economy*)
CAF	Corporación Andina de Fomento – Banco de Desarrollo de América Latina (*Andean Development Corporation – Development Bank of Latin America*)
CAGR	Compound Annualised Growth Rate
CAIT	Climate Analysis Indicators Tool
CAN	Censo Agropecuario Nacional (*National Agriculture Census*)
CCT	Conditional Cash Transfer
CEA	Consorcio de Ganaderos para Experimentación Agropecuaria (*Livestock Center for Agricultural Experimentation*)
CEA	Conferencia Estadística de las Américas (*Statistical Conference of the Americas*)
CEACR	Committee of Experts on the Application of Conventions and Recommendations

CEDLAS	Centro de Estudios Distributivos, Laborales y Sociales (*Centre for Distributive, Labour and Social Studies*)
CEPEJ	European Commission for the Efficiency of Justice
CEPII	Centre d'Études Prospectives et d'Informations Internationales (*Center for Prospective Studies and International Information*)
CIAT	Centro Interamericano de Administraciones Tributarias (*Inter-American Centre of Tax Administrations*)
CNEP	Consejo nacional de empresas públicas (*National Council of Public Enterprises*)
CO_2	Carbon dioxide
COMJIB	Conferencia de Ministros de Justicia de los Países Iberoamericanos (*Conference of Ministers of Justice of the Ibero-American countries*)
CONACOM	Comisión Nacional de Competencia (*National Competition Commission*)
CONACYT	Consejo Nacional de Ciencia y Tecnología (*National Council for Science and Technology*)
CONATEL	Comisión Nacional de Telecomunicaciones (*National Telecommunications Commission*)
CPI	Consumer Price Index
CREMA	Contratos de Rehabilitación y Mantenimiento (*Rehabilitation and Maintenance Contracts*)
DECE	Dirección de Evaluación de la Calidad Educativa (*Directorate for Evaluation of Educational Quality*)
DGEEC	Dirección General de Estadística, Encuestas y Censos (*General Directorate of Statistics, Surveys and Censuses*)
DIBEN	Dirección de Beneficencia y Ayuda Social (*Directorate for charity and social assistance*)
DINAC	Dirección Nacional de Aeronáutica Civil (*National Directorate of Civil Aeronautics*)
DINATRAN	Dirección Nacional de Transporte (*National Directorate of Transport*)
DNCP	Dirección Nacional de Contrataciones Públicas (*National Directorate of Public Procurement*)
DSIP	Dirección del Sistema de Inversión Pública (*Directorate of the Public Investment System*)
ECE	Encuesta Continua de Empleo (*Continuous Labour Force Survey*)
ECI	Economic Complexity Index
ECLAC	United Nations Economic Commission for Latin American and the Caribbean
e-GDDS	Enhanced General Data Dissemination System
EIEP	Encuesta de Innovación Empresarial de Paraguay (*Entrepreneurial Innovation Survey*)
EIF	Encuesta sobre Inclusión Financiera (*Survey on Financial Inclusion*)
EMIS	Education Management Information System

ENEP	Equipo Nacional de Estrategia País (*National Team of Country Strategy*)
EPH	Encuesta Permanente de Hogares (*Permanent Household Survey*)
EPL	Employment Protection Legislation
EPP	Ejército del Pueblo Paraguayo (*Army of the Paraguayan People* [rebel group])
EU	European Union
EUR	Euro
FAO	Food and Agriculture Organization of the United Nations
FAOSTAT	Food and Agriculture Organization Corporate Statistical Database
FARC	Fuerzas Armadas Revolucionarias de Colombia (*Colombian Revolutionary Armed Forces* [rebel group])
FDI	Foreign Direct Investment
FEEI	Fondo para la excelencia de la educación y la investigación (*Fund for excellence in Education and Research*)
FOCEM	Fondo para la Convergencia Estructural del MERCOSUR (*Fund for the Structural Convergence of MERCOSUR*)
FONACIDE	Fondo Nacional de Inversión Pública y de Desarrollo (*National Fund for Public Investment and Development*)
FONAVIS	Fondo Nacional de la Vivienda Social (*National Fund for Social Housing*)
FRL	Fiscal Responsibility Law
GDP	Gross Domestic Product
GERD	Gross expenditure on research and development
GFP	Global Forum on Productivity
GHG	Greenhouse Gas
GIZ	Deutsche Gesellschaft für Internationale Zusammenarbeit GmbH (*German Corporation for International Cooperation GmbH*)
GNESD	Global Network on Energy for Sustainable Development
GNI	Gross National Income
HHI	Herfindahl-Hirschmann Index
ICSE	International Standard Classification of Status in Employment
ICT	Information and Communication Technology
IDB	Inter-American Development Bank
IDD	Income Distribution Database
IDEA	Institute for Democracy and Electoral Assistance
IEA	International Energy Agency
IFC	International Finance Corporation
IGME	Inter-Agency Group for Child Mortality Estimation
ILO	International Labour Organization
IMF	International Monetary Fund
INCOOP	National Co-operative Institute

INDERT	Instituto Nacional de Desarrollo Rural y de la Tierra (*National Institute for Land and Rural Development*)
INFONA	Instituto Forestal Nacional (*National Forest Institute*)
INFRALATAM	Database on investment in economic infrastructure in Latin America and the Caribbean
IOSCO	International Organization of Securities Commissions
IPS	Instituto de Previsión Social (*Social Security Institute*)
IRACIS	Impuesto sobre la Renta Comercial, Industrial o de Servicios (*Tax on Commercial, Industrial or Services Income*)
IRAGRO	Impuesto sobre la Renta de las Actividades Agropecuarias (*Income Tax for Agricultural Activities*)
IRM	Independent Reporting Mechanism
ISC	Impuesto Selectivo al Consumo (*Selective Consumption Tax*)
ISCED	International Standard Classification of Education
ISSAT	International Security Sector Advisory Team
IT	Information Technology
ITU	International Telecommunications Union
KILM	Key Indicators of the Labour Market
LAC	Latin America and the Caribbean
LAIA	Latin American Integration Association
LLECE	Laboratorio Latinoamericano de Evaluación de la Calidad de la Educación (*Latin American Laboratory for Education Quality Assessment*)
MDCR	Multi-dimensional Country Review
MEC	Ministerio de Educación y Cultura (*Ministry for Education and Culture*)
MECIP	Modelo Estándar de Control Interno de las Entidades Públicas Paraguayas (*Standard Model of Internal Control of Paraguayan Public Entities*)
MERCOSUR	Mercado Común del Sur (*Southern Common Market*)
MH	Ministerio de Hacienda (*Ministry of Finance*)
MIC	Ministerio de Industria y Comercio (*Ministry of Industry and Commerce*)
MOPC	Ministerio de Obras Públicas y Comunicaciones (*Ministry of Public Works and Communications*)
MSPBS	Ministerio de Salud Pública y Bienestar Social (*Ministry of Public Health and Social Well-being*)
MTESS	Ministerio de Trabajo, Empleo y Seguridad Social (*Ministry of Labour, Employment and Social Security*)
MW	Megawatts
NDP	Net Domestic Product
NEET	Not in education, employment or training
NPPC	National Plan for the Prevention of Corruption
NSS	National Statistical System

OBEI	Observatorio de Economía Internacional (*Observatory of International Economy*)
ODA	Official Development Assistance
OECD	Organisation for Economic Co-operation and Development
OFIP	Observatorio Fiscal y Presupuestario (*Fiscal and Budgetary Observatory*)
OGP	Open Government Partnership
OLADE	Organización Latinoamericana de Energía (*Latin American Energy Organization*)
OP	Operational Programmes
PAHO	Pan American Health Organization
PGR	Procurador General de la República (*Attorney General of the Republic*)
PISA	Programme for International Student Assessment
PISA-D	PISA for Development
PIT	Personal Income Tax
PLRA	Partido Liberal Radical Auténtico (*Authentic Radical Liberal Party*)
PM	Particulate Matter
PMR	Product Market Regulation
PND	Plan Nacional de Desarrollo (*National Development Plan*)
PPCDAm	Action Plan for Deforestation Prevention and Control in the Legal Amazon
PPP	Purchasing Power Parity
PPP	Public-Private Partnership
PREAL	Programa de Promoción de la Reforma Educativa en América Latina y el Caribe (*Program for the Promotion of Educational Reform in Latin America and the Caribbean*)
PROCIENCIA	Programme for the development of science and technology
PROT	Planos Regionais de Ordemanmento do Território (*Regional Development Plans*)
PWT	Penn World Tables
PYG	Paraguayan Guaraní
R&D	Research and Development
REDIEX	Red de Exportaciones e Inversiones (*Export and Investment Network*)
ROA	Return on assets
RSU	Residuos sólidos urbanos (*urban solid waste*)
SAS	Secretaría de Acción Social (*Social Action Secretariat*)
SCJ	Superior Council of the Judiciary
SDDS	Special Data Dissemination Standard
SEAM	Secretaría del Ambiente (*Secretariat of the Environment*)
SEDLAC	Socio-Economic Database for Latin America and the Caribbean
SENAC	Secretaría Nacional Anticorrupción (*National Anti-corruption Secretariat*)

SENACSA	Servicio Nacional de Calidad y Salud Animal (*National Service for Animal Health and Quality*)
SENADIS	Secretaría Nacional por los Derechos Humanos de las Personas con Discapacidad (*National Secretariat for the Human Rights of Persons with Disabilities*)
SENASA	Servicio Nacional de Saneamiento Ambiental (*National Service of Environmental Sanitation*)
SENAVE	Servicio Nacional de Calidad y Sanidad Vegetal y de Semillas (*National Service for Plant and Seed Quality and Health*)
SENAVITAT	Secretaría Nacional de la Vivienda y el Hábitat (*Secretariat for Housing and Habitat*)
SET	Subsecretaría de Estado de Tributación (*Undersecretary of State for Taxation*)
SFN	Servicio Forestal Nacional (*National Forest Service*)
SFP	Secretaría de la Función Pública (*Civil Service Sercretariat*)
SGP +	Generalised System of Preferences Plus
SICCA	Sistema Integrado Centralizado de la Carrera Administrativa (*Centralized Integrated System of the Administrative Career*)
SIEC	Sistema de Información de Estadística Continua (*Continuous Statistical Information System*)
SII	Sistema de Intercambio de Información (*Information Exchange System*)
SINAFOCAL	Sistema Nacional de Formación y Capacitación Laboral (*National training and skill formation system*)
SNA	System of National Accounts
SNEPE	Sistema Nacional de Evaluación del Proceso Educativo (*National system for the evaluation of educational processes*)
SNIP	Sistema Nacional de Inversión Pública (*National Public Investment System*)
SNPP	Sistema Nacional de Promoción Profesional (*National professional promotion system*)
SOE	State-owned enterprise
STP	Secretaría Técnica de Planificación (*Technical Secretariat of Planning*)
SUACE	Sistema unificado de apertura y cierre de empresas (*Unified system for opening and closing businesses*)
TERCE	Tercer estudio regional comparativo y explicativo (*Third Regional Comparative and Explanatory Study*)
TFP	Total Factor Productivity
UIS	UNESCO Institute of Statistics
UN	United Nations
UNA	Universidad Nacional de Asunción (*National University of Asunción*)
UNCAC	United Nations Convention Against Corruption
UNCTAD	United Nations Conference on Trade and Development

UNDP	United Nations Development Programme
UNESCO	United Nations Educational, Scientific and Cultural Organization
UNICEF	United Nations Children's Fund
UNODC	United Nations Office on Drugs and Crime
US	United States of America
USD	United States Dollars
USF	Unidades de salud de la familia (*Family healthcare units*)
UTA	Unidades de Transparencia y Anticorrupción (*Transparency and Anti-Corruption Units*)
VAT	Value-added tax
VUE	Ventanilla Única del Exportador (*One-stop shop for the exporter*)
WEF	World Economic Forum
WEO	World Economic Outlook
WHO	World Health Organization
WLT	World Land Trust
WWF	World Wildlife Fund

Editorial

Paraguay's economic and social progress has accelerated since 2003. After a prolonged period of economic and political instability, the country has experienced stronger growth than most countries in the region, with GDP growing at 4% in 2016 and showing resilience in face of the difficulties of its neighbours and key trading partners. Building on strong economic performance, the country has more than halved its poverty rate and expanded access to health and education.

The reforms undertaken since the democratic transition in 1989 set the stage for the country to make the most of the tailwinds brought about by the increase in commodity prices during the 2000s. They helped establish sound macroeconomic management, culminating in the adoption of an inflation-targeting regime in 2011 and the fiscal responsibility law of 2013. The country also opened up, joining Mercosur and gradually extending its network of free-trade agreements.

However, ensuring sustained economic and social progress in the medium term will require further reforms to help steer the economy's structural transformation and deliver more inclusive development with a strong focus on people's well-being. Inequality remains a major challenge for Paraguay. Despite recent improvements, income inequality remains higher than the regional average. Marked inequalities, especially between urban and rural areas, also characterise quality of life, including in access to social insurance or to clean water and sanitation. GDP growth and exports are still largely dependent on the highly productive commercial agriculture sector, which creates relatively few jobs. Low diversification partly explains the high level of informality in the country that, in turn, fuels inequality and weakens state capacity.

Paraguay will need to overcome seven key constraints to bring about such transformation. The infrastructure gap constrains new investment and leads to a territorial concentration in economic activity. A systemic approach to increasing educational attainment and forming more relevant skills is also necessary. Further efforts are necessary to strengthen governance so that public affairs are, and are perceived to be, efficient and fair. Unlocking finance for development through domestic resource mobilisation and crowding in private investment can help sustain economic growth. Informality has led to a fragmented social protection system, which limits the efficiency of public action to reduce poverty, provide public services or redistribute. Inequality has a strong territorial component, which calls for designing a territorial approach to development policy to build upon local development plans and the comparative advantages and characteristics of each territory. Finally, Paraguay will need to update its statistical system for generating the evidence that would allow accurately and timely monitoring of its development.

Delivering on Paraguay's ambition for 2030, as set out in its National Development Plan, requires an ambitious reform agenda. This Multi-dimensional Country Review mobilises expertise from across the OECD to help the country meet its objectives. This first volume presents a diagnosis of the main impediments to Paraguay's development. Subsequent volumes will provide in-depth analysis of the main constraints and outline policy recommendations to address them.

Mario Pezzini
Director of the OECD Development Centre and Special Advisor to the Secretary-General on Development

Martine Durand
OECD Chief Statistician
Director of the Statistics Directorate

Alvaro Pereira
OECD Chief Economist a.i.
Head of the Economics Department

Facts and figures of Paraguay

Numbers in parentheses refer to the OECD average

The land, people and electoral cycle

Population (thousands - 2015)[a]	6 756	Official languages	Spanish, Guaraní
Under 15 (% - 2015)[a]	31 %	Form of government	Constitutional Republic
Population density	16.6	Last presidential election	2018
Land area (km²)	406 752		

The economy

GDP, current prices (billion USD - 2016)	27.4[b]	Main exports (% of total merchandise exports - 2016)	
GDP growth rate 2016 (%)	4.1[b]	Soybeans and derivatives	36%[c]
Inflation rate 2016 (%)	4.1[c]	Beef meat	14%[c]
GDP growth 2006-2015 (%, annual average)	5.1[b]	Value-added (% of GDP, 2016)[b]	
Tax to GDP ratio (% of GDP - 2015)	17.9[d] (34.3%)	Agriculture	20 (1.5 – 2015)
Trade in goods and services (% of GDP)		Industry	30.3 (24.3 – 2015)
Exports – 2016	42.1[b] (28.5 - 2015)	Services	49.8 (74.2– 2015)
Imports – 2016	39.4[b] (28 - 2015)		

Well-being

Consumption possibilities			
GDP per capita, 2016 (USD, 2011 constant PPP)	8 878[b] (38 725)	Share of population living below the poverty line (%, 2016)	28.9[h]
Income inequality (adult equivalent disposable income), 2015	52 (32)[e]		
Work			
Labour force participation (%, 15 to 64 year old, 2016)	72.7[f] (71.3 – 2015)[g]	Unemployment rate (% - 2016)	6.0[n] (6.3)
Employment to population ratio (% of 15 and over, 2016)	66.3[m] (55.7)	Youth unemployment rate[o] (%, 15 to 29, 2016)	10.6 (12.5)
Housing			
Households with improved sanitation facilities (%, 2015)	88.6 (98.8)	Satisfaction with the availability of affordable housing[j] (%, 2015)	54
Education			
Expected years of schooling[k]	12.3 (17.4)	Adult literacy rate (%, 2016)	94.6
Health			
Life expectancy (at birth, in years, 2016)	73.6[i] (79.9)	Satisfaction with the health system (%)[j]	43
Vulnerability			
Intentional homicide rate (per 100 000)	8.4	Health insurance coverage (% of the employed population, 2016)[f]	29
Social connections		*Empowerment and participation*	
Population stating they have someone to count on in case of need (%)	91[j] (88)[j]	Ranking in the Transparency International's Corruption Perception Index, 2015[l]	123/176
Life evaluation			
Life satisfaction (average on 1-10 scale)	5.6[j] (7.3)		

The environment

Average exposure to PM2.5 concentrations, micrograms per cubic metre, 2015	14.3 (12.3)	CO_2 emissions (kg per 2011 PPP USD of GDP)	0.09 (0.27)[b]
Forest area (% of land area, 2014)	39.4[b] (31.3)[b]		

Notes:

The Central Bank of Paraguay is undertaking a revision of National Accounts, changing the base year to 2014 and adopting SNA 2008. At the time of writing, the revised data were not available in long series or at the necessary level of disaggregation. This report therefore relies on national accounts data with the 1994 base year.

a) DGEEC. Paraguay. Proyección de la Población Nacional, Áreas Urbana y Rural por Sexo y Edad, 2000-2025. Revisión 2015.
b) World Bank (2017), *World Development Indicators Database* (database), Washington DC, *http://data.worldbank.org*.
c) Central Bank of Paraguay (2017), *https://www.bcp.gov.py/*.
d) Ministry of Finance of Paraguay (2017), *Informe de las Finanzas Públicas de la República del Paraguay*, Ministerio de Hacienda, Gobierno Nacional de Paraguay, Asunción.
e) OECD project 2015/16 "Monitoring Inequalities and Fostering Inclusive Growth in Emerging Economies" estimates based on micro-data from the main household surveys for Argentina, Bolivia, Dominic Republic, Ecuador, Panama, Paraguay, Peru and Uruguay, as available through CEDLAS (Centre for Distributive, Labor and Social Issues in Latin America, Universidad Nacional de La Plata, Argentina).
f) Calculations based on Encuesta Permanente de Hogares (2016).
g) OECD Labour force participation database, *http://dotstat.oecd.org/?lang=en*.
h) DGEEC (2017), *Principales Resultados de Pobreza y Distribución de Ingreso*, *www.dgeec.gov.py*.
i) MSPBS/DIGIES/DES, Subsistema de Información de Estadísticas Vitales.
j) Gallup World Poll, *www.gallup.com/services/170945/world-poll.aspx*.
k) UIS (UNESCO).
l) Transparency International.
m) MTESS (2017), Boletín Estadístico de Seguridad Social 2016, Ministerio de Trabajo, Empleo y Seguridad Social.
n) DGEEC (2017), Principales Indicadores de Empleo, EPH 2016, *www.dgeec.gov.py*.
o) OECD/ECLAC/CAF (2016), *Latin American Economic Outlook 2017: Youth, Skills and Entrepreneurship*, OECD Publishing, Paris, *http://dx.doi.org/10.1787/leo-2017-en*.

Administrative regions of Paraguay

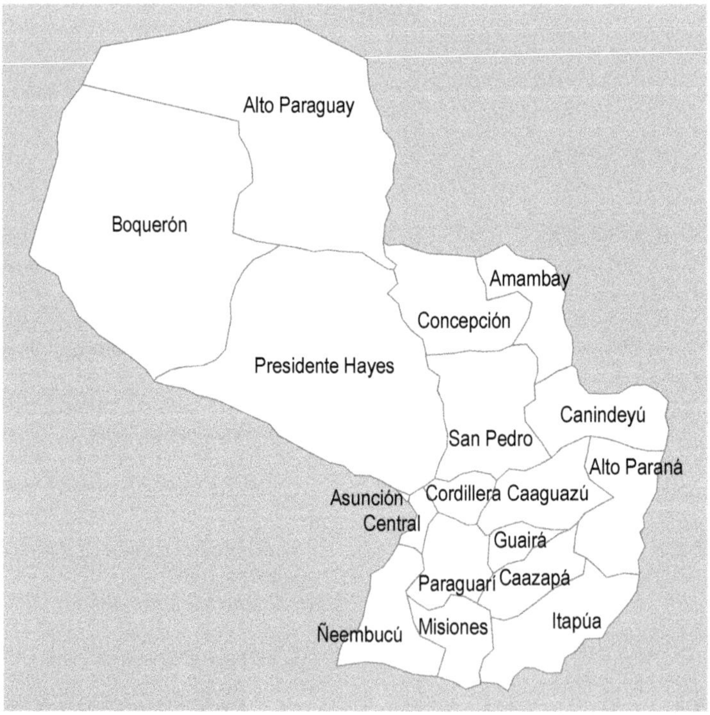

Executive summary

Paraguay has performed well over a range of development outcomes since 2003, after emerging from a prolonged period of economic and political instability. The economy has grown at 4.6% per annum in real terms, the poverty rate has fallen from 58% to 27%, and employment creation has progressed at 2.8% per annum, more rapidly than the growth of the working age population. The country's development has benefited from a favourable external environment, with large increases in the prices of major agricultural export products and from a large demographic dividend. Structural reforms undertaken since the democratic transition in 1989 and intensified in the recent period have enabled the country to take advantage of the tailwinds of the 2000s. Maintaining the pace of development and increasing its inclusiveness will require Paraguay to face a number of institutional, economic and social constraints that challenge its development model.

In 2014, Paraguay adopted its first National Development Plan (PND). Elaborated through a wide national consultation process, the PND is an ambitious agenda for mid-term development with a 2030 horizon along three strategic axes: i) poverty reduction and social development, ii) inclusive economic growth, and iii) inserting Paraguay into the world.

This report is the first volume of the Multi-dimensional Country Review (MDCR) of Paraguay. The MDCR is undertaken to support Paraguay in developing and implementing a strategy to achieve its development outcomes. This volume describes the driving forces of development in the country, benchmarks development outcomes and identifies the main constraints on sustainable progress in growth and citizen well-being.

Main findings

Economic growth is among the strongest in Latin America but is also very volatile, mainly because of the importance of agriculture in the economy and the concentration of exports in primary agricultural products and their derivatives. Despite this volatility, an inflation-targeting regime has managed to bring inflation volatility down, and the fiscal framework is sound, with low levels of debt and one of the lowest public deficits in the Latin America region. Productivity has grown steadily in the past decade, despite investment levels remaining below those of the region and the OECD by about 4% of GDP in the past decade. Structural transformation is progressing, with employment in agriculture falling by 10 percentage points over the past ten years. However, as employment shifts in part to low productivity activities in the service sector, labour reallocation contributes less to growth than it would otherwise.

Living standards have improved, but inequality remains a major challenge. Economic growth and macroeconomic stabilisation have contributed to raising the living standards of Paraguayans and to lowering the poverty rate from 45% in 2007 to 27% in 2015. Solid job creation has contributed to improving incomes. The expansion of free health care provision has contributed to improved accessibility of service. Income inequality is among the highest in the benchmark group and there are marked inequalities in non-monetary dimensions, including access to social insurance or water and sanitation, especially between urban and rural areas. Vulnerability is also a factor of inequality: perceived insecurity is relatively high in the country, and homicides are concentrated in a few departments, in particular in border areas.

The current economic expansion has put increasing pressure on the rich environmental endowment of the country. Paraguay has one of the cleanest energy mixes in the region, which has allowed it to maintain low carbon intensity and manage air pollution, and is endowed with diverse ecosystems and abundant resources for primary production. However, deforestation is one of the most critical environmental issues in the country, driven by increased land use for agriculture and livestock development.

Governance institutions are still undergoing fundamental transformations and further institutional strengthening is necessary to increase trust and ensure the rule of law. The Paraguayan democracy is still in a consolidation phase. Trust in major institutions is lower than in benchmark countries, especially in the case of the judiciary. Citizens' support for and satisfaction with democracy, as expressed in surveys, are also low compared to other Latin American countries. They have increased in the past decade however, showing resilience in the face of episodes of political instability. High levels of perceived corruption hinder trust in public institutions, constrain business opportunities, and erode social capital. A comprehensive integrity system is being developed, with focus on transparency, but ensuring its effectiveness remains a big challenge.

Financing flows for development are low in Paraguay compared to both the benchmarking countries and the OECD despite recent improvements in both public and private flows. Given the country's prudent fiscal stance and low reliance on public debt, public finance for development comes mostly from fiscal space. Government expenditure is relatively low, at 25% of GDP compared to 34% in Latin America and 45% in OECD countries. This is the consequence of low tax revenues and high non-discretionary expenditure, representing almost half of total public expenditure. At 5.5% of GDP, private flows are also relatively low. Foreign direct investment (FDI) flows have increased, but, at 1.16% of GDP, remain small.

Main constraints to development in Paraguay

The Paraguayan government faces two major challenges in achieving the country's vision for the future given its development model: to steer the economy to deliver sustainable growth in the medium term and to improve the country's capacity to stem inequality. An agriculture-based development model makes these tasks particularly difficult. Mechanised agriculture generates few jobs and concentrated incomes. Low diversification explains in part the high level of informality in the country. Informality in turn fuels inequality and weakens the capacity of the state both to alter the distribution of income and to steer the structural transformation of the economy.

To deliver sustainable growth in the medium term, the country has to overcome the obstacles to increasing investment and unblock avenues for increasing competitiveness. The country's limited fiscal space constrains public investment and there is also unexploited potential to increase private investment flows, given the solidity and profitability of the banking sector. Investment in infrastructure is particularly necessary given the country's geography, and could open up profitable opportunities. Two critical factors to unlock competitiveness are to improve educational outcomes and to improve state capacity in a number of areas including land management and administration, integrity, regulatory quality, and environmental protection.

The country also has to overcome obstacles to improving the inclusiveness of its development path. Diversification and improvements to educational outcomes are necessary to improve the distribution of market incomes. However, the capacity of the state to affect inequality in living standards is constrained by its limited capacity to deliver quality public services to all, in particular across territories, and the low impact of the fiscal taxation and transfer system on poverty and inequality. The prevalence of informality and the fragmented nature of the social protection system hinder the efficiency of state action towards inequality in living standards.

Multi-dimensional Review of Paraguay
Volume 1. Initial Assessment

Chapter 1

Overview: Meeting Paraguay's development ambition

Paraguay has performed well in a range of development outcomes since 2003. The country has set out an ambitious development vision with the horizon of 2030 and a National Development Plan to meet that ambition. Challenges remain to sustain economic performance, increase the inclusivity of the country's development pattern and buttress the process of institutional development. The objective of the Multi-dimensional Country Review (MDCR) is to support Paraguay in achieving its development objectives. The first volume identifies the key constraints to development in the country. This chapter presents the country's development performance from a comparative and historical perspective, assesses performance across a range of well-being outcomes and, on the basis of the main results of the volume, identifies the key constraints to development in the country.

Paraguay has performed well in a range of development outcomes in recent years although major challenges lie ahead to meet the country's ambitious development vision. Economic growth in the country has outpaced that of the region, driven by the tailwinds of rising export prices. Its proceeds have contributed to a large reduction in poverty. Well-being outcomes have improved notably in some areas, such as access to health or educational attainment. Challenges remain to sustain economic performance, increase the inclusivity of the country's development pattern, and buttress the process of institutional development that has followed the democratic transition.

The Multi-dimensional Country Review (MDCR) of Paraguay is undertaken to support the country in achieving its development objectives. The MDCR is a process implemented in three phases, each leading to the production of a report. This first volume of the MDCR of Paraguay aims to identify the binding constraints to achieving sustainable and equitable improvements in well-being and economic growth. The second phase will further analyse the key constraints identified in order to formulate policy recommendations that can be integrated into Paraguay's development strategy. The third and final phase of the MDCR will provide support to the implementation of these recommendations.

This overview chapter analyses the performance of Paraguay across key well-being dimensions and brings together the results of the thematic chapters to identify the key constraints to development in the country. First, it presents briefly the historical and structural context of Paraguay's development path, and describes the country's development vision as set out in its National Development Plan (PND). Second, the chapter analyses the country's performance across a range of well-being indicators. Third, it summarises the assessments contained in the five thematic chapters. Finally, it concludes by summarising the main constraints to development in Paraguay.

Paraguay's recent development performance

Since 2003 Paraguay has performed well in a range of development outcomes. Economic growth was mediocre throughout the 1990s and the economy suffered a long crisis in the early 2000s but after recovering in 2003 real gross domestic product (GDP) has grown at 4.6% per annum and, although it has slowed since 2013, the economy grew 4.0% in 2016 in the face of negative growth in the Latin American region. The proportion of the population in poverty has fallen substantially, from 58% in 2002 to 27% in 2015. The economy has become increasingly interconnected with the rest of the world and labour productivity has grown fairly rapidly, at 3.8% on average since 2004.

The recent period is a break from the economic history of the country since the middle of the 20th century. Following the civil war of 1947, and the fall in demand for agricultural commodities, the country's economy slowed and fell behind its neighbours (Figure 1.1).[1] The economy awoke from its slumber with the massive investment in the construction of the Itaipú dam, one of the largest hydroelectric power plants in the world, shared by Brazil and Paraguay, between 1973 and 1982, and the expansion of the agricultural frontier during the 1970s, resulting in average growth of 8.8%, including 20% growth in the construction sector. However, the economy returned to slow growth after the Itaipú boom, suffering from the Latin American "lost decade" in the 1980s and from political and economic instability from the democratic transition in 1989 until the crisis of the early 2000s (Arce, Krauer and Ovando, 2011; Fernández Valdovinos and Monge Naranjo, 2004).

Figure 1.1. **GDP and GDP per capita growth in Paraguay (1960-2016)**

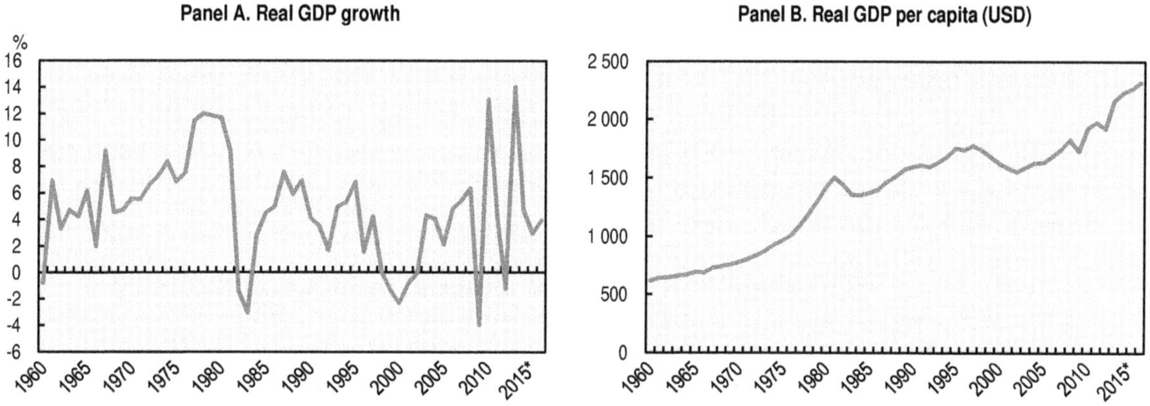

Note: Data for years 2014, 2015 and 2016 are preliminary. The data correspond to the National Accounts series with base year 1994.
Source: Banco Central de Paraguay (2017), *https://www.bcp.gov.py/anexo-estadistico-del-informe-economico-i365.*
StatLink http://dx.doi.org/10.1787/888933748705

Development in the country since 2003 has benefitted from favourable external and internal contexts. On the external front, the prices of key export products soared. The prices for soybeans and soybean oil more than tripled and the price of beef more than doubled between 2001 and the early 2010s and have remained at historically high levels despite a sharp fall in 2014. On the domestic front, Paraguay is in the midst of a long demographic transition and 28% of its population is young (15 to 29 years old). The low unemployment rate offers great potential for a demographic dividend to be reaped in the form of increased growth and economic dynamism.

Reforms undertaken since the democratic transition, and intensified during the most recent period, have contributed to the country's capacity to benefit from a favourable external environment. Although they did not deliver a growth acceleration during the 1990s, key macroeconomic reforms undertaken during the decade set the stage for an improvement in macroeconomic management and introduced the essential building blocks of the country's development model as it is today. Among the fundamental reforms in the 1990s were the unification of the exchange rate, a simplified tax code with greater emphasis on indirect taxation, fiscal adjustment and reform to public finances, and the joining of MERCOSUR common market created in 1991.

Continuing reforms have buttressed macroeconomic stability as one of the key features of the Paraguayan economy. An inflation-targeting regime with an explicit target since 2011 has succeeded in progressively lowering inflation and its volatility. Public sector external debt is very low at 23% of GDP (at the end of 2016), and the fiscal framework is sound. A fiscal responsibility law passed in 2013 limits the public deficit to 1.5% of GDP, even though the first years of its implementation have been challenging (see Chapter 2).

Priorities for government action have also shifted since 2003, with notable increases in public expenditure in social areas and on infrastructure. Paraguay does not produce reports or consolidated statements of public social expenditure for the whole of the public sector (it does report social expenditure for the central administration), nor are the domains that official figures classify as social comparable to those of OECD data. Nevertheless, available evidence shows an increase of social expenditure from 4.0% to 11.8% of GDP between 2003 and 2016 (Figure 1.2). This figure excludes a doubling of expenditure by social security institutions (from 2.1% to 4.4% of GDP) and significant increases in expenditure by autonomous bodies.[2] In practice, this led to a massive expansion in the coverage of the two main anti-poverty programmes. The conditional cash transfer *Tekoporã* increased in coverage from 4 000 families in 2005 to 77 000 in 2009 to 140 000 as of 2016. Similarly, the non-contributory social pension, which covered less than 1 000 beneficiaries in 2010, covered 168 000 at the end of 2016 (see Chapter 3). Public infrastructure spending has soared, especially since 2011, doubling in nominal terms, and placing Paraguay above most countries in the region in terms of infrastructure investment as a share of GDP (see Chapter 2).

Figure 1.2. **Public expenditure classified as social in Paraguay (2003-16)**

Central government expenditure (including transfers, excluding autonomous bodies), percentage of GDP

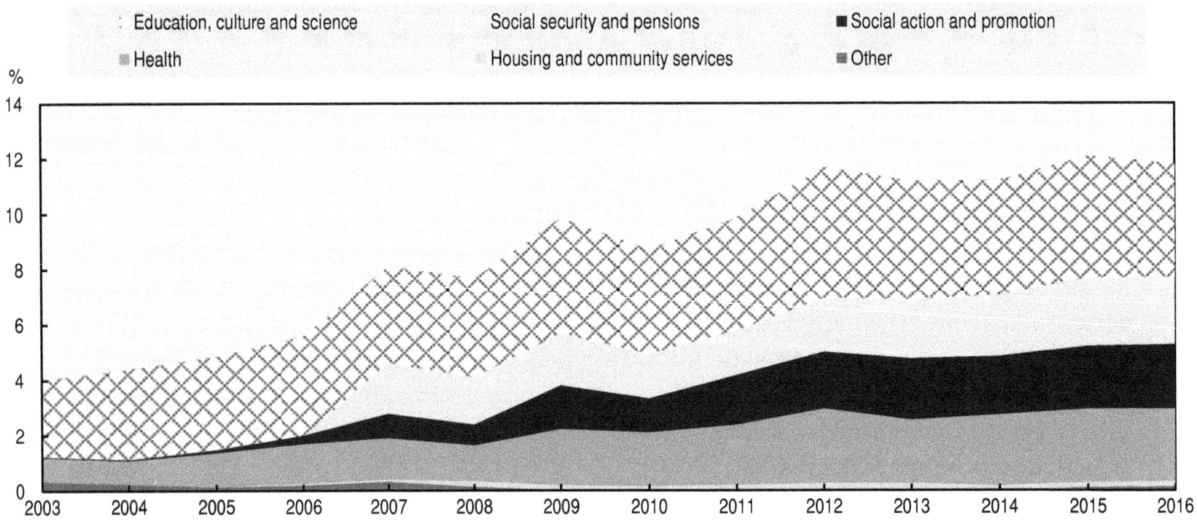

Note: Social security expenditure is included in social action and promotion prior to 2005.

Source: Ministerio de Hacienda (2017).

StatLink http://dx.doi.org/10.1787/888933748724

Beyond its geographical position, in the heart of South America and without direct access to the sea, Paraguay's current and future growth path depends on a number of structural factors. Among them the most determinant are the importance of agriculture and animal husbandry in the country's economy and society, the territorial distribution of the population and the on-going demographic transition, and Paraguay's position as a major hydroelectricity producer.

Economy and society in Paraguay are characterised by the size of agriculture in the country's economy. The share of the primary sector in the economy has remained relatively stable and large since the 1970s, with decade averages of between 24% and 28% of GDP. It even increased in the first decade of the 2000s with the increase in commodity prices before falling back in the first half of the 2010s with the fall in prices (Chapter 2). The contribution of livestock has increased in the past 25 years from 3.3% of GDP to 5.9% in 2016, while agriculture contributed 11.4% of GDP in 2016 (at current prices). Even these figures under-represent the importance of agriculture and animal husbandry in the country. Indeed, agro-industry also accounts for more than half of manufacturing value added, as well as significant shares of transport and service output. The agro-industrial value chain is estimated to generate 28.9% of GDP (Investor, 2015), and Masi (2014) estimates that in the boom year of 2013, agro-industry contributed 57% of GDP growth. This explains why the variability in agricultural output, largely driven by weather conditions, has an impact on the economy over and above its direct contribution to GDP.

The territorial distribution of the population and its recent evolution are also major on-going changes. The colonial occupation of Paraguay was heavily concentrated in frontier areas focused on defence, and, in the early years of independence, port towns (Asunción and Concepción on the Paraguay river, Encarnación on the Paraná river). Since independence, the settlement of the country has progressed via largely agricultural colonisation and the development of border towns, of which Ciudad del Este is the largest. As a result, the rate of urbanisation has lagged behind that of other countries in the region, and reached 60% of the population in 2015. More than half of the urban population is concentrated in the metropolitan area of Asunción and another 13% in Ciudad del Este and its metropolitan area. Urbanisation has progressed rapidly since 1980, driven by increased migration from rural to urban areas. Since 2000 the combination of internal migration and falling fertility has led to a stagnating and ageing population in rural areas (Investor, 2015). The pattern of urbanisation is also changing. In the ten years between the 2002 and 2012 censuses, the rate of growth of greater Asunción (1.8% per annum) and Ciudad del Este (2.2%) was much slower than that of the rest of the urban areas (3.5%) in the country, signalling renewed dynamism among intermediary urban centres in Paraguay.

Figure 1.3. **Rural and urban population in Paraguay**

Millions

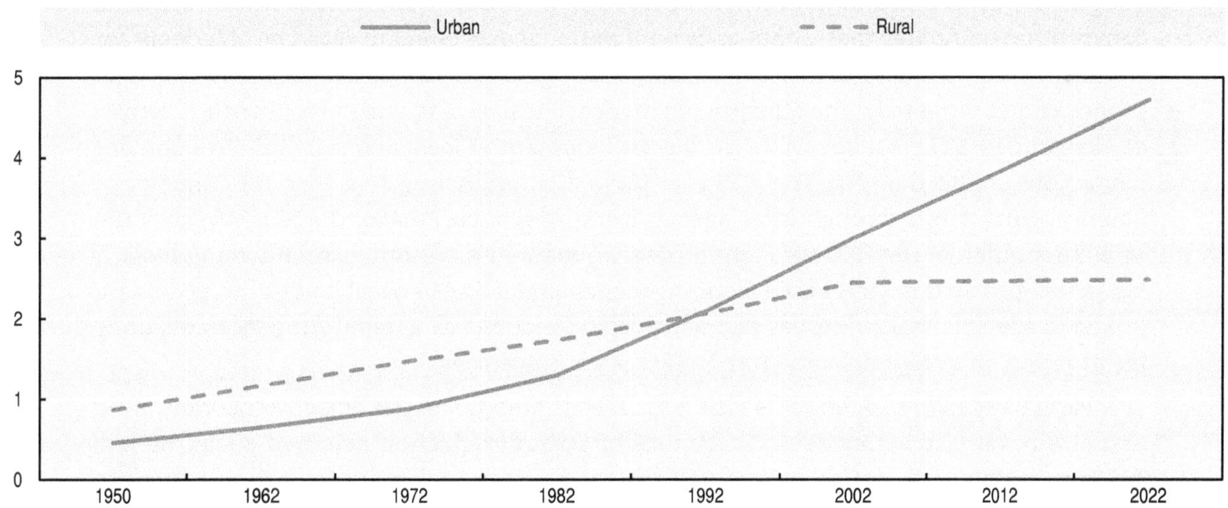

Source: DGEEC (2015).

StatLink http://dx.doi.org/10.1787/888933748743

The ongoing demographic transition is a major opportunity for development. Paraguay is a very young country. According to official demographic projections, 28% of the population are aged between 15 and 29 and that indicator is currently at its maximum. The demographic transition is under way and is relatively slow. While gross death rates are projected to be at their minimum in 2017, birth rates are not projected to converge with death rates until well into the second half of the century. As a result young cohorts arriving into the labour market are large and will be in the years to come, offering opportunities for growth but also straining the capacity of the economy to provide good formal jobs to all.

Paraguay's hydroelectric production capacity is also a major characteristic of the country's economy. The two binational power plants, shared respectively with Brazil (Itaipú) and Argentina (Yacyretá), together house installed capacity of 17 200 megawatts (MW) which are shared between Paraguay and its neighbours. Since Paraguay only uses a fraction of its share of electricity, the rest is exported, making it the largest exporter of clean electricity in the world. The two binationals contribute about 10% to GDP. Royalties and compensations from the two dams also generate public revenues (11% of total public revenues in 2016 [Chapter 2]), of which a sizeable proportion is channelled to local governments and earmarked for capital expenditures and social infrastructure. Paraguay's generation capacity also endows the country with spare capacity in low-cost electricity, a major asset for the attraction of foreign investment.

Paraguay's development ambition: The National Development Plan

In 2014, Paraguay adopted its first National Development Plan (*Plan Nacional de Desarrollo*, PND) (Gobierno Nacional de Paraguay, 2014). Entitled "Building the Paraguay of 2030" (*Construyendo el Paraguay del 2030*), the PND is an ambitious agenda for mid-term development with a 2030 horizon. The PND is directed along three strategic axes: (i) poverty reduction and social development; (ii) inclusive economic growth; and (iii) inserting Paraguay into the world. It follows four cross-cutting themes (equality of opportunity, efficient and transparent public management, territorial development and land management, and environmental sustainability). Together, these form 12 strategies with a monitoring framework based largely on numerical targets.

The PND is a strategic document, backed by a legislative framework and linked to the budget. It was adopted by presidential decree in December 2014. Article 177 of the 1992 constitution mandates that compliance with national development plans be obligatory for the public sector. Adherence to the PND is part of the guidelines for the development of budget proposals put forward by the Ministry of Finance. The planning authority (*Secretaría Técnica de Planificación*, STP) is responsible for the development of local and sectoral development plans adhering to the PND. The STP also plays a co-ordinating role with the Ministry of Finance, carried out through inter-agency working groups. Finally, the STP supports the implementation of the PND through the development of monitoring and planning tools. It has developed an outcome-based planning management tool in which budget proposals are linked to specific PND objectives and which also functions as a monitoring tool, collecting information on output delivery from implementing agencies.

Paraguay's plan to achieve its vision for 2030 is ambitious. The objective of eradicating extreme poverty is within reach if the rate of poverty reduction achieved since the late 1990s is maintained, but this alone will require constant policy innovation to reach the poorest and increase their living standards. Achieving average GDP growth of 6.8% in the medium run will also be challenging in a more difficult external environment. Paraguay's growth performance in the past ten years has been better than most comparator countries, but below that objective (Chapter 2). Some of the most ambitious objectives do not have numerical targets. For example, consolidating the network of transport while reducing costs and integrating the country with the rest of the world requires large infrastructure investments. The same is true for a number of objectives that will require significant progress in institutional development, such as achieving universal social security coverage or establishing land management and zoning plans in all municipalities.

The National Development Plan can contribute to policy continuity. The PND's development was based on a wide consultation process with the central and local administrations, civil society and other stakeholders. It is supported by a national committee of citizens from the private sector, academia, and civil society, the *Equipo Nacional de Estrategia País* (ENEP). ENEP, with its wide representativity of Paraguayan society, acts as a guardian of the PND and follows its implementation. Given its long horizon and its institutional backing, the PND can contribute to avoiding policy reversals, by establishing long-term policy objectives that cut across line ministries and agencies.

The MDCR assists Paraguay in meeting its development goals

Development is inherently multi-dimensional and cannot be reduced to a single objective or indicator, even factors as determinant as economic growth or as socially relevant as poverty. The OECD's MDCRs analyse development challenges from a wide variety of perspectives, using a combination of tools: a gap analysis across a dashboard of indicators, detailed cross-country benchmarking with a set of comparator countries, and a visioning exercise to identify priority outcomes for citizens in the country.

Following the adoption of Agenda 2030 by the United Nations as global development agenda (UN, 2015) and given the alignment of Paraguay's PND with the objective framework of the Sustainable Development Goals, this report adopts the five areas of critical importance of Agenda 2030 as guiding themes for each chapter: prosperity, people, planet, peace and institutions, partnership and financing development.

To assess accurately Paraguay's economic and social strengths and weaknesses, the MDCR goes beyond benchmarking them relative to averages and adopts a comparative approach with the help of a group of benchmarking countries, selected jointly by the team undertaking the review and Paraguay. The choice of these countries is based on factors such as income per capita, size, structural characteristics and the degree to which experiences from some of these countries could be useful models for policy development in Paraguay. The comparator countries selected are: Argentina, Australia, Brazil, Canada, Chile, Colombia, Costa Rica, Indonesia, Israel, Mexico, Peru, Poland, Portugal, Thailand, and Uruguay.

In addition to this quantitative dimension, the MDCR includes a series of participatory workshops. These workshops enable the OECD team to connect with diverse perspectives in the country and to bring together different elements of Paraguayan society to reflect on the challenges of development, as well as on the context in which policy responses will be implemented. They serve as a platform for dialogue and a means to test recommendations and ensure they are adapted to the context and are relevant. A multi-stakeholder workshop was organised in Asunción in March 2017 with participants from the public and private sectors and civil society (see Box 1.1).

Paraguay has taken steps to engage with the OECD to find further support for its development objectives. This engagement is piloted by an inter-agency commission under the co-ordination of the STP. It takes several forms, including the simultaneous implementation of an MDCR and of a Public Governance Review, which will analyse in detail the issues of co-ordination by the centre of government, planning and budgeting, open government, human resource management and multi-level governance. Paraguay is also stepping up its participation in OECD committees and analysing the OECD's normative body to support its own reform agenda.

Box 1.1. **Paraguay: Future and challenges**

As part of the OECD Multi-dimensional Country Review (MDCR) methodology, a series of workshops are organised throughout the review to connect with a diversity of perspectives of Paraguayan society and identify challenges and solutions to inclusive, sustainable development together with local stakeholders and experts. A first workshop entitled "Paraguay: Future, challenges and global environment" was organised in Asunción on 23 March 2017. The workshop was co-hosted by the *Secretaría Técnica de Planificación* (STP), and brought together over 40 participants from the public sector, the private sector, academia and civil society.

The workshop aimed to capture citizen aspirations for the future of their country, and discuss major obstacles to realising progress. The first session of the day focused on developing success stories of Paraguay in 2030, and capturing citizen normative preferences for the future (see Annex 1.A1). Participants were divided into groups and were asked to develop narratives from citizens' perspectives of a Paraguay in 2030 where all policies had succeeded. Participants subsequently extracted the different categories in their stories, which were subsequently clustered into policy areas modelled on the OECD's "How's life" framework.

Participants' stories described a whole range of different citizen profiles: men and women, young and old, some with graduate education and others not having completed high school education, some in high skilled professions like engineers and others in manual labour, some from Asunción and others from different regions, including indigenous groups. All fictional citizens enjoyed middle class family lives, with stable decent work based on existing industries, leisure time, good health and education for workers and their children.

The stories described an integrated Paraguay, importance was placed on good connectivity between Asunción and the rest of the country. Diet, fresh food and healthy living were also features of many of these fictional citizens' lives, as was the use of electric cars and bicycles. Several of the stories described decent livelihoods from farm holdings well integrated in value chains. This involved the efficient organisation of producers, access to financing, and favourable export opportunities. Finally, most stories described a meritocratic system, where citizens who benefited from free education were offered opportunities through scholarships and could travel abroad for their further education but returned to their home country where they found good jobs and were able to provide a prosperous future for their children.

All 11 dimensions of the OECD's "How's life" framework were identified in participants' stories, yet two new dimensions were added: culture and identity, and inequality which was noted as a transversal theme. Participants engaged in a rich discussion around the major obstacles to realising progress and the development objectives of the PND. The most frequently mentioned obstacles holding the country back related to the social sphere with issues such as regional and economic inequality, vulnerability, poor healthcare provision and outcomes for citizens, and skills. Participants also emphasised low investment and insufficient regard for Paraguay's cultural heritage and identity, and the lack of accommodation of indigenous culture in Paraguay's cultural identity.

When discussing the root of these obstacles, lack of policy planning, anticipation, and proper implementation were cited. Participants also highlighted the poor management of resources, corruption, lack of compliance with the law, and authorities' limited capacity to enforce it. The question of skilled human resources was also raised, and weakness in delivery of social services was in part attributed to a lack of trained professionals across several fields. Finally, participants noted that policy often sought to treat all citizens equally, and as a result was not always inclusive, just as institutions were seldom designed to accommodate diversity, perpetuating inequalities.

How's life in Paraguay? An overview of the OECD well-being framework

Development is often considered synonymous with economic growth, and yet growth in GDP is only one element of development. If aggregate increases in productivity and material wealth do not produce meaningful gains in the overall well-being of a country's population, development has failed in both human and economic terms. Economic growth is only a means to an end – the sustainable and equitable improvement of people's lives. To assess comprehensively life within a country, it is necessary to go beyond macroeconomic indicators and monitor well-being across the many different areas that matter for citizens.

Part of the OECD MDCR benchmark analysis examined a range of well-being indicators in Paraguay. Well-being is a multi-dimensional concept and can be difficult to define in isolation as it covers many areas of people's lives. However, the core idea is relatively intuitive: well-being encompasses those aspects of life that people would consider essential to meet one's needs, pursue one's goals and feel satisfied with life (Box 1.2).

Figure 1.5 shows Paraguay's performance across a range of indicators that are representative of the ten dimensions of the OECD's well-being framework. Paraguay's actual performance (the blue bars) is shown in contrast to its expected performance given its level of economic development (the black circle). Results that are outside the circle therefore represent better-than-expected outcomes; results inside the circle show lower-than-expected outcomes; and the longer the bar, the better Paraguay's performance in that indicator in relation to its expected outcome.

Box 1.2. **Using the OECD's "How's Life" framework to measure well-being in developing countries**

The OECD has developed a framework for measuring well-being in OECD countries based on national initiatives undertaken in several countries and several years of collaboration with experts and representatives from national governments (OECD, 2011). This "How's Life" framework has also been adapted to measure well-being in non-OECD countries, taking into account the literature on measuring development outcomes and embracing the realities of these countries. Its dimensions have been redefined better to match the availability of data, the priorities and critical concerns of these countries (Boarini, Kolev and McGregor, 2014).

This adjusted framework, like the original one, measures well-being outcomes in two broad fields. The first, material conditions, comprises the dimensions of consumption possibilities, work and housing conditions and infrastructure. The second, quality of life, comprises health status, education and skills, social connections, empowerment and participation, vulnerability and life evaluations, feelings and meaning — i.e. the main aspects of subjective well-being (Figure 1.4). These ten dimensions are used to measure current well-being. They are complemented with another set of indicators to measure the sustainability of current well-being in the future. The framework emphasises the importance of preserving the natural, human, economic and social resources that are essential for ensuring the well-being of future generations.

The OECD well-being framework is informed by a number of analytical principles. First, it is concerned with the well-being of individuals rather than aggregate economic conditions. Second, it focuses on well-being outputs rather than inputs, recognising that outcomes may be uncorrelated with the resources devoted to achieving them. Third, it emphasises the need to measure the distribution of well-being outcomes to identify inequalities across

Box 1.2. **Using the OECD's "How's Life" framework to measure well-being in developing countries** *(cont.)*

and within population groups. Finally, it considers both objective and subjective indicators, as people's own evaluations and feelings about their lives matter as much as the objective conditions in which they live (OECD, 2011).

Figure 1.4. **OECD well-being framework for developing countries**

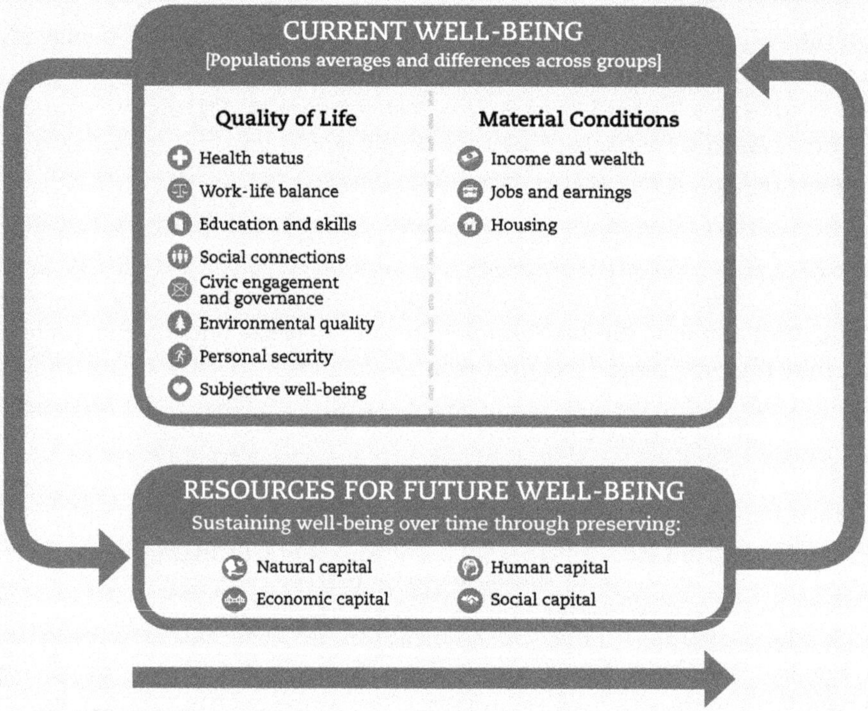

Sources: Boarini, Kolev and McGregor (2014); OECD (2011), DOI: *http://dx.doi.org/10.1787/9789264121164-en*.

When it comes to well-being, Paraguay has areas of strengths and weaknesses (Figure 1.5). Paraguay performs reasonably well in the areas of work, social connections and life evaluations but it underperforms in the areas of consumption and empowerment. In most dimensions, the overall situation is relatively good compared to countries of the same level of development. However, many areas are characterised by high levels of inequality. Incomes, access to improved sanitation, health insurance coverage and satisfaction with transport infrastructure differ markedly between rural and urban dwellers (Chapters 3 and 5). Less educated and poorer citizens have worse perceptions of key public services and institutions like the health and justice systems than those who are better educated of better off.

Figure 1.5. **Current and expected well-being outcomes for Paraguay: Worldwide comparison**

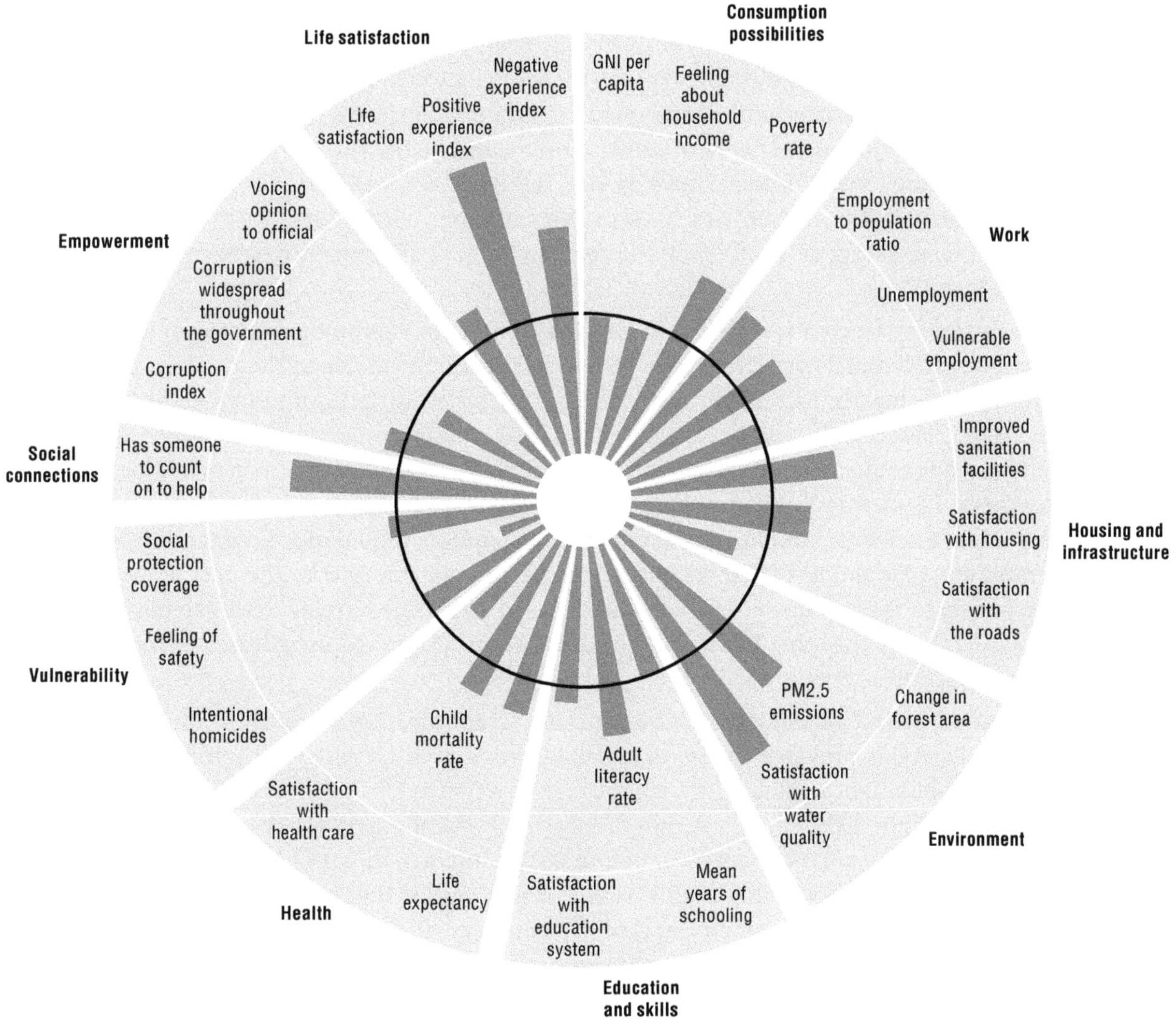

Note: The bars represent the observed well-being values for Paraguay and the circle shows the expected values based on Paraguay's level of GDP per capita obtained from a set of bivariate regressions with GDP as the independent variable and the various well-being outcomes as dependent variables from a cross-country dataset of around 150 countries with a population over a million. All indicators are normalised in terms of standard deviations across the panel. The observed values falling inside the circle indicate the areas where Paraguay performs poorly in terms of what could be expected from a country with a similar level of GDP per capita. All indicators had been normalised so that the longer the bar, the better the outcome.

Source: Gallup (2016), Gallup World Poll, *http://www.gallup.com/services/170945/world-poll.aspx* (accessed 1 February 2017), World Bank (2016), *World Development Indicators* (database), Washington DC, *http://data.worldbank.org*, UNESCO Institute of Statistics (UIS), PISA scores (2009), and Transparency International (2016), Corruption Perception Index *http://www.transparency.org*.

StatLink http://dx.doi.org/10.1787/888933748762

People have jobs but income is relatively low, transport infrastructure is poor, and there is a sizeable quality deficit in housing

Gross national income (GNI) per capita captures the gross flow of income to individuals from earnings, self-employment and income from capital.[3] In 2015, Paraguay's GNI was USD 8 176 (2011 constant PPP) which is slightly below what is expected for countries with similar GDP per capita. In turn, the Paraguayan values are somehow below the Latin American and Caribbean average of USD 12 107 (2011 constant PPP). Similarly, satisfaction with living standards is relatively low. Only 53% of Paraguayans reported in 2015 that they can either get by on, or live comfortably with, their household income, a figure within the same range as the average for the past 7 years. Yet, reaching 7% in 2014 the poverty rate at the international poverty line of USD 3.10 in PPP was lower than what could be expected given the level of development and below the LAC average (11.4%). Poverty according to the national poverty line fell from 45% in 2007 to 27% in 2015 and extreme poverty fell from 14.0% to 5.4% in the same period (Chapter 3). If the 10-year trend continues, Paraguay is on track to meeting its goal of achieving extreme poverty below 3% by 2030.

Labour force participation is high in Paraguay. The ratio of employment to population is 66% among individuals over the age of 15 and has remained stable in the past ten years. In turn, despite having increased from 5% in 2013 to 6% in 2016, unemployment was comparatively low, both in terms of the country's level of development and when compared to the average for Latin America and the Caribbean (6.8%). The share of those in vulnerable employment, i.e. unpaid family workers and own-account workers, is around 40% and is slightly lower than what could be expected given Paraguay's level of development. Indeed, vulnerable employment has fallen by almost ten percentage points over the past ten years, thanks largely to the expansion of wage and salaried work. The employment gap between women and men, on the other hand, is larger than in most OECD and benchmark economies and has evolved little over time.

Access to decent housing and infrastructure is another key dimension of material conditions. Paraguay provides access to improved sanitation facilities in their houses[4] to 88.6% of its population, a value above what could be expected for its level of development, and up from 62% in 2005. Given the rate of improvement, the goal of achieving universal improved sanitation could be met even before 2030. Similarly, in 2015 54% of Paraguayans were satisfied with the availability of affordable housing, a value that is also above what could be expected given the development level of the country. Official estimates of the housing deficit suggest the deficit pertains to quality, in particular in terms of access to piped water and to the public sanitation grid. Only 17% of the housing deficit is quantitative, that signals the need for building new housing units (Chapter 3). Conversely, for the same year only 44% of people in Paraguay reported being satisfied with the roads, a value that is below what could be expected given the country's level of development as well as the LAC average (53%). Satisfaction with roads has deteriorated in the past ten years, with 55% of people reporting being satisfied in 2005, which reinforces the significant infrastructure challenge the country faces (Chapters 2 and 5).

Moving ahead: Closing gaps in environment, vulnerability and empowerment

Based on the experience of countries with similar GDP, Paraguay displays mixed results in terms of its environmental performance. It performs better than expected on PM2.5 levels – a measure of particulate matter (PM) of 2.5 micrometres, a size that has severe health effects – with a value of 14.3 micrograms per cubic metre in 2015. In turn, Paraguayans are remarkably satisfied with the water quality as reported by 88% of the population and considerably above what could be expected for its development level. Conversely, the country scores well below expectations on the change of its forest area that, according to 2015 data, experienced a reduction of 17.1% over ten years.

While having a good education makes it easier for people to get a good job, a good education is more than a passport to work. The opportunity to learn new skills can intrinsically be rewarding, and education is generally valued by people as an outcome in its own right. Paraguay performs reasonably well given its level of development. Mean years of schooling of the population aged 25 and above are 8.68 and the adult literacy rate is 95%. Progress in adult literacy has been slow (3 percentage points between 2005 and 2015) but the target of universal literacy by 2030 is within reach. Conversely, weaknesses in the production of key education statistics, in particular enrolment rates, make it very challenging to assess progress in access to education. This is a source of concern given that the PND establishes five numerical targets to be met in enrolment rates (for early childhood education, pre-school, and the three cycles in basic education). In the absence of better measures of the quality of the education system, the reported level of satisfaction is considered. In 2015, two-thirds of Paraguayans reported being satisfied with the education system, a value that is above what would be expected for a country with Paraguay's level of development and that has been consistently high over the past years, probably reflecting the density of the school network.

Good health is a major determinant of quality of life and a core dimension of well-being. In addition to its intrinsic value, it is vital for people's ability to work and participate in social life. Life expectancy at birth in Paraguay is 73.6 years (70.8 years for men and 76.5 years for women) according to the most recent projections (DGEEC, 2015). In this regard, Paraguay performs relatively well given its level of development. Progress in life expectancy has been slow (2.4 years gained on average in ten years); indeed too slow to meet the target of 79 years by 2030. The recorded child mortality rate per 1 000 live births in 2015 was 16.4, still higher than the average for Latin America and the Caribbean.[5] However, fewer than half of Paraguayans (43%) reported being satisfied with the health system, a figure that is below what could be expected given the country's level of economic development and similar to the value from ten years ago (48%) (Gallup, 2016).

In the OECD well-being framework vulnerability is understood as the exposure to risks such as food or income insecurity, job loss, illness, or physical violence. Paraguay's results in this dimension of the framework are either as expected or below expectations given its level of development. In 2014, its rate of intentional homicides per 100 000 people was 8.4 – much lower than the LAC average (25.04 per 100 000 people), a full 9 points below the level ten years ago, and as expected given Paraguay's level of economic development; however, the average could hide some worrisome values in specific regions (see Chapter 5). At the same time, people's perceived level of safety is relatively low: in 2016 only half of Paraguayans surveyed reported that they felt safe walking home alone at night, which is much lower than the expected value. Beyond, personal security economic insecurity is another source of vulnerability with the capacity to affect the quality of life. Slightly more than half of Paraguayans were covered by social protection, labour and transfer programmes in 2011, a level that is a little higher than what could be expected for a country with a similar level of development. Despite this good relative performance, health insurance coverage has stagnated below 30% of the population since 2013. Even if it were to continue on the upward trend of the first decade of the 2000s (4.4 percentage points over 10 years), the target of universal social security coverage would not be reached by 2030. This gap in social security is largely due to the persistence of informality (Chapter 3).

Social connections in Paraguay are relatively strong. Good proxies of the strength of close personal networks in a country are the proportion of people feeling that they can count on others in times of need and the amount of time people spend with friends and family. In Paraguay, 91% of those surveyed said that they have at least one friend or a relative that they can turn to for help in a time of need, a value which is above the LAC average (84%).

Paraguay has significant weaknesses in the area of empowerment and participation. According to Transparency International's Corruption Perception Index (Transparency International, 2016), which ranks countries based on how corrupt their public sector is perceived to be by business people and country analysts, Paraguay ranks relatively low (123/176) for countries where data are available. This is in line with its level of economic development. Notwithstanding Paraguay's relatively low score, its performance in the Corruption Perception Index has improved markedly since it entered the ranking in 2002 as one of the countries with the highest perception of corruption among those ranked (98/102). Between 2010 and 2016, the country gained 23 places in the ranking while the total number of countries remained stable. However, according to the Gallup World Poll, 74% of the population think corruption is widespread in government and only 19% believe that elections are honest (see Chapter 5). In respect of participation, just 8% of people have voiced their opinion to a public official, the lowest value amongst LAC countries. Finally, only 28% of the population trust the government (see Chapter 5).

Life evaluation is measured through three distinct channels to disentangle people's daily experiences (feelings and emotions) from overall life satisfaction. These measures are based on the idea that people are the best judges of how their own lives are going (OECD, 2011). Using the Cantril Ladder, a measure which asks respondents to rate their lives as a whole on a scale of 0 to 10, with 0 representing the worst possible evaluation and 10 representing the best, average life satisfaction in Paraguay is 5.6, as compared with a Latin American average of 5.9 but still above what is expected for a country with a similar level of development. Using a set of ten positive and negative "experiences", Paraguay shows more unbalanced results (higher-than-expected on the positive experiences but lower-than-expected on the negative experiences). These experiences include, on the one hand, feeling well-rested, laughing and smiling, enjoyment, feeling respected, and learning or doing something interesting, and stress, sadness, physical pain, worry and anger on the other. The high overall level of subjective well-being relative to the level that could be predicted based on the country's GDP per capita is a feature that Paraguay shares with most other Latin American countries.

The well-being framework within each dimension: The case of gender inequalities

The OECD well-being framework also takes account of inequalities within each dimension, consistent with the idea that community welfare reflects both average outcomes and how they are distributed across people with different characteristics. For instance, gender inequality is a cross-cutting issue that should be gauged across every dimension of well-being. Women tend to have lower outcomes in most of the dimensions of well-being and lag significantly in the areas of jobs, vulnerability life evaluation and consumption possibilities (Figure 1.6). In particular, in respect of jobs, they are more likely to be out of the labour market and have a higher risk of being unemployed.

Figure 1.6. **Difference of well-being outcomes by gender**

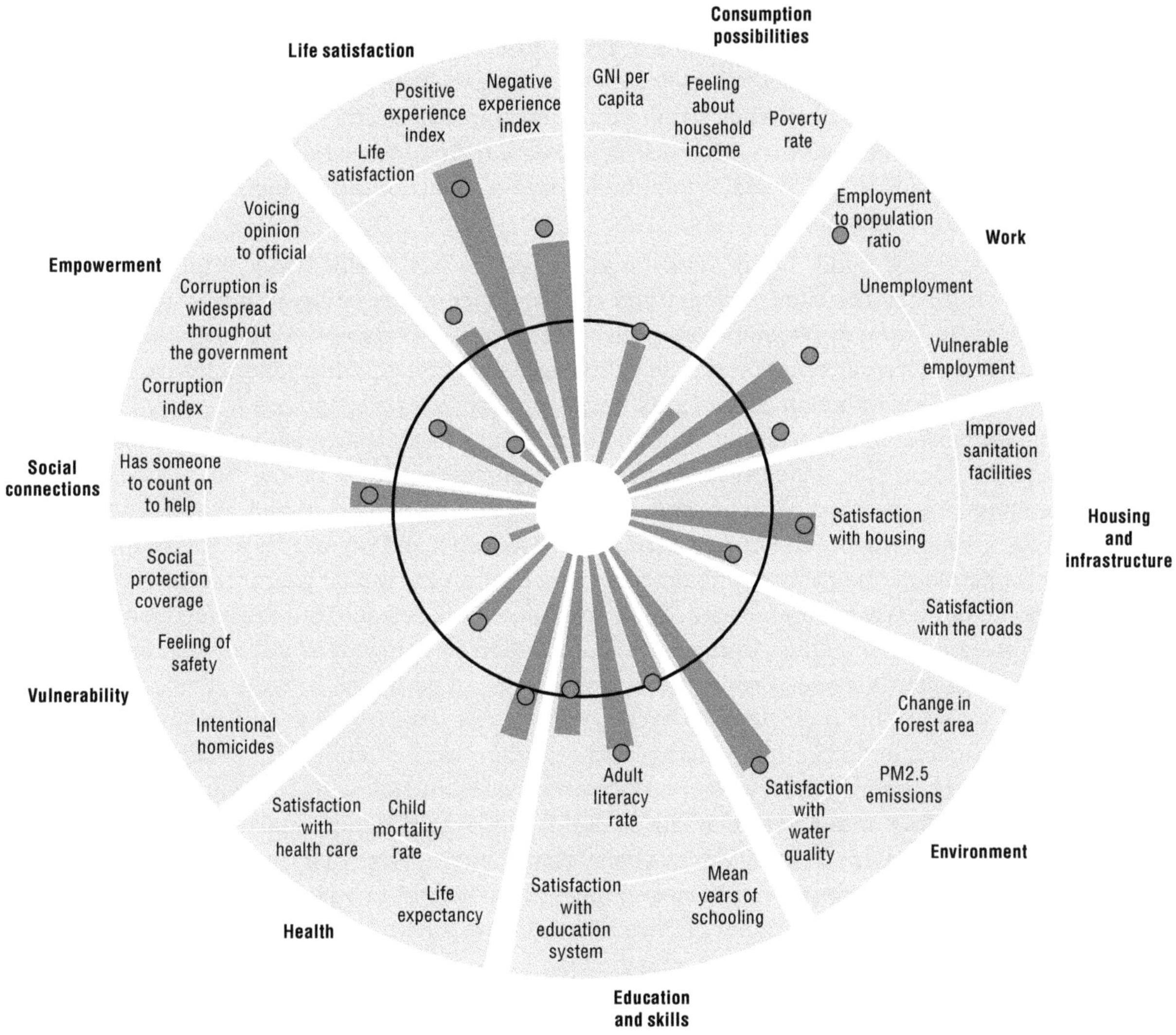

Note: The bars represent the observed well-being values for women in Paraguay. The dots stand for the observed well-being values for men. The circle shows the expected values based on Paraguay's level of GDP per capita obtained from a set of bivariate regressions, with GDP as the independent variable and the various well-being outcomes as dependent variables from a cross-country dataset of around 150 countries with a population over one million. All indicators are normalised in terms of standard deviations across the panel. The observed values falling inside the circle indicate the areas where Paraguay performs poorly in terms of what could be expected from a country with a similar level of GDP per capita. All indicators have been normalised so that the longer the bar, the better the outcome.

Source: Gallup (2016), Gallup World Poll, *http://www.gallup.com/services/170945/world-poll.aspx* (accessed 1 February 2017), Work Bank (2016), *World Development Indicators* (database), Washington DC, *http://data.wroldbank.org*, UNESCO Institute of Statistics (UIS), PISA scores (2009), and Transparency International (2016), Corruption Perception Index *http://www.transparency.org*.

StatLink http://dx.doi.org/10.1787/888933748781

Assessment and key constraints to development in Paraguay

Prosperity

The Paraguayan economy remains among the strongest growing in the region but with significant volatility. This growth volatility is mainly due to its reliance on agriculture and livestock production as leading economic activities. Over the past few decades, Paraguay's exports have been marked by low levels of diversification and are mainly concentrated in products such as soybeans, beef meat and electricity. However, in recent years, some diversification across export destinations has been observed, shifting from the neighbouring countries towards the European Union and Asia. Moreover, there has been a gradual increase in the technological content of exports; the growth in export during the 2000s has been accompanied by an increase in the share of agriculture-based manufacturing products from 25% to 35% of total exports. Labour reallocation from agriculture to other sectors, especially manufacturing and services, shows that structural transformation is proceeding at pace. As a result a number of sectors (livestock, construction, financial services) have seen their shares of value added grow, while manufacturing has contributed an increasingly larger share to aggregate growth.

Monetary policy and the inflation-targeting regime have helped to control inflation volatility with both the explicit target and the tolerance range being gradually adjusted downwards. To support the monetary policy framework, efforts to develop the financial system and the interbank market should be strengthened and liquidity conditions carefully monitored. The introduction of the Fiscal Responsibility Law (FRL) and the Advisory Fiscal Council represent an important step in terms of fiscal sustainability, as part of a broader package of reforms in macro-fiscal policy. The implementation of the FRL has been challenging and the possibility of amending the law is being considered as it does not allow for the implementation of counter-cyclical measures and represents a constraint on public investment. Any changes should be analysed carefully, should guarantee credibility, and should be clearly communicated. The fiscal framework is sound but tax collection and capital investment should be improved. Tax collection in Paraguay is still low compared to benchmark countries despite recent improvements, in particular in tax collection from domestic activity. This is particularly because of low tax rates (more details in Chapter 6) although evasion and informality also play a role. Government efforts to contain current spending are noteworthy, having declined in recent years and allowing for a slight increase in social spending and government investment. However, although starting to pick up, the level of investment in Paraguay has been considerably lower than in OECD and Latin American countries. Paraguay still faces significant challenges in budgetary execution and management of public investment projects. Further government efforts to facilitate capital investment would contribute to boosting growth.

Strengthening productivity and competitiveness is also essential for sustaining long-term growth but several challenges remain. Although Paraguay has shown strong growth in recent years, the income gap remains high compared to OECD countries and most of the difference is explained by labour productivity. Despite government efforts and implemented measures, several challenges still remain to boost productivity and competitiveness. Resources invested in research and development activities in Paraguay are low relative to benchmark countries while private sector investment and involvement should be strengthened. There is also wide scope to boost productivity by improving the quality of education and reducing skills mismatches while high-quality infrastructure and connectivity are fundamental to both raising productivity levels and improving social inclusion. The institutional and regulatory framework should be set in a way that boosts further competition and government efforts to help to reduce barriers to investment, trade and entrepreneurship are therefore welcome.

People

Paraguay's growth performance has led to improvements in incomes but inequality remains substantial. The recent period of economic growth has contributed to raising the living standards of many Paraguayans. In the period 2007-14, income growth "lifted all boats", contributing to a significant fall in income poverty, which fell from 45% in 2007 to 27% in 2015. Macroeconomic stabilisation also contributed to containing poverty by limiting food price inflation. In contrast to the fall in poverty, inequality remains high in Paraguay and a major concern of citizens. Income inequality has fallen in the past five years but less than in other Latin American countries in the past decade. The territorial dimension is an important contributor to inequality. Levels of monetary and non-monetary deprivation are higher in rural areas, in terms of income poverty but also of access to water and sanitation or health insurance. Public social programmes have expanded notably in the years since 2009. Among them, the social pension and the main conditional cash transfer (CCT) programme (Tekoporã) have noticeable effects on income poverty, although they remain small. In fact, taken as a whole, the fiscal taxation and redistribution system in Paraguay has very limited impacts on inequality and poverty. The impact of social policy in other areas of well-being is larger and better documented, in particular in terms of children's use of health and education services. The expansion of free universal health care provision by the Ministry of Health has also contributed to improved outcomes by reducing gaps in the accessibility of service, in particular between urban and rural households. A notable expansion in housing programmes, whose budgets have more than doubled in real terms, has made it possible to build 10 000 dwellings a year since 2015.

Employment outcomes are quantitatively good, although informality and job quality remain major challenges. Net job creation over the medium term has been good, overtaking rapid growth in the working age population. As a result, unemployment is low and labour force participation remains stable at levels comparable to benchmark countries, although female labour force participation is low and volatile. The sector distribution of employment points to a dynamic structural transformation process, with agricultural employment falling by ten percentage points in favour of services and construction. These changes have been particularly notable in rural areas, including with the development of secondary sector jobs. This transformation has seen a steady increase in salaried work in both the public and the private sectors. In spite of these changes, job quality remains an issue for many workers: domestic workers, unpaid family worker and own-account workers account for 46% of employment and almost two-thirds in rural areas. Informality, which concerns 64% of workers outside agriculture is a major issue, and explains why 44.5% of employees do not earn the minimum wage and why social security coverage is low. Informality poses a challenge due to the absence of a suitable social protection regime (pension and health insurance) for independent workers. The share of informal employment has fallen by a percentage point per year on average in the past five years, a relatively slow pace compared to the process of structural transformation and the prevalence of informality. Labour market institutions are relatively weak, with low rates of unionisation and little collective bargaining. While employment protection legislation is not particularly stringent, the combination of high minimum wages relative to market wages, and of contribution rules in social security make formalisation costly for employees.

Education outcomes have progressed but need further improvement. Although it performs at the expected level for its level of development, the country is among those with the lowest adult educational attainment among the benchmark countries, with 8.7 years of education among adults on average. The cohorts educated since 1990 have significantly higher attainment but estimates of school life expectancy for Paraguay are lower than for benchmark countries, which casts doubt on whether this will be sufficient to catch up. Although limitations in statistical capacity hamper the analysis of access to education, survey data suggest that access to primary and lower secondary education is nearly generalised, with the exception of indigenous areas, thanks in part to previous education reforms aiming at expanding coverage. Gaps in access to school remain significant for pre-primary education and upper secondary education, and in both cases gaps between rural and urban areas remain wide. Progress in recent years has been notable in secondary school and especially in tertiary education, where access has grown rapidly although, at 35%, gross enrolment rates remain low compared to benchmark countries. The quality of education remains a major challenge. Learning outcomes underperform with respect to the expected proficiency as described in the national curriculum (for almost three quarters of grade 3 students) and relative to benchmarking countries in the region. Among the main challenges facing the education sector are gaps in the qualification of teaching staff and in infrastructure. Improving the skills of teachers is one of the key objectives of Paraguay's recently created national programme for postgraduate scholarships abroad (BECAL), which also finances postgraduate studies for researchers and science and technology specialists. The *Fondo Nacional de Inversión Pública y de Desarrollo* (FONACIDE), created in 2012, channels resources from the royalties obtained from the binational plant of Itaipú to education, research and social infrastructure. FONACIDE has been instrumental in sustaining the increase in funding to support education, especially through financing investment in schools. In spite of a recovery in public expenditure in education and earmarking of funds for social infrastructure, limited absorption capacity is a constraint on the speed at which these challenges can be overcome.

The efficiency of social service delivery is limited by the fragmentation of the social protection system and informality. The prevalence of informal employment and contribution rules for own-account workers limit the coverage of contributory social security to 22% for the pension system and 29% for health insurance. The pension system is characterised by the multiplicity of regimes, subject to light regulation and with varying degrees of financial health. The generous provisions of the general regime contrast with the low coverage and the expansion of the non-contributory pension financed by the general budget. The health system is also fragmented both on the financing side and in service delivery. Despite advances in free universal health care provision, the elimination of user fees in Ministry of Health services and programmes to grant free drugs to certain categories, health is largely financed by households, and out-of-pocket payments were estimated to be as high as 49% in 2014. High out-of-pocket payments create obstacles to effective use of health services and reinforce inequalities in health status. Social assistance and income support programmes are also fragmented, with overlapping objectives and differences in targeting methods. The consolidation of anti-poverty measures under an umbrella programme (*Sembrando oportunidades*), the ongoing implementation of a single targeting tool and improved *ad hoc* co-ordination are contributing to greater efficiency. However, given the relatively weak impact of transfers on monetary poverty, there is potential for greater effectiveness in institutionally co-ordinated action. To succeed in addressing informality, co-ordination in programme design, implementation and enforcement is a necessity.

Planet

Geography has endowed Paraguay with one of the most biodiverse ecosystems in the world. With access to a large tropical forest and a vast number of water endowments, the country provides abundant resources for agriculture and livestock development. With one of the cleanest energy mixes in the region, based on the use of hydropower, Paraguay has managed to keep the economy's carbon intensity at low levels and allowed the country to manage air pollution. Total greenhouse emissions also remain relatively low. However, the current economic expansion, largely based on the use of land for agriculture and livestock development, has put increasing environmental pressure on the country. Deforestation remains one of the most critical issues in terms of environmental sustainability.

While costs are low by comparison with other countries, access to public services, including water, sanitation and waste management, is still limited for a large part of the population, and regional disparities in the quality and distribution of these services persist. The rapid urbanisation process has increased pressure in Asunción and intermediary cities, and water shortages and poor water quality are major concerns for the authorities, particularly in urban areas. In rural areas, natural disaster prevention has gained importance after two recent episodes where agricultural production was affected.

To maintain the current economic momentum and guarantee that it benefits the entire population, Paraguay needs to incorporate the sustainable use of environmental resources and capabilities into its development agenda. There are considerable needs in terms of environmental protection that are not being met. The regulatory framework against deforestation is insufficient and is not being implemented, and more support to strengthen the institutional setting is needed, particularly at the local level. Waste management is another issue of concern, and is mostly based on landfilling as the primary disposal method.

With access to abundant clean hydropower energy, Paraguay could be at the forefront of environmental policy in the region, promoting renewable energy, building an energy-efficient technology, improving energy utilisation in transport, among other areas. However, only 29% of total energy consumption comes from this clean electricity, the bulk coming from fuel and biomass. Transport, which accounts for nearly 90% of Paraguay's greenhouse gas (GHG) emissions, is one area where improvements could be introduced, introducing electricity-based systems and incentives to reduce biomass consumption in the industry sector. Improving land management will be fundamental to the implementation of a strategic plan for the environment.

Peace and institutions

Paraguay's vision for 2030 is that of a democratic, supportive state, subsidiary, transparent and geared towards the provision of equal opportunities. Governance institutions in the country are still undergoing fundamental transformations. Today, democracy in the country is still in a consolidation phase. The process of consolidation since the transition to democracy in 1989 has been convoluted. Fewer than half of Paraguayans consider that democracy is preferable to any other form of government and fewer than one quarter of citizens are satisfied with how democracy works in the country. Satisfaction with democracy almost doubled between 2006 and 2015 in spite of several episodes of political instability, signalling a certain degree of resilience of democratic institutions. Further strengthening the justice system is crucial for ensuring the rule of law. Only 28% of Paraguayans trust the judiciary, compared to 42% in benchmarking countries and 54% in the OECD. Those in urban areas and with higher education have higher levels of trust, as they are able to overcome barriers to access justice. The justice problem faces a number of constraints, including the range of functions that the Supreme Court fulfils on top of its core function of administering justice, the relatively small number of judges, and the pervasive influence of entrenched informal institutions that limit judicial independence.

Perceived personal insecurity is comparatively high in Paraguay, although violence is unequally spread and more prevalent in border areas. Homicide rates have fallen considerably in the past years, and homicides are concentrated in a small number of departments in border areas and the area of operation of the Paraguayan People's Army guerrilla group. Despite ongoing efforts, smuggling, drug trafficking, counterfeiting and money-laundering continue to take advantage of porous borders and weak law enforcement.

The capacity of government is limited by its relatively small size. Government expenditure reached 25% of GDP in 2015, compared to 34% in LAC countries and 45% in OECD countries. Public employment is also relatively low. Strategically planning for the right mix of skills in the civil service in the years to come will help the government meet strategic objectives as well as increase efficiency, responsiveness and quality in service delivery. In turn improvements in service delivery and maintaining commitment to inclusiveness, transparency and efficiency are needed for increasing levels of trust in government, which remain low. Indeed, satisfaction with service delivery is a significant challenge in Paraguay. While satisfaction with the education system is relatively high, satisfaction with health care, transport infrastructure and the transport system is low relative to benchmarks and particularly so for rural dwellers and for the most disadvantaged.

Paraguay has advanced towards the development of a comprehensive and coherent integrity system, with transparency playing a major role, but ensuring its effectiveness remains a big challenge. Perceptions of corruption by citizens are high, relative to regional peers and have evolved little in the past ten years. The government has taken a number of initiatives as part of a National Plan for the Prevention of Corruption. Among them, a key institutional pillar is the creation of a national anti-corruption agency (SENAC) which has been successful in co-ordinating and ensuring that all institutions in the executive branch establish an anti-corruption unit, and in raising awareness about public sector integrity issues. Transparency efforts play a major role in the fight against corruption. Paraguay has made strides against corruption in public procurement by making all procurement information available on line and including a whistle-blowing function in the procurement agency's electronic platform. The mandatory provision of information on the use of public resources, including the remuneration of civil servants, and the law on transparency and access to information adopted in 2014 also underpin the government's strategy for increasing citizen oversight of public affairs. Significant challenges remain, however, including ensuring political will to follow through on complaints raised, of which only a small number have so far led to administrative investigation, and the limitations in the scope of SENAC's action, which focuses only on embezzlement, but not other forms of corruption, and the absence of a specific provision for whistle-blower protection.

The development of the open government strategy in Paraguay has spearheaded a whole-of-government approach to promote transparency, empower citizens, fight corruption and harness new technologies for strengthening governance. Following a first action plan in which most of the actions were effectively linked to the development of information systems and less to mechanisms for civic participation and accountability, and which was faced with a degree of resistance, the action plan for the 2014-16 period was conceived through a participatory approach with 12 government institutions and nine civil society organisations. Progress in the form of legal and institutional reform has been notable and the country ranks fourth among Latin American countries with information in the OECD Index on Open Government Data and above the OECD average in the same index. While considerable efforts have been made to enhance openness by making information available, challenges remain to tailor public information to citizens' needs and strengthen accountability mechanisms.

Partnerships and financing for development

Analysis of financing flows for development shows that they are low in Paraguay compared to both the benchmarking countries and the OECD. Given the country's prudent fiscal stance and low reliance on public debt, public financing comes mostly from fiscal space. Fiscal space is helped by idiosyncratically high non-tax revenues from the two binational power plants, but constrained by relatively low tax revenues, reflecting low tax rates and evasion rates above the regional average. The weight of non-discretionary expenditures, which represent almost half of total public expenditure, also limits fiscal space. The country has recently made notable progress on both fronts. Tax revenues have increased by 5.4% of GDP since 2000 and the country has implemented major fiscal reforms, including the progressive implementation of the personal income tax since 2012, the expansion of VAT to the agricultural sector and the introduction of a tax on profit from agricultural activities in 2014. Measures are also being taken to limit the growth of the public wage bill, to reduce the weight of non-discretionary expenditures, which has led to public investment and capital expenditure growing at much higher rates than current expenditures, even if the weight of the latter remains high at 85% of total expenditure.

Private development flows, at 5.5% of GDP are relatively modest compared to public financing flows of 11.8% of GDP. Foreign direct investment (FDI) flows remain small: they accounted for 1.16% of GDP in 2016, the third lowest in the region. The importance of FDI is growing, however, and the government's investment attraction strategy is bearing fruit. Net FDI flows averaged 1.7% in 2010-16, an improvement compared to previous periods, and inward flows increased by 5% in 2016, against the trend in the South American region, where they fell by 9%. The recent dynamism in FDI flows has been partially driven by efforts to create an attractive regulatory framework and measures to attract investment. These measures have contributed to transforming the composition of investment with a notable increase in the maquila industry, increased diversification in countries of origin, and the development of sectors with greater job creation prospects such as automotive components.

The stability of the Paraguayan financial system is a major asset for development, but it needs to be further developed and become more inclusive. The banking sector is well capitalised, with sufficient access to sources of deposit financing and highly profitable. Credit growth has accelerated in recent years, with 26% average banking credit growth over the 2005-15 period, and banking credit to the private sector reached 43% in 2015. To better finance development, the regulation of the financial sector as a whole needs to be strengthened beyond that of the banking sector. Moreover, high interest rate spreads and reliance on short-term finance reflect constraints in the quality and availability of creditor information as well as the reliance on consumption credits. Financial inclusion is still very low and unequal in the country in spite of rapid growth in credit. Together, these constraints prevent the financial sector from making an even greater contribution to the country's development.

Key constraints to development in Paraguay

The main constraints to development identified by the first phase of the MDCR are interrelated and stem from the institutional and economic history of Paraguay, as well as from its growth model. The country's development path has been largely dependent on the development of highly productive mechanised agriculture and extensive animal farming, in a context of highly concentrated ownership of factors of production, especially land. As a result, the primary distribution of income in the country is unequal, the distribution of opportunities across the territory is uneven, and there are strong pressures on environmental resources. The country's economy has developed alongside a state with relatively limited reach, with relatively low taxation and public expenditure, where a number of markets are lightly or not regulated and where direct control of economic endeavours by the state is rare, with exceptions in network industries and energy in particular. In such a context, power relations that permeated the state under the authoritarian regime through a number of informal practices, and which remain to some extent, limit the efficiency of public service delivery, the equality of treatment and the efficacy of enforcement.

Table 1.1. **Key constraints to development in Paraguay**

Main constraints identified	Related outcomes	Chapters in this volume
Low levels of diversification, reliance on agriculture	Growth is volatile	Chapter 2
	Deforestation pressures	Chapter 4
Low levels of investment	Infrastructure gaps	Chapter 2
	Potential growth is lower than it could be with larger investment flows	Chapter 6
Infrastructure gaps	Competitiveness harmed by transport costs	Chapter 2
	Limited connectivity	Chapter 3
	Territorial inequalities	Chapter 4
	Health impacts	
Limited fiscal space	Limited public investment	Chapter 2
	Limited capacity in government agencies	Chapter 5
Prevalent informality	Low fiscal revenue	Chapter 2
	Prevalence of low quality and low paying jobs	Chapter 3
Competitiveness and FDI attractiveness	Limited innovation capacity	Chapter 2
	Relatively small inward FDI flows	Chapter 6
Unexploited development potential in the financial sector	Low private development finance flows	Chapter 6
	Regulatory gaps in the financial sector	
	Inequality in financial inclusion	
Low educational attainment and poor learning outcomes	Persistence of inequality	Chapter 3
	Lower innovation and productive upgrading potential	Chapter 2
Fiscal tax and transfer system has little impact on inequality	Income inequality	Chapter 3
Fragmented social protection system	Low coverage of social insurance	Chapter 3
	Limited effectiveness of social expenditure	Chapter 6
	Risks to public finances due to pension liabilities	
Weak institutional framework for environmental protection	Deforestation	Chapter 4
Weaknesses in land management and administration	Territorial inequalities reinforced by lack of urban planning	Chapter 4
	Weakness of local public finances	
	Limited access to capital for farmers	
Prevalence and perceptions of corruption	Inequality in access and use of public service, including in the justice system	Chapter 4
	Lowers investment attractiveness and makes doing business more difficult	Chapter 2
Limited capacity of government to deliver quality public service to all	Inequality in access and satisfaction with public services	Chapter 5
Weaknesses in coverage and quality of regulation	Administrative burdens create barriers to entrepreneurship	Chapter 2
	Competition and consumer protection regulations are insufficiently developed	Chapter 6
	Financial sector regulation has limited scope	

Source: Authors.

The Paraguayan government faces two major challenges in achieving the country's vision, given its development model: to steer the economy to deliver sustainable growth in the medium term and to improve the country's capacity to stem inequality. The agriculture-based development model as it has developed makes both of these tasks more difficult. Mechanised agriculture generates few jobs and the absence of diversification explains in part the high levels of informality in the country as many create their own jobs in low-value added services sectors. Informality fuels inequality in earnings and implies lower efficiency in tax collection, further weakening the capacity of the state both to alter the secondary distribution of income and to steer the structural transformation of the economy.

This system is evolving through changes in fiscal policy and emerging diversification. A major shift occurred in 2014 with the fiscal reform, extending VAT to agricultural produce and reforming the tax on profits from agricultural activity. Together, these reforms significantly raised the fiscal contribution of the sector to the public purse, although it remains smaller than its share of value added. Another key development is the progressive structural transformation taking place. The development of the agribusiness value chain itself can increase indirect job creation in firms offering services to agricultural producers (technical assistance, marketing of inputs like seeds, finance, transport and others) although many of these activities require qualified labour. While the thrust of industrial policy in Paraguay rests on exploiting comparative advantage by moving up the value chain in agricultural products and development agro-industry and related services, non-traditional sectors have also developed recently, especially as *maquilas* integrated into global value chains.

One of the major challenges for Paraguay is to buttress sources of economic prosperity that will sustain growth in the medium term. The current high contribution of total factor productivity to economic growth is an encouraging symptom of the ongoing structural transformation and institutional development in the country. However, the contribution of capital accumulation is lower than could be expected in the country given its position relative to the region and the scope for productive investments with both economic and social returns, as the large infrastructure needs suggest. The efforts on the part of the public sector in this regard are noteworthy. Within the limits imposed by the fiscal responsibility law, public investment has grown rapidly in recent years, and efforts are under way to increase tax revenues and improve the balance in the composition of expenditure. A large share of non-tax revenues is earmarked for infrastructure spending, shielding it from political intervention. However, given the size of the Paraguayan state, this will not suffice. Given the country's very prudent approach to international debt, the government is implementing means of intervention that will crowd in private financing, such as public-private partnerships.

The second major challenge is to increase the inclusiveness of the development path. Further improvements in infrastructure would contribute to integrating territories better. This would increase economic opportunities and the ability to deliver public services in remote areas. In terms of social policy, the flagship social assistance programmes have grown rapidly in the past few years, but the fragmentation of social protection limits its efficiency and undermines equality of opportunity. The prevalence of informal work is a key cause of this fragmentation, of which one important dimension is between social security –which covers formally employed workers– and non-contributory systems – which cover informal workers or the poor.

Improving educational outcomes is a crucial element in fulfilling the potential of all citizens. It is also a critical ingredient to reduce inequality in the distribution of market incomes. As structural transformation and internal migration progress, the capacity of new entrants into the manufacturing and, especially, the services sectors, to enter more productive segments, is of great importance also to ensuring that structural transformation contributes to productivity growth in the country. Recent successes in ensuring the quality of education and in expanding vocational training and professional education should be greatly expanded; they can contribute to making education more pertinent for the labour market.

Increasing inclusiveness also requires more inclusive patterns of production. They can generate livelihood opportunities to vulnerable groups across the country's territories. Indeed, the PND considers regional development and productive diversification jointly as one of the 12 strategies for implementation. The strategy is currently focused on increasing productivity and developing opportunities for smallholder agriculture. The development of formal manufacturing jobs in rural areas and the importance of non-farm activities in stimulating rural development in the region and elsewhere suggest that such a strategy should consider activities in the agri-food value chain besides agriculture, and beyond.

The main constraints identified can be bundled together into two overlapping domains: constraints that limit structural transformation and sustainable growth, and constraints that limit the capacity of the state. In each of these domains, three priority areas for action can be identified:

Structural transformation that unlocks new sources of growth can be encouraged by:

- Continued efforts to close the quantitative and qualitative gap in **infrastructure**, which is a major component of the historical investment deficit in Paraguay and affects the potential return of new investments as well as their geographic location.
- A systemic approach to **education** reform, so as to increase attainment and ensure a better match between the skills generated by the education system and the demands of the economy.
- Further efforts to strengthen **governance** so as to ensure that public affairs are, and are perceived to be, efficient and fair.

The capacity of the state to steer the economy in a sustainable growth path and to further social development can be strengthened by:

- Further unlocking **finance for development** through domestic resource mobilisation and crowding in private investment flows.
- Addressing **informality** and **the fragmentation of the social protection system** that has emerged as a result and which limits the efficiency of public action in poverty reduction and redistribution. Addressing this issue requires reforms in the areas of old age pensions, health and social assistance, as well as an integrated approach to informality.
- Developing a **territorial approach** to public policy that accounts for the specific comparative advantages and circumstances of each territory and builds upon local development plans.

Notes

1. This period corresponds to what is termed "the great delay" (*El gran retardo*) by Arce, Krauer and Ovando (2011).
2. Figure 1.2 does include transfers from the central administration to decentralised bodies and autonomous bodies, but available data do not account for expenditure by all such bodies.

3. Economy-wide and household level income measures can differ significantly, in terms of both levels and changes, particularly in countries that are relying heavily on natural resources and where a significant part of income from production is transferred abroad. Note that the ideal measure of household living standard is a measure of household net adjusted disposable income but since many developing countries lack such measure the report uses the gross national income.
4. Improved sanitation facilities are flush or pour flush toilets (to piped sewer system, septic tank and pit latrine), ventilated improved pit latrines, pit latrines with slab, or composting toilets.
5. Country estimates based on recorded deaths are not comparable due to differential underreporting. According to the estimates by the UN Inter-agency Group for Child Mortality Estimation, the child mortality rate in Paraguay (21‰) was 3‰ higher than the regional average (18‰) (UNICEF, 2015).

References

Arce, L. D., J. C. Herken Krauer, and F. Ovando (2011), "La Economía del Paraguay entre 1940-2008: Crecimiento, Convergencia Regional e Incertidumbres" [The Paraguayan economy between 1940 and 2008: Growth, regional convergence and uncertainties], Working Paper No. 5, *Paraguay. 200 Years of Independent Life. From Instability and Stagnation to the Challenge of Sustainable Growth and Social Equity Series*. Tinker Foundation and CADEP, Asunción.

BCP (2017), Statistical annex to the economic report (database), Banco Central de Paraguay, *https://www.bcp.gov.py/anexo-estadistico-del-informe-economico-i365*.

Boarini R., A. Kolev and A. McGregor (2014), "Measuring well-being and progress in countries at different stages of development: Towards a more universal conceptual framework", *http://dx.doi.org/10.1787/5jxss4hv2d8n-en*.

DGEEC (2015), *Paraguay. Proyección de la Población Nacional, Áreas Urbana y Rural por Sexo y Edad, 2000-2025. Revisión 2015* [Paraguay, Projections of national population, for rural and urban areas, by gender and age, 2000-2025. 2015 Revision], Dirección General de Estadística, Encuestas y Censos, Fernando de la Mora, October, *www.dgeec.gov.py/Publicaciones/Biblioteca/proyeccion%20nacional/Estimacion%20y%20proyeccion%20Nacional.pdf*.

Fernández Valdovinos, C. G. and A. Monge Naranjo (2004), "Economic Growth in Paraguay", *Economic and Social Study Series*, RE1-04-009, Inter-American Development Bank, Washington DC.

Gallup (2016), Gallup World Poll, *http://www.gallup.com/services/170945/world-poll.aspx* (accessed 1 June 2017).

Gobierno Nacional de Paraguay (2014), *Plan Nacional de Desarrollo. Construyendo el Paraguay del 2030*, Gobierno Nacional de Paraguay, *http://www.stp.gov.py/pnd/wp-content/uploads/2014/12/pnd2030.pdf*.

Investor (2015), *Agricultura y desarrollo en Paraguay*, Unión de Gremios de la Producción, Asunción.

Masi, F. (2014), "2015: El crecimiento económico y el factor agroalimentario", *Economía y Sociedad* No. 27, CADEP, Asunción, *www.cadep.org.py/2015/10/economia-y-sociedad-n31-2/*.

Ministerio de Hacienda (2017), "Evolución del Gasto Social 2003 a 2017" [Social Expenditure 2003 to 2017], Asunción, *http://www.hacienda.gov.py/web-presupuesto/index.php?c=275*.

OECD (2015), *PISA 2015 Results (Volume I): Excellence and Equity in Education*, OECD Publishing, Paris, *http://dx.doi.org/10.1787/9789264266490-en*.

OECD (2011), *How's Life? Measuring Well-being*, OECD Publishing, Paris, *http://dx.doi.org/10.1787/9789264121164-en*.

Transparency International (2016), Corruption Perception Index (database), *http://www.transparency.org*.

UN (2015), "Transforming our world: the 2030 Agenda for Sustainable Development", Outcome document of the United Nations summit for the adoption of the post-2015 development agenda, A/RES/70/1, United Nations, New York, *http://www.un.org/ga/search/view_doc.asp?symbol=A/RES/70/1&Lang=E*.

UNESCO (2017), UIS.stat (database), United Nations Educational, Scientific and Cultural Organization, *http://data.uis.unesco.org/Index.aspx* (accessed September 2017).

UNICEF (2015), "Levels & Trends in Child Mortality", Estimates developed by the Inter-Agency Group for Child Mortality Estimation (UN IGME), UNICEF, WHO, World Bank, UNPD.

World Bank (2016), *World Development Indicators* (database), Washington DC, *http://data.worldbank.org*.

ANNEX 1.A1

Stories from a successful Paraguay in 2030

During the workshop "Paraguay: Future, challenges and global environment", participants prepared stories describing the life of ordinary citizens in Paraguay in 2030 in a future where development policy has succeeded. These stories are summarised here.

"Aracy González is 40 years old and is a civil servant. She lives in San Lorenzo but works in Asunción. She has a healthy breakfast and uses public transport to get to work. Schoolchildren, sportsmen and professionals also use public transport, all keen to go to work. While she travels, she obtains useful information for her job via IT. Her working time is flexible, she can go to the office only 2 or 3 days a week. Her work is measured by her productivity and not the amount of time she is at the office. All the work is done electronically. On her way back from work, she picks up her children at the community centre. There is no informal work. All amenities are handy in the community: education, leisure activities, etc. She fulfilled her objectives and is happy."

"Jasmine is 32 years old and from Carapeguá. She studied Administration at a university outside Asunción. There is a pig slaughterhouse in Carapeguá where she has been hired as head of department. She gets up at 4 am and works until 2pm and has a car of her own. Jasmine benefits from social security, a reformed IPS capitalised with resources from Itaipú. She has 2 children, 4 and 6 years old. Her husband works in a 7 hectare farm. He works in a programme for the production of pig feed. He gets home in time to welcome the boys after school, who study until 4:00 pm. Once a year they enjoy a vacation in the coast of Brazil. They live with their parents who do not have insurance but do receive certain subsidies form the government. Jasmine likes her home and is happy that she did not have to sell her lands and move to the city, though she does enjoy occasional trip to Asuncion to visit the malls and shops. Jasmine participates in a women's club and the boys go fishing on weekends."

"Estanislao Bacete is 33 years old and lives in Bache San Pedro. He did not go to university. He is married to Juana, who is 30 years old. They have 2 children of 8 and 10 years: Juanita and Pedrito. They are farmers, but live comfortably as their harvest has low production risks, and is integrated in a value chain. The family enjoy a healthy diet, with a balanced family breakfast every morning with fresh milk. The children go to school on public transport and the school has a single shift. Juanita is to participate in the Mathematical Olympiads in Mexico. Her dream is to get a scholarship to study economics in Chicago. Estanislao enjoys a quiet life, with stable income, health and vacations. He feels like an integrated citizen who can provide for his family."

"Mariana is 30 years old, and is currently studying for a masters' degree in civil engineering abroad. Originally from Aripahuari, she has been offered a job in Asunción upon return from her studies to fulfil her scholarship's requirement. Mariana has a son. She could not bring him to school but the father took leave to take care of the child. He has a good job opportunity, has medical benefits, security, and efficient public transport to reach the city. They live in a city where you can get around by bicycle or walking. The father was unemployed for a year but wants to raise capital to start a company. Mariana is happy because the family is able to avail of welfare and she is in a situation where she can realise her professional dream and can contribute to her country."

"Juan Perez is 43 years old, has a wife and two children. He owns his own house with all services and 8G internet. In 2030 education in Paraguay is free: one of Juan's sons attends a public school, and the other is studying electromechanics at a university. Both travel to class on a metrobus. After training in Spain, Juan's wife passed competitive exams and got a job as a teacher in the same school as her younger son. The family have access to social security. They are happy because they have access to good health conditions, infrastructure and social protection."

"Hilda is 60 years old. She has five children, and two of her children have a neurological condition. Hilda makes *chipas* she sells at the market and her husband is a fisherman. With seed capital, she started a company and established her home as a guest house. The department of Alto Paraguay where they live has developed considerably; the infrastructure is in good condition. She offers visitors a taste of the cultural and gastronomic heritage of Paraguay. Hilda receives training in management of her inn. She is happy because she has a source of income for her children in the future. In fact, she has the same income as her husband."

"Rosa María González, 37, is a fourth grade teacher at the local public school in Coronel Oviedo. She is married and has two sons, and graduated with a bachelor's degree at the age of 23 with a scholarship. Rosa María is currently saving to do a masters' degree. She is happy for her children and is proud of their achievements. Rosa's husband is a systems analyst and works in his own micro-enterprise. Prior to this he studied abroad. They have a house with a vegetable garden and own an electric vehicle. Her 9 and 6 year olds follow music and robotics lessons. Rosa is happy because they can access health and education. Two weeks ago they returned from vacations, and Rosa is planning to take them to their health check-ups. They travel in comfortable and reliable public transportation."

"Esperanza, 18, did not finish high school. She is the eldest daughter of couple of farmers. Her parents were able to form a cooperative of producers thanks to subsidies they received. The producers' cooperative was successful and they were subsequently able to set up a cassava starch factory. The business is well embedded in a value chain. Esperanza's parents also work in corporate social responsibility programs. The local health care facility has been upgraded. With her father's improved income, Esperanza was able to access a university. In 2030 with her degree, she was able to find work in a factory."

Multi-dimensional Review of Paraguay
Volume 1. Initial Assessment

Chapter 2

Towards shared prosperity in Paraguay

This chapter first analyses Paraguay's macroeconomic performance, looking into the drivers of recent economic growth as well as recent developments in economic and trade diversification. Second, the inflation-targeting regime and the fiscal framework are discussed. Third, the chapter examines the levels of both capital and public investment, discussing some of the main challenges regarding budget management and execution, particularly for infrastructure investment projects and as investment contribution to growth. Finally, it looks into remaining challenges faced by Paraguay to further boost productivity and competition such as innovation, skills mismatch, infrastructure and the institutional framework.

Paraguay's macroeconomic performance has been robust but is highly dependent on a few agricultural products and trading partners

Growth remains strong but volatile because of the high reliance on agriculture and trade

The Paraguayan economy has remained among the strongest-growing economies in the region but with significant volatility (Figure 2.1). Between 2006 and 2015, Paraguay's gross domestic product (GDP) grew at an annual average of 5.1%, mainly supported by solid external trade and favourable commodity prices. GDP growth has slowed in the last few years (2014-15) in part because of a decline in commodity prices. More recently in a context of economic downturn for both the region and the main trading partners (Argentina and Brazil), Paraguay registered high growth rates, as GDP increased by 4.0% in 2016 (including binationals), explained largely by exports and investment, while consumption remained sluggish (Figure 2.2). Growth volatility is mainly the result of its heavy reliance on agriculture and livestock production as well as electricity generation, which are the leading economic activities, representing around 60% of all Paraguayan exports in 2016.

Figure 2.1. **Paraguay's economic growth remains strong relative to benchmark countries**

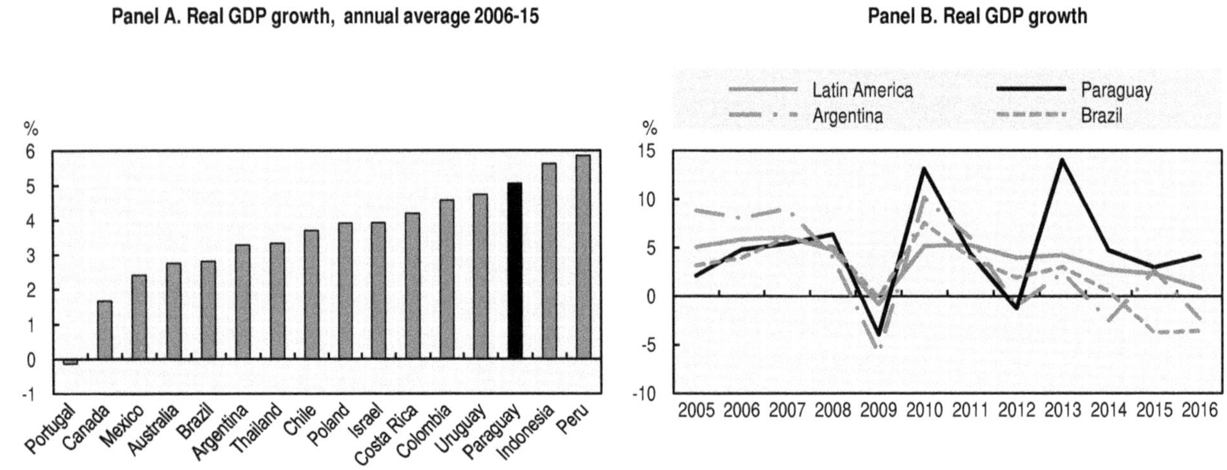

Note: Panel A: Purchasing power parity (PPP), constant 2011 international USD.

Source: Panel A: World Bank (2017a), *World Development Indicators Database* (database), Washington DC, *http://data.worldbank.org*. Panel B: International Monetary Fund (2017), *World Economic Outlook* (database), *https://www.imf.org/external/pubs/ft/weo/2015/01/weodata/index.aspx*.

StatLink http://dx.doi.org/10.1787/888933748800

Reliance on agriculture and few export products to drive growth exposes the economy to weather and commodity price shocks as well as regional spillovers. The agricultural sector accounted for around 18.7% of GDP in 2016 (trade accounted for 14.3% and industry for 10.7%). Paraguay's exports are concentrated in a few products (soybeans, beef meat, electricity) and a few export destinations (Brazil with about 35% of exports, the European Union (EU) with about 14%, Asia 12%, Argentina 10% and Russia 8%) (Figure 2.3). The current account is estimated to have recorded a surplus of around 1.7% of GDP in 2016 given a strong improvement in the trade balance, caused in part by an increase in re-exports and contraction of imports (BCP, 2016).

Figure 2.2. **Economic growth is highly dependent on agriculture and trade**

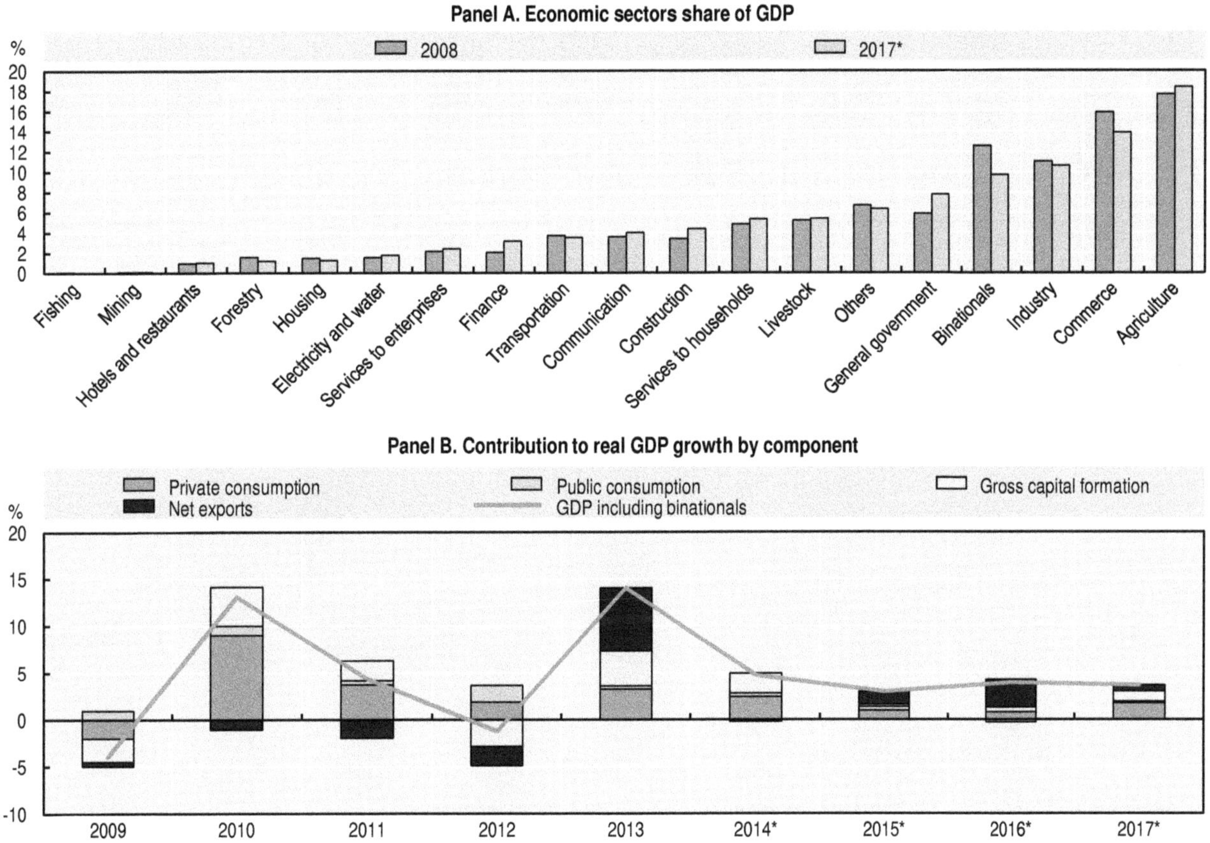

Note: * Preliminary figures.

Source: Central Bank of Paraguay (2017), *https://www.bcp.gov.py/*.

StatLink http://dx.doi.org/10.1787/888933748819

Sectoral growth patterns in recent years show that diversification is contributing to greater resilience in aggregate performance. At 4.8% in compound annual terms, real GDP growth was comparable in 2007-11 and 2011-16. Agriculture grew 7.4% in the former period, but only 4.7% in the latter,[1] although given its large contribution to GDP, it remained the sector with the largest contribution to growth. Faster growth in manufacturing (which grew at 6.1% compared to 1.4% in the first period) contributed to stabilising total growth and to increasing productive diversification. During the period 2011-16, a number of sectors grew more rapidly than agriculture thereby increasing diversification, including livestock (6.9%), construction (8.9%) and financial services (8.6%).

Figure 2.3. **Economic and exports diversification remains low**

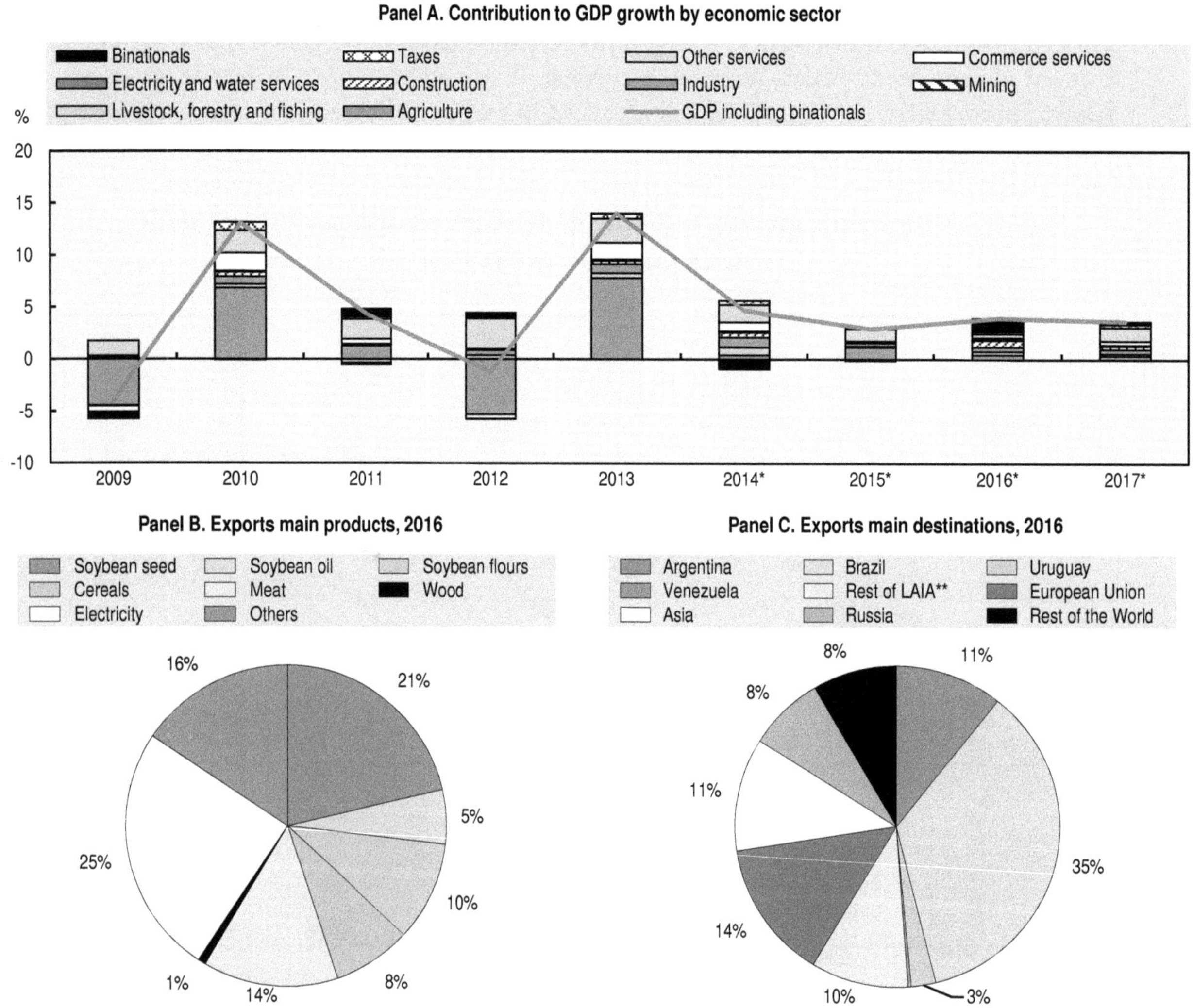

Note: * Preliminary figures. Panel C: **Rest of LAIA is Latin American Integration Association.

Source: Central Bank of Paraguay (2017), *https://www.bcp.gov.py/*.

StatLink http://dx.doi.org/10.1787/888933748838

Exports are concentrated in primary products but sophistication is slowly increasing

Exports are concentrated in primary agricultural products and processed agricultural products. Oilseeds, vegetable oils and meat products together account for over two thirds of Paraguay's exports. In 2014, soybeans and their derivatives accounted for over 40% of the country's exports. Bovine meat accounted for approximately 14%, while other grains such as maize and rice accounted for 6% (Center for International Development at Harvard University, 2017).In 2016, soybeans and their derivatives accounted for 37% of the country's exports. Beef meat accounted for approximately 14%, while cereals such as maize and rice accounted for 8% (BCP, 2017).

The concentration has increased since 2000 due to trends in prices, which also drove the rapid increase in total exports. However, in 2015, international and regional events reversed this trend. Between 2000 and 2016 the value of exports increased more than their volume, which suggests that growth in exports in this period was mainly due to the increased prices of its main commodities (Figure 2.4 and Figure 2.5). Total goods exports fell by 16% in 2015. The fall can be explained by the decline of three of Paraguay's main exports: oilseeds accounted for approximately 62% of the fall, vegetable oils for 4%, and meat products for 14%. Taken together, these products accounted for 52% of the country's total exports (without electricity) in 2015 (OBEI, 2016).

Figure 2.4. **Paraguay's exports increased more in value than in volume**

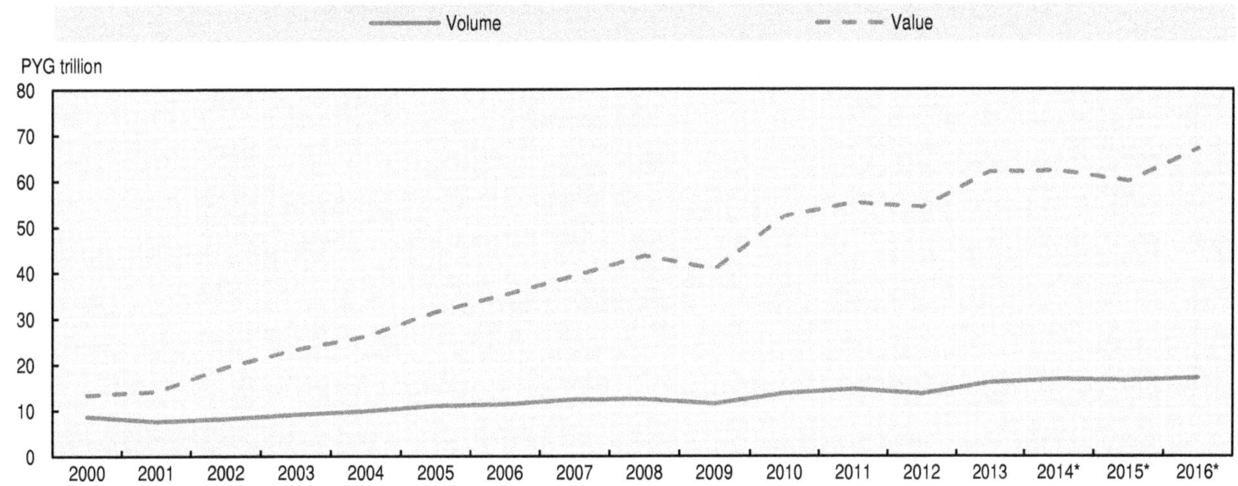

Note: * Preliminary figures.

Source: BCP (2017), *https://www.bcp.gov.py/*.

StatLink http://dx.doi.org/10.1787/888933748857

Figure 2.5. **Prices for some of Paraguay's main commodities have increased**

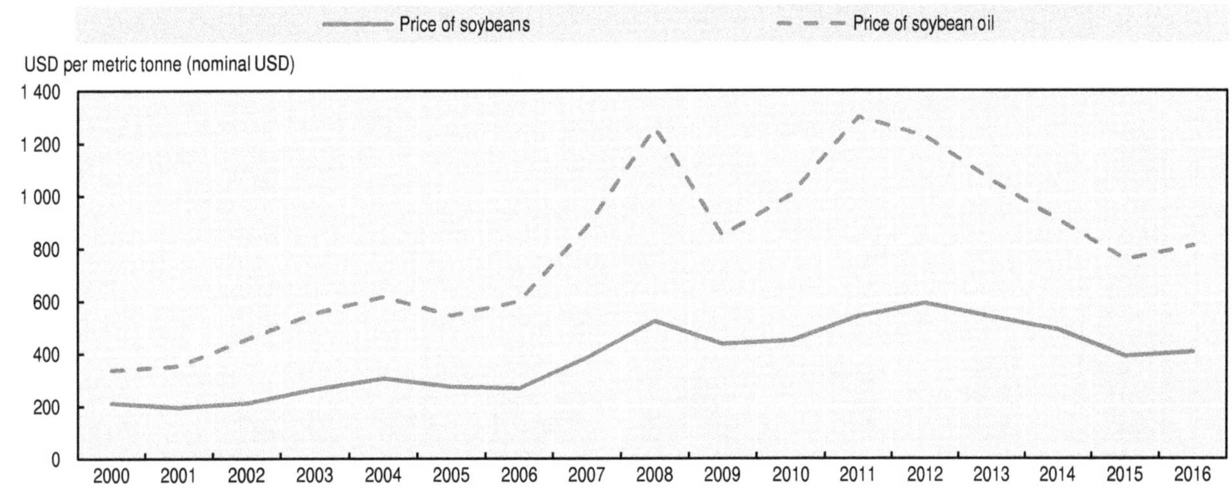

Source: World Bank (2017b), *Commodity Price Data* (database), *http://data.worldbank.org*.

StatLink http://dx.doi.org/10.1787/888933748876

Moreover, 60% of total exports value was concentrated in the top 1% of exporting firms in 2016. This concentration of exports among a few firms is consistent with an increasing trend in exports that parallels a decreasing trend in the number of exporting firms (CEPAL, 2016). Moreover, the export concentration is more marked in specific sectors. Since the beginning of the 2000s, exports of primary products and manufacturing outputs have been increasing at similar rates (Figure 2.6).

In terms of its trading partners, the number of Paraguay's export destination countries remains limited, yet some diversification is observed (Figure 2.7). Asian economies have gained weight in Paraguay's exports, as have European markets and the Pacific Alliance countries.

Within Asian economies, Paraguay's main recipients of exports are: Bangladesh, India, Israel, Korea, Thailand and Viet Nam, which jointly accounted for 76% of exports to Asia in 2016.

Figure 2.6. **The value of exports of primary commodities and manufactured goods has increased at a similar rate**

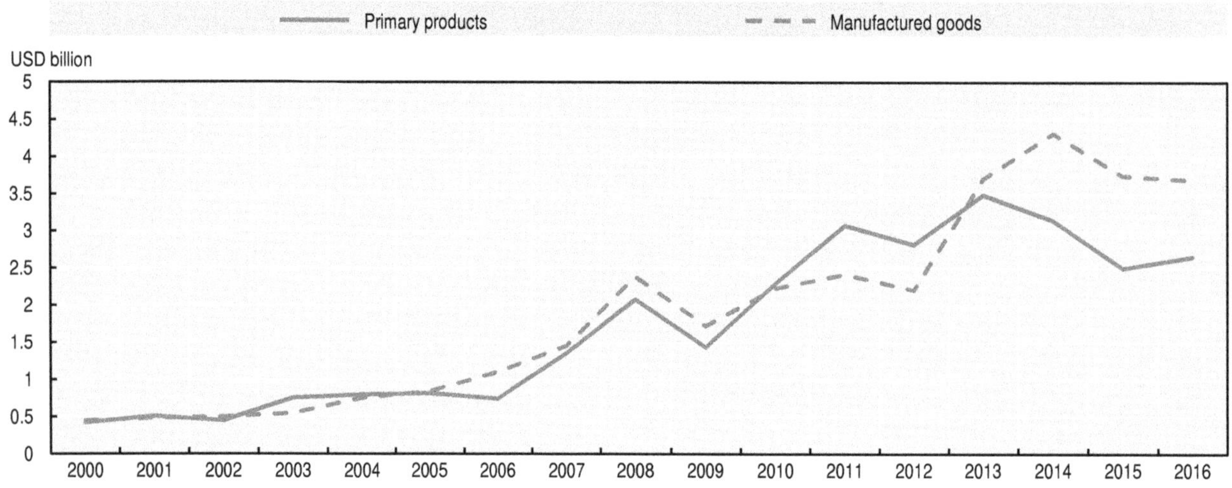

Source: Central Bank of Paraguay (2017), *https://www.bcp.gov.py/*.

StatLink http://dx.doi.org/10.1787/888933748895

Figure 2.7. **Diversification is observed in export destination countries**

Exports by trading partners

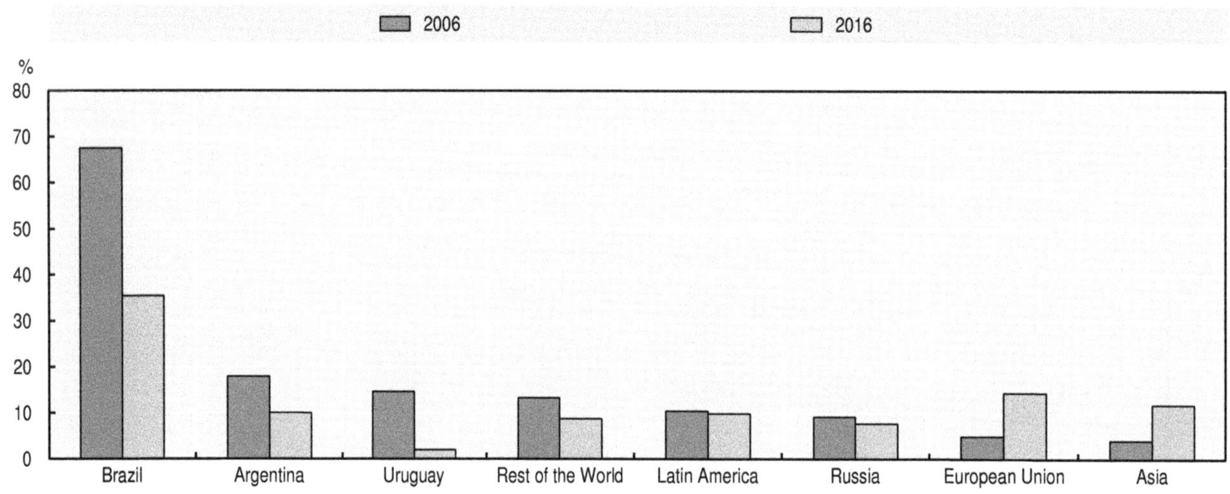

Source: Central Bank of Paraguay (2017), *https://www.bcp.gov.py/*.

StatLink http://dx.doi.org/10.1787/888933748914

In 2016 Asian economies accounted for over 11% of Paraguayan exports, and the EU for approximately 14%. Overall, Paraguay exports less today to its South American neighbours than previously and has been increasingly redirecting its exports out of the Mercosur block and into Asian and new European trading partners. China's demand for agricultural and food products, including meat, is likely to increase considerably in the next few years (OECD/CAF/ECLAC, 2015). In particular, China's beef consumption is expected to grow by between 10% and 20% over the next decade, offering new opportunities for exporters such as Paraguay. Taking advantage of some of these possible opportunities would contribute to strengthening the already increasing trend in the value of low and medium technological content such as primary products and agricultural manufactures (Figure 2.8).

Figure 2.8. **Technological content in exports is increasing**

Exports by technological content

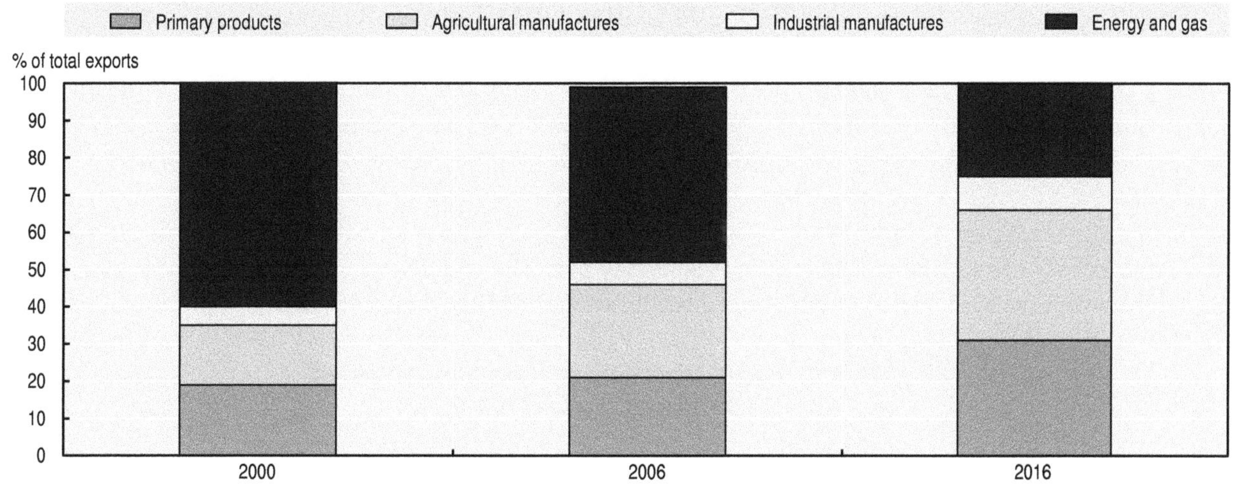

Source: Central Bank of Paraguay (2017), *https://www.bcp.gov.py/.*

StatLink http://dx.doi.org/10.1787/888933748933

The level of sophistication and complexity of Paraguayan exports is low. In 2015, Paraguay was ranked as 91st in terms of economic complexity, out of 141 countries, defined as a measure of the knowledge in a society that gets translated into the products it makes. A country is considered "complex" if it exports not only highly complex products, but also a large number of different products (AEC, 2017). The country-level economic complexity is measured through the Economic Complexity Index (ECI). Although between 2000 and 2014, there was a positive change in Paraguay's Economic Complexity Index (ECI), the country's index remains negative, with an ECI of -0.51 (Figure 2.9). Moreover, when compared to other countries in the region and countries with a similar economic structure, such as Brazil, Colombia, and Argentina, Paraguay ranks as one of the last in terms of the ECI.

Figure 2.9. **The level of sophistication and complexity of Paraguayan exports is low**

Economic complexity index

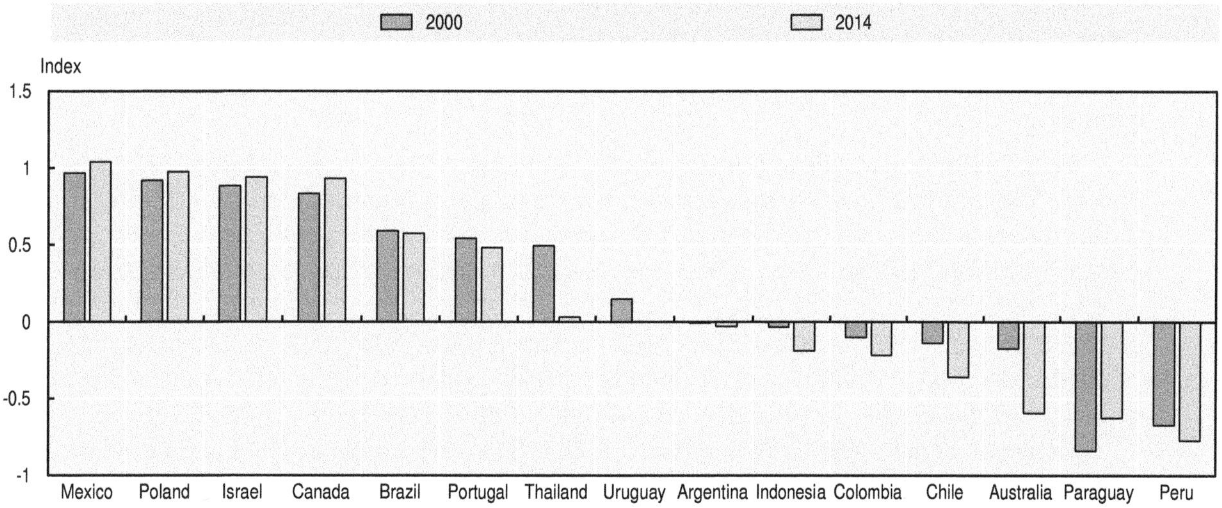

Source: Center for International Development at Harvard University (2017), *http://www.atlas.cid.harvard.edu.*

StatLink http://dx.doi.org/10.1787/888933748952

The country's low economic complexity rank is partly explained by its reliance on primary products. Primary products with low levels of sophistication accounted for roughly 54% of Paraguay's total exports in 2016. As an example, in the case of soybeans, the country's largest export crop, over 60% is exported as grain, while less than 40% is industrially treated prior to its commercialisation (BCP, 2017). Both raw primary products and manufactured outputs have increased their share of exports over the past decades. Nonetheless, it is important to acknowledge that in 2016, energy accounted for over 25% of Paraguay's exports. During this year, the country exported approximately 75% of its total energy production, making Paraguay a significant regional exporter of clean and renewable energy. Increasing investment from hydroelectric companies may pave the way for the country to expand its involvement in exports of higher complexity, while moving away from primary products.

Figure 2.10. **Paraguay's exports are concentrated**

Concentration index, 2000-15

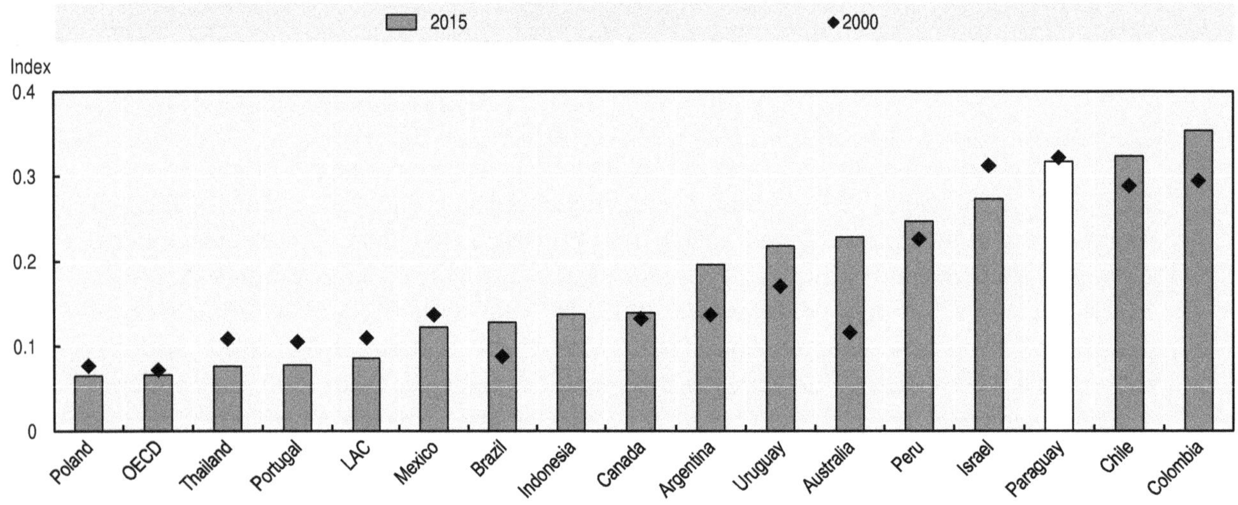

Note: The concentration index, also referred to as Herfindahl-Hirschmann Index (HHI), is a measure of concentration of exports. Values range between 0 and 1; a value of 1 suggests that a specific country's exports and imports are highly concentrated in a few products. On the contrary, a value of 0 means that a country's exports and imports are highly diversified and relying on many different products.

Source: UNCTAD (2017), UnctadStat (database), *http://unctadstat.unctad.org/ReportFolders/reportFolders.aspx.*

StatLink *http://dx.doi.org/10.1787/888933748971*

Structural transformation is progressing, but is not the main driver of productivity growth

While Paraguay's sector composition of GDP has remained relatively stable over the past decades, the contribution of the primary sector to the economy remains important. Whereas during the 1970s the average contribution of the primary sector (including agriculture, livestock, forestry and fishing industries) to the economy was 22%, a similar average annual contribution was registered during the 1980s (19%), 1990s (19%) and 2000s (22%). Between 2010 and 2015, the contribution from the primary sector dropped in current prices from 20.5% at the beginning of the decade, to 17.5% in 2015, a phenomenon partially explained by the fall in commodity prices. While the average participation has been stable, during specific years (2007, 2010 and 2013), when Paraguay's annual GDP growth reached 11%, the contribution of the primary sector was above 50%. The agro-industry sector represents around 40% of Paraguayan exports, but it has also shown signs of dynamism towards other sectors, with a contribution to the tertiary sector, in particular transport, commerce and financial services (CADEP, 2014a). This explains why fluctuations in the agricultural sector (due to climatic changes) can go beyond the primary sector and impact on other parts of the economy. Employment shifts from agriculture towards manufacturing, construction and services have been substantial. Paraguay's share of employment in agriculture and related activities remains large, accounting for nearly one-fourth of the labour force (from 24% of the labour force to 20% in 2015). Manufacturing employs a smaller share (nearly 12%, excluding electricity generation), whereas the services sector employs between 50% and 60% of the labour force, including commerce, tourism, business, social and personal services, transportation and communication. In terms of output, the contributions of agriculture and related sectors in 2015 (20%), manufacturing (13%) and services (altogether, 53%) are comparable to their employment share.

Structural transformation has the potential to increase productivity growth in Paraguay. The distribution of the workforce according to the labour productivity of broad industrial groups shows that there are significant productivity gains to be realised through labour reallocations from less to more productive sectors. Labour productivity in the sector where it is lowest, trade and hospitality services, is only 60% of the average, and the sector employed 27% of the workforce in 2015. Relative productivity across sectors also shows two particularities of the Paraguayan economy. The first is the high productivity of agriculture: labour productivity in agriculture is only 5% below average productivity. The second is the high labour productivity of the utilities sector, driven by the reliance of the country of hydropower. The data in Figure 2.11 do not include revenues from the binational dams in the value added of utilities. If it were included, productivity in the utilities sector would be 16 times the country average. The analysis on the basis of sector-level data is limited by the level of detail available in labour statistics. For example, Figure 2.11 bundles personal and business services or all sectors in manufacturing, whose productivity levels are very different. More importantly, it considers the agricultural sector as a whole, while there exist large productivity and yield gaps between mechanised agriculture and smallholder production.

Figure 2.11. **Productivity and the distribution of labour in Paraguay, 2015**

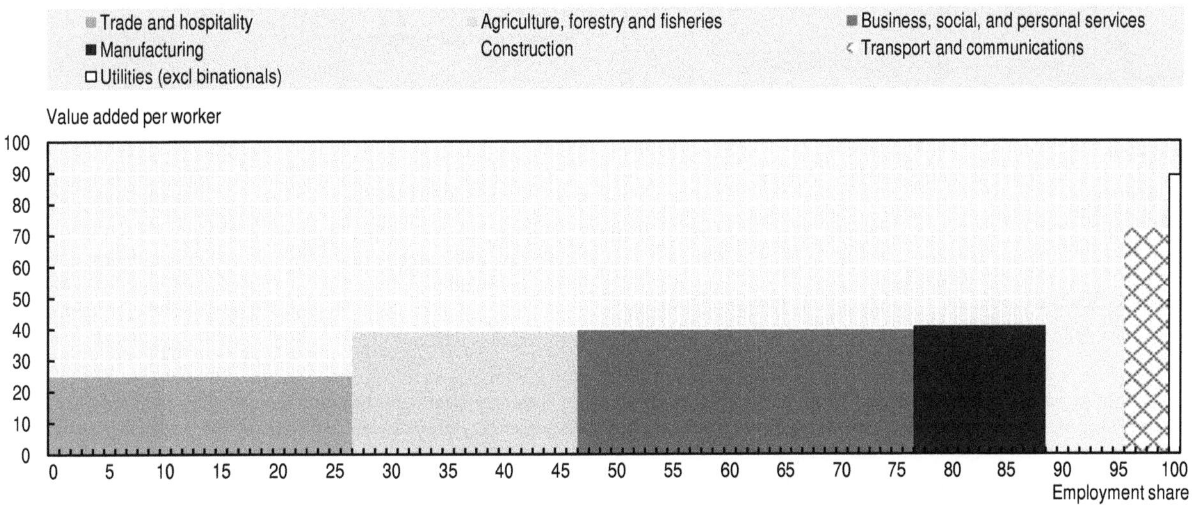

Source: Authors' calculations, based on Central Bank of Paraguay (2017), *https://www.bcp.gov.py/* and General Directorate of Statistics, Surveys and Censuses (DGEEC) data.

StatLink http://dx.doi.org/10.1787/888933748990

Labour reallocation in Paraguay has been mostly from agriculture-related sectors to the rest of the economy (Figure 2.12). Job creation in Paraguay between 2010 and 2015 has been notable, even with the country's high levels of labour force participation and low unemployment rates. The average annual employment growth for the whole economy of 1.8% hides some interesting dynamics at the sectoral level. Whereas the primary sector experienced an average annual 3% slowdown over the period, the manufacturing industry experienced a major increase in employment of 3.9%. This increase can be partially explained by the investment attraction policy implemented in recent years. Services sectors have also experienced an increase in employment ranging from 0.8% (on average) for construction, to 3.3% for commerce and tourism and 5.0% for business, social and personal services. Differences in overall labour productivity levels per sector are moderate, with business and personal services leading, followed by manufacturing and construction then by agriculture and related services. In contrast to other economies, labour productivity in the agriculture sector remains substantial in Paraguay, even in a context of decreasing yields of the agriculture sector. Therefore, the shift of a share of the agricultural labour force towards other sectors does not have a large positive impact on overall labour productivity, because part of that reallocation is towards less productive sectors.

Figure 2.12. **Productivity increases are led by within-sector growth rather than by labour reallocation**

In percentage, 2010-15

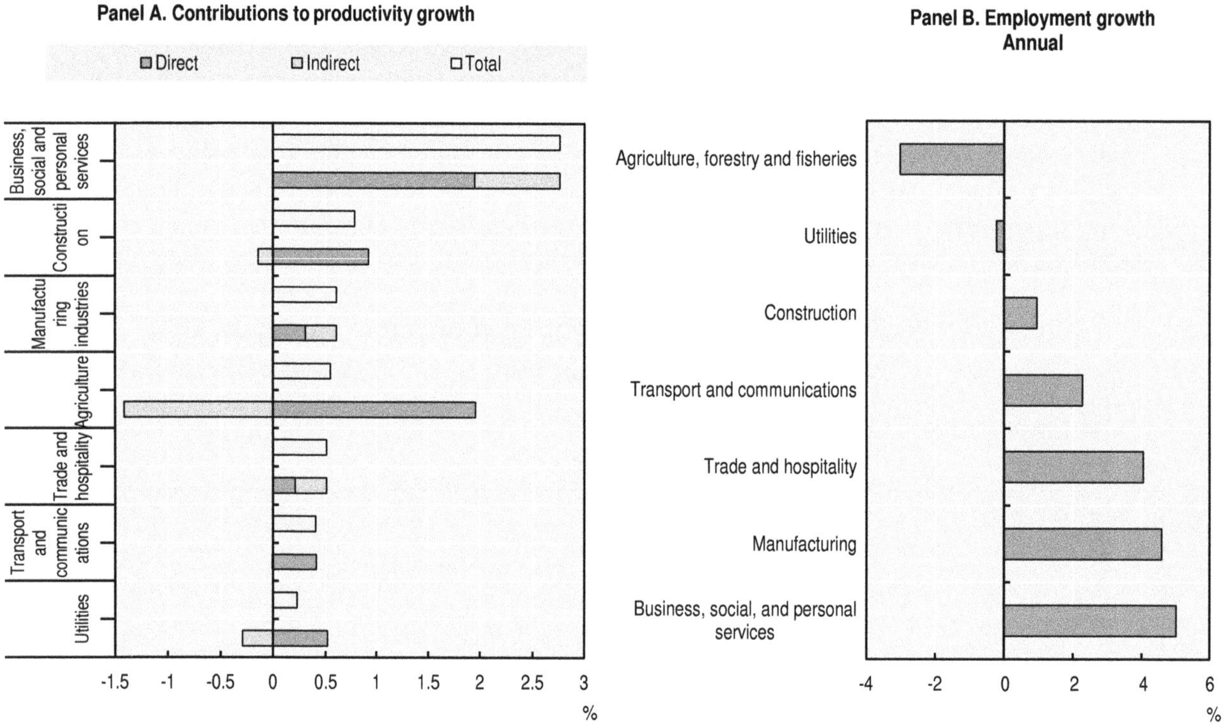

Note: In Panel A, overall productivity growth is decomposed into a within-industry effect (direct), measuring the average yearly growth of output per employed person; and a between-industry effect (indirect) measuring compositional shifts in sectoral shares of employment and relative price changes, as in Diewert (2014).

Source: Authors' calculations, based on Central Bank of Paraguay (2017), *https://www.bcp.gov.py/* and General Directorate of Statistics, Surveys and Censuses (DGEEC) data.

StatLink http://dx.doi.org/10.1787/888933749009

Productivity gains in all major sectors in the past 5 years have been achieved with falling labour elasticities. Figure 2.13 shows the growth in value added and in employment across the sectors with the largest employment shares in the economy. A positive employment elasticity of growth indicates that increased output is associated with increased employment, unlike the case of the agriculture sector, where it has been accompanied by falling employment.

An elasticity lower than 1 indicates that output is growing more quickly than employment, signifying both increases in productivity and in employment. While manufacturing and construction were associated with large gains in employment during the past decade, elasticities have fallen below 1 since 2010 – in the case of construction, much below 1. The trend in the trade and restaurant sector, where elasticity is above 1 and growing is a call to attention. Since this is the sector with the lowest productivity in the economy, and its employment share is growing, a further fall in productivity is a cause for concern. This is in contrast to the rest of the services sector, where fast employment growth is accompanied by steady productivity growth. Fostering labour reallocation towards more productive services is therefore an avenue to increase overall productivity in the economy.

Figure 2.13. **Employment elasticity across selected sectors in Paraguay (2003-15)**

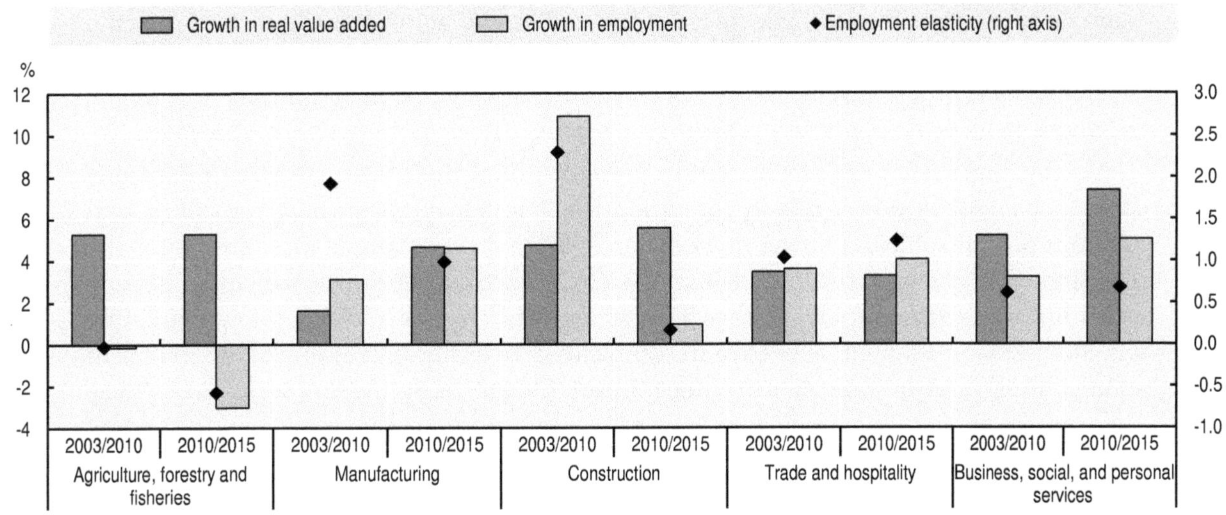

Note: Growth rates are compound annual growth rates for real value added (in 1994 constant prices) and employment by sector. The elasticities are calculated as the ratio of compound annualised growth rates (CAGR) for the two series.

Source: Author calculations based on BCP (2017) and EPH (DGEEC, 2017).

StatLink http://dx.doi.org/10.1787/888933749028

The agriculture, livestock and forestry sectors in Paraguay account for nearly a quarter the country's GDP and more than 40% of its exports. The Paraguayan economy is highly dependent on the sector, with agriculture accounting for 17% of its GDP between 2008 and 2016, and livestock and forestry 5% and 1%, respectively (BCP, 2017). Still, this large share hides considerable differences between large, commercially-oriented producers and subsistence producers. According to the 2008 agricultural census, Paraguay accounted more than 250 000 family farms, 17% concentrated in the areas of San Pedro, Caaguazú (15%), Itapúa (12%), Paraguarí (9%) and Caazapá (8%). Data on productivity by farm size is not available for recent years. However, the yield differential between small and large farms in the 2008 Agricultural Census suggests that, overall, large farms are more productive (CADEP, 2014b). Commercial agriculture has also moved away from less-profitable products in international markets today, such as cotton and sesame, towards soy, maize and wheat. In contrast, products like cassava, beans, white maize, cotton, sesame, fruits and vegetables, constitute the main farming crops in family agriculture and key staples within households' consumption baskets.

Providing proper support to family agriculture could improve living conditions of the rural population. While services in the agriculture sector are not particularly developed in Paraguay, other forms of support have been introduced, in line with Paraguay's National

Development Plan (section 2.26). The Ministry of Agriculture co-ordinates three main lines of action directed at family agriculture: first, employing direct-seeding systems for crops used for self-consumption, specifying minimum coverage and using coverage for the conservation of minerals and soil biomass; second, rotating crops to avoid the propagation of diseases and plagues, and to replace nutrients in the soil; third, using a silvo-pastoral system for cattle, which combines forestry and grazing of animals to enhance soil protection while guaranteeing a long-term income for cattle-dependent households. All three initiatives, while still modest in coverage, aim at promoting a more sustainable approach to agricultural practices. In recent years other forms of support to family agriculture have been introduced, in the form of promotion activities and market creation. The creation of a "quality seal" for family agriculture products is one of the innovations in the sector. Also, through public procurement, the government is trying to create demand for agricultural products, for example to supply schools. Some specific products in the agro-business sector are being developed. One example of this is stevia, a sweetener, which is traded to China and Malaysia. Organic sesame production has also gained traction recently thanks to demand from Japan, and there could be an opportunity to develop a competitive value chain in the sector.

Developing the service sectors within the agricultural chain is an area where Paraguay could focus in the future. While the provision of services in some areas of agriculture and livestock are consolidated in the most dynamic sectors (for example distribution for the meat industry or research and development [R&D] for the soybean sector), other sectors lack a proper services supply in areas such as logistics, transport, distribution, marketing and R&D. More investment is needed in technical services for agricultural value chains. In addition to services, mechanisms to reduce the volatility of the agriculture sector are lacking. The transfer of agro-climatic risks among small agriculture producers is a recent area of intervention of the Ministry of Agriculture, which assumes the production risk of vulnerable agriculture-dependent families (also guaranteeing some fiscal predictability).

Paraguay's industrial sector has gained dynamism in recent years. While traditionally, the country's industrial development was limited to the processing of primary products from the agricultural and forestry industries, more recently the metal-mechanics, auto parts and pharmaceutical sectors have gained prominence. Electricity generation remains the most important contributor to the country's GDP in the industry sector. However, in recent years, sectors such as clothing, footwear, auto parts, electrical appliances and chemical products have resurged, thanks to Paraguay's competitive advantages, which include low labour costs (20% lower than its neighbour Brazil), access to low-cost and clean electricity, and a favourable tax regime for companies. The maquila regime and a more solid investment promotion strategy have also been critical in explaining the expansion of the manufacturing sector. The government has made efforts to diversify domestic production and develop the manufacturing and services sectors, mainly by promoting added value in primary goods, by introducing investment attraction instruments and by developing an infrastructure plan. Initiatives for the internationalisation of firms, such as those managed by REDIEX, have aimed at supporting strategic sectors in manufacturing and logistics services (see Chapter 6).

The development of tourism is another opportunity for Paraguay to consolidate a diversification strategy. Both foreign and domestic tourism flows have increased in recent years, particularly in the area of ecological tourism. The core of international tourism in Paraguay comes from Mercosur neighbours Argentina and Brazil, with 848 000 and 190 000 registered visitors in 2015 from a total of 1 214 000 visitors, which represents an impressive increase with respect to previous years. The number of Argentinian visitors has almost quadrupled since 2010. The rest of visitors come mainly from the Americas (Bolivia, United States, Uruguay), and Europe (Germany, France, Spain). The emergence of tourism as a promising sector is also the result of the national plan for the development of tourism (*Plan Maestro de Desarrollo Turístico*), which covers several strategic areas. The *posadas turísticas* (tourist guesthouses) programme aims at empowering local communities to develop domestic tourism. Ecotourism (*turismo de naturaleza*) has gained ground in recent years. Other forms of tourism, such as religious tourism (the Jesuit Mission *Guaraní de la Santísima Trinidad* attracts 30 000 visitors per year) and conference-related tourism, have raised the profile of Paraguay in the region. The decentralisation of tourism-related activities remains an essential objective for the government in coming years. To this end an ambitious capacity building programme is being implemented with municipalities.

The inflation-targeting regime has helped to control inflation volatility

An implicit inflation-targeting regime since 2004 has helped to control inflation volatility. An explicit inflation target started in 2011 which together with the tolerance range have been adjusted downwards. The tolerance range was lowered from +/-2.5 percentage points (pp) to +/-2 pp in January 2014. In December 2014, the inflation target was shifted from 5% to 4.5% for the years 2015 and 2016. In February 2017, the inflation target was shifted from 4.5% to 4%, keeping the tolerance range at +/-2 pp. Inflation in 2016 averaged 3.9%, well within the Central Bank tolerance range, while inflation expectations are well anchored (Figure 2.14). The Central Bank expects headline and core inflation to remain within the tolerance range. The most relevant risk to this forecast remains future exchange rate developments, which could be partly affected by monetary policy decisions from the United States Federal Reserve, however monetary policy is expected to remain accommodative. After cutting the policy interest rate by 50 basis points in 2016 to 5.5%, rates are likely to remain on hold given that inflation and inflation expectations remain within the tolerance range while the international context remains uncertain.

Figure 2.14. **The inflation-targeting regime has helped to control inflation**

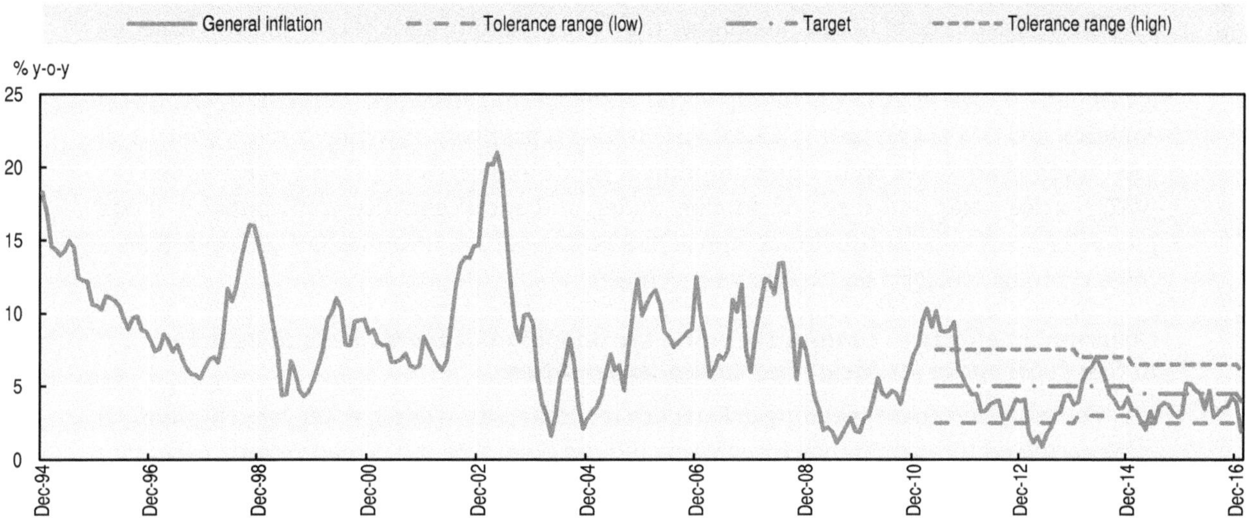

Source: Central Bank of Paraguay (2017), *https://www.bcp.gov.py/*.

StatLink http://dx.doi.org/10.1787/888933749047

Excess liquidity in the interbank market could diminish the effectiveness of the monetary policy transmission channels. Paraguay's banks hold a high volume of excess reserves and there is less need for interbank transactions. Therefore, while interbank market rates follow policy rates relatively well, they have little influence on banks' interest rates, making the monetary transmission channel weaker and limiting the effectiveness of monetary policy (IMF, 2016a). To support the monetary policy framework, efforts to develop the financial system and the interbank market should be strengthened and liquidity conditions carefully monitored.

Paraguay follows a flexible exchange rate policy with occasional interventions by the Central Bank. Interventions are of two types: regular pre-announced interventions (*operaciones compensatorias*) to sterilise government receipts (royalties, issued bonds) and exceptional interventions (*operaciones complementarias*) used in situations of volatility and exchange rate fluctuations that do not respond to market fundamentals. Limiting discretionary interventions only to extraordinary disorders in the markets with clear communication and intervention rules is crucial to reinforcing the inflation-targeting scheme.

Dollarisation of the economy has diminished in the last decades but is still high and has recently increased. Around 48.2% of credits are denominated in dollars as are 46.4% of the deposits in the banking system. Although there are no evident currency mismatch risks, close monitoring and supervision should be guaranteed and macro prudential tools could be used to reduce potential risks. Simulations of exchange rate depreciation shocks show that most banks appear able to withstand depreciation shocks of 10% to 25%; however, larger depreciations result in more notable decreases in capitalisation (IMF, 2016b).

The fiscal framework is sound but tax collection and capital investment should be improved

Tax collection is low mainly because of low tax rates, but efforts to fight evasion and informality should be strengthened

Paraguay's tax rates and revenues are low by regional standards and when compared with OECD economies. Total tax revenues, as a share of GDP, continue to be low and concentrated in indirect taxes. However, since 2000 tax revenues have increased by 5.4 percentage points of GDP, a rate higher than the growth of 4.9% of GDP in Latin America during the same period. In spite of recent improvements, tax-to-GDP ratios continue to be low, 17.9% of GDP in 2015 (including social security contributions), compared with Latin America and OECD averages of 22.8% and 34.3% respectively. Paraguay's main sources of total revenue are taxes on the consumption of goods and services (mainly value added tax [VAT], excise taxes and taxes on foreign trade), and social security contributions. These groups of taxes and contributions represent 83% of total tax revenues (see Chapter 6 for a more thorough analysis on Paraguay's revenues).

Government efforts to contain spending are ongoing but more needs to be done to free fiscal space for social and capital expenditure

Central government spending in Paraguay is characterised by a greater concentration on current expenditure rather than investment, but the government has made efforts to contain employees' compensation expenditures. Following the passage of the Fiscal Responsibility Law (FRL), the government has taken steps to reduce non-discretionary expenses related to the public-sector payroll by controlling salary expenditures, a hiring freeze and the reallocation of existing resources within the public sector to improve performance and productivity. In 2015, total expenditure amounted to 18% of GDP, higher than the previous year (16.6% of GDP). Preliminary estimates for 2016 showed a slight decrease to 17% of GDP. In terms of the components of expenditure, figures for 2016 showed that employee compensation accounted for 43% of total expenditure (including investment) while investment accounted for only 15% (an increase from the 2012 level of 13%). There was also an increase in the proportion of interest payments, rising from 1% to 3% of total expenditure. The government's efforts to contain spending on employees' compensation are noteworthy, as it fell from 9.4% of GDP in 2012 to 8.6% of GDP in 2016. This has allowed a slight increase in social benefits as well as in government investment in recent years (rising from 2.6% of GDP in 2012 to 2.9% of GDP by 2016) (Figure 2.15).

Box 2.1. **Main macro-fiscal reforms in Paraguay 2011-17**

A number of reforms undertaken between 2011 and 2017 have contributed to stable and resilient growth in the country and have encouraged private investment. Some of the most important reforms are:

- **The adoption of an inflation targeting scheme**, announced in May 2011 by the Central Bank of Paraguay. The original target was 5% annual inflation. The target was lowered a year after to 4.5% and has recently been lowered to 4%, with a tolerance range of +/- 2 percentage points.
- **The creation of the National Public Investment System** (SNIP). Created in 2012 with Decree 8 312/12, the SNIP seeks to optimise the use of public investment resources through methodologies, norms, capacity-building and a project bank, as well as the necessary components for appropriate project development, social assessment, presentation, monitoring and evaluation of projects.
- **The implementation of the Personal Income Tax**, with the entry in force of Law 4 673/12 in August 2012.
- **The reform of IRAGRO and implementation of Agricultural VAT.** Law 5 061/13 introduced important changes to the taxation of the agricultural sector, including its income taxation (IRAGRO) and its coverage by VAT, in order to formalise the sector and increase tax receipts.
- **The Fiscal Responsibility Law**, law 5 098/13, adopted in October 2013, seeks to achieve prudent management of public finances to ensure sustainability and macroeconomic stability in the medium term.
- **The Public Private Partnerships law**: adopted in November 2013, law 5 102/13 "For promotion of investment in public infrastructure and the expansion and improvement of goods and services provided by the State" seeks to promote public/private participation in public infrastructure investment.
- **Law on turnkey contracts**: Law 5 074/13, adopted in October 2013 modified and extended the public works regime. This reform allows the execution of turnkey infrastructure projects for which payment only takes place after the completion and delivery of the project.
- **The increase in the VAT rate for financial transactions**, from 5% to 10% for financial transactions carried out by entities regulated under the general banking law (law 861/96). This reform unified the rate between regulated and unregulated entities.
- **The extension of VAT to credit granted by cooperatives**, included in the reform of cooperative law (law 5 501/15, adopted in 2015). This reform seeks to improve the management of the collection and control of the tax.
- **The increase in the tax on tobacco**, the ceiling of the tax (ISC Tabaco) was first increased from 13% to 20% (Law 5 538/15). Decree 4 694/15 established a 16% tax applied from 2016.
- **The investment guarantee and employment generation law**, adopted in December 2015, law 5 542/15 seeks to encourage domestic and foreign capital investment in productive projects in the country, so as to invigorate the economy and contribute to sustainable development, though the generation of new sources of employment, growth in manufacturing and technology adoption.
- **The modification of the Personal Income Tax regulations**, in decree 6 650/16 and Resolution 104/16 which specify deductible expenses and investments in the context of the Personal Income Tax, in order to limit abuses and allow for a more equitable application of the law.

Source: Ministry of Finance, Paraguay.

Figure 2.15. **Paraguay's central government spending is mostly concentrated on current expenditure**

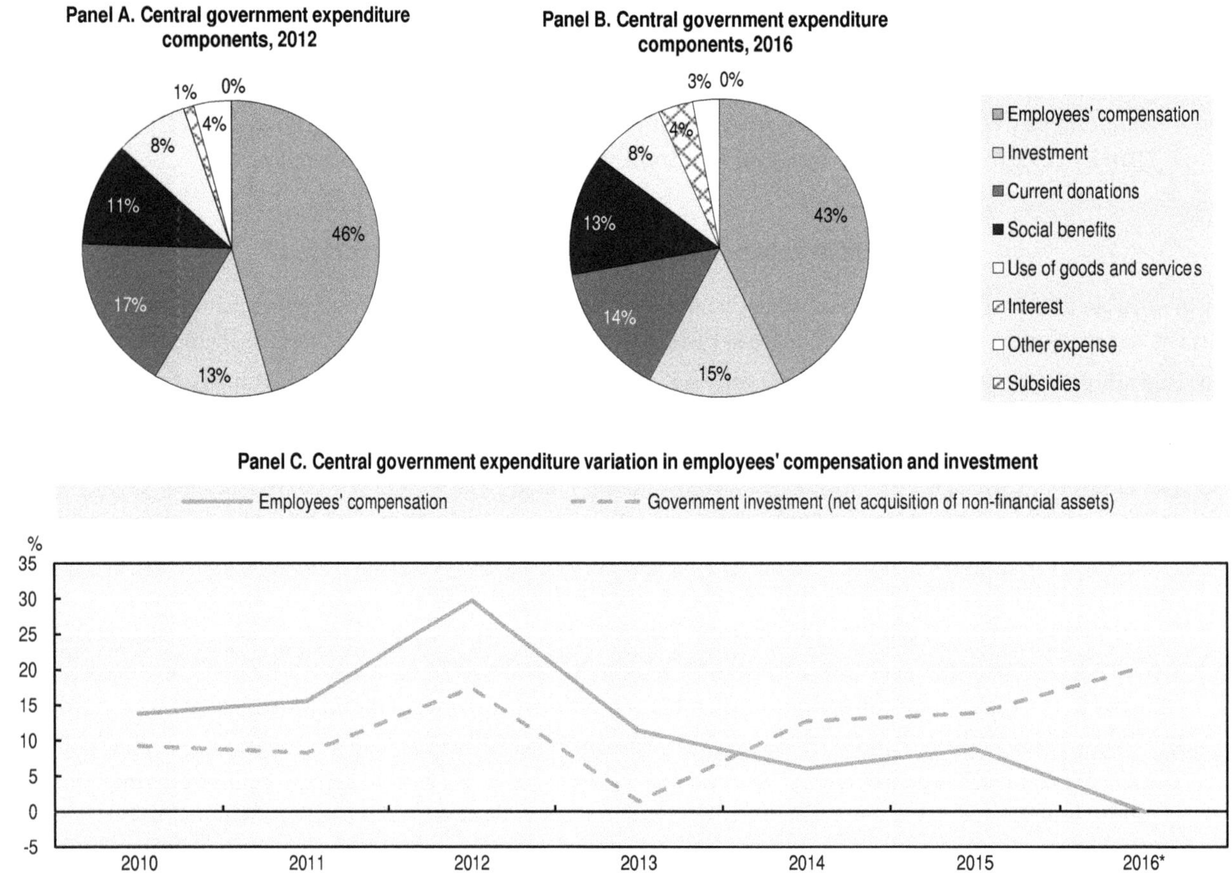

Note: * Preliminary figures.

Source: Ministry of Finance of Paraguay (2017b).

StatLink http://dx.doi.org/10.1787/888933749066

The implementation of the Fiscal Responsibility Law has been challenging

The introduction of the FRL and the Advisory Fiscal Council represents a major step in terms of fiscal sustainability. The FRL (Law 5098/2013) was passed in 2013 and has been in force since 2015, seeking to ensure the prudent management of public finances, sustainability and macroeconomic stability in the medium term. The FRL governs the preparation and approval of budgets, but not their execution. The law limits the central government deficit to no more than 1.5% of GDP (Figure 2.16). Escape clauses allow Congress to approve a deficit of up to 3% of GDP in cases of national emergency, international crisis or negative growth. In some cases, this increase would also require the approval of the national economic team. The FRL also stipulates that all public-sector real current primary expenditure growth rate must not exceed 4% and growth in public sector salaries must be in line with minimum wage developments. This law also requires a three-year fiscal programme not exceeding an average deficit (budgeted) of 1% of GDP (this rule only applies to the *ex-ante* medium-term budget plan). The Comptroller General is responsible for monitoring compliance.

In addition, by Decree 6498/2016 an Advisory Fiscal Council to the Ministry of Finance was created to contribute to the discussion, analysis and transparency and provide recommendations on fiscal issues. The council is a high-level and independent body, composed of three experts in macroeconomic and fiscal issues from the private sector or academia, appointed for periods of up to three years. The effectiveness of fiscal councils relies on several factors, such as full autonomy, credibility and active and unrestricted dissemination of their analysis. Experience and empirical evidence suggest that independent fiscal councils can reduce macroeconomic forecasting bias and support the government's capacity to comply with a numerical rule. However, fiscal institutions are a necessary condition for achieving disciplined fiscal performance but not a sufficient one. Strong and sustained political commitment to a medium-term fiscal goal and to the fiscal council mandate are needed to achieve durable improvements in fiscal performance (Hagemann, 2010; IMF, 2013).

Figure 2.16. **The implementation of the FRL has been challenging**

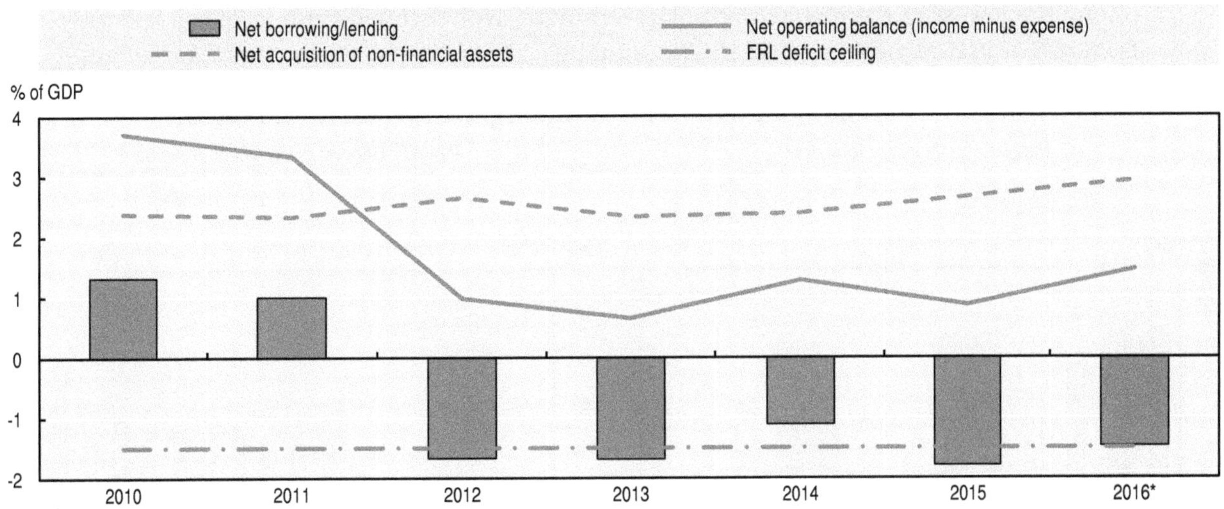

Note: *Preliminary figures.

Source: Ministry of Finance of Paraguay.

StatLink http://dx.doi.org/10.1787/888933749085

The FRL has helped to keep Paraguay´s public deficit one of the lowest among benchmark countries and in the Latin American region. However, the implementation of the FRL has been challenging and its efficiency is being strengthened. In the first year of the FRL implementation, which came into force with the 2015 annual budget, the central government's overall balance recorded a deficit of 1.8% of GDP, above the 1.5% ceiling. However, excluding expenditures on infrastructure financed by sovereign bonds issued in the international capital markets, which was permitted only for 2015, the deficit recorded in the central government's overall balance stood at 0.5% of GDP, meeting the FRL's ceiling of 1.5% of GDP for 2015. In 2015, the difference with respect to the FRL ceiling (0.3% of GDP) was mainly explained by the carry-over of some transfers, namely Yacyreta dam's royalties transfers (USD 30 million) and the 4G bid (USD 60 million). In 2016, the budget was approved in accordance with the FRL targets and without exclusions of capital expenditures. The central government deficit for 2016 was 1.4% of GDP, while the operating balance (before deducting capital expenditure) was 1.5% of GDP (MH, 2015).

The authorities are exploring the possibility of amending the FRL as the current framework does not allow the implementation of counter-cyclical measures while the low level of the deficit ceiling could represent a constraint on public investment. Escape clauses seem limited and since the FRL applies only to the budget approval process, it might not prove effective in containing actual fiscal outcomes. Sanctions are based on personal accountability but there is no clear understanding of who the responsible civil servants are or who determines the responsibility. Any changes to the current FRL should be considered carefully, should ensure debt sustainability, guarantee credibility, and should be clearly communicated.

Fiscal space has improved thanks to well-managed low levels of gross debt

Fiscal space exists in Paraguay thanks to well-managed low levels of gross debt (Figure 2.17). The main guidelines in the government's public debt policies are the ratio of total outstanding public-sector debt to GDP, and the ratio of total principal, interest payments and other financial costs (including interest, commissions and others) on public sector external debt to registered exports of goods. On 31 December 2016 those ratios were 23.1% and 3.4%, respectively (MH, 2017c). The central government's debt amounted to 19.9% of GDP in 2016, among the lowest in the region. Central government debt declined from levels of around 25.8% of GDP in 2004 to around 9.3% in 2011, although it has followed a rising trend since then.

Figure 2.17. **Paraguay's public debt is among the lowest in the region**

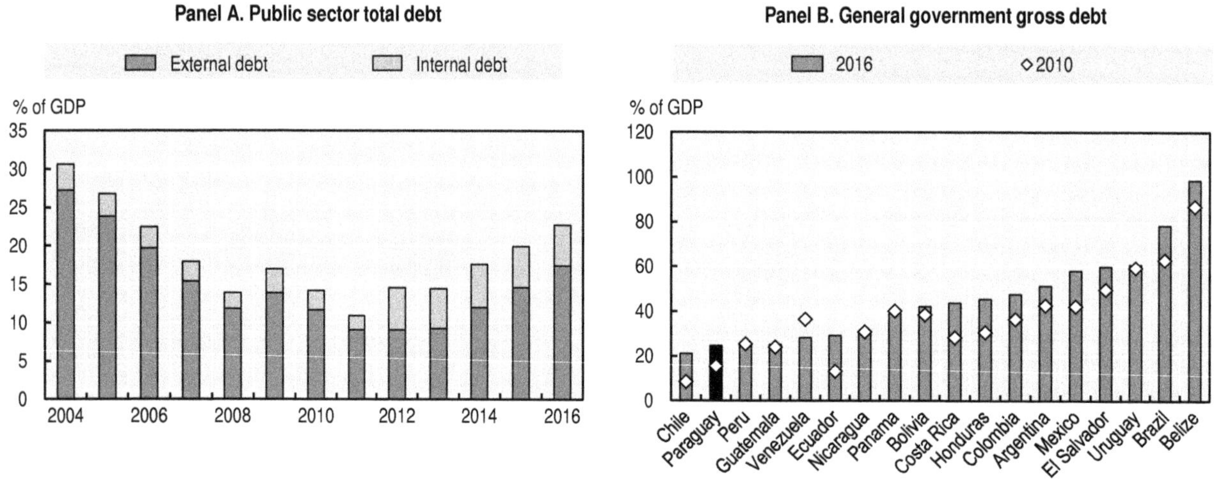

Source: Panel A: Ministry of Finance of Paraguay. Panel B: International Monetary Fund (2017), *World Economic Outlook* (database), *https://www.imf.org/external/pubs/ft/weo/2015/01/weodata/index.aspx.*

StatLink http://dx.doi.org/10.1787/888933749104

Public debt was traditionally concentrated in loans from international financial institutions and bilateral credits (56% and 21% of total debt respectively in 2011). Beginning in 2012, as a result of good fiscal and economic conditions, funding sources were diversified with the issuance of sovereign bonds, which by 2016 accounted for 38.8% of total public debt, followed by multilateral loans with 34%. For the first time in 2013, the government issued sovereign bonds in the international market for USD 500 million (ten-year); in 2014 for USD 1 billion (30 year); in 2015 for USD 280 million; in 2016 for USD 600 million and in 2017 for USD 500 million (MH, 2017b). The level of exposure to risks related to changes in international interest rates has declined, as the share of loans contracted with fixed rates has been rising from 58% in 2011 to 70.3% by 2016 while the sovereign credit ratings have continuously increased (MH , 2017b; CADEP, 2017). Moody's improved Paraguay's rating from Ba3 in February 2014 to Ba1 in March 2015; Standard & Poor's rating improved from BB- to BB in June 2014; and Fitch improved the rating from BB- to BB in January 2015.

A high share of public debt is denominated in foreign currency, principally in US dollars. Despite a recent increase in the share of debt denominated in local currency, by the end of 2016, 76.5% of total public debt was denominated in foreign currency (72.1% in dollars, 2.9% in yen and 1.5% in other currencies) (MH, 2017c). The exchange rate risk is relatively low given that Paraguay´s income in US dollars is greater that the annual debt payment amounts. This income comes from compensations and royalties from the binationals and from the sale of energy.

Efforts to further expand public investment should be strengthened

Although starting to pick up, investment has been very low

In the last decade, the level of investment in Paraguay has been considerably lower than in OECD and Latin American countries (Figure 2.18, Panel A). While investment in Paraguay was around 15.9% of GDP on average from 2005 to 2016, average investment in Latin American and OECD countries for the same period was about 20% of GDP. Paraguay's investment level in 2016 was slightly higher than that of 2005, showing a rising trend in recent years, while the average for Latin American countries has been declining. In spite of this recent recovery of investment after a decline in 2012, investment in 2016 was only about 17.6% of GDP, one of the lowest levels when compared to other benchmark countries (Figure 2.18, Panel B). Nevertheless, in respect of the source of composition of investment, although public capital expenditures increased from 2.4% of GDP in 2010 to 2.9% of GDP in 2016, they represent less than 20% of total gross fixed capital formation in the country. Some factors limiting public investment are the institutional and fiscal framework as well as low tax collection.

Figure 2.18. **Investment in Paraguay has been considerably lower than OECD and Latin American countries**

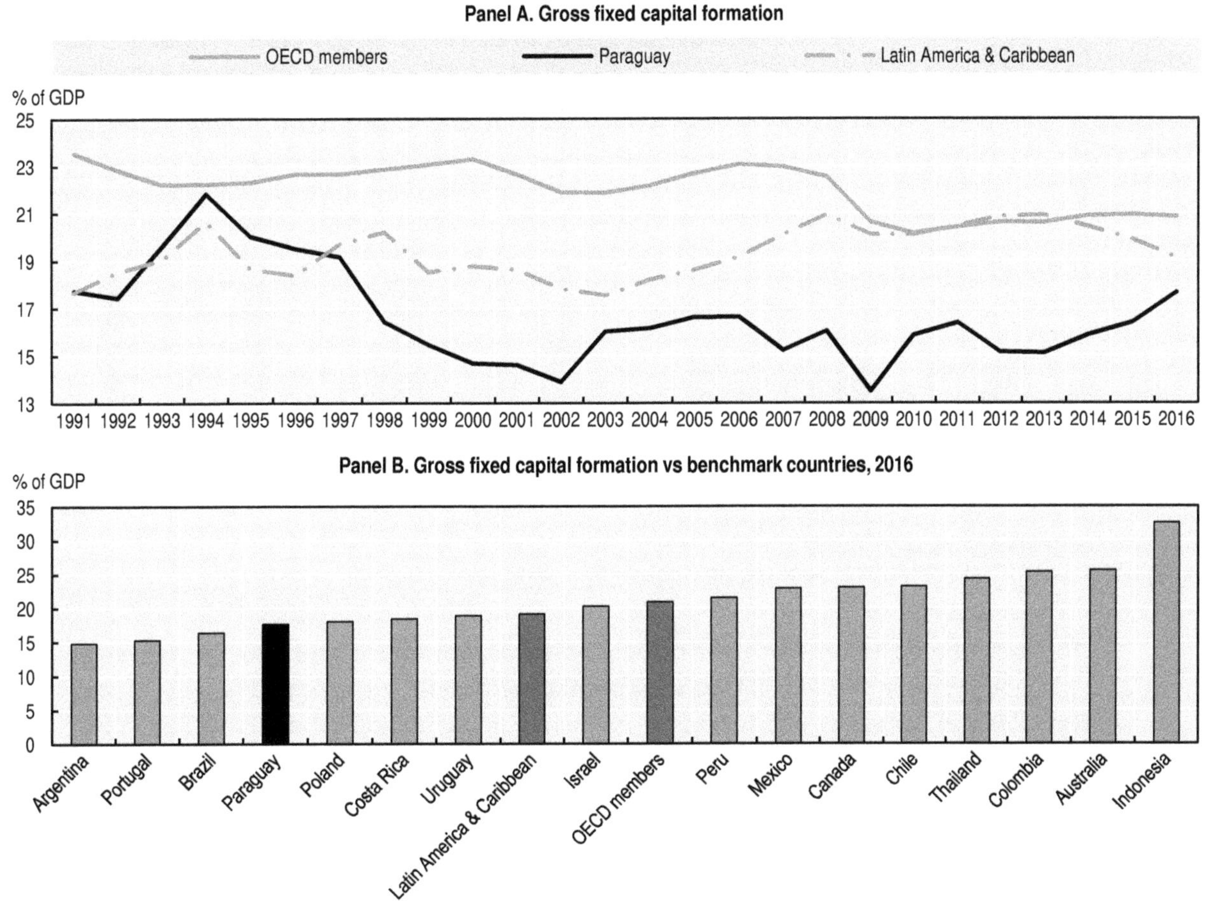

Source: World Bank (2017a), *World Development Indicators* (database), *http://data.worldbank.org.*

StatLink http://dx.doi.org/10.1787/888933749123

Particularly in respect of infrastructure investment, Paraguay performs slightly better than the average of Latin American countries (Figure 2.19, Panel A) and managed to increase the level of infrastructure investment from 3.3% of GDP in 2010 to 4.4% of GDP in 2015, (Figure 2.19, Panel B) which is significantly higher than the Latin American average. On the other hand, private infrastructure investment in Paraguay (0.61% of GDP over the period 2008-14) remains below the average for Latin America (1.3% of GDP for the same period).

Figure 2.19. **Public investment in infrastructure is much higher than in the region**

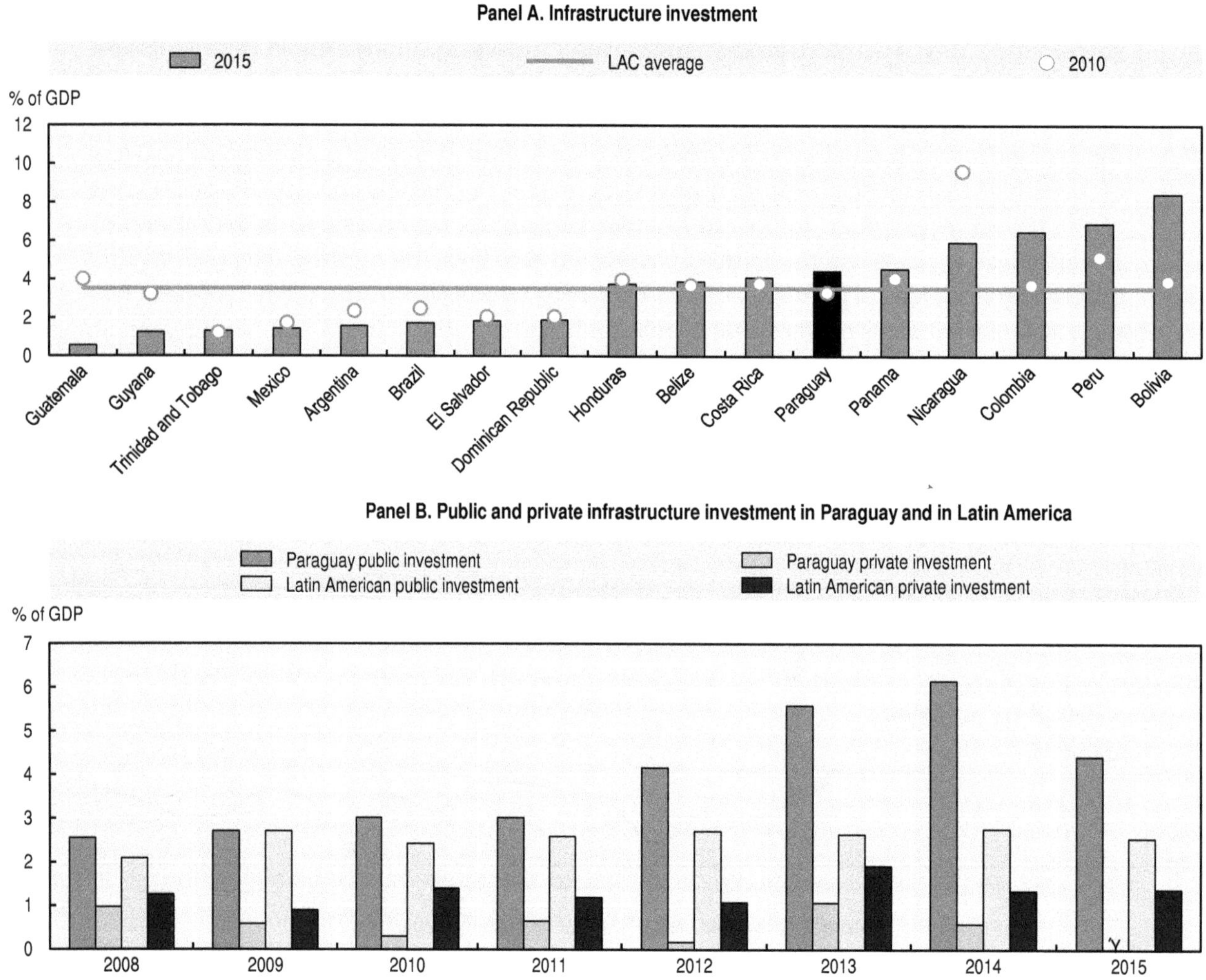

Note: * No data is available for Paraguay in 2015.

Source: ECLAC/IDB/CAF (2016), INFRALATAM Database, *http://en.infralatam.info/home* (accessed 23 May 2017).

StatLink http://dx.doi.org/10.1787/888933749142

To reach the government target of expanding capital expenditure to the target of USD 1 billion per year (AIP, 2016), the Paraguayan government has taken advantage of low interest rates and has been quite successful in raising capital in international sovereign debt markets of USD 2.4 billion since 2013. These funds are intended to cover infrastructure and capital spending and to refinance part of the public debt in accordance with the Budget Law (70% has been used to finance investment and 25% to pay for debt). The Ministry of Public Works and Communications (MOPC) has received 42% of investment resources (mostly used for paving and building roads and bridges), followed by the *Administración Nacional de Electricidad* (ANDE) which has received 13% (MH, 2017a).

Some challenges remain in terms of management and budget execution of infrastructure projects

Low public capital reflects not only years of underinvestment, but also inefficiencies in infrastructure investment, in terms of institutions, management, and budget execution of infrastructure projects. According to Roldos, Santoro and David (2016), Paraguay could be developing more infrastructures for the same amount invested and there is considerable scope for enhancing its efficiency regarding project selection and evaluation, multiyear budgeting processes, and regulation of infrastructure companies (Roldos, Santoro and David, 2016).

In 2011, the process of setting up the bases for the National Public Investment System (SNIP) was initiated, establishing the creation of the Directorate of the Public Investment System (DSIP) to manage the SNIP and optimise the use of public resources intended for investment. The SNIP oversees the investment process, establishing clear regulations, ensuring compliance and co-ordinating efforts to execute projects. Since 2012, the SNIP has approved 119 new projects for a total amount of USD 5.5 billion, also providing training in the design, evaluation and management of investment projects to around 950 officials (SNIP/MH/GN, 2015).

Public investment projects are financed from three main sources: resources from the government (financial code FF10), primarily taxes and royalties; resources from public credit (code FF20), meaning government loans from international organisations as well as resources from bonds issuance; and institutional resources (code FF30), those generated and managed by the public institutions themselves. The latter includes projects of different public entities financed by the Fund for the Structural Convergence of Mercosur (FOCEM), a transferring mechanism of financial resources funded by member country contributions. The DSIP is responsible for co-ordinating, evaluating and monitoring projects financed by FOCEM (SNIP/MH/GN, 2015).

Paraguay still faces challenges in budgetary execution and management of public investment projects. The total budget for public investment reached PYG 8 922 billion (Paraguayan guaraní) in 2015. However, the budget execution reached only PYG 3 264 billion, which represents 37% of the total budgeted. Projects financed through FF10 are those with the higher rate of execution (SNIP/MH/GN, 2015). In spite of government efforts to provide training for officials linked to the development, evaluation and execution of investment projects, large gaps in institutional capacity are visible, varying among public entities. Whereas the Ministry of Public Works has improved in terms of capacity, other ministries and government entities still lack the staff and institutional capacity to carry out projects. There is considerable room for the country to improve the SNIP through clear and uniform regulation as well as technical assistance and capacity training. The existence of multiple institutional frameworks for prioritising and managing public infrastructure spending can generate inconsistencies and inefficiencies in the relevant processes. For example, social infrastructure funded by FONACIDE (see Chapter 3) follows a different process than projects in the SNIP and is under the responsibility of other ministries and agencies. There are ongoing changes in the health and education sectors to have the MOPC handle the execution of these projects (for example hospital construction). The OECD *Policy Framework for Investment* is a relevant tool as it provides a checklist of key policy issues for consideration by any government interested in creating and enabling environment for all types of investment (OECD, 2015).

Box 2.2. **Building a governance framework for public investment: Portugal's experience**

Since the 1980s, Portugal has been using European funds to cope with its infrastructure and development deficits. These resources have been an important financial resource to address the country's major development gaps. Originally driven by the need to manage EU structural funds, Portugal has developed a regional approach to public policy and a governance framework for public investment management that go far beyond the management of European funds.

Portugal has been one of the most significant recipients of the European Union (EU) Cohesion Policy, receiving more than EUR 50 billion of EU structural funds between 1989 and 2006 and broadly comparable budgets for the 2007-13 (EUR 21.5 billion) and 2014-20 (EUR 25 billion) periods.

In the early stages, coinciding with the integration of the country into European institutions, the emphasis in programming, management and resource allocation was on large independent projects. Major infrastructure projects with expected potential for economic growth, in particular in energy and transport absorbed most of the resources.

The strategic framework for public investment has developed gradually into an integrated programmatic framework. While formally framed by Regional Development Plans (*Planos Regionais de Ordenamento do Território*, PROT), the framework was originally limited in its reach, in particular in terms of specifying objectives and targets. The progressive integration into development programme logic has enabled greater attention to the requirements and complementarities between interventions and sectors, and the development of robust planning and prioritization mechanisms. For example, in the social arena, programmes framed to address skills needs and school drop-outs invested not only in building schools but also in the rationalisation of the network of schools, the diversification of offers and special programmes for priority areas. At the regional level, public investment is subordinated to regional strategies, defined and implemented with the involvement of local authorities in areas where they have responsibilities.

Operationally, the framework is organised in four national and cross-sectoral Operational Programmes (OP) on competitiveness and internationalisation, social inclusion and employment, human capital, and sustainability and efficiency in the use of resources. These are completed by seven regional OP for five continental regions and the two island autonomous regions (Açores and Madeira).

The global public investment framework is organised in three interconnected systems:

- A management system with management authorities for each OP that can delegate responsibilities to technical agencies and are overseen by a National Development Agency.
- An audit and control system, headed by a national authority (the General Inspection under the Ministry of Finance), with direct links to control departments in each OP, is supported by an autonomous branch of the National Development Agency.
- An evaluation and monitoring system, headed by another branch of the National Development Agency, based on an evaluation plan involving each OP and a system of indicators covering all the steps in each project, as well as aggregate financial, output and outcome indicators.

An integrated information system, certified by the audit and control authority, is the basis for all operations and gathers the necessary data for the whole framework.

In order to achieve more integrated governance, a new delivery framework was developed that involves a new layer of governance through co-ordination bodies. An inter-ministerial co-ordination commission has a political supervisory and co-ordination role at the national level. At the OP level, strategic advisory committees facilitate the involvement of different ministries into strategic decisions, increase political accountability and ensure clear separation of functions between strategic design and delivery and between management and political supervision.

Source: Authors on the basis of inputs provided by Portugal, Portugal 2020 (*https://www.portugal2020.pt/Portal2020/modelo-de-governacao*), and OECD (2010).

Public investment often involves different levels of government, whether through shared policy competencies or joint funding arrangements. Effective public investment requires substantial co-ordination across levels of government to bridge information, policy or fiscal gaps that may occur, as well as governance capacities at different levels to design and implement public investment projects. In this context, the OECD *Recommendation on Effective Public Investment across Levels of Government* would prove helpful for the government of Paraguay to orient the efforts or improve multilevel governance of public investment. Bolstering capacity at the subnational level deserves particular attention as in some cases financial resources, professional skills or institutional quality may be lacking. Good practices for budgeting and financial accountability should also be implemented and required (OECD, 2014).

Given the significant gap in infrastructure and financing resources, the law on "Promotion of investment in public infrastructure and the expansion and improvement of goods and services by the state" was approved in 2013, which permits projects under the form of public-private partnerships (PPP). In this context, there is an interinstitutional framework involving the Ministry of Finance (MH), the secretariat of planning for economic and social development (STP), the attorney general of the republic (PGR), and the Ministry of Public Works and Communications (MOPC), co-ordinated by the STP, in charge of evaluating and approving investment projects.

Finally, projects are approved by decree (SNIP/MH/GN, 2015; STP, 2017). The government has also encouraged foreign participation (e.g. Spain, South Korea, Argentina, Brazil) and currently, the portfolio of projects in public-private partnership (PPP) form has reached more than USD 2 billion with one signed contract of USD 500 million (extension of routes 2 and 7) and the modernisation of the international airport which is under review (STP, 2014; STP, 2017). Private sector participation can bring more benefits than additional capital alone; for instance, a more competitive environment, sharing of technological expertise and managerial competences. Paraguay would benefit from taking into account the OECD *Principles for Private Sector Participation in Infrastructure* which assists governments in assessing their policies in light of their own national circumstances and needs (OECD, 2007). Measures to ensure high standards of public and corporate governance, transparency, and rule of law would be essential to attract participation by the private sector. Likewise, authorities responsible for privately operated infrastructure projects should have the capacity to manage commercial processes while sharing objectives throughout all levels of governments and parts of the public administration.

Given the current fiscal framework, the government has sought alternative sources to fund investment

The FRL was implemented with the 2015 annual budget as part of Paraguay's efforts to strengthen its fiscal framework in terms of discipline and transparency. However, the question has arisen as to whether the FRL design is adequate, given Paraguay´s large investment needs, mainly in infrastructure. The stock of public capital in Paraguay stood at 44% of GDP in 2015 against an average of 79% for emerging markets and 84% for Latin America (Roldos, Santoro and David, 2016). Paraguay's minimum infrastructure investment needs require investment of about USD 1 billion annually.

In a context of debate about the appropriateness of the current FRL and the constraints it imposes on infrastructure investment in Paraguay, the authorities are analysing potential reform options and are currently receiving technical assistance from multilateral financial institutions to consider these options. Among the options that could be considered is the adoption of a structural balance rule to replace the current nominal balance rule, which would allow for a more stable path of current expenditure (Eyraud, David and Bardella, 2016). Given the investment gap that Paraguay faces, the country could also consider a reform that allows for greater capital expenditure. It has been suggested that it could consider reforming the deficit rule by excluding public investment expenditure from the deficit calculation. Any such rule would require, at the minimum, a debt ceiling, as it would not on its own, ensure debt sustainability, as noted by David and Novta (2016).

Likewise, the composition of expenditures would vary significantly under different rules. David and Novta (2016) estimate that capital expenditures would be less than what authorities would like to implement, based on the net domestic product (NDP), if real current primary spending grows at 4% and the authorities comply with an overall deficit ceiling. When primary current expenditures grow steadily at 4% in real terms and the deficit ceiling is 3%, then capital expenditures would decline from 4% of GDP in 2015 to about 2.5% of GDP in 2026. Levels of public investment would be even lower with a tighter 1.5% deficit ceiling, declining to 2% by 2026. The authorities could maintain higher levels of capital expenditure, but would have to reduce current primary spending to satisfy the overall balance of 1.5% or 3%, respectively (David and Novta, 2016). In this regard, Paraguay has been implementing other financing mechanisms such as public and private partnerships and tenders with financing (Law 5074).

An increase in investment would contribute to boosting growth

Investment is crucial for growth and sustainable development. An increase in investment allows the expansion of productive capacity, jobs generation and income growth. Investment in strategic sectors such as infrastructure is particularly essential. For instance, investment in roads would allow for a reduction in transport costs which have been estimated to have a considerable impact on GDP. Ludeña and Ruiz Díaz (2008) find that in Paraguay a reduction in transport costs of 54% would contribute to a 0.24% increase in GDP, an increase in exports and imports (by 1.38% and 6.35%, respectively) and an improvement of 3.88% in the terms of trade. Other studies show that an increase of 1% of GDP in public investment can spur up to 0.5% higher GDP or more after four years; in other words, a return of 15% a year (Roldos, Santoro and David, 2016). An increase in public investment would support demand and employment in the short run and catalyse private investment and innovation to increase potential output in the long term (Calderón and Servén, 2004).

Estimates by David (2017) of cumulative fiscal multipliers in Paraguay show that multipliers for capital expenditure are substantially higher than multipliers for current expenditure. Over long horizons, the cumulative response in GDP relative to the cumulative government spending increases to 0.2-0.5 for current expenditure and 1.4-2.1 for capital expenditure, although statistical significance varies on whether total GDP or non-agro, non-energy GDP is considered (Table 2.1).

Table 2.1. **Capital expenditure multipliers are substantially higher than those of current expenditure**

Estimates of government spending multipliers in Paraguay (cumulative)

	Total GDP	Non-agro non-energy GDP
Current expenditure		
t = 0	0	0
t = 8	0.2*	0.2**
t = 20	0.5**	0.5**
Capital expenditure		
t = 0	0.1	0
t = 8	1.4**	0.5
t = 20	2.1**	0.8

Note: * Indicates statistical significance at the 10% level. ** Indicates statistical significance at 5% level.
Source: IMF (2017).

Sustaining development and long-term growth would require strengthening productivity and competitiveness

Strengthening productivity and competitiveness is essential for sustaining long-term growth but several challenges remain

Although Paraguay has shown strong growth in recent years, the income gap remains high compared to OECD countries. For Paraguay, as well as other peer countries, most of the difference in GDP per capita with OECD countries is explained by labour productivity. The difference in income per capita can be broken down into gaps in labour productivity and gaps in labour utilisation (measured as employment as share of population). Labour productivity was close to 81% lower than in the top OECD economies in 2014, much lower than the Latin America region average labour productivity, which is around 70% lower than that of the top OECD countries and the lowest amongst other benchmark countries (Figure 2.20) (OECD/IDB/GFP, 2016).

While labour productivity remains low compared with OECD countries, it has improved in very recent years (Figure 2.21). Although as measured as GDP per person employed in constant purchasing power parity it performs more poorly than the Latin America region average, in recent years it has shown a significant improvement. Most of the labour productivity gap is explained by the low performance in human capital. Labour productivity in Paraguay has experienced relatively high growth rates, on average 3.8% since 2004, mainly driven by total factor productivity (TFP) and capital accumulation per worker, while the contribution of human capital has been marginal. These high growth rates in TFP and capital accumulation have recently declined and have not been enough to close the gap with more developed economies. Improvements in the quality of human and physical capital and the promotion of policies enhancing the agriculture sector and a reallocation of resources from low-productivity to high-productivity industries are fundamental to boosting sustainable productivity and economic prospects in Paraguay (OECD/IDB/GFP, 2016).

However, several challenges remain to boost productivity and competitiveness. The general position of Paraguay in the Global Competitiveness Index has been improving, from a ranking of 124 in 2008 to 117 in 2016-17. However, relative to the Latin American average there are several dimensions in which Paraguay lags behind: innovation, infrastructure, institutions, technological readiness and higher education and training. The five most problematic factors for doing business are corruption, an inadequate supply of infrastructure, an inadequately educated workforce, inefficient government bureaucracy and access to financing (Figure 2.22) (WEO, 2016).

Figure 2.20. **Although Paraguay has shown strong growth in recent years, the income gap remains high compared to OECD countries**

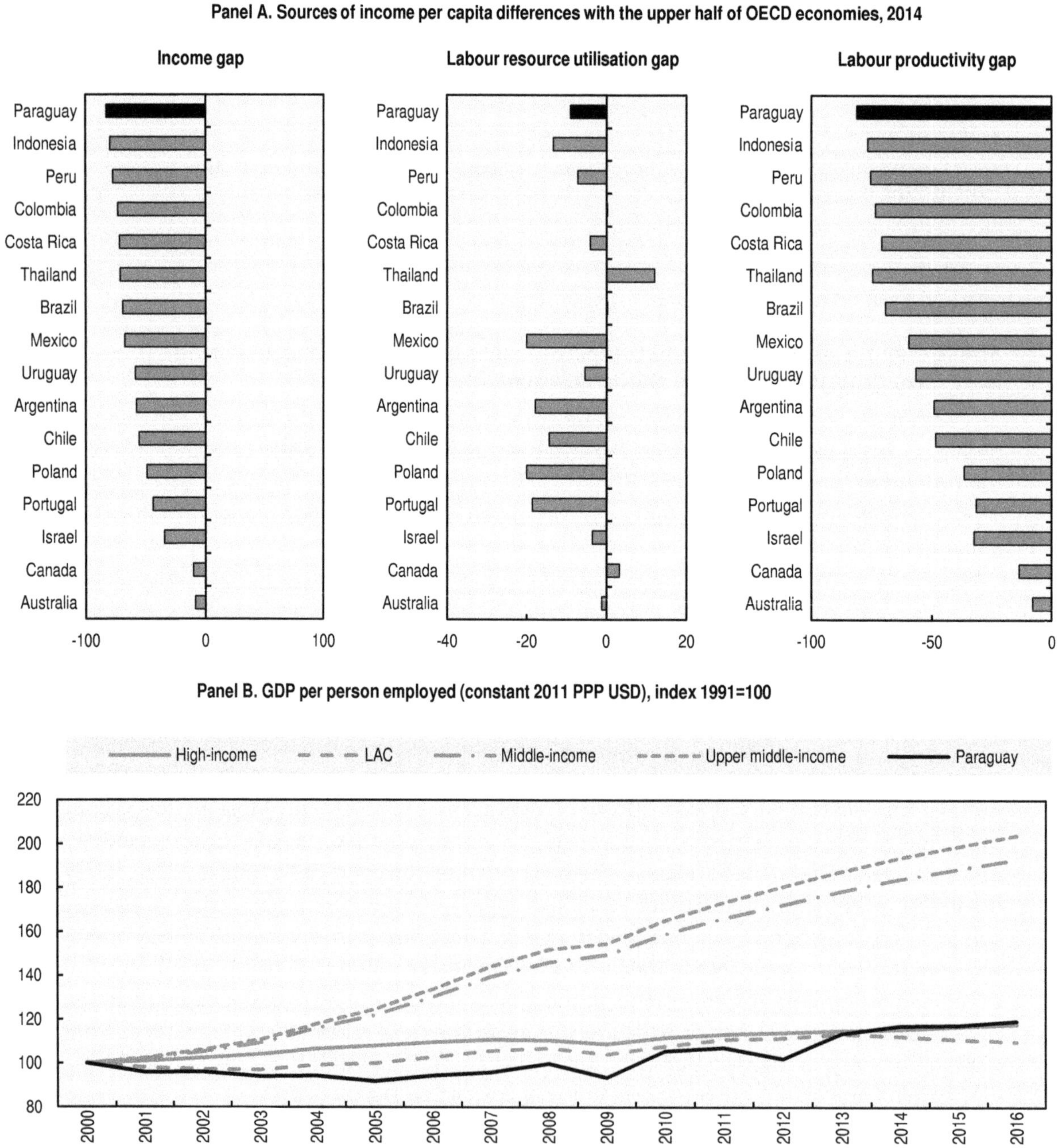

Source: Panel A. OECD calculations based on data from Penn World Tables PWT 9.0 (Feenstra, Inklaar and Timmer, 2015); Panel B: World Bank (2017a), *World Development Indicators Database* (database), Washington DC, *http://data.worldbank.org*.

StatLink *http://dx.doi.org/10.1787/888933749161*

Figure 2.21. **Labour productivity in Paraguay has experienced relatively high growth rates**

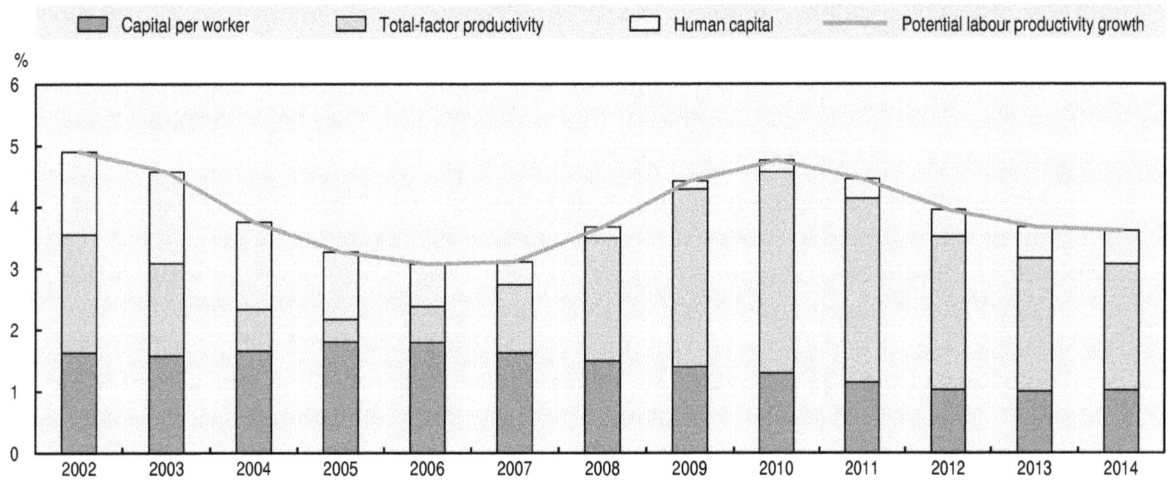

Source: OECD calculations based on Feenstra, Inklaar et Timmer (2015), *http://www.ggdc.net/pwt/* and Barro and Lee (2013).

StatLink http://dx.doi.org/10.1787/888933749180

Figure 2.22. **Several challenges remain to boost productivity and competitiveness**

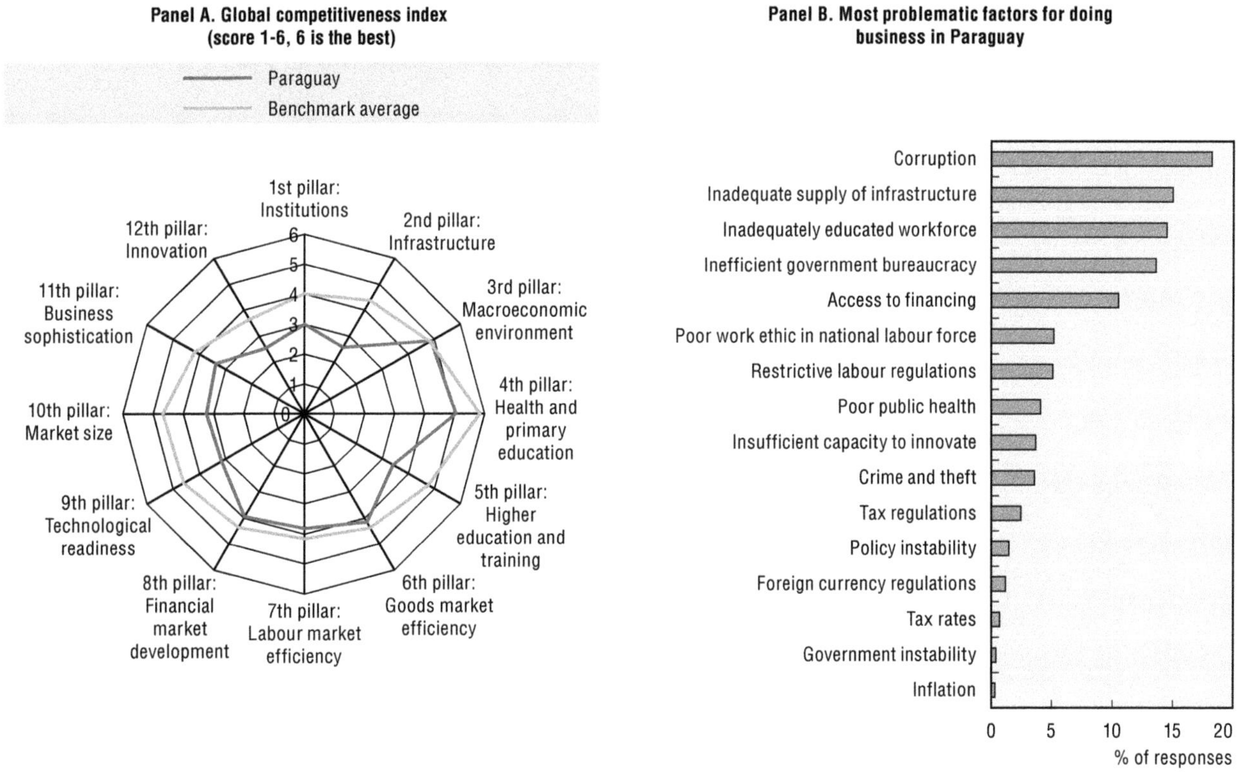

Note: Panel B: From a list of 15 factors, respondents were asked to select the five most problematic for doing business in their country and to rank them between 1 (most problematic) and 5. The bars in the figure show the responses weighted according to their rankings.

Source: Panel A. WEF (2017), *The Global Competitiveness Report 2006-2016* (database). Panel B: WEF, Executive Opinion Survey 2016.

StatLink http://dx.doi.org/10.1787/888933749199

Greater investment in innovation could contribute to improving competitiveness

Among the limiting factors of competitiveness are the low capacity of technological development and the lack of innovation to diversify into more productive sectors and make processes more efficient. Empirical evidence shows that the application of technological advances leads to a more effective use of resources and to the transformation of new ideas into new products, solutions, processes and services, generating competitive advantages for companies (Grazzi and Pietrobelli, 2016). Greater investment in innovation, combined with the development of complementary activities, such as information and communication technologies and training, can contribute to reducing productivity gaps and improving competitiveness (Crespi and Zuñiga, 2010; OECD, 2009).

Resources invested in gross expenditure on research and development (GERD) activities in Paraguay are low relative to benchmark countries while private sector investment and involvement should be strengthened (Figure 2.23, Panel A). Paraguay's gross expenditure on research and development (R&D) by 2012 reached 0.09% of GDP (0.13% by 2015 based on National Council for Science and Technology [CONACYT] national data), far from the level of investment in other countries in the region (Peru 4.1% of GDP, Brazil 1.2% of GDP) (UIS, 2017). The level of human resources devoted to R&D is also amongst the lowest relative to benchmark countries, with fewer than one researcher per thousand employed (Figure 2.23, Panel B). Overall, this low investment and low level of human resources result in a significantly low number of patents applications. In respect of the private sector involvement in R&D activities, the business contribution to GERD is less than 1%, with more than 80% financed by the government (Figure 2.23, Panel C). Likewise, most of the resources are being used by higher education and government institutions (Figure 2.23, Panel D). The contribution of business enterprises both for financing and performing of R&D investment is close to zero.

Figure 2.23. **R&D resources are low relative to benchmark countries**

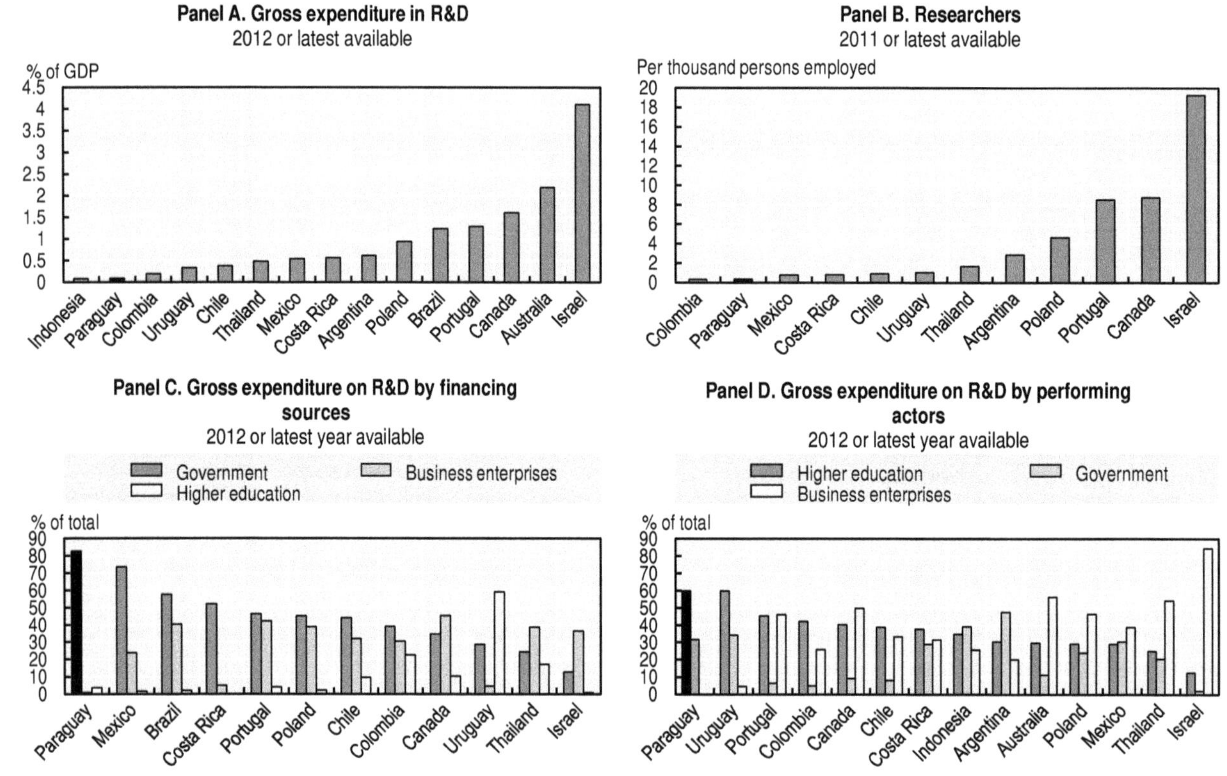

Source: UIS (2017), UNESCO Institute for Statistics Database, *http://uis.unesco.org/*.

StatLink *http://dx.doi.org/10.1787/888933749218*

In a context in which slightly more than half of Paraguayan companies carried out at least one innovation activity, the largest firms with export activity stood out for innovative effort. CONACYT, as the responsible entity for the design and implementation of Paraguay's innovation policy, together with the Inter-American Development Bank (IDB) and the General Directorate of Statistics, Surveys and Censuses (DGEEC), carried out the Entrepreneurial Innovation Survey 2010-12 (EIEP) and data from the period between 2013 and 2015 will be included in the forthcoming 2016 edition of this survey. According to the survey, 52% of Paraguayan firms performed some innovation activity in the period 2010-12 (higher for big firms, 72%), with an average investment of 2.6% of sales in 2012. Export orientation is also a factor driving innovative behaviour, as 71.8% of the exporting companies carried out innovation activity, compared to 49.7% for non-exporters (CONACYT/DGEEC, 2013).

In terms of investment, almost half of the sampled firms invested in innovation (for big companies the proportion rises to more than 60%). However, in the composition of innovation investment of the Paraguayan companies, there was a large participation of activities with a very limited impact in the generation of knowledge, since 76.6% of the investments went to the acquisition of capital goods. On the other hand, activities of internal research and development were relatively low, with a share of just over 8%. As a percentage of sales, the average investment in 2012 was 3.9%, with noticeable differences according to size of firms; large companies registered one percentage point more than medium firms and 0.7 percentage points with respect to the small ones (Angelelli, Luna and Vargas, 2016). Those companies that do not trade in the international market invested more intensely in innovation. The main source of financing for innovation investment is the company's own resources, which represent 74% of the funds. The second most used source consisted of commercial banks with 21.4%, while the share of public sector participation was practically null (0.3%) (Figure 2.24) (CONACYT/DGEEC, 2013; Angelelli, Luna and Vargas, 2016).

Among the main obstacles to innovation in Paraguay, more than 30% of companies attributed high or medium importance to the lack of public policies and public support, followed by the shortage of skilled workers and the difficulties of access to financing. Large companies pointed to the shortage of trained personnel as the most frequent obstacle, while for small firms, financial difficulties and access to finance represented greater problems (Figure 2.24, Panel C) (CONACYT/DGEEC, 2013).

The low innovation capacity in Paraguay reflects a weak innovation model and institutional framework. Articulation between the various actors and institutions (firms, academic institutions, research centres, etc.) dedicated to promoting innovation, research and development is deficient. According to the EIEP 2013 survey (CONACYT/DGEEC) only a small number of companies claimed to maintain links with other actors or institutions to develop their innovation activities. As part of the objectives of the National Development Plan, CONACYT is making efforts to integrate private sector and academic priorities into the national innovation strategy. The National Development Bank (*Banco Nacional de Fomento*) is also playing a role in supporting start-ups, ecosystems, pre-incubators and incubators in different sectors, which are mostly linked to the public university system. One of the current difficulties of the National Innovation System is the identification of priority sectors/projects; through a sectoral assessment, the agency is currently identifying priority industries where innovation resources will be focused. In 2015, about 37% of R&D investment was devoted to agricultural sciences, 22.4% to medical sciences and 14.7% to technology and engineering (CONACYT, 2015). In terms of resources, CONACYT manages the fund for excellence in education and research (FEEI-FONACIDE) which provides resources to

13 programmes, including the Paraguayan programme for the development of science and technology – PROCIENCIA. CONACYT also manages a project for technological development, innovation and conformity assessment as part of the fund for the structural convergence of MERCOSUR (FOCEM).

Figure 2.24. **Eliminating remaining barriers would bolster firm-level innovation**

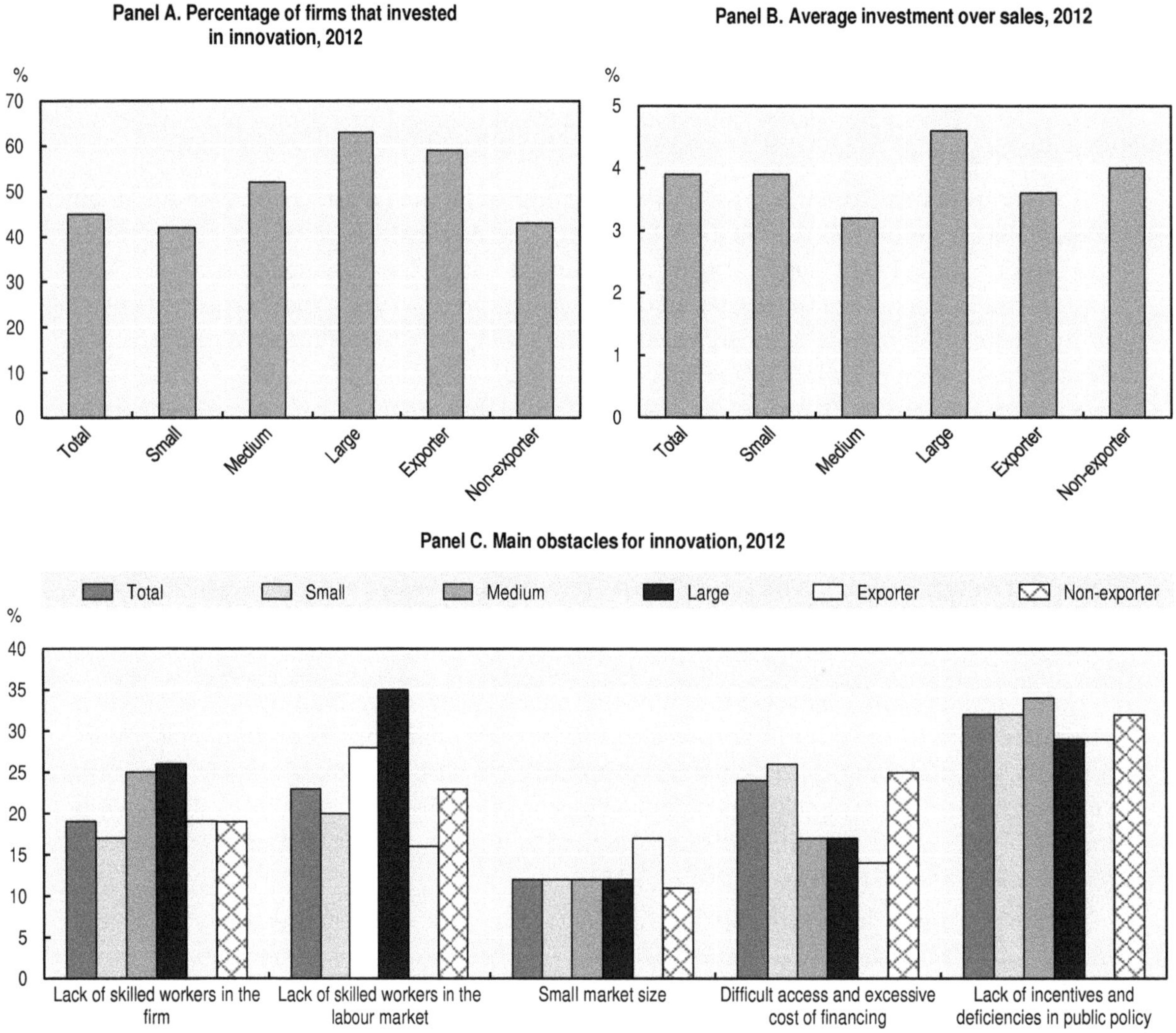

Source: CONACYT/DGEEC (2013), Encuesta de Innovación Empresarial del Paraguay 2010-2012, *http://www.dgeec.gov.py/eiep/*.

StatLink *http://dx.doi.org/10.1787/888933749237*

Improving the quality of education and reducing skills mismatches would help to boost competitiveness and innovation

There is wide scope to boost productivity by improving the quality of education and reducing the skills mismatch. As mentioned above, the third most problematic factor for doing business in Paraguay according to the Global Competitiveness Index is the inadequately educated workforce. Although Paraguay has achieved an average per capita increase of 1.5 years of education over ten years (2004-14), completion of secondary and tertiary education is relatively low for adults of 30 to 64 years old (36.6% and 12.5%, respectively) compared to the Latin America regional average (38.6% and 13.4%, respectively) and the OECD average (76% and 34%, respectively) (OECD/CAF/ECLAC, 2016) (see Chapter 3). Some of the recent policies to develop skills in Paraguay include technical and vocational training aiming to promote and develop workers' training and specific skills. However, the number of students in secondary education enrolled in technical and vocational programmes by 2013 (15.6% of total secondary students) although larger than the Latin America average (14.5%) was still below the OECD average (26%). Efforts to introduce a dual education system and provide vocational training that matches the needs of those sectors being developed continue but should be strengthened and systematised.

Infrastructure and connectivity development faces several challenges

High-quality infrastructure and connectivity are fundamental to both raising productivity levels and improving social inclusion as they allow for lower costs, higher competitiveness and support the delivery of, and access to, public services. Such connectivity, as well as improved logistics performance, is also critical to reinforcing trade in goods and services across value chains, and thereby to spreading economic benefits from trade. As a landlocked country, Paraguay's competitiveness is heavily dependent on its own transport and logistics infrastructure and that of neighbouring countries to connect to regional and international markets (OECD, 2016b). More than 75% of Paraguay's exports are time-sensitive (OECD/CAF/ECLAC, 2014), which makes it extremely important to have appropriate transport connectivity. Although in past years Paraguay's investment in infrastructure has been similar to the average of Latin American countries, the quantity and quality of that infrastructure are still barriers to inclusive growth.

Assessing the quality and quantity is difficult as there are no comprehensive internationally comparable data based on objective criteria (Pisu, Hoeller and Joumard, 2012). Survey data on the perceived quality of infrastructure ranked Paraguay 122nd worldwide in 2016. The perceived quality of overall infrastructure has improved in the last decade but remains below that of OECD countries and among the lowest when compared with its benchmark economies. While overall perceived quality of infrastructure on average in benchmark economies improved by 1.6% between 2006 and 2016, Paraguay's perceived infrastructure quality increased by 24% in the same period (Figure 2.25) (WEO, 2016).

Figure 2.25. **Perceived quality of infrastructure has improved but remains below that of OECD countries**

Perceived quality of overall infrastructure

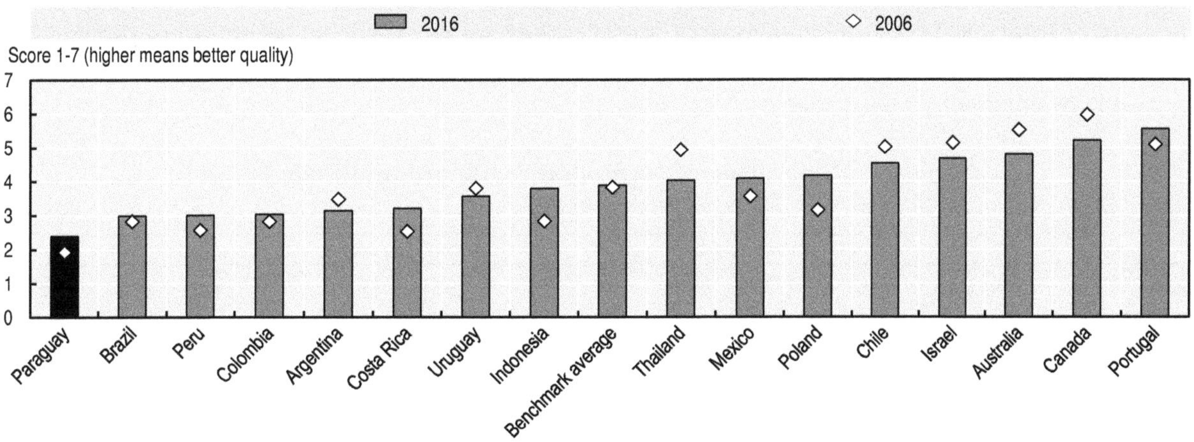

Source: WEF (2006), *The Global Competitiveness Report 2006-2007*, *http://www3.weforum.org/docs/WEF_GlobalCompetitivenessReport_2006-07.pdf*; WEF (2016), *The Global Competitiveness Report 2016-2017*, *http://www3.weforum.org/docs/GCR2016-2017/05FullReport/TheGlobalCompetitiveness Report2016-2017_FINAL.pdf*.

StatLink http://dx.doi.org/10.1787/888933749256

In respect of the quality of different infrastructure sectors, Paraguay performs poorly relative to other OECD benchmark economies and, although to a lesser extent, to other Latin American benchmark economies. In all the sectors, Paraguay ranks at the bottom of benchmark economies except for mobile telephone subscriptions (Figure 2.26). However, the perceived quality of almost all sectors has improved since 2006 apart from air infrastructure and energy supply.

Figure 2.26. **Perception of low quality of infrastructure is generalised in all sectors**

Perceived quality of infrastructure by sectors

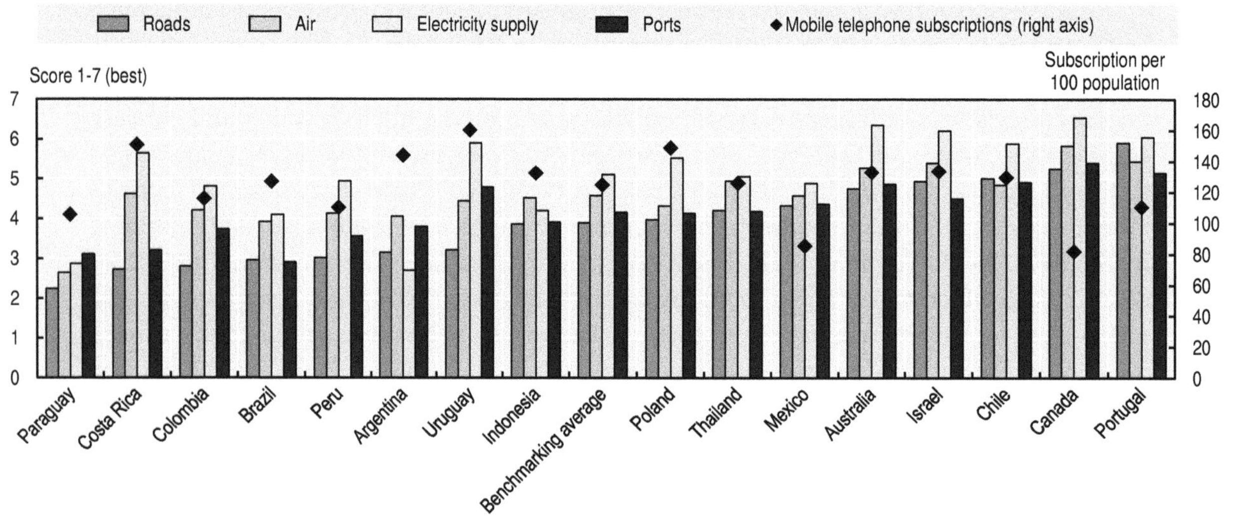

Source: WEF (2016), *The Global Competitiveness Report 2016-2017*, *http://www3.weforum.org/docs/GCR2016-2017/05FullReport/TheGlobalCompetitivenessReport2016-2017_FINAL.pdf.*

StatLink *http://dx.doi.org/10.1787/888933749275*

Road quality perception is the lowest amongst benchmark economies (Figure 2.25) and the lowest compared to the quality of other infrastructure sectors in Paraguay. Table 2.2 shows the kilometres of roads by type of material. The total road network seems reasonable according to the regional averages. However, the number of kilometres of asphalted roads is relatively low (CAF, 2009). Paraguay has 74 251 km of national, departmental and local or rural roads, of which only 6 167 (8%) are asphalted and including enriched roads, paved roads total 8 307 (11%), while almost 89% of all roads are dirt roads which in times of rain present traffic difficulties. Consequently several localities in the interior are isolated, with no possibility of access to basic services.

Table 2.2. **Kilometres of asphalted roads are relatively low**

Road network (Inventoried)

	Paved (km)	Not paved (km)	Total
National	3 108	16	3 124
Departmental	3 879	9 696	13 575
Local or rural	1 320	56 232	57 552
Total	8 307	65 944	74 251
Share	11%	89%	100%

Source: Ministry of Public works and Communication (MOPC).

The 2013 National Development Plan reported that 89% of the roads may have traffic difficulties because of deterioration, rain, etc. while 18% of paved roads were severely damaged and only 30% of rural roads were subject to some conservation or improvement programmes (Gobierno Nacional, 2014). The case of local roads is alarming given that almost 97% consist of dirt roads on which traffic is non-existent in periods of rain. A new generation of contracts (*contratos CREMA, [Contratos de Rehabilitación y Mantenimiento]*) has aimed to cover both road rehabilitation and maintenance. These contracts are yielding positive results for road infrastructure. The road capacity in some cities such as Asunción has not increased significantly while the fleet of vehicles grows year by year. Despite the low quality of the road network, the total number of vehicles in circulation rose by more than 70% from 2006 to 2013 (DINATRAN, 2007; DINATRAN, 2014). According to the traffic lights control centre of Paraguay, the collapse of communication channels and the subsequent congestion around the capital city limit the maximum speed of access to main cities to an average of 11 kilometres per hour.

Rail transport disappeared because of the creation of the reservoir of the Yacyretá dam in 2010, financing problems and the lack of adequate technical capacity to reactivate the system (Gobierno Nacional, 2014). Starting in 2015, a passenger service between Posadas in Argentina and Encarnación in Paraguay was introduced (4.83km between the two stations). The number of passengers increased from almost 920 000 in 2015 to 1 336 000 by 2016, around 45%. (Railway Gazette, 2015). The line crosses the River Paraná by means of the San Roque González de Santa Cruz Bridge, where freight trains had resumed operating in 2012. The benefit of integrating rail systems with neighbouring countries would be substantial as it would enable a connection with ports, generating benefits to the country's foreign trade; it would help diversify its transport corridors of imports and exports, and complement road transport with a lower price option and ability to transport a higher volume (IDB/ MOPC, 2013).

River navigation is of the greatest importance for Paraguay's foreign trade. Approximately 75% of export and import cargos are transported by the Paraguay-Paraná waterway connecting to the ocean ports of Buenos Aires and Montevideo. The main challenge lies in maintaining adequate navigability, especially on the Paraguay River. The most frequent obstacles are the lack of dredging and signalling that would allow navigation all year round (even during drought months) and at night (IDB/ MOPC, 2013). With the third largest fleet for navigation (*barcazas*) after the United States and China (MOPC, 2016a), Paraguay is focusing on its waterways infrastructure to become a connectivity hub in the region. A *barcaza* carries the equivalent of 60 trucks and 15 railway cars (Muñoz, 2012) per trip while it represents cost reductions, fuel savings and decongestion of traffic. Other means of transport should complement the Paraguay-Paraná waterway; land routes and railway lines must ensure a practical, fast and cheap access to both rivers. Paraguay has emphasised the development of multi-modality among different transportation systems, developing waterways and the land-water connection.

As in the case of ports infrastructure, Paraguay ranks at the bottom of the benchmark countries. However, the improvement in perceived quality has been impressive, increasing by almost 30% between 2006 and 2016, compared to around 12% for benchmark economies. Paraguay has had great growth in terms of investment in private ports. Until the mid-1990s, port activity was monopolised by the government through the National Administration of Navigation and Ports (ANNP). In 1994, a law on private ports was enacted which made it possible for the private sector to invest and operate ports. Since then, more than 40 private ports have been installed (there are also eight public ports) (IDB/MOPC, 2013). However, the lack of an integrated and efficient transport policy generated a disorderly growth with many ports being established in the environs of the city of Asunción and creating urban development problems (Gobierno Nacional, 2014). This growth in port activity has not been accompanied by public transport infrastructure support, which currently creates traffic and urban development congestion in the region.

In terms of air transport quality, Paraguay ranks at the bottom when compared with benchmark economies and perceived quality decreased by 11% from 2006 to 2016, while the decrease in quality for average benchmark countries was of less than 2%. Paraguay has a serious shortage in its main air terminal as institutional problems in the sector make it difficult to adopt reforms that allow for modernisation of the airport infrastructure. In addition, international airlines that connected directly with airports in the United States and Europe (Gobierno Nacional, 2014) have abandoned their services. Still, in 2016, for the first time, more than a million passengers used the Silvio Pettirossi airport, an increase of around 14% relative to 2015.

The two international airports are the Silvio Pettirossi Airport serving the city of Asunción and the Guaraní Airport serving Ciudad del Este. The number of passengers at Silvio Airport Pettirossi for the year 2016 was 1 033 168, while at the Guaraní Airport there were 43 622. In respect of cargo the former handled 14 109 tonnes and the latter 6 506 tonnes (DINAC, 2016). Currently, a public-private partnership contract is being processed for the modernisation and expansion of the Silvio Pettirossi airport, which involves an investment of USD 150 million (MOPC, 2016b). The concession has not yet been implemented because of complaints of irregularities.

Paraguay has established a national transport strategy, but its implementation faces challenges. According to the National Development Plan 2030 the weakness of government, both in its planning and regulatory role, is a common factor in all modes of transport (Gobierno Nacional, 2014). This is perceived as the main cause of the delays in the provision of infrastructure and the poor quality of transport services. There is a National Transport Plan (*Plan Maestro de Transporte*) designed at the sectoral level which aims to organise the development of transport and logistics infrastructure, which was updated for the last time in 2012. There is also a National Logistics Plan with the aim of rationalising processes, increasing opportunities for exporters, and capturing regional supply and value chains through efficient logistics mechanisms and reduction of costs for commercial transactions. The extra costs coming from the import and export of goods represent a weakness for Paraguay's export competitiveness. Better institutional organisation will create a harmonised and strategic timetable of infrastructure works. Clear leadership from the government will also facilitate the regulation of public-private partnerships (see Chapter 6).

The telecommunications infrastructure has improved considerably in recent years, but further inclusiveness and improvements are needed. In Paraguay, mobile telephone subscriptions per hundred of the population increased almost four times from 30 in 2006 to 105 in 2015, an increase slightly lower than that of the Latin American region average. Broadband penetration is still very low, with only 1.1 subscriptions per 100 inhabitants while the average for benchmark countries is 16.5. Fewer than half of the population (44%) use the Internet, a similar level to the average of Latin American countries but lower than the 60% Internet users in benchmark economies (WEO, 2016). Although it has increased in recent years, the use of information and communication technology (ICT) in Paraguay remains well below that in the benchmark economies, including Latin American and OECD economies (Figure 2.27).

Figure 2.27. **Telecommunications infrastructure has improved in recent years, but there is further room for improvement**

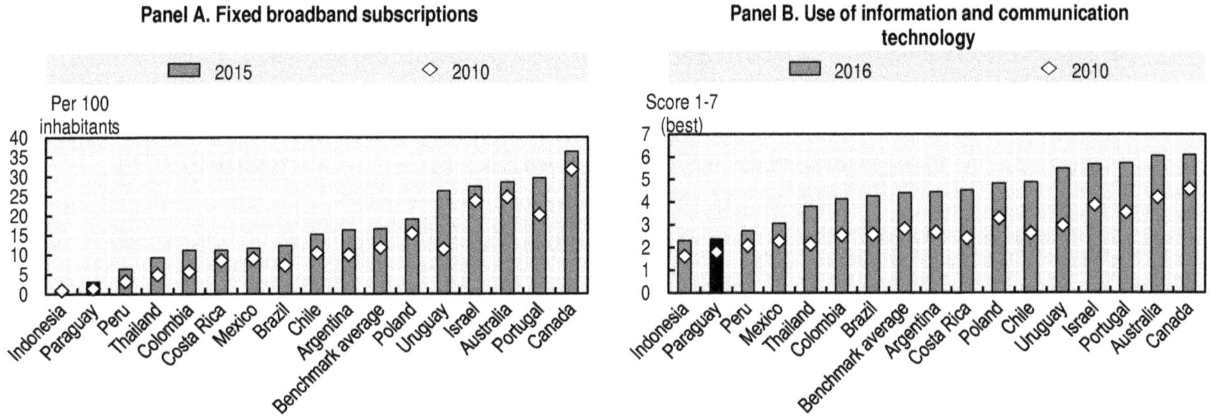

Source: Panel A: International Telecommunication Union (ITU) Statistics (2017), *http://www.itu.int/en/Pages/default.aspx*. Panel B: WEF, *The Global Competitiveness Report 2006-2016* (database).

StatLink http://dx.doi.org/10.1787/888933749294

The National Telecommunications Plan 2006-16 developed by the National Telecommunication Commission (CONATEL) points that a concern for the government in coming years would be to provide connectivity to education, health and safety institutions while on the supply side, one of the main concerns is to provide good-quality connectivity through fixed-broadband as well as to decrease the cost of international connectivity (CONATEL, 2016). These connections today are provided at a very high cost, impacting on losses of competitiveness and limitations for access to the Internet, both for public services and for private enterprises.

Paraguay's gross electricity production capacity (close to 64 000 GWh/year in 2016) is one of the largest in the world per capita (9 290 kWh per inhabitant in 2016) as a result of the production of binational hydroelectric plants. Electricity is an important export product to the partner countries of the Itaipú (Paraguay/Brazil) and Yacyreta (Paraguay/Argentina) binational hydroelectric plants; less than 16% is used by the national electricity market. The main national electricity company is the National Electricity Administration (*Administración Nacional de Electricidad*, ANDE) which participates in the generation, transmission, distribution and commercialisation of electric energy in the country. The other two public sector companies are the binational companies that operate the hydroelectric plants of Itaipú and Yacyreta, in which Paraguay participates through ANDE with the 50% of the capital in both cases. Electricity generated in Paraguay is mostly hydroelectric (MOPC, 2017).

Access to electricity is higher than the Latin American average and similar to the average of benchmark economies. According to latest comparable data, in 2014, 99% of the population had access to electricity (97.7% in rural areas, 99.9% in urban areas). In terms of electric power transmission and distribution losses, Paraguay ranks relatively well when compared to other Latin American countries, relative to its total electricity output (Figure 2.28). Paraguay registered losses of 6.6% of the output in 2014 while the average for the Latin America region was 15.6% and 9.2% for the average of benchmark economies. However, if only the domestic market is concerned and exports are excluded, losses are above those of all benchmark countries, at 23.5% in 2015, the bulk of which are distribution losses. Regarding the quality of electricity supply, Paraguay ranks at the bottom relative to other benchmark countries while service interruption rates in the metropolitan area have worsened (ANDE, 2015). Quality perception decreased by 15% from 2006-16, while for benchmark countries it increased by around 1.5% (WEO, 2016).

Figure 2.28. **The government aims to expand and improve electricity supply**

Electric power transmission and distribution losses

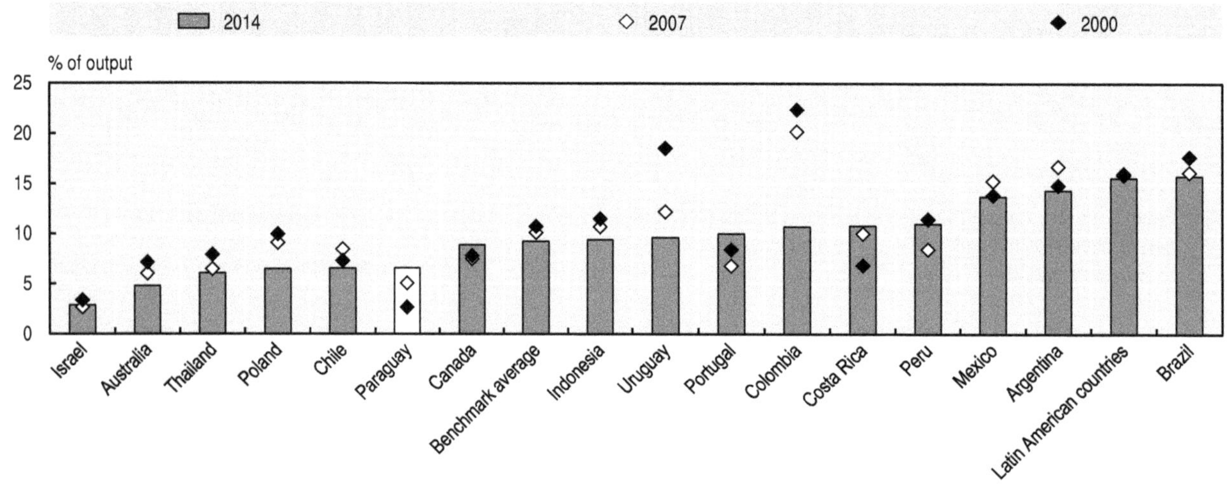

Source: World Bank (2017a), *World Development Indicators* (database), *http://data.worldbank.org*.

StatLink http://dx.doi.org/10.1787/888933749313

The government aims to expand and improve electricity supply to meet the country's requirements. To this end, within the Plan for Electrical Losses Reduction, in 2014, ANDE carried out several activities such as improvement of obsolete rural distribution lines, improvement of the quality of measurement and monitoring. ANDE has been granted several loans by multilateral organisations, treasury bonds, FOCEM funds, etc. Investments in the electricity sector are essential to help improve the performance of productive sectors and the country's competitiveness.

The institutional and regulatory framework should be set in a way that boosts competition

According to OECD's Product Market Regulation (PMR) indicator 2013 (Koske et al., 2015), regulation in Paraguayan product markets was slightly more stringent than the regional average and much more so than OECD average (Figure 2.29). Restrictions in the form of barriers to trade and investments were especially high (Figure 2.30). Markedly reducing barriers to trade and investment will broaden the scope for knowledge diffusion and technological transfers across borders and boost productivity through more efficient resource allocation. More specifically, among barriers directly hampering trade and investment, barriers to trade facilitation and barriers to foreign direct investment (FDI) were significantly higher than the OECD and Latin America average in 2013.

In recent years, there have been major efforts by the government to attract investment which include special regulations and fiscal regimes that promote a favourable environment for both local and foreign investment. They include the tax incentive scheme for national and foreign capital investment (Law No. 60/90), the *maquila* Regime, the *zonas francas* Regime (Law No. 523/95) and the law on guarantees for investments and the promotion of employment and socio-economic development (Law No. 5542/2015), among others. According to the Ministry of Industry and Commerce, the number of *maquiladoras* (foreign-run factories) increased significantly from 46 in 2013 to 126 in 2016. The sectors with the greatest dynamism are automotive parts, plastics, textiles, and footwear. Important offices have also been opened, such as the one-stop shop for exporters (*ventanilla unica del exportador* – VUE) which aims to facilitate cross-border commerce, and the unified system for opening and closing businesses (*sistema unificado de apertura y cierre de empresas* – SUACE) which significantly shortens the time needed for administrative procedures.

Figure 2.29. **There is scope for easing regulation in product markets**

Product Market Regulation (PMR) stringency indicator (scale 0-6, higher is more restrictive), 2013

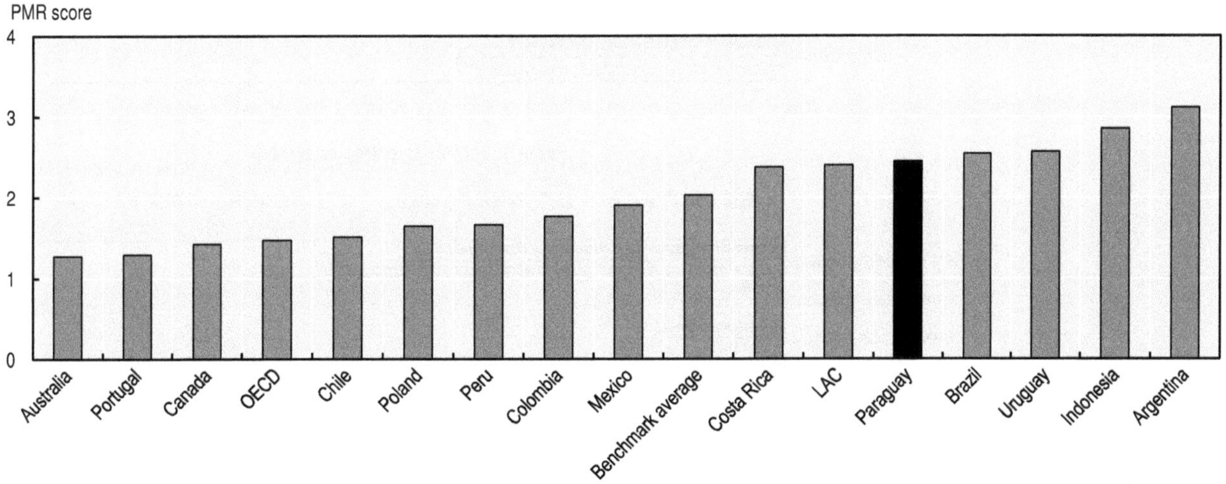

Source: OECD Product Market Regulation Indicators (database) available at *http://stats.oecd.org/Index.aspx?datasetcode=PMR*; Koske et al. (2015).

StatLink http://dx.doi.org/10.1787/888933749332

Barriers to entrepreneurship in Paraguay seem to be lower than in the Latin American region as a whole. However, among barriers directly hampering entrepreneurship, administrative burdens for sole proprietor firms and corporations, as well as communication and simplification of rules and procedures were significantly higher than in the average of benchmark countries (OECD/IDB/GFP, 2016). Markedly reducing barriers to entrepreneurship will improve the business environment and enhance competitive pressures, in addition to reducing labour market informality. OECD best practices indicate that establishing one-stop agencies and adopting the "silence is consent" rule can significantly lower these barriers (OECD, 2016a). In this sense, the government of Paraguay recently created a one-stop-shop (*sistema Unificado de Apertura y Cierre de Empresas, SUACE*) as a unified system to reduce time and facilitate the opening and closing of companies. Regarding access to finance for small and medium-sized enterprises (SMEs), the government is working to launch credits with differentiated interest rates and repayment periods adapted to the specific needs of SMEs. The Ministry of Industry and Commerce is currently working on developing the regulation for a SMEs Guarantees Fund to facilitate access to credit by using this fund as collateral with the help of the *Agencia Financiera de Desarrollo* (AFD).

Figure 2.30. **Barriers to trade and investment as well as administrative burdens restrict competition**

Product Market Regulation (PMR) stringency indicator (scale 0-6, higher is more restrictive), 2013

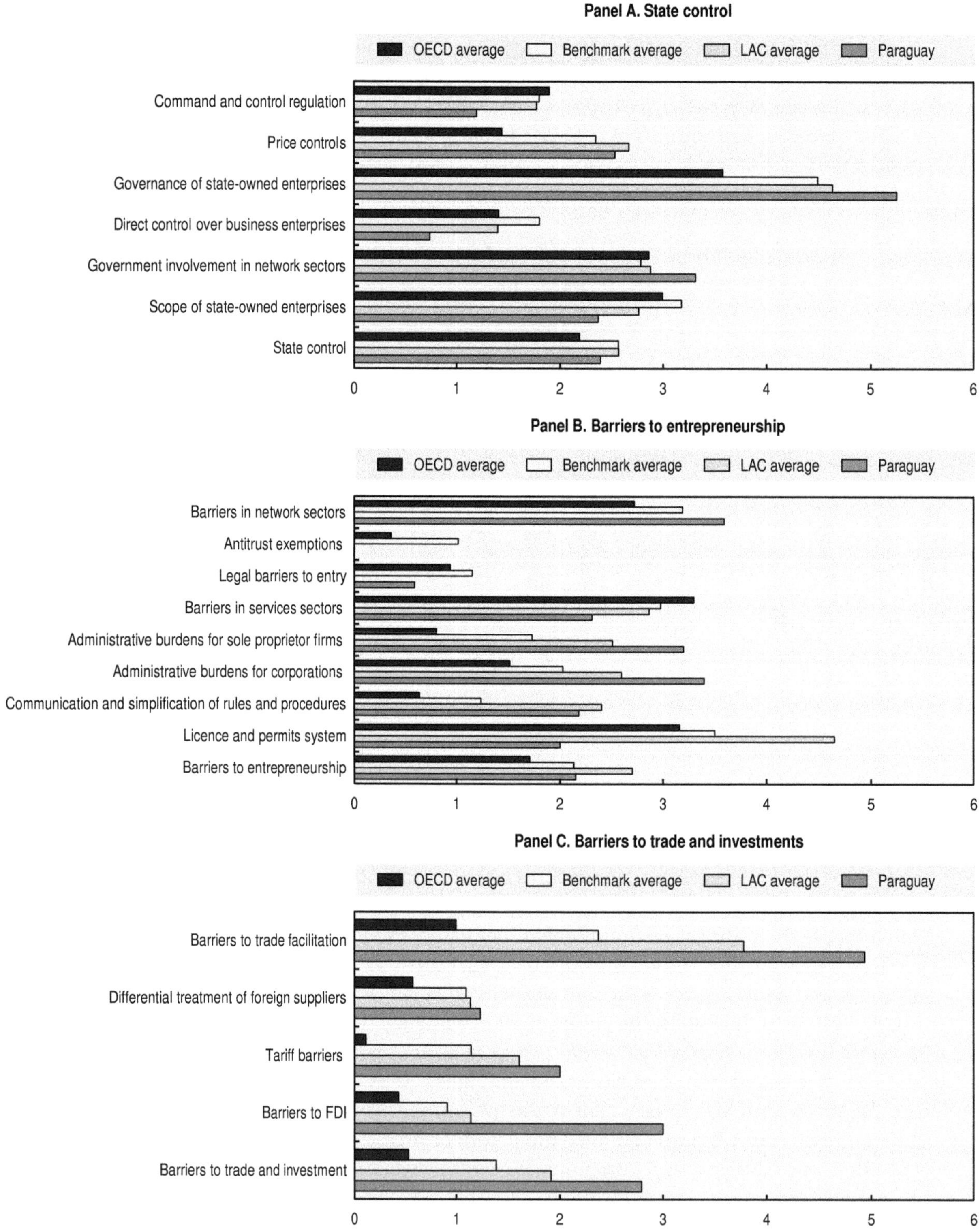

Source: OECD Product Market Regulation Indicators (database) available at *http://stats.oecd.org/Index.aspx?datasetcode=PMR*; Koske et al. (2015).

StatLink http://dx.doi.org/10.1787/888933749351

It is worth noting that overall state controls are less restrictive than in other benchmark and Latin American countries. However, government involvement in network sectors and poor governance of state-owned enterprises (SOEs) are particularly problematic. SOEs have played a significant role in the Paraguayan economy, accounting for roughly 9.94% of GDP and 23% of public sector expenditures in 2016 (Republic of Paraguay, 2017). The performance of SOEs has been affected by inefficient management and planning practices, lack of tariff adjustments, and low investment. Some of the sectors still operated by the government are electricity, telecommunications, and water. Because of their major role, Paraguay must establish clear governance models to allow SOEs to perform at the most efficient level with a strong commitment to accountability. In an effort to promote the efficient management of SOEs, the government of Paraguay created in 2013 the SOEs' national council (*consejo nacional de empresas públicas*, CNEP), made of representatives from the Ministry of Finance, the Ministry of Public Works, the Ministry of Industry and Trade and the Attorney General. The CNEP's role is to act as the SOEs' shareholder on the government's behalf and to supervise SOEs' corporate governance and financial and business management (Republic of Paraguay, 2017). It has promoted planning, management and control measures strengthening the institutional framework for supervision and seeking to ensure the sustainability of the implemented reforms. The CNEP´s review of the status of existing corporate governance practices resulted in the issuance of Executive Branch Decree No. 6381/16 (Code Arandú), which formalises the mandatory adoption of uniform principles of corporate governance to ensure SOEs follow the highest international standards, such as the OECD *Principles of Corporate Governance for SOEs* and *Guidelines for Best Corporate Governance of CAF State Companies* (Republic of Paraguay, 2017). Paraguay is also a regular participant in the Latin American Network on Corporate Governance of State-Owned Enterprises and if sound corporate governance practices were applied, SOEs would become more transparent, more accountable and more efficient in their management.

The institutional framework for the implementation of competition policy in Paraguay is embryonic. Law No. 4956 defines the main pillars for a competition policy, but little support from a budgetary point of view has been given to the National Competition Commission (CONACOM) in charge (currently the agency has only ten staff). Recently established, the agency is in charge of investigating cases of abuse of dominant position, supervising mergers and acquisitions, and identifying anti-competition practices. The commission's board is composed of members from both the public and private sectors. Issues related to consumers' welfare and unfair competition are discussed elsewhere. The agency is currently identifying key sectors for intervention; the financial system, telecommunications, health and the hydrocarbons sectors are identified as sectors where the enforcement of competition law seems most urgent. Sanctions can be applied to companies for anti-competitive practices (with fines up to 150% of the illicit profits or up to 20% of the gross sales of products subject to the infringing practice in the relevant market, [Decree 1490/14]). In February 2017, after an eight-month process, CONACOM legislated on its first case of economic concentration since its creation more than three years ago (Sosa & Vera, 2016).

Notes

1. Paraguay's agricultural sector suffered a significant contraction in 2012 due to drought linked to the "la Niña" phenomenon, which affected the 2011/12 crop. Production and value added recovered in 2013. The year 2011 is chosen as a pivot year, as a more typical year.

References

AIP (2016), MOPC *Pretende Invertir 1000 Millones de Dólares por Año en Obras*, Agencia de Información Paraguaya, *www.ip.gov.py/ip/105184* (accessed June 2017).

ANDE (2014), *Memoria Anual 2014*, Administración Nacional de Electricidad, Sede Central de la ANDE.

ANDE (2015), *Resumen Estadístico 2011-2015*, Administración Nacional de Electricidad.

Angelelli, P., F. Luna and F. Vargas (2016), "Características, determinantes e impacto de la innovación en las empresas paraguayas", *Documento para Discusión* No. IDB-DP-478, Banco Interamericano para el Desarrollo, Washington, DC.

Arce, L., González, C., Masi, F., Servin, B. and Setrini, G. (2010), "Comercio y pobreza en el Paraguay: el caso de una cadena de valor agroindustrial", Comisión Económica para América Latina y el Caribe, Santiago de Chile.

Barro, R. and Jong-Wha Lee (2013), "A New Data Set of Educational Attainment in the World, 1950-2010", *Journal of Development Economics*, Vol. 104, pp.184-198, Elsevier.

BCP (2017), *Anexo Estadístico – Informe Económico* (database), Banco Central de Paraguay, Asunción.

BCP (2016), *Informe de Política Monetaria Diciembre 2016*, Banco Central de Paraguay, Asunción.

CADEP (2017), *Deuda Pública*, Cartilla Fiscal 19, Centro de Análisis y Difusión de la Economía Paraguaya CADEP, Observatorio Fiscal y Presupuestario OFIP, Iniciativa Think Tank, Asunción.

CADEP (2014a), "Economía y Sociedad, Análisis de Coyuntura Mensual", Centro de Análisis y Difusión de la Economía Paraguaya, No. 27, Asunción.

CADEP (2014b), "Cadenas de Valor y Pequeña Producción Agricola en el Paraguay", *http://www.cadep.org.py/cadenas/*

CAF (2009), "Paraguay. Análisis del sector transporte. 2009", *Serie Informes Sectoriales. Infraestructura*, Corporación Andina de Fomento (CAF), Caracas.

Calderón, C., and L. Servén (2004), "The effects of infrastructure development on growth and income distribution", *World Bank Policy Research Working Paper* No. 3400, World Bank, Washington, DC.

Center for International Development at Harvard University (2017), *The Atlas of Economic Complexity* (datebase), *http://www.atlas.cid.harvard.edu.*

CONACYT (2015), *Estadísticas e Indicadores de Ciencia y Tecnología de Paraguay 2014-2015*, Consejo Nacional de Ciencia y Tecnología (CONACYT), Asunción.

CONACYT/DGEEC (2013), *Encuesta de Innovación Empresarial del Paraguay 2010-2012. Resultados*, Consejo Nacional de Ciencia y Tecnología (CONACYT), Dirección General de Estadística, Encuestas y Censos (DGEEC), Asunción, *www.dgeec.gov.py/eiep/.*

CONATEL (2016), *Plan Nacional de Telecomunicaciones Paraguay 2016-2020*, Comisión Nacional de Telecomunicaciones (CONATEL), Asunción.

Crespi, G. and P. Zuñiga (2010), "Innovation and productivity: Evidence from six Latin American countries", *IDB Working Paper* Series No. IDB-WP-218, Inter-American Development Bank, Washington, DC.

Cresta, J. (2017), *Análisis de la Eficiencia de las Empresas Públicas de Paraguay*, Centro de Análisis y Difusión de la Economía Paraguaya (CADEP), Asunción.

David, A (2017), "Fiscal policy effectiveness in a small open economy: Estimates of tax and spending multipliers in Paraguay", *IMF Working Papers*, WP/17/63, International Monetary Fund, Washington, DC.

David, A. and N. Novta (2016), "A balancing act: Reform options for Paraguay's Fiscal Responsibility Law", *IMF Working Papers*, WP/16/226, International Monetary Fund, Washington, DC.

DGEEC (2017), *Encuesta Permanente de Hogares* [Permanent Household Survey] (database), Dirección General de Estadística, Encuestas y Censos, Fernando de la Mora, *http://www.dgeec.gov.py/microdatos/index.php*, accessed August 2017.

Diewert, W. Erwin (2014), "Decompositions of Productivity Growth into Sectoral Effects", *Journal of Productivity Analysis*, April, 1–21, doi:10.1007/s11123-014-0392-0.

DINAC (2016), *Informe Estadístico del Transporte Aéreo. Enero a Diciembre de 2016. Aeropuerto Internacional "Silvio Pettirossi"*, Dirección Nacional de Aeronáutica Civil (DINAC), Asunción.

DINATRAN (2014), *Anuario Estadístico de Transporte 2013*, Dirección de Planificación Integral de Transporte (DINATRAN), San Lorenzo.

ECLAC (2016), *Dinámica de las empresas exportadoras en América Latina: El aporte de las PYMES*, Economic Commission for Latin America and the Caribbean, Santiago.

ECLAC/IDB/CAF (2016), INFRALATAM Database, *http://en.infralatam.info/home* (accessed 23 May 2017), Santiago.

Eyraud, L., A. C. David and F. Bardella (2016), "Paraguay: Establishing a Structural Balance Rule and a Public Debt Objective", Technical Assistance Aide-Memoire, November 2016.

Feenstra, R, R.Inklaar and M. Timmer (2015), "The Next Generation of the Penn World Table", *American Economic Review*, 105(10), 3150-3182, available for download at *www.ggdc.net/pwt*.

Gobierno Nacional (2014), *Plan Nacional de Desarrollo Paraguay 2030*, Gobierno Nacional de Paraguay, Asunción, *http://www.stp.gov.py/pnd/wp-content/uploads/2014/12/pnd2030.pdf*.

Grazzi, M. and C. Pietrobelli (eds.) (2016), *Firm Innovation and Productivity in Latin America and the Caribbean. The Engine of Economic Development*, Inter-American Development Bank, Washington, DC.

Hagemann, R. (2010), "Improving fiscal performance through fiscal councils", *OECD Economics Department Working Paper* No. 829, OECD Publishing, Paris, *http://dx.doi.org/10.1787/5km33sqsqq9v-en*.

IDB/MOPC (2013), *Plan Nacional de Logística-Paraguay 2013*, Inter-American Development Bank, Ministerio de Obras Públicas y Comunicaciones (MOPC).

IMF (2017), *World Economic Outlook* (database), Washington DC, *https://www.imf.org/external/pubs/ft/weo/2015/01/weodata/index.aspx*.

IMF (2016a), "Paraguay, 2016 Article IV Consultation", *IMF Country Report*, No. 16/11, International Monetary Fund, Washington, DC.

IMF (2016b), "Paraguay, Selected Issues", *IMF Country Report*, No. 16/117, International Monetary Fund, Washington, DC.

IMF (2013), *The Functions and Impact of Fiscal Councils*, International Monetary Fund, Washington, DC.

International Telecommunication Union (ITU) Statistics (2017), Geneva, *http://www.itu.int/en/Pages/default.aspx*.

Koske, I. and al. (2015), "The 2013 update of the OECD product market regulation indicators: policy insights for OECD and non-OECD countries", *OECD Economics Department Working Papers*, No. 1200, OECD Publishing, Paris.

Law 5098/2013, *Ley No. 5098 de Responsabilidad Fiscal*, Gaceta Oficial, Asunción.

Ludeña, C. and F. Ruiz Díaz (2008), "Sobrecostos de transporte: ¿maldición geográfica o falla de política de infraestructura? Una estimación para Paraguay desde un modelo de equilibrio general", *Cuaderno de Economía, Publicación del Departamento de Economía*, Facultad de Ciencias Empresariales, Universidad Católica del Uruguay, Montevideo.

MH (2017a), *En qué Invierte el Gobierno los Bonos Soberanos?*, Ministerio de Hacienda, Gobierno Nacional de Paraguay, Asunción.

MH (2017b), *Informe de las Finanzas Públicas de la República del Paraguay*, Ministerio de Hacienda, Gobierno Nacional de Paraguay, Asunción.

MH (2017c), *Estadísticas de la Deuda Pública* (database), Ministerio de Hacienda, Dirección de Política de Endeudamiento, Gobierno Nacional de Paraguay, Asunción, *http://www.economia.gov.py/index.php/dependencias/direccion-de-politica-de-endeudamiento/estadistica/deuda-publica-clasificacion-saldo-desembolso-servicio* (accessed June 2017).

MH (2015), *Situación Financiera Administación Central. Diciembre 2015*, Ministerio de Hacienda, Gobierno Nacional de Paraguay, Asunción.

MOPC (2017), *Electricidad – Generación* website, Ministerio de Obras Públicas y Comunicaciones (MOPC), *http://www.ssme.gov.py/vmme/index.php?option=com_content&view=article&id=1216&* (accessed June 2017).

MOPC (2016a), *Ministro destaca avance del transporte urbano en Paraguay y la Hidrovía como eje para el desarrollo*, Noticias website, Ministerio de Obras Públicas y Comunicaciones (MOPC), *http://www.mopc.gov.py/ministro-destaca-avance-del-transporte-urbano-en-paraguay-y-la-hidrovia-como-eje-para-el-desarrollo-n3646* (accessed June 2017).

MOPC (2016b), *MOPC ejecuta seis proyectos estratégicos que representan USD 1.292 millones de inversión*, Noticias website, Ministerio de Obras Públicas y Comunicaciones (MOPC), *http://www.mopc.gov.py/mopc-ejecuta-seis-proyectos-estrategicos-que-representan-usd-1292-millones-de-inversion-n3300* (accessed June 2017).

Muñoz, J. (2012), "El transporte por la Hidrovía Paraguay-Paraná", *Revista de la Bolsa de Comercio de Rosario*, Rosario.

OBEI (2016), *Informe de Comercio Exterior 2015-2016*, Observatorio de Economía Internacional, Asunción.

Observatorio Turístico de Paraguay (2017), Estadísticas Turísticas Básicas, Secretaría Nacional de Turismo, *http://www.observatorionacionaldeturismo.gov.py/index.php/estadisitcas/informes-anuales*.

OECD (2016a), *OECD Economic Surveys: Costa Rica 2016: Economic Assessment*, OECD Publishing, Paris, *http://dx.doi.org/10.1787/eco_surveys-cri-2016-en*.

OECD (2016b), "*Promoting Productivity for Inclusive Growth in Latin America*", *Better Policies Series*, OECD Publishing, Paris, *www.oecd.org/economy/promoting-productivity-for-inclusive-growth-in-latin-america.pdf*.

OECD (2015), *Policy Framework for Investment, 2015 Edition*, OECD Publishing, Paris, *http://dx.doi.org/10.1787/9789264208667-en*.

OECD (2014), *Recommendation of the Council on Effective Public Investment Across Levels of Government*, OECD Publishing, Paris, *www.oecd.org/regional/regional-policy/Principles-Public-Investment.pdf*.

OECD (2010), "Portugal", in *Regional Development Policies in OECD Countries*, OECD Publishing, Paris, *http://dx.doi.org/10.1787/9789264087255-26-en*.

OECD (2009), *Innovation in Firms: A Microeconomic Perspective*, OECD Publishing, Paris, *http://dx.doi.org/10.1787/9789264056213-en*.

OECD (2007), *OECD Principles for Private Sector Participation in Infrastructure*, OECD Publishing, Paris, *www.oecd.org/daf/inv/investment-policy/38309896.pdf*.

OECD/CAF/ECLAC (2016), *Latin American Economic Outlook 2017: Youth, Skills and Entrepreneurship*, OECD Publishing, Paris, *http://dx.doi.org/10.1787/leo-2017-en*.

OECD/CAF/ECLAC (2015), *Latin American Economic Outlook 2016: Towards A New Partnership with China*, OECD Publishing, Paris, *http://dx.doi.org/10.1787/9789264246218-en*.

OECD/CAF/ECLAC (2014), *Latin American Economic Outlook 2015: Education, Skills and Innovation*, OECD Publishing, Paris, *http://dx.doi.org/10.1787/leo-2015-en*.

OECD/IDB/GFP (2016), *Boosting Productivity and Inclusive Growth in Latin America*, OECD Publishing, Paris, *www.oecd.org/latin-america/Boosting_Productivity_Inclusive_Growth.pdf*.

Pisu, M., P. Hoeller and I. Joumard (2012), "Options for benchmarking infrastructure performance", *OECD Economics Department Working Papers*, No. 956, OECD Publishing, Paris, *http://dx.doi.org/10.1787/5k9b7bnbxjwl-en*.

Railway Gazette (2015), Posadas - Encarnación passenger service restored, retrieved from *http://www.railwaygazette.com/news/passenger/single-view/view/posadas-encarnacion-passenger-service-restored.html*.

Republic of Paraguay (2017), *Offering Memorandum. 4.700% Bonds due 2027*, República de Paraguay, Asunción.

Roldos, J., M. Santoro and A. David (2016), *Investing in Paraguay's Future*, Blog Diálogo a Fondo, International Monetary Fund, Washington DC.

SNIP/MH/GN (2015), *Dirección del Sistema de Inversión Pública Informe Anual 2015*, Sistema Nacional de Inversión Pública, Ministerio de Hacienda, Gobierno Nacional de Paraguay, Asunción.

Sosa, C. and C. Vera, (2016), *Hito de la Competencia. La primera autorización de concentración económica en Paraguay*, Berkemeyer Attorneys and Counsellors website, *http://www.berke.com.py/sitio/article/179* (accessed June 2017).

STP (2017), Registro Público de Proyectos de Participación Público-Privada, Cartera de Proyectos APP website, Secretaría Pública de Planificación del Desarrollo Económico y Social (STP), *www.stp.gov.py/v1/proyectos-de-participacion-publico-privada/#INICIATIVA PÚBLICA* (accessed June 2017).

STP (2014), *Informe de Gestión. Proyectos de Alianza Público Privada. 2015*, Secretaría Técnica de Planificación del Desarrollo Económico y Social (STP), Asunción.

UIS (2017), Science, Technology and Development, *UNESCO Institute for Statistics* (database), *http://data.uis.unesco.org/* (accessed 4 May 2017).

UNCTAD (2017), *Merchandise: Product Concentration and Diversification Indices by Economy, Annual, 1995-2015* (database), United Nations Conference on Trade and Development, Geneva.

Urmeneta, R. (2016), *Dinámica de las Empresas Exportadoras en América Latina: El Aporte de las PYMES*, Economic Commission for Latin America and the Caribbean (ECLAC), United Nations, Santiago.

WEF (2017), *The Global Competitiveness Report 2006-2016* (database), World Economic Forum, Geneva.

WEF (2016), *The Global Competitiveness Report 2016-2017*, World Economic Forum, Geneva. *http://www3.weforum.org/docs/GCR2016-2017/05FullReport/TheGlobalCompetitivenessReport2016-2017_FINAL.pdf.*

WEF (2006), *The Global Competitiveness Report 2006-2007*, World Economic Forum, Geneva.

WEF, Executive Opinion Survey 2016, World Economic Forum, Geneva.

World Bank (2017a), *World Development Indicators Database* (database), Washington DC, *http://data.worldbank.org.*

World Bank (2017b), *Commodity Price Data* (database), *http://data.worldbank.org.*

Multi-dimensional Review of Paraguay
Volume 1. Initial Assessment

Chapter 3

People: Improving citizen well-being in Paraguay

This chapter focuses on key aspects related to the well-being of citizens in Paraguay. It analyses the country's performance in terms of poverty and of inequality between people. While poverty has fallen significantly in the past ten years, inequality is persistently high. The chapter goes on to analyse key mechanisms to address inequality in the short and medium terms: employment and labour markets, education and the social protection system.

The statistical data for Israel are supplied by and under the responsibility of the relevant Israeli authorities. The use of such data by the OECD is without prejudice to the status of the Golan Heights, East Jerusalem and Israeli settlements in the West Bank under the terms of international law.

Improving the well-being of everyone in a sustainable manner is the ultimate development goal. Paraguay has made significant progress in reducing poverty. High economic growth and strengthened social spending have contributed to this achievement. On the other hand, income inequality and inequalities between urban and rural areas remain large. Improving education and labour market outcomes is critical to ensuring that the good economic fortunes of the country benefit all.

This chapter examines performance and the constraints on improving people's well-being across a number of dimensions. The chapter first examines Paraguay's performance in terms of poverty and inequality, with special attention paid to territorial inequalities, the income and non-monetary dimensions of which are considerable. The chapter then turns to selected topics of critical importance to the ability of the Paraguayan economy and state to reduce inequality. Promising job opportunities provide an avenue for increasing the incomes of the poor, and while Paraguay has a very good job creation record, the country still faces challenges in generating good-quality jobs in the formal economy. Education is also a key component in ensuring that future generations have more equal opportunities. Paraguay still faces challenges in meeting its objective of universal access to 12 years of education for all students, and this problem is exacerbated by significant gaps in the quality of learning outcomes. Finally, the institutional arrangements and the prevalence of informality lead to a fragmented social protection system.

Paraguay's growth performance has led to improvements in incomes but inequality remains large

The recent period of economic growth in the country has contributed to raising the living standards of many Paraguayans, including those of the poorest. While household consumption expenditure in Paraguay is among the lowest in the comparison group, the economic performance over the past five years has been very encouraging. This has translated into an adequate growth in household consumption expenditure (2.3% annual in purchasing power parity [PPP] terms), above that of most OECD comparators, but below that of other fast-growing countries in the region and beyond.

Economic growth has contributed to growth in personal incomes, albeit less than in comparable countries. Incomes started growing in real terms when growth picked up in 2003, but it was only after 2006 that growth in personal incomes accelerated and stabilised. In the period 2007-14 economic growth has been associated more directly with improvements in people's living standards. While historically the relative disconnect between gross domestic product (GDP) growth and household incomes means that over the whole period, growth did not always benefit consumers as much as it could have, it has an advantage, since macroeconomic volatility did not lead to volatility in median incomes as measured by national household surveys (Figure 3.2).

Figure 3.1. **Household consumption and growth**

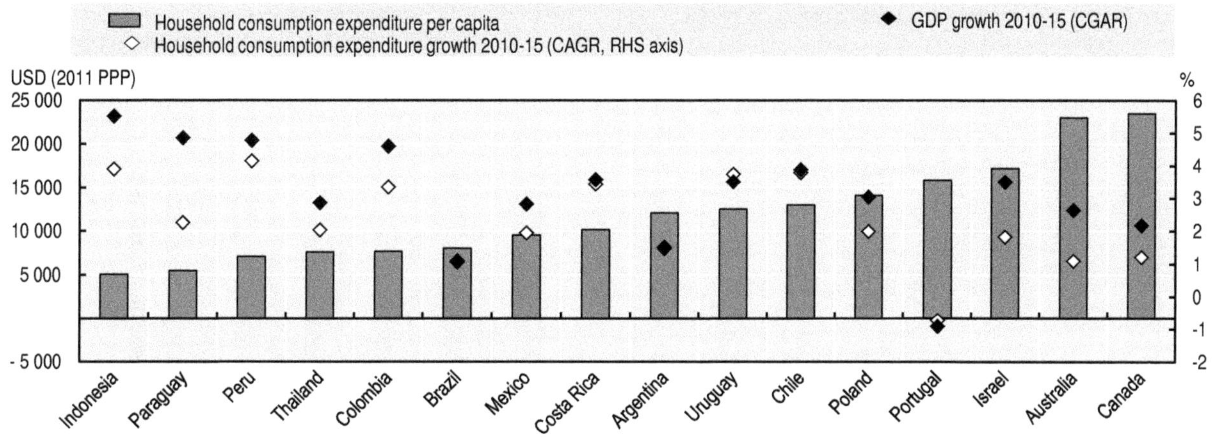

Source: World Bank (2017a), *World Development Indicators*, *https://data.worldbank.org/*.

StatLink http://dx.doi.org/10.1787/888933749370

Figure 3.2. **Growth in median household incomes has picked up**

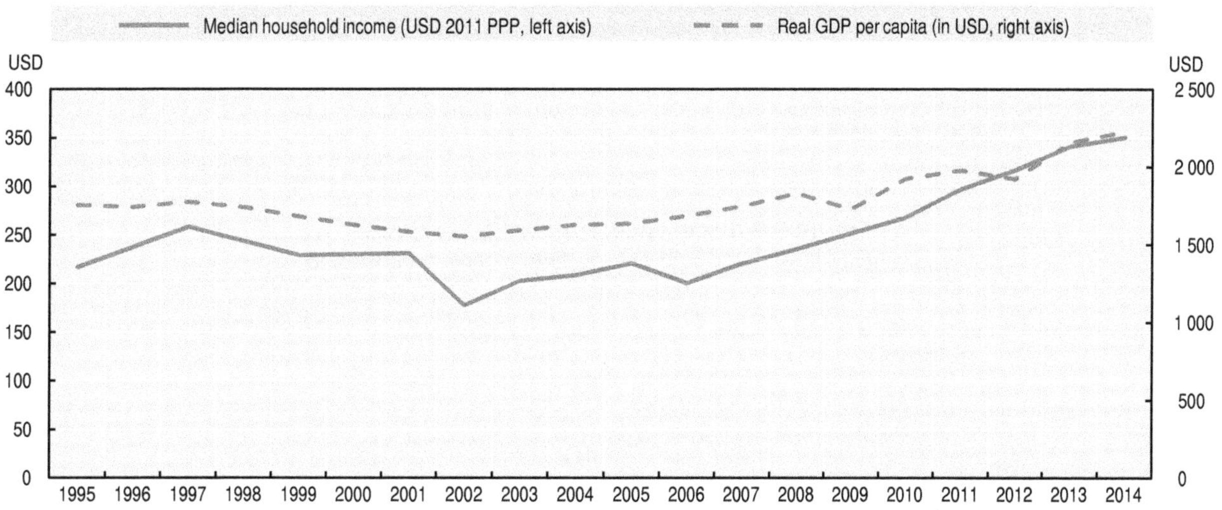

Source: Median household income from World Bank (2017b) PovcalNet, *http://iresearch.worldbank.org/PovcalNet/home.aspx*, real GDP per capita from BCP (2017) Anexo estadístico del Informe Económico, *https://www.bcp.gov.py/anexo-estadistico-del-informe-economico-i365*.

StatLink http://dx.doi.org/10.1787/888933749389

Inequality has fallen but remains high

The pattern of income growth in Paraguay has led to a slight fall in the level of income inequality since the turn of the century, with a Gini coefficient dropping from 0.55 in 2000, to 0.48 in 2016, according to national sources. In terms of OECD comparable data, inequality in per capita equivalent disposable income fell from 0.57 in 1999 to 0.52 in 2014. This is a significant fall in inequality as shown by the trend in Panel A of Figure 3.3, even though it is smaller than the fall in inequality observed for the Latin American region as a whole (Figure 3.3, Panel B).

The distributional pattern of growth has changed dramatically since the end of the crisis of the 1990s. Growth was more pro-poor during the period 1999-2007, but at very low average rates; indeed average real growth was slightly negative, at -0.6%. Since 2007, growth has been much stronger and affected all parts of the income distribution almost equally, although the poorest decile benefitted slightly more than average (Figure 3.4, Panel B).

Figure 3.3. **Inequality level and evolution in Paraguay and benchmark economies**

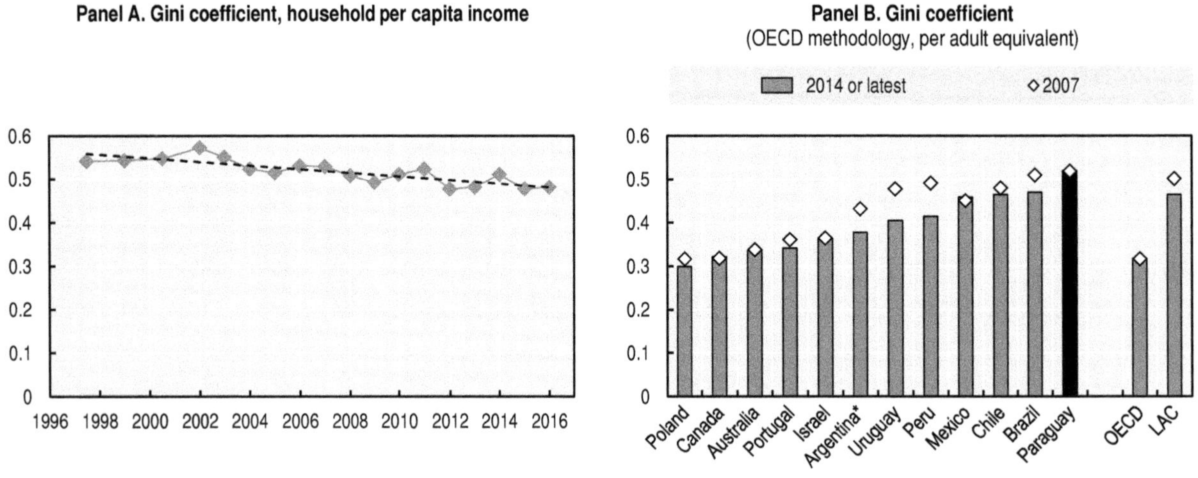

Notes: Panel B estimates are based on the same definitions and methodologies used to generate estimates for OECD countries, as available through the OECD Income Distribution Database (IDD) *http://oe.cd/idd*. Due to differences in survey methodologies and questionnaires design (e.g. in terms of the recording of taxes paid and transfers received and paid by households), estimates for these Latin American countries are not fully comparable to those available for OECD countries. Data for Brazil are for years 2013 and 2006.

* Data for Argentina refer to urban areas only, and data for 2007-2014 for Argentina cannot be compared to data before 2007 or after 2015.

Source: Panel A: DGEEC, Paraguay, Panel B, OECD project 2015/16 "Monitoring Inequalities and Fostering Inclusive Growth in Emerging Economies" estimates based on micro-data from the main household surveys for Argentina, Bolivia, Dominican Republic, Ecuador, Panama, Paraguay, Peru and Uruguay, as available through CEDLAS (Centre for Distributive, Labor and Social Issues in Latin America, Universidad Nacional de La Plata, Argentina).

StatLink *http://dx.doi.org/10.1787/888933749408*

Figure 3.4. **Incidence of growth by decile**

Annualised per adult equivalent growth in disposable income

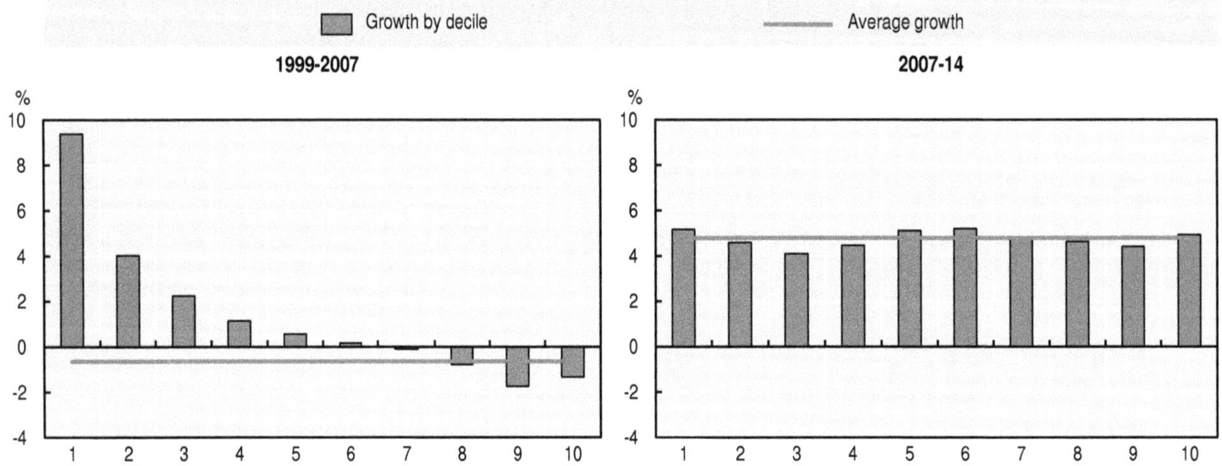

Source: Calculations based on OECD project 2015/16 "Monitoring Inequalities and Fostering Inclusive Growth in Emerging Economies" estimates based on micro-data from the main household surveys for Argentina, Bolivia, Dominican Republic, Ecuador, Panama, Paraguay, Peru and Uruguay, as available through CEDLAS (Centre for Distributive, Labor and Social Issues in Latin America, Universidad Nacional de La Plata, Argentina). Nominal data are deflated by the IPC for Greater Asunción obtained from the BCP.

StatLink *http://dx.doi.org/10.1787/888933749427*

Inequality in Paraguay has a marked geographical component. Income is highest in Asunción, the capital, although the premium over average income fell from over 110% in 2001 to 73% in 2011 (CEDLAS and the World Bank, 2017). On the other hand, the ratio between overall rural and urban incomes was stable between 2001 and 2015, with rural incomes oscillating between a minimum of 55% of urban incomes and a maximum of 70%. Remarkably, urban residents in the Central region, which includes most of Greater Asunción, and the rest of the country's cities, had similar average incomes 10% above the national average, while those in rural Central had 80% and those in other rural areas 72%, possibly reflecting easier access to market close to Greater Asunción than further inland. The rural to urban gap has been fairly stable since 2002, with rural incomes standing at about 60% of average urban incomes.

Territorial inequality is an important contributor to inequality and deprivation in Paraguay. Extreme poverty is largely a rural phenomenon, reaching only 1.6% in urban areas, compared to 12.2% in rural areas. As Figure 3.5 shows, levels of monetary and non-monetary deprivation are higher in rural areas, with marked differences in access to water and sanitation. Basic services that require less heavy investment, such as electricity and telephony are more present in rural areas.

Figure 3.5. **Monetary and non-monetary deprivation in urban and rural areas**

2015 or latest available

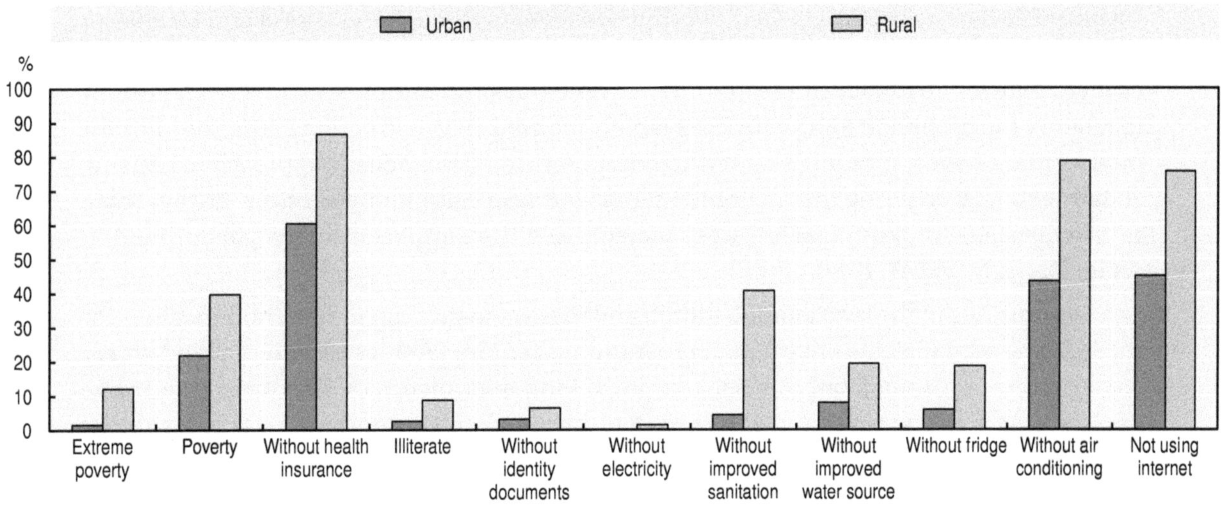

Source: Data provided by DGEEC (2015; 2017).

StatLink http://dx.doi.org/10.1787/888933749446

The housing deficit is a key aspect of territorial inequalities

Access to decent housing and infrastructure is s fundamental element of material well-being and one where territorial inequalities are large in Paraguay. SENAVITAT (*Secretaría Nacional de la Vivienda y el Hábitat*), the national housing authority, estimates the housing deficit to concern over 800 000 housing units, or 73% of the total. Within that deficit, 13% corresponds to needs for new housing (on the basis of overcrowding or the presence of multiple households in a single house). The rest of the deficit is qualitative, and represents chiefly needs for improvements to housing, in particular to access to piped water and to the public sanitation grid, which only covers 10% of the population.

In spite of the development of the construction sector, needs remain significant. Overall, SENAVITAT estimated a need to build just under 100 000 dwellings on the basis of the 2002 census (SENAVITAT, 2016). That figure was projected to reach 190 330 by 2020 (SENAVITAT, 2012). The need for housing is also reflected in the extent of informal settlements, which according to estimates, number over 1 000 in the Central department alone (which includes areas surrounding the capital Asunción). In addition to the large estimated needs for the poor, there are difficulties for the lower middle classes (in the 1 to 3 minimum-wage band) in accessing housing, because construction firms concentrate on the higher end of the market and because of the difficulties in access to credit for those households.

Public intervention in housing is largely focused on construction of housing units. SENAVITAT has built 20 299 dwellings since 2013, benefitting 80 000 people and has reached the capacity to generate 10 000 units a year since 2015, of which about 90% go to families in extreme poverty. This is the result of a significant increase in public expenditure in housing and community services after 2011. Financial commitments towards housing from SENAVITAT more than doubled in real terms between 2011 and 2016 when they reached just under 600 million PYG. According to the law that governs access to the national fund for social housing (FONAVIS) (Law No 3637), households with a total income below one minimum wage can receive a 95% subsidy on the acquisition of a dwelling. The state also grants subsidised long-term loans for the acquisition of housing through the *Agencia Financiera de Desarrollo* (AFD) to creditworthy households through the *Micasa* and *Mi Primera Casa* programmes. However, these tend to reach higher income individuals able to pay. Law No 3909 of 2010, which created the current housing authority, SENAVITAT, gives it regulatory functions, but SENAVITAT has largely focused on construction in the past. Recent interventions have increasingly aimed at incorporating a more holistic approach to housing construction, by ensuring that not only utilities but also community services, are available to new dwellers, in particular in larger projects like the San Francisco neighbourhood in Asunción (SENAVITAT, 2017).

Weaknesses in the land administration and management system present difficulties for the housing sector. Most construction programmes require families to own the land where construction is planned, but inconsistencies in land administration instances (the Public Register and the Cadastre) and the spread of informal settlements make this condition difficult to meet. There are a number of government interventions to address this problem, mostly through *ex post* regularisation of land tenure. Among them, the Tekoha programme, implemented by the SAS (*Secretaría de Acción Social*), grants property rights to beneficiaries through the regularisation and sale of land. The programme has widened its scope, serving 22 693 families by February 2017, although it remains small compared to the size of other social programmes and the potential size of the problem.

Poverty reduction accelerated but has stalled in recent years

Paraguay has managed significantly to reduce poverty and extreme poverty since the turn of the century. The poverty headcount fell from 45% in 2007 to 27% in 2015 according to the national poverty line;[1] and extreme poverty from 14% to 5.4% in the same period (DGEEC, 2017). The fall in poverty has been continuous since the 2002 crisis, but has slowed in recent years. The pattern is identical if other poverty lines are used. On the basis of the World Bank moderate poverty line, set at USD 3.10 in 2011 PPP, poverty fell from 18% in 2001 to 7% in 2014. The stagnation in poverty rates is a cause for concern, given the still relatively rapid growth in population. Indeed, the absolute number of poor and extreme poor in the country is estimated to have increased between 2015 and 2016 on the basis of an improved methodology.

Figure 3.6. **Poverty in Paraguay**

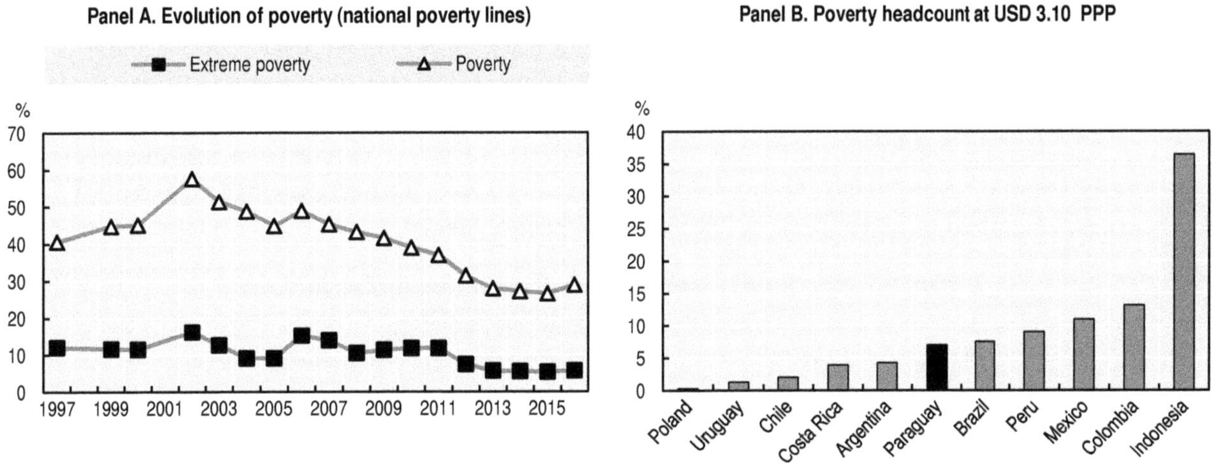

Source: Panel A: DGEEC (2017a). Panel B: World Bank (2017a), *World Development Indicators, data.worldbank.org.*

StatLink http://dx.doi.org/10.1787/888933749465

The fall in poverty has been largely driven by growth in incomes across the population rather than by increased redistribution. This is suggested by the growth incidence curves in Figure 3.4. Given that poverty occupied the first four deciles until the mid-2000s, rapid growth across the distribution was a stronger force than the very progressive but low-growth pattern of the early 2000s. Correspondingly, if the evolution of poverty is decomposed into a growth and a distribution component, all the fall in poverty can be attributed to growth, given the increase in inequality during the period (ECLAC, 2016).

Macroeconomic stabilisation played a major role in sustaining the fall in poverty. The World Bank (2015) found that poverty levels prior to the fall in poverty of the first half of the decade were very sensitive to food prices. This explains the increase in poverty and extreme poverty in 2006-07 when the increase in food prices was more than double the general rate of inflation. It is worth noting that the food consumer price index (CPI) for Asunción is used to update the extreme poverty line, so that actual food affordability in other parts of the country may vary, depending in particular on the quality of market integration.

Paraguay's tax and expenditure system only has modest effects on inequality and poverty

Taxes and public transfers in Paraguay have a very small effect on income inequality. Of the group of benchmark countries with comparable data from the OECD Income Distribution Database, Paraguay is not only the country with the highest level of inequality in disposable income, but also the one where the tax and transfer system has the lowest incidence in the distribution (-1.6%, compared to -7% in Uruguay and a maximum of -38% in Portugal). The data for Paraguay in Figure 3.7 do not account for the redistributive effect of social security contributions; as such, they understate market income inequality relative to other countries, and possibly understate distribution. The reliance on indirect taxes and flat tax rates explains the low impact of taxes on the income distribution. Giménez et al (2017) estimate a total effect of direct taxes corresponding to 0.13% of market income inequality.

Public transfers in Paraguay do have an impact on poverty. The Tekoporã conditional cash transfer (CCT) and the social pension (*Adulto Mayor*) lead, respectively, to falls in the moderate poverty rate of 0.3 and 1.1 percentage points, (Giménez et al, 2017). There are several other programmes which effect direct transfers to households, although their impact cannot be assessed through the same methodology in the absence of identifiable benefits in national household surveys. They include *Abrazo*, a programme to fight child labour, which focused originally on children working on the streets but as of 2015 covered over 3 000 families, and provided conditional cash transfers to 2 000 of them and to 7 700 children.[2] They also include programmes aimed at supporting households' productive activities, in particular in smallholder agriculture. Of these, the programme of direct purchase of smallholder agricultural produce by the Ministry of Agriculture is noteworthy as it provides preferential access to certain public purchases (including for school meals).

Figure 3.7. **Inequality before and after taxes and transfers**

Gini coefficient, 2014 or latest available

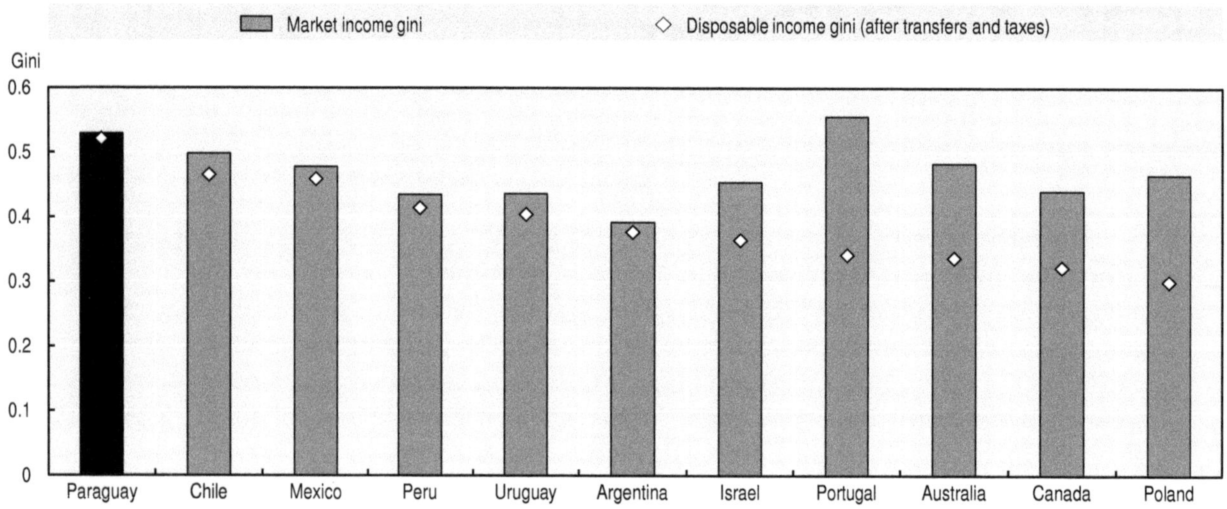

Note: The data displayed are Gini coefficients for the entire population of income per adult equivalent.

Source: IDD database for OECD countries, calculations based on SEDLAC/Word Bank for Latin American countries.

StatLink http://dx.doi.org/10.1787/888933749484

The conditional cash transfer programme Tekoporã is one of the cornerstones of Paraguay's poverty agenda. The Tekoporã programme has grown considerably since its creation in 2005, in particular under the Lugo presidency and under the current administration. In December 2016, the programme covered 685 578 people, about the same as the number of extreme poor in the country. Tekoporã was evaluated in 2016 by Rossi (2016). The programme has significant impact in terms of health and education outcomes. Programme participants are 8% more likely to have vaccination cards, and attend school 13% more often than non-participants. The programme also leads to increases in the use of health services, with an increase in 25% of prenatal controls. Effects on health and education contribute to reducing the inter-generational transmission of poverty. However, the programme's poverty impact is relatively modest. Giménez et al. (2017) estimate that after accounting for Tekoporã transfers, poverty and extreme poverty fall by less than one percentage point (0.3 and 0.7 percentage points respectively). The falls in the poverty gap are larger (1.2 percentage points for both). This is due to limitations in both the size of the transfer and the coverage of the programme. The programme is targeted on the basis of a quality of life index, which can explain in part that, when compared to household income alone, Giménez et al. (2017) find it only covers 30% of households in the first income decile and 20% of households in the second income decile. This is a low figure by international standards, although it is an improvement on the results of a similar study that estimated that in 2010 only 24% of the extreme poor received direct transfers (Higgins et al, 2013).[3] Moreover, the size of transfers is relatively modest: Rossi (2016) notes that the average participant household received each month about 60% of the cost of a basic food basket for one person. The programme therefore would need to grow further in coverage and generosity to have a larger impact on monetary poverty. The evaluation also highlights a number of possible improvements in process that would contribute to its efficiency (Rossi, 2016).

Figure 3.8. **Budget and coverage of Tekoporã**

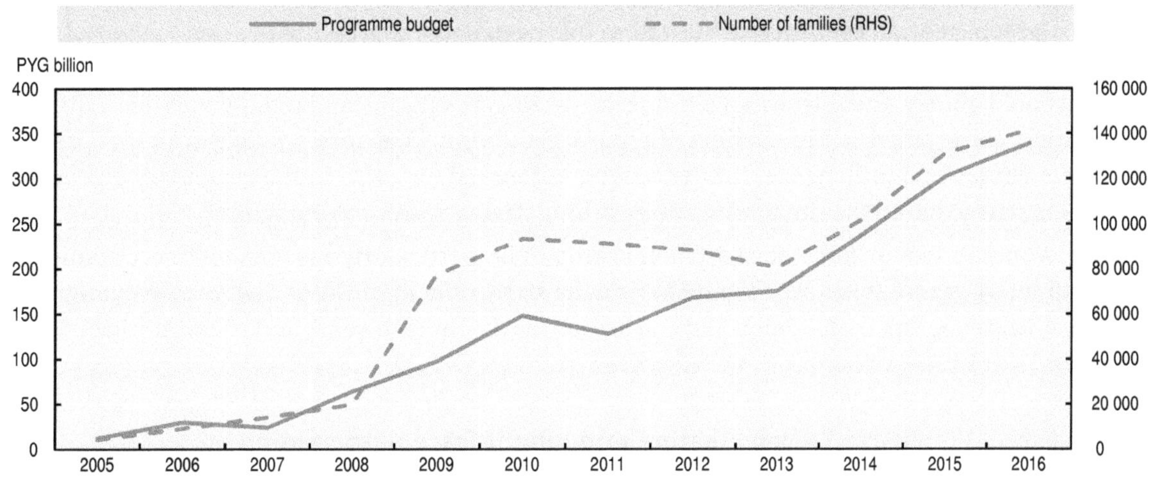

Source: SAS, Ramirez (n.d.), budget information provided by the Ministry of Finance.

StatLink http://dx.doi.org/10.1787/888933749503

The administration is responding to the stagnation in the fall of poverty by innovating its approach to targeting and delivering anti-poverty programmes. On the one hand, programmes are being extended beyond cash transfers to include a productive investment component (*Tenonderã* and *Familia por Familia*). Given the rate of poverty in rural areas, the effectiveness of the new approaches will hinge on the success of policies to increase productivity in smallholder agriculture. The *Tenonderã* programme is the largest of such initiatives. The programme provides grants for productive activities chosen by the beneficiary household (the majority choose small livestock raising) along with capacity-building in social, life and business skills. It can be seen as a graduation programme from the CCT *Tekoporã*, as it targets households who have been in the CCT programme for three years. *Tenonderã* and *Familia por Familia* target poor farmers, often with subsistence production, which is a different population than the established smallholders most likely to receive assistance from the Ministry of Agriculture. *Tenonderã* initiated operations in 2014 and covered 11 540 households by the end of 2016 (SAS, 2016) for a budget of 13 billion guaraní (PYG), about 3% the size of *Tekoporã*. On the other hand, new programmes are extending the range of personal and social support that accompanies recipients, which is already a feature of Tekoporã, to include financial literacy and life skills, and piloting new ways of implementing them (under the pilot methodology *Familia por familia*).

The administration is also responding to the persistence of poverty by increasing its institutional capacity. The *Sembrando Oportunidades* programme, led by the STP, in the national anti-poverty programme. It seeks to co-ordinate the action of multiple agencies and programmes to deliver better livelihoods for the poor. Among other elements, it introduces a single targeting instrument and has a strong focus on productive inclusion through agriculture. *Familia por Familia* is one intervention of the programme. The programme also includes the development of a monitoring framework and tool, which is linked to the budget and to the PND and allows geolocalised monitoring of interventions.

Employment and labour outcomes: The challenge of informality and job quality

Paraguay is undergoing a demographic transition and has a major opportunity to accelerate growth and strive for a more equal society, but also faces the challenge of creating high-quality jobs for large cohorts of young entrants into the labour market.

Job creation has been adequate, sustained by growth in the services sector

Net job creation over the medium term has been good, overtaking the rapid growth in the working age population (2.5% p.a, in 2003-15). Job creation, as measured by the main household survey, the Encuesta Permanente de Hogares (EPH), is markedly volatile.[4] This volatility corresponds to the volatility of activity in the various sectors, not only in agriculture, where climatic conditions can influence labour demand, but also in the secondary sector. This is partly due to the importance of agro-industrial activities in Paraguay.[5]

Women's labour force participation seems to be particularly responsive to economic conditions (Figure 3.9, Panel B), significantly more so than for men. Given that unemployment is low, this suggests that women exit the labour market in lean years and re-enter in boom years.

Figure 3.9. **Job creation and labour force participation**

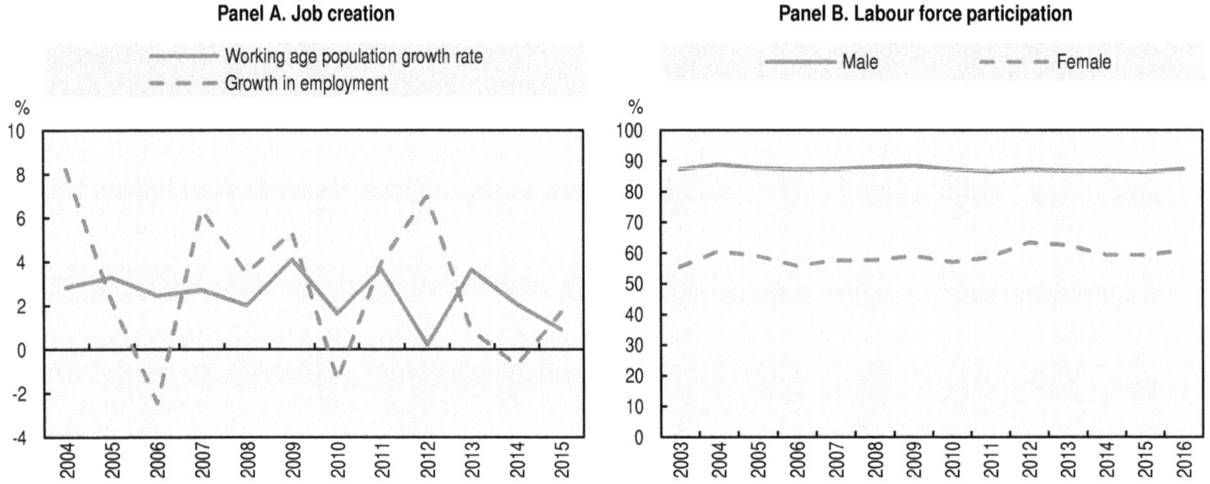

Note: Labour force participation in panel B is for individuals aged 15 to 64.

Source: DGEEC data based on Encuesta Permanente de Hogares (various years) for panel A (DGEEC, 2017b). Own calculations based on updated EPH data (DGEEC, 2017b) for panel B.

StatLink http://dx.doi.org/10.1787/888933749522

Unemployment is low and labour force participation remains stable. Labour force participation in Paraguay was 70.5% for the age group over 15 years old in 2016, stable compared to 2005 figures.[6] This figure is slightly below the average of labour force participation rates for the OECD (71.3% in 2015) but in line with other countries of the region. When a wide age group is considered, including older citizens, measured labour force participation is lower than for the 15 to 64 group, as would be expected, although a third of people over 65 are still active in the labour market. In 2016, unemployment concerned only 6% of the labour force and most of the persons remain unemployed for a short period of time (less than three months). Around 6.0% of the unemployed (about 10 000 people) were looking for a job for more than two years.

Figure 3.10. **Unemployment is low and labour force participation stable**

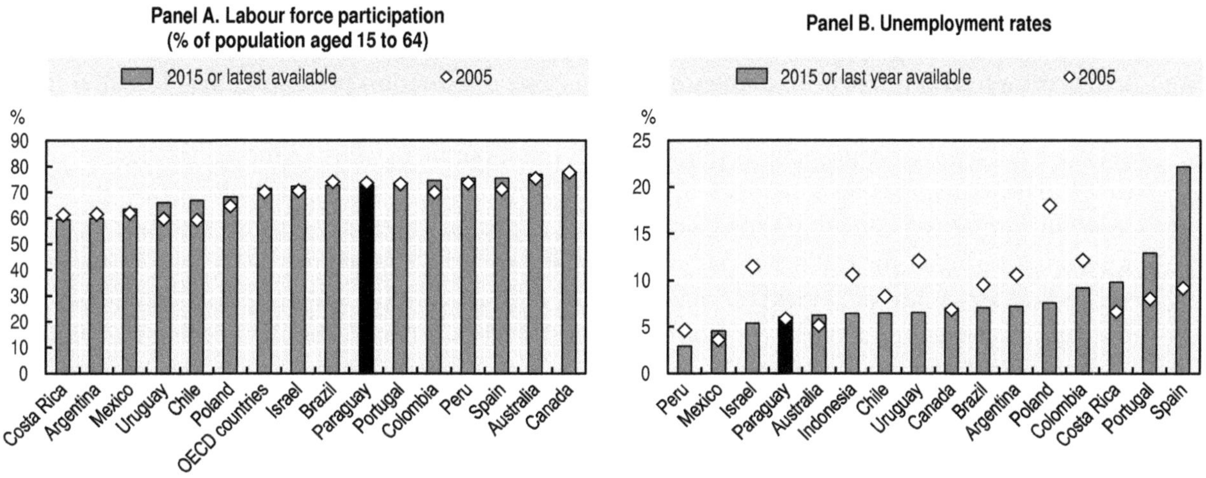

Source: OECD Labour force participation database, *http://dotstat.oecd.org/?lang=en*, SEDLAC for Argentina, Peru and Uruguay, and EPH for Paraguay (DGEEC, 2017b).

StatLink *http://dx.doi.org/10.1787/888933749541*

The participation of women in the labour force is low. Only 50% of women (and 61% of women aged 15 to 64) are active in the labour market, one of the lowest rates among the benchmark countries. This rate increases with the level of education but there is still some margin for improvement at the country level. As many as 57% of employed women among salaried workers are working in agricultural activities in the economy (CEDLAS and the World Bank, 2017). In this regard, Paraguay may want to consider reviewing how countries have implemented 2013 Recommendation of the OECD Council on Gender Equality in Education, Employment and Entrepreneurship (OECD, 2013a).

Figure 3.11. **Despite improvements, women's labour force participation is still low**

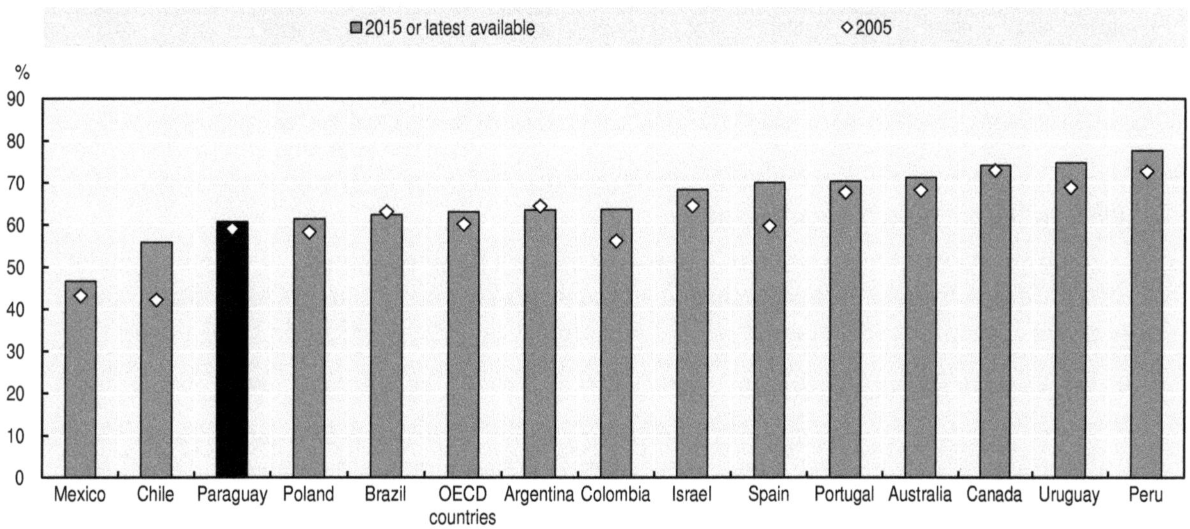

Note: Data correspond to women aged 15 to 64 for all countries except Argentina, Peru and Uruguay, where they are for women aged 15 and over.

Source: OECD Labour force participation database, *http://dotstat.oecd.org/?lang=en*, SEDLAC for Argentina, Peru and Uruguay, and EPH for Paraguay.

StatLink *http://dx.doi.org/10.1787/888933749560*

The structure of employment across the economy shows a slow but regular decline in the primary sector. From 2006 to 2016, the proportion of people working in the agricultural sector declined by ten percentage points, compensated for by job increases in hospitality and commercial services (+3.3 percentage points), in construction (+2.2 percentage points) and in other services, including financial services, real estate and community and personal services (+3.6 percentage points) (Figure 3.12). Manufacturing employment has stayed, in relative terms, around a modest 10% of total employment. Changes have been more rapid in rural areas. If 90% of those working in the primary sector live in rural areas, the reverse is not true for the secondary and tertiary sectors. One-third of the jobs in the secondary sector are now located in rural areas, highlighting the growing importance of the agro-business industry in the country. Even if the number of people working in the secondary sector remains higher in urban areas, it increased significantly in rural areas between 2003 and 2015 (+ 71%).

Figure 3.12. **The employment structure evolves slowly**

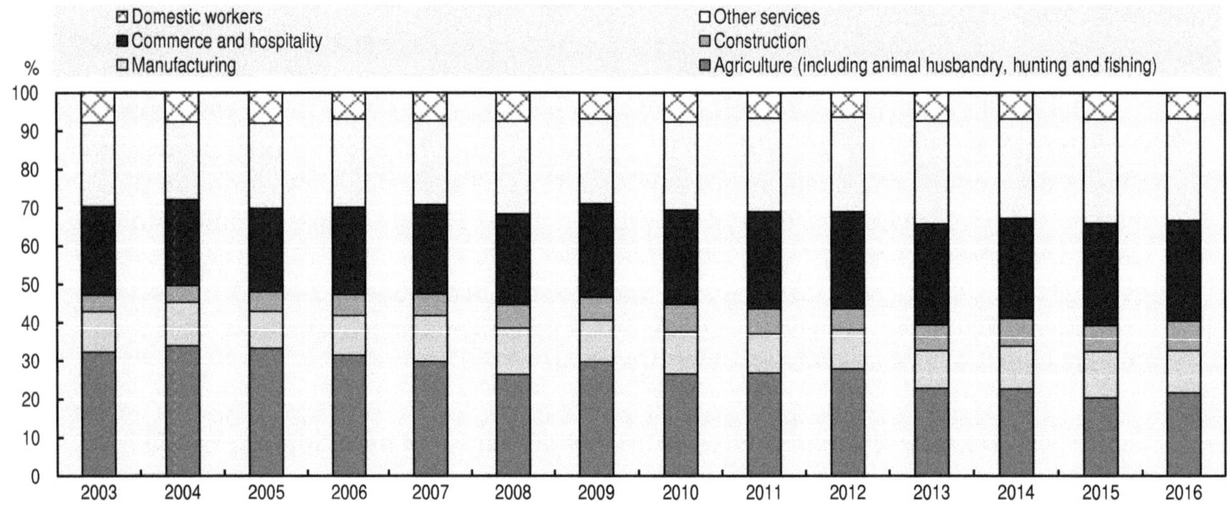

Note: The category "other services" includes electricity, gas and water provision, transport, storage and communications; finance, insurance and real estate; and communal, social and personal services (excluding domestic service).

Source: Calculations based on the Encuesta Permanente de Hogares (years 2003 to 2016) (DGEEC, 2017b).

StatLink http://dx.doi.org/10.1787/888933749579

Job quality remains a major issue

Job quality remains an issue for many workers. Despite some changes in the employment structure over the last decade, domestic workers, unpaid family workers and own-account workers account for 46% of employment and almost two thirds of jobs in rural areas.

Salaried work has increased

The past few years have seen a slow but regular increase in salaried work. In 2014, almost half the working population were salaried (Figure 3.13). The increases in both public sector (by 40% over the 2010-15 period) and private sector jobs have contributed to this trend. Between 2002 and 2013, more than 1 million salaried jobs were created in the country, two-thirds of them in the private sector. This regular increase in salaried work concerns all the country. In urban areas, this increase is led by the growing number of jobs in the tertiary sector (+865 000 between 2002 and 2015). In rural areas, the increase in salaried work can be partially explained by the formalisation of work in the secondary sector.

Figure 3.13. **Structure of employment, by status**

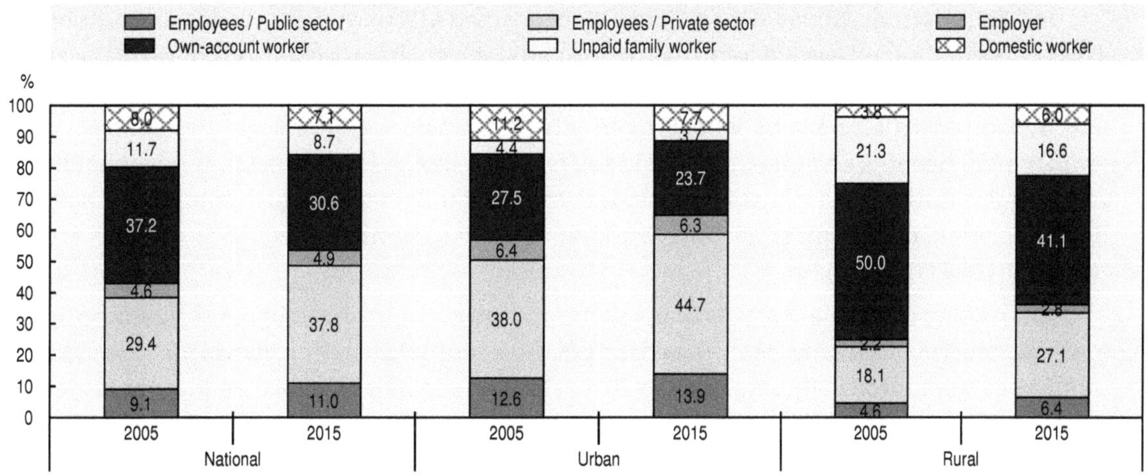

Note: Data do not include the departments of Boquerón and Alto Paraguay.

Source: Encuesta Permanente de Hogares 2005 and 2015 (DGEEC, 2017b).

StatLink http://dx.doi.org/10.1787/888933749598

Public employment has also grown significantly in the past ten years. The human resource management capacity of the Paraguayan state has grown significantly in recent years, but consolidated data on public employment for the early 2000s are patchy and a lack of complete information means it is not possible to examine the evolution of public employment from administrative data. Survey data (Figure 3.13) show that public and private salaried employment grew at a rate of 5.4% per annum between 2002 and 2015, compared to 3% for total employment. Thanks to an improvement in reporting, data provided by the *Secretaría de la Función Pública* (SFP) on public employment now cover 365 reporting institutions out of 409 registered institutions, accounting for 297 891 public employees as of 2016 (SFP, 2017).

Figure 3.14. **The share of salaried work is rising but remains low**

Proportion of employees in the labour force (%), 2015 or latest available data

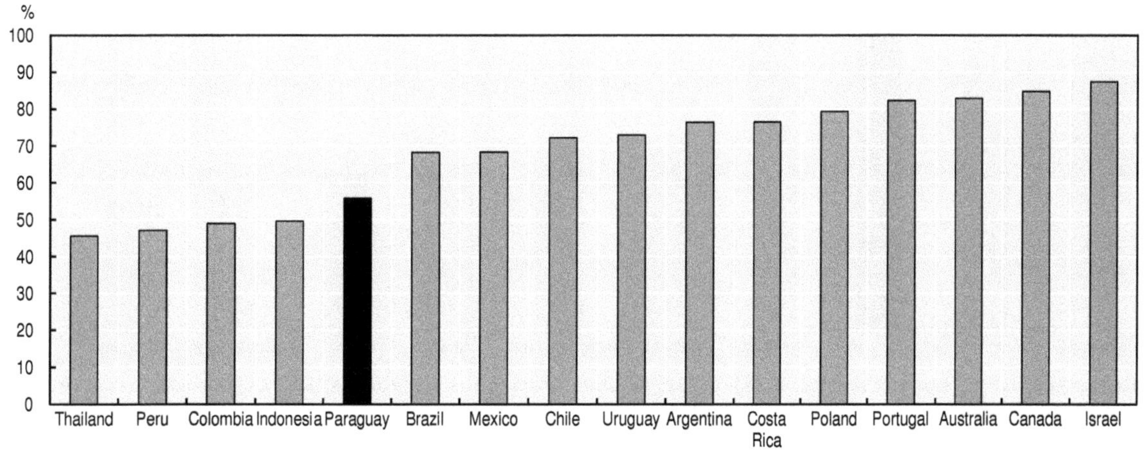

Note: The employed comprise all persons of working age who, during a specified brief period, were in one of the following categories: a) paid employment (whether at work or with a job but not at work); or b) self-employment (whether at work or with an enterprise but not at work). Data are disaggregated by status in employment according to the latest version of the International Standard Classification of Status in Employment (ICSE-93). Status in employment refers to the type of explicit or implicit contract of employment the person has with other persons or organisations. The basic criteria used to define the groups of the classification are the type of economic risk and the type of authority over establishments and other workers which the job incumbents have or will have.

Source: ILOSTAT, *http://www.ilo.org/ilostat*, based on Labour Force Surveys (Encuesta Permanente de Hogares for Paraguay).

StatLink http://dx.doi.org/10.1787/888933749617

Informality is a major challenge for job quality

In 2015, informal employment in Paraguay concerned 64% of workers outside agriculture. This represents a high level of informality compared to benchmark countries but still lower than informal rates in Indonesia and Peru. Informal employment is a job-based concept and encompasses all persons whose main jobs lack basic social or legal protections or employment benefits and may be found in the formal sector, informal sector or households. In Paraguay, informal employment includes unpaid family workers (by definition), most domestic workers, and most of those working as own-account workers (77% of them are informal, [DGEEC, 2016]).

Informality is prevalent across many sectors of the economy. Although it is significantly lower among public employees, by the criteria of the household survey just over 60 000 public employees were informally employed in 2016. This corresponds to public employees under contract (as opposed to civil servants), whose labour relationship is governed by the Civil code (Art. 5 of Law 1626/00). Informal employment is high for those working in the private sector (65%). In terms of sectoral distribution, the construction and commerce sectors also present high levels of informal jobs (respectively, 89% and 72% in 2016). Informality is higher among young (below age 24) and older workers (above age 60), women, the less educated and those working in rural areas. For instance, 79.4% of the jobs occupied by women in rural areas were informal in 2014.

Informality has fallen in recent years. It dropped from 69.2% of non-agricultural employment to 64.3% between 2010 and 2015. Given the fall in agricultural employment, which is largely unprotected, this in fact understates the rate of formalisation in the economy.

Figure 3.15. **Informality is high**

Informal employment (percentage of non-agricultural employment), 2016 or latest available year

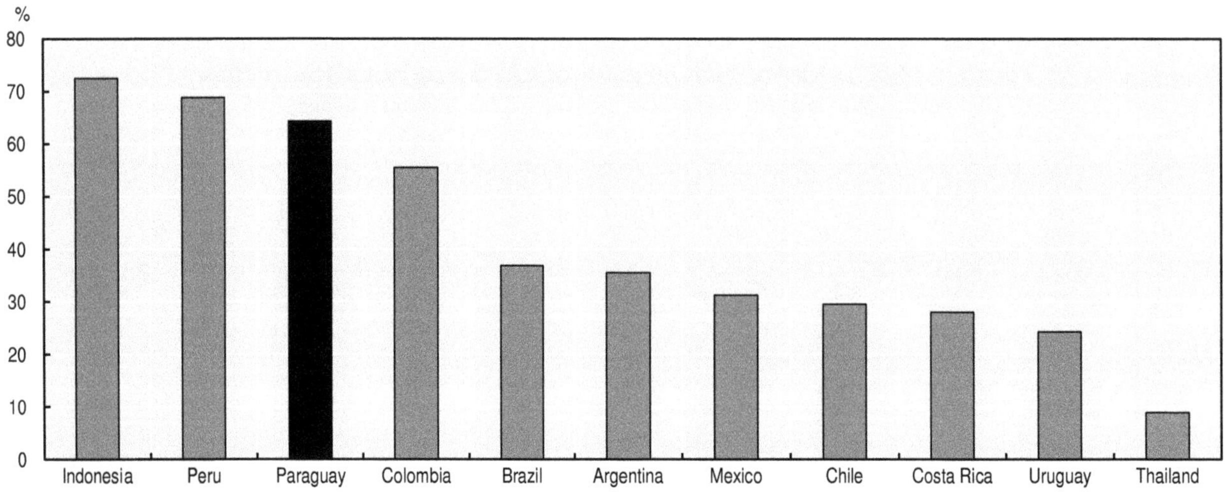

Note: Non-agricultural employment rates are based on 2016 for Chile, Costa Rica and Mexico, 2015 for Colombia, Paraguay, Uruguay, 2014 for Argentina and Thailand; 2013 for Brazil and Peru; 2009 for Indonesia.

Source: ILO, Key Indicators of the Labour Market (KILM) database, *http://www.ilo.org/ilostat/*.

StatLink *http://dx.doi.org/10.1787/888933749636*

Earnings

A considerable proportion of workers earn less than the national minimum wage. In the public sector, 9.6% of workers earned less than the minimum wage in 2016, but this share rises to 44.5% of workers in the private sector. Half of informal employees earn less than the minimum wage, even when domestic workers are excluded. These proportions have registered a decrease over the past five years, (by eight and seven percentage points for public sector employees and private sector employees respectively), but remain substantial in the light of the level of development of the country. Moreover, the minimum wage fell in real terms by over 2% during the period, which diminishes the impact on workers' purchasing power.

The minimum wage has not changed much in real terms over the past 25 years. In 2015 it was estimated at USD 342 (PYG 1 964 507). In real terms, the minimum wage stood in early 2017 at a similar level to that of 1991. The general wage index has only gained 12 percentage points over the increase in the consumer price index (CPI) in the past 13 years, a very modest evolution in the face of rapid growth. Moreover, there are very large differences in labour earnings between rural and urban areas (the gap is about 43% in monthly labour earnings).

Figure 3.16. **Evolution of the real minimum wage**

In 1980 PYG

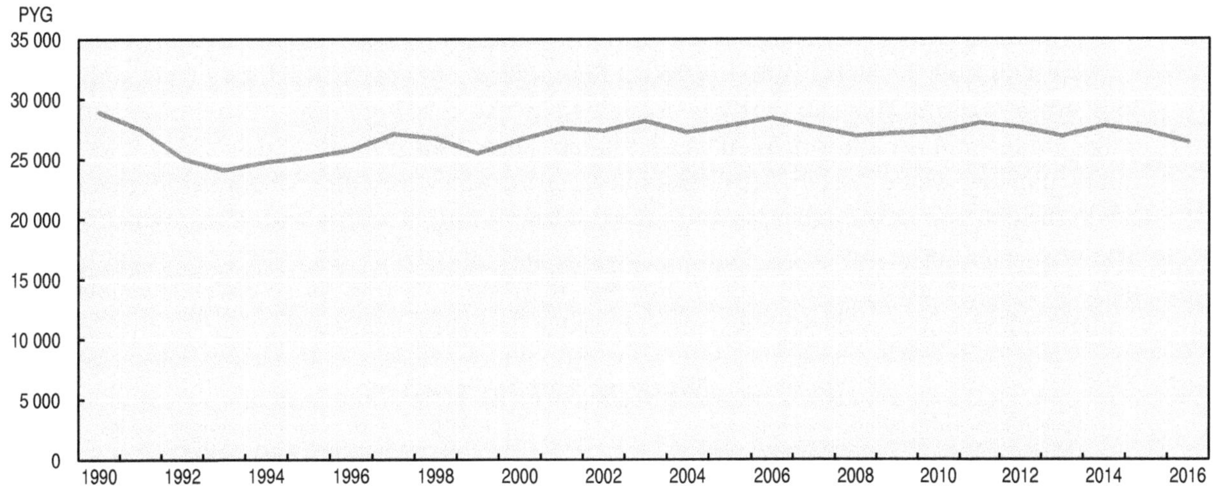

Source: BCP.

StatLink http://dx.doi.org/10.1787/888933749655

The minimum wage in Paraguay is very high by international comparison. OECD data compare minimum wages to average or median wages of the relevant population (salaried workers). In Figure 3.17, minimum wages are compared to mean monthly wages of salaried workers according to the labour force survey, which covers the greater Asunción area and is therefore not representative. Even then, the minimum wage stood at 81% of the mean wage, far above comparator countries. The minimum wage is also high relative to the country's level of development. It is of the same order of magnitude as GDP per capita. The only country in the comparison group that comes close to having such a high minimum wage relative to its economy is Costa Rica, where the minimum wage is 64% of GDP per capita.

Working time

Most Paraguayans work long hours. National data show that more than half of workers work more than 45 hours a week. Only 28% work fewer than 39 hours a week (DGEEC ECE [*Encuesta Continua de Empleo*], 2016). Compared to benchmark countries, the number of weekly hours worked per employed person is highest in Paraguay (46 hours a week).

Figure 3.17. **Minimum wages in Paraguay and comparator countries**

Minimum wage as a share of mean wage

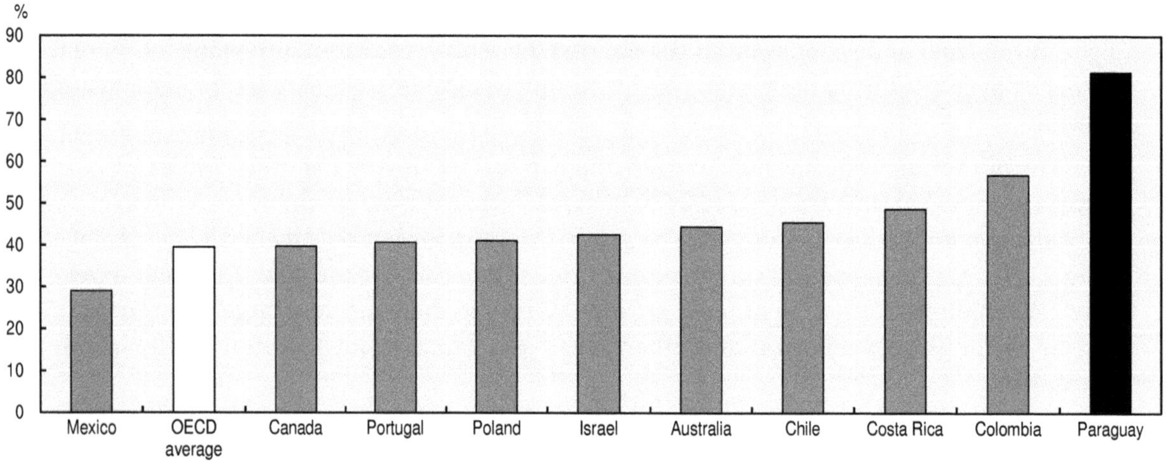

Source: OECD dotstat for OECD countries, Costa Rica and Colombia. Calculations on the basis of ILOstat for Brazil.

StatLink http://dx.doi.org/10.1787/888933749674

Underemployment is a significant issue in Paraguay although measures are very imperfect. Indeed, the level of time-related underemployment appears high given relatively long average hours. This can partly be explained by the very high level of the minimum wage. Underemployment is defined as a situation where a worker either is working fewer hours than they would like (*visible* underemployment) or one where their labour earnings are not sufficient to meet a standard, usually the minimum wage (*invisible* underemployment). The high level of the minimum wage in Paraguay both relative to the country's economy and its labour market, makes this a high bar to reach. In Paraguay so-called invisible underemployment is twice as prevalent as invisible underemployment.

Figure 3.18. **Working time in Paraguay**

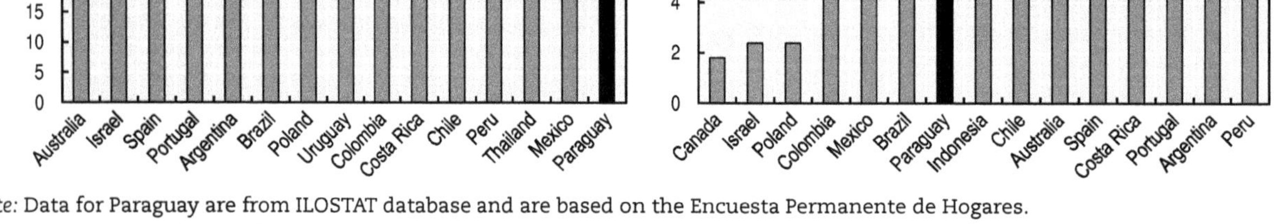

Note: Data for Paraguay are from ILOSTAT database and are based on the Encuesta Permanente de Hogares.

Source: ILOSTAT database and SEDLAC.

StatLink http://dx.doi.org/10.1787/888933749693

The insertion of the young in the labour market is a major challenge

In spite of the low unemployment rate, unemployment in Paraguay for the young is triple that of prime-age adults. The 15-to-29 age group faces an 11% unemployment rate, similar to that of the Latin American region as a whole (Figure 3.19). Compared to the rest of the region, however, young Paraguayans are less likely to remain idle. The share of 15-29 year-olds who are not in employment, education or training (NEET) is 17.2%, below the level of ten years ago and three percentage points below the average for the region.

Figure 3.19. **Unemployment rates among the young and adult populations in LAC and the OECD**

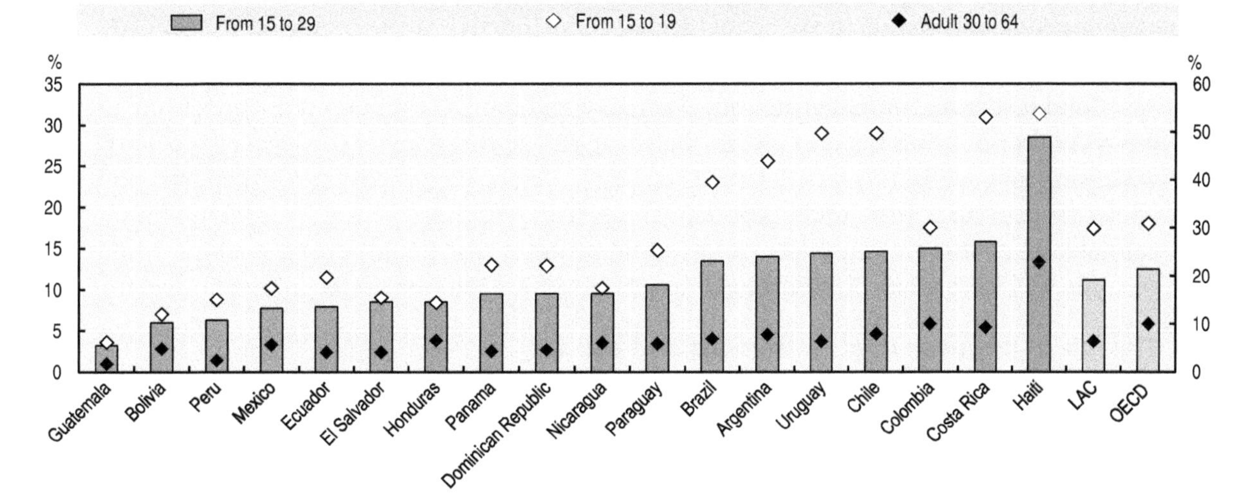

Note: LAC average excludes Haiti.

Source: OECD/CAF/ECLAC (2016).

StatLink http://dx.doi.org/10.1787/888933749712

Gender gaps in employment performance emerge early in Paraguay. Young women are more likely to continue studying, as shown also in education outcomes (see next section). However, they are much more likely not to be in employment, education or training. They are also more likely to be unemployed if they are looking for a job (14% compared to 8% for young men) (OECD/CAF/ECLAC, 2016). Conversely, young men are much more likely to work informally. Informality rates for the 20-24 group are significantly higher than average (73% compared to 63% for the whole labour force)

Figure 3.20. **Activity status of youth by gender**

Percentage of youth aged 15-29, 2014

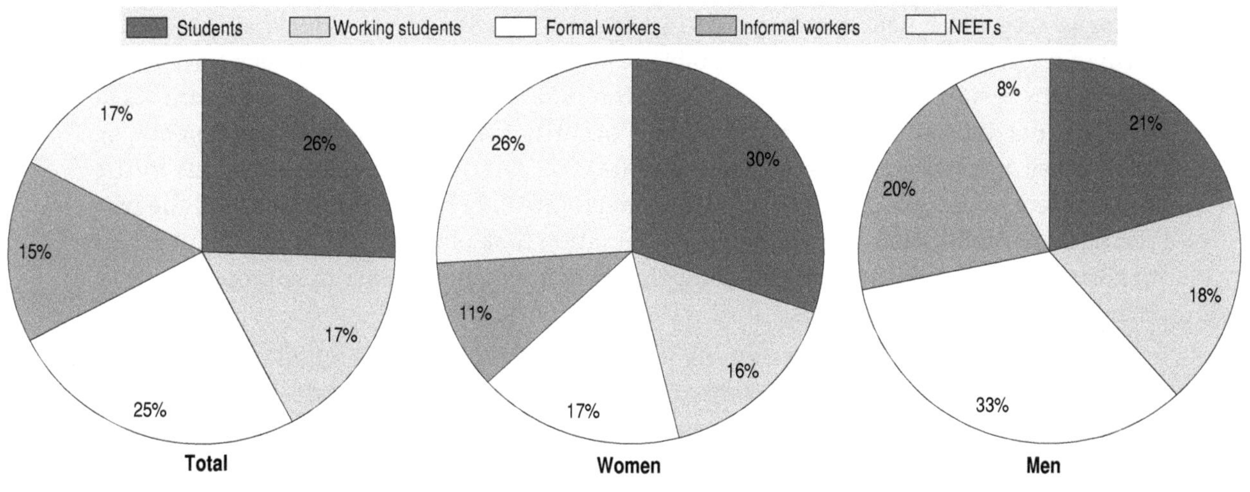

Source: OECD/CAF/ECLAC (2016).

StatLink http://dx.doi.org/10.1787/888933749731

Analysis of school-to-work transitions in Paraguay suggests that informality is not a deliberate choice of the young. In other countries in the region where informality is high, a substantial proportion of the young exit school and enter informality: in Mexico, 20% of males do. By contrast, in Paraguay, only a small proportion of school leavers, aged between 15 and 29, enters informal work directly in the year after leaving school (7%), and a higher proportion than in other countries goes to formal work. However, larger shares of young men and women leave school and become inactive or unemployed[7] (OECD/CAF/ECLAC, 2016).

Child labour also remains an issue. Paraguay and the ILO estimate that almost half of five to 17 year-olds in rural areas work, including 42% of those under the legal age to work, which in Paraguay is 14 years (ILO/DGEEC, 2016). Significant proportions of children and adolescents in rural areas undertake dangerous tasks. For those above the legal minimum age, jobs are almost entirely informal – a formalisation of traditional apprenticeships would go some way towards incorporating young school leavers into the social protection system.

The role of labour market institutions and policies

Paraguay's labour market institutions are relatively weak. The Ministry of Labour was created in 2013. Before that the functions of the ministry were performed by the Ministry of Justice, with mainly an enforcement function, and a limited one at that. Active labour market policies under the ministry are currently focused on the young as well as on women. This is justifiable in the light of the issues regarding their incorporation into the labour market, all the more so as this generation is much better educated than the previous one. Indeed, 60% of 25 to 29-year olds have completed secondary education and 17.3% tertiary education, compared to 36.6% and 12.5% of adults, respectively. In both these indicators, young Paraguayans have overtaken the regional average.

Collective bargaining is weak, given the relatively small share of workers that is unionised (4.9% according to the ILO). The Ministry of Labour has directed efforts to the modernisation of the system of registration of trade unions. There has been less progress in easing the obstacles to freedom of association and union activity. In particular, the lack of effective protection of workers against anti-union discrimination has been pointed out repeatedly by the ILO's Committee of Experts on the Application of Conventions and Recommendations (CEACR) as a weakness of Paraguayan labour law (Lachi, 2014). Social dialogue received a new impetus in 2014 with the creation of areas for dialogue in the form of tripartite thematic discussion tables and a consultative council, which have led to noteworthy results, including consensus on the reform of the system for minimum wage adjustments and on the creation of a social security system for microentrepreneurs, as well as key agreements at the sectoral level (MTESS, 2017). Enforcement functions in the ministry are under-resourced. The labour inspectorate only has 31 inspectors, and the first recruitment on the basis of competitive examination took place in 2015, with the intention of professionalising the service. This compels any enforcement activity to be targeted, rather than systemic.

Employment protection is relatively low and unlikely to cause limited mobility in the labour market. Traditionally, employment protection legislation (EPL) is designed to protect jobs and have only a limited impact on employment and unemployment rates (OECD, 2013b). However, it can affect job creation and labour mobility. The OECD has developed a framework for measuring EPL that assesses the strictness of the procedures and costs involved in dismissing individuals or groups of workers and those involved in hiring workers on fixed-term or temporary work agency contracts. This analytical framework is based on 21 indicators that measure from zero (not strict at all) to six (very strict) the strictness of the legislation. Paraguay scores 1.75 out of 6 regarding the strictness of EPL for individual and collective dismissals, a low score which can be explained by the fact that there is no additional procedure for collective dismissals. Regarding legislation for temporary work contracts, Paraguay also displays legislation that favours employers.

Figure 3.21. **Employment protection in Paraguay and benchmark economies**

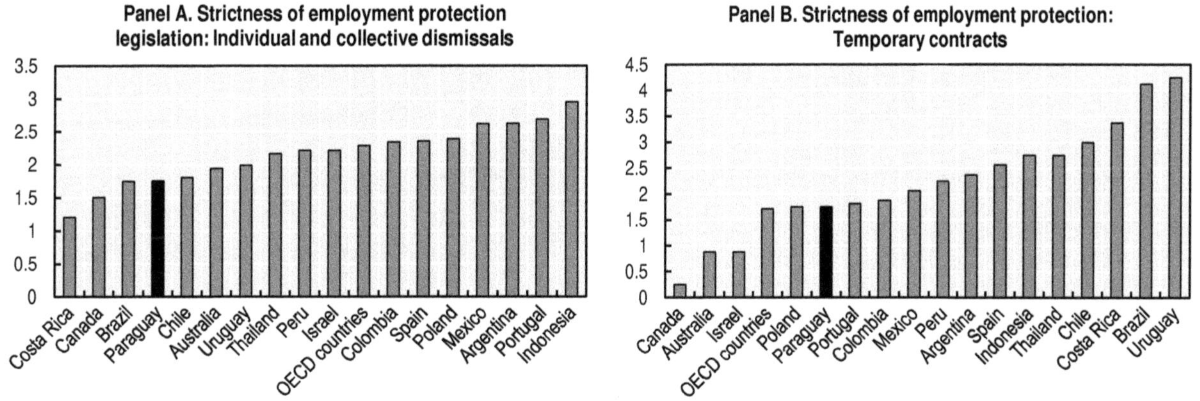

Source: OECD Indicators of Employment Protection Legislation, *http://www.oecd.org/els/emp/oecdindicatorsofemploymentprotection.htm.*

StatLink http://dx.doi.org/10.1787/888933749750

On the other hand, the combination of contribution rules and high minimum wages makes formalisation costly for employees. Higher theoretical formalisation costs are associated with higher levels of informality among wage-earning workers in Paraguay and Latin America. Theoretical formalisation costs measure the cost for a worker to join social security programmes given required income thresholds and minimum contribution levels, expressed as a proportion of their current earnings. Individuals at the lower end of the income distribution are therefore more likely to be informal because of higher costs. In the case of Paraguay, poor workers at the lowest end of the income distribution would have to forego 88% of their wages to join social security programmes, which is higher than the theoretical cost for a poor worker in Latin American countries (72% of the worker's wage) (Figure 3.22).

Despite recent improvements in initial education, Paraguay faces a significant skills shortage. The training system is relatively small, which makes it insufficient to address this challenge. The reach of the national training system (SINAFOCAL) and the public training organisation (SNPP) is too small to provide training to a large section of the population. SINAFOCAL oversees the training system as a whole (including SNPP and private providers of training). It estimates that a quarter of adults over 25 had received training during their careers by 2014, of which a large fraction (39%) in the five years preceding the survey. In contrast, in OECD countries, 50% of adults participate in formal or informal training over a given year, and 10% do so in the formal education system (*Education at a Glance* [OECD, 2016]). By contrast, SNPP provides training to about 5% of the active population (181 529 workers were trained in 2016, for an estimated active population of about 3.5 million people, [SNPP, 2016]). The training system is being developed, with a four-fold increase in the budget of SNPP in the past eight years.

Figure 3.22. **Higher theoretical formalisation costs are associated with higher levels of informality**

Theoretical formality costs and informality rates for dependent workers in Latin American countries, by decile, 2013

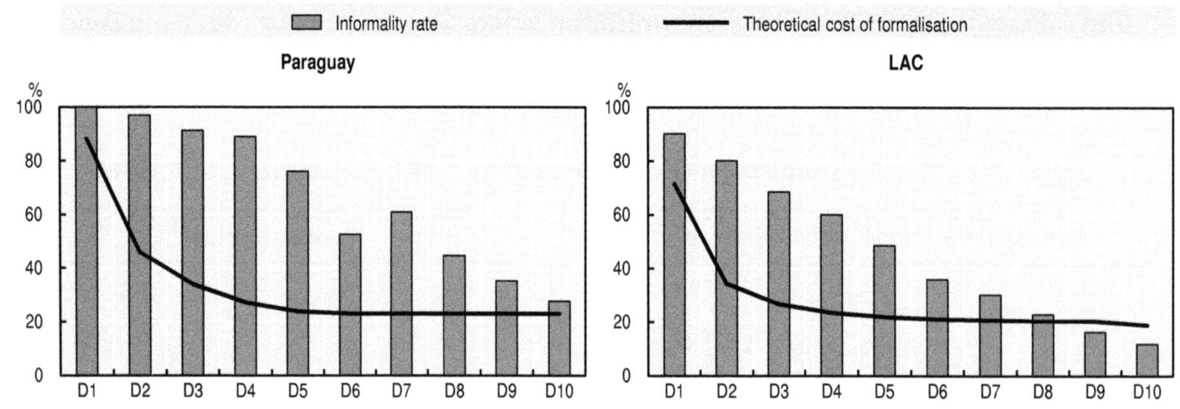

Source: OECD/CIAT/IDB (2016), *Taxing Wages in Latin America and the Caribbean.*

StatLink http://dx.doi.org/10.1787/888933749769

Education outcomes have improved but reforms are unfinished

Educational attainment in Paraguay is low in spite of recent improvements. The country lagged significantly behind the benchmark countries in 1990. In 2010, the average educational attainment of a working age Paraguayan over 25 was 7.3 years according to international databases (Cohen and Leker, 2014) and 7.7 years according to national survey data,[8] below the level of most benchmark countries and significantly below the level of attainment corresponding to compulsory education. Since 1990, there has been considerable progress: indeed, average educational attainment for the 20-24-year-old cohort was estimated to be 10.9 years in 2010 by Cohen and Leker (2014) and 10.2 on the basis of survey data, a very significant progress over the same cohort 20 years before, and on a par with a number of Latin American benchmarking countries (Colombia, Brazil, Mexico).

Despite recent progress, the prospects for future catch-up in educational attainment remain uncertain. Indeed, school life expectancy, which measures the expected educational attainment of today's entrants to the education system, is the lowest in the group of comparator countries (Figure 3.23, Panel B).

School enrolment and student retention are still problematic in some areas

The 2010 reform that made education compulsory and free from pre-school to end of secondary school is a landmark of Paraguay's development ambition with respect to its education system. The system is structured into four main blocks: initial education covers all pre-primary education, of which only the year of pre-school (age 5) is compulsory, basic education consists of three three-year cycles of which the first two make up primary education (and correspond to level 1 of the International Standard Classification of Education [ISCED]) and the third makes up lower secondary (corresponding to ISCED level 2). Finally, *middle* education is a 3-year cycle corresponding to ISCED level 3 (upper secondary education).

Weaknesses in the production of education statistics hamper the analysis of access to education across cycles as well as that of its evolution over time. Available data on access to education present a mixed picture and are inconsistent across sources. Enrolment rate data as made available by the Ministry of Education and Culture (MEC) situate Paraguay at the bottom of the group of comparator countries (Figure 3.24) and show declining net and gross enrolment rates for primary education. However, falling net enrolment rates in primary education reflect both falling numbers of enrolled students and population estimates that find the corresponding cohort to be growing slowly (between 0.2% and 0.3%). The Ministry of Education and MEC (2014) note that the falls in enrolment rates are due to overestimates in the population projections for the age group.[9] Enrolment rates are also at odds with data from household surveys, which indicate that 98% of six to nine year olds and 97% of ten to 14 year-olds attend school (DGEEC, 2015).[10] The Ministry of Education is currently working to improve its capacity to generate primary information on access to education through the improvement of its information system, in particular of the unified registry of students.

Figure 3.23. **Educational attainment in Paraguay remains low despite recent improvements**

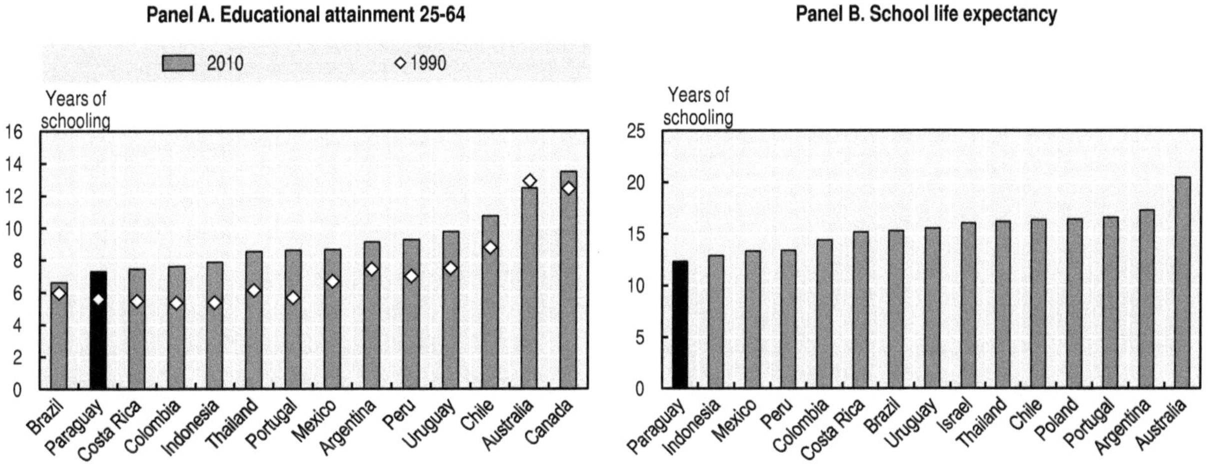

Source: Panel A: Cohen-Soto database (Cohen and Soto, 2007) as updated by Cohen-Leker (2014), available at *https://www.parisschoolofeconomics.eu/en/cohen-daniel/international-educational-attainment-database/*. Panel B: UIS, UNESCO (uis.unesco.org).

StatLink http://dx.doi.org/10.1787/888933749788

Combining the available administrative data with survey data allows to draw comparative perspectives and to establish a diagnostic. Available survey data do not include information on enrolment by grade, but include information on attendance and on the last grade completed. The survey is carried out during the end of the school year, which can also potentially lead to differences in how answers are given to questions on current enrolment. Unfortunately, data available over time are not representative of the whole country, as the main household survey (the *Encuesta Permanente de Hogares*, EPH) did not cover two of the country's departments (1.1% of the population as of 2012) or its indigenous areas (1.8% of the population as of 2012) until the most recent iterations. Elías, Walder and Sosa (2016) note that estimates from the survey lead to estimates of the population of students that are 9% higher than shown by administrative records in the Ministry of Education. For this reason, the analysis in this chapter relies on proportion estimates alone, which excludes any estimates of proxies for gross enrolment rates. Age-specific attendance ratios were estimated to reflect the likelihood that children of specific age-groups are enrolled in formal education (including special education programmes for the disabled but excluding adult education). Similarly, net attendance ratios were calculated to reflect that likelihood that children are attending the cycle of education that corresponds to their age.

Together, the available data suggest that enrolment in basic education remains a significant challenge in Paraguay, especially in secondary education. In the case of primary education, net enrolment rates calculated on the basis of administrative data and survey data offer conflicting results. Net enrolment rates based on administrative data are very low compared to benchmark countries. In contrast, survey data suggest that schooling is close to universal for children of primary school age, with 98% of children in school and about 1% entering school with delay. In the case of lower secondary education, and despite the gap between administrative and survey data, the picture is more consistent. In both cases, participation in school has increased slightly (the coverage gap is 8% on the basis of survey data), whilst significant progress has been made in increasing the number of students who are at the right grade for their age.

Figure 3.24. **Net enrolment rates and net attendance ratios in basic education (%)**

2015 or latest available data

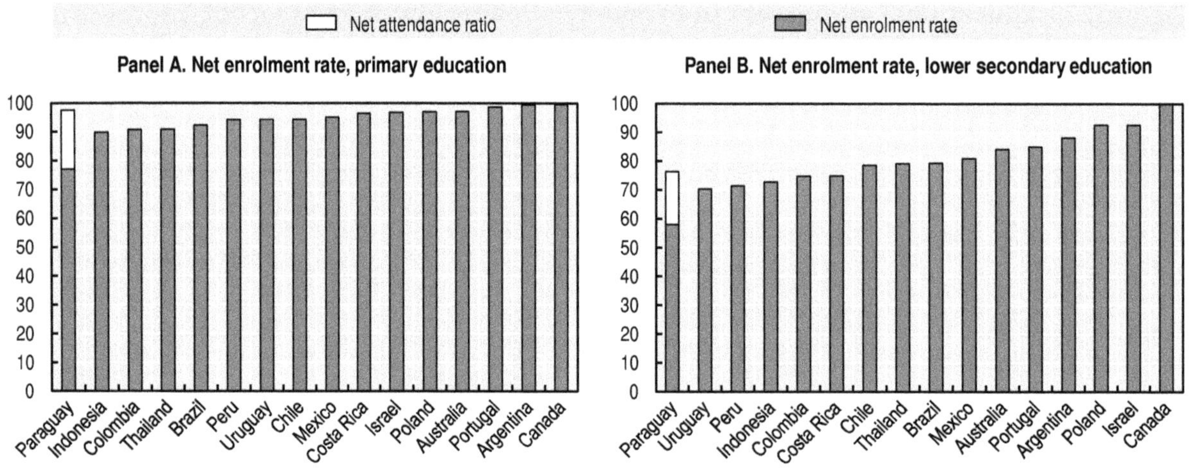

Note: Net enrolment rates are estimates provided by the Ministry of Education on the basis of administrative records and population projections, following UNESCO methodology. Net attendance ratios are age-specific net attendance ratios calculated on the basis of survey data.

Source: Ministerio de Educación y Cultura (MEC) for Paraguay, UIS (UNESCO) for benchmark countries; author's calculations on the basis of the *Encuesta Permanente de Hogares* (DGEEC, 2017b) for net attendance ratios.

StatLink http://dx.doi.org/10.1787/888933749807

Figure 3.25. **Age-specific and net attendance ratios in Paraguay, by level of education (%)**

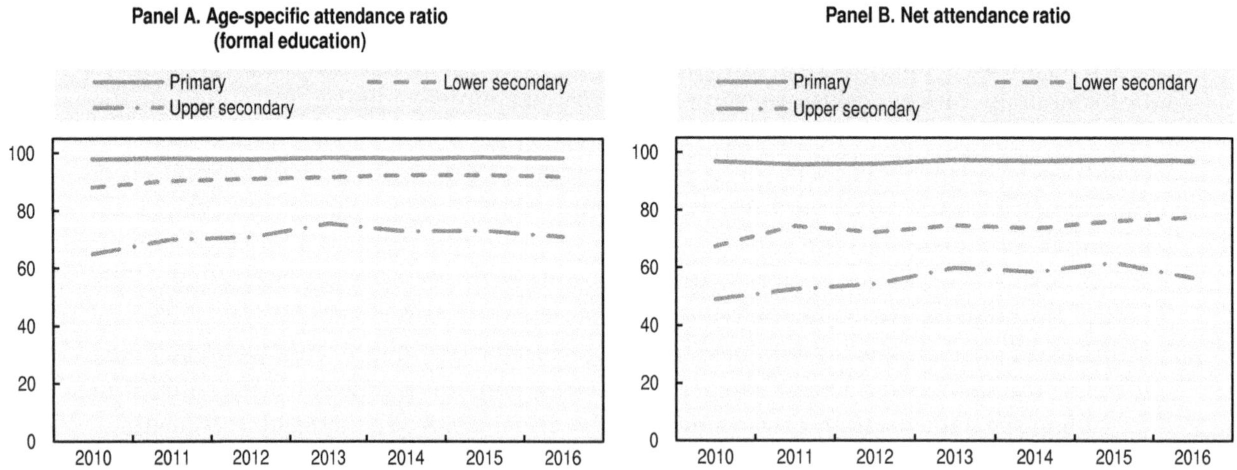

Note: Panel A represents the estimated share of children who are attending formal education (at any level and grade) grouped by the cycle that corresponds to their age as of March 31 on the year of the survey: primary (6 to 11), lower secondary (12 to 14) and upper secondary (15 to 17). Panel B represents the share of children who are attending the cycle corresponding to their age (irrespective of the grade).

Source: Authors' calculation on the basis of the *Encuesta Permanente de Hogares* (DGEEC, 2017b).

StatLink http://dx.doi.org/10.1787/888933749826

Compulsory education in Paraguay begins at the age of five, which leads to a relatively high pre-school enrolment for that age group. Attendance at pre-school is compulsory and has been free when provided in public schools since 2010. In contrast, the supply of early childhood education for children before the age of five is meagre. At 60%, the net enrolment rate for pre-school (age five) is low but in the range of benchmark countries. However, given the low supply of early childhood education, overall pre-primary (including all education before age six) enrolment remains at the bottom of the range of benchmark countries. After focusing on pre-school (with an objective of reaching universal enrolment by 2024), the Ministry of Education is currently expanding the supply of pre-primary education.

In terms of coverage, most progress has been made in secondary and tertiary education. Gross enrolment rates in secondary education have increased by 10 points to 62% over the past ten years. Moreover, a significant part of this increase has been in vocational upper secondary schooling, which increased from 9% to 15% of the age group between 2000 and 2012. In tertiary education, Paraguay has followed in the footsteps of the region with a rapid increase in access to tertiary education, although gross enrolment rates (at 35% in 2010) remain low compared to benchmark countries.

Figure 3.26. **Gross enrolment rates in tertiary education**

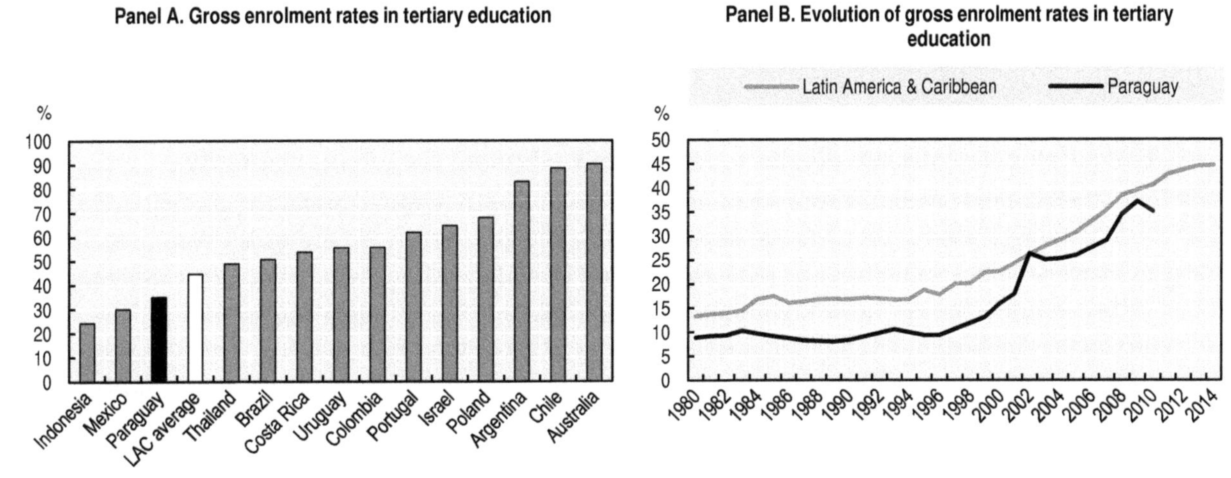

Source: UIS (UNESCO, 2017).

StatLink http://dx.doi.org/10.1787/888933749845

Paraguay has had success in lowering the high repetition rates and in increasing completion rates for basic education (from primary to lower secondary). According to UNESCO (2017) data, repeaters were 4% of primary students in 2007, compared to 8% in 2001, although the rate did not evolve significantly between 2007 and 2012. The cohort entering education in 2007 had a significantly higher chance (56%) of completing nine years of education than that entering formal education in 2002 (48%). The bulk of the improvement happened for cohorts entering school between 2005 and 2007, which explains why it is not yet visible for completion rates at 12 years of education.

Together, available data sources suggest that the main challenges in access to schooling are in pre-primary and upper secondary school, although observers point to deficiencies in lower secondary schooling in some areas (Elias, Walder and Sosa, 2016). A significant challenge remains to retain students until they have completed nine years of formal schooling (*Basic Education* in the Paraguayan system) and even more so to retain them until they have completed 12 years of formal schooling. Lowering dropout rates requires also addressing shortcomings in learning outcomes and in late enrolment, which requires not only material, but also organisational and pedagogical actions.

Figure 3.27. **School attendance by age group in Paraguay**

2015

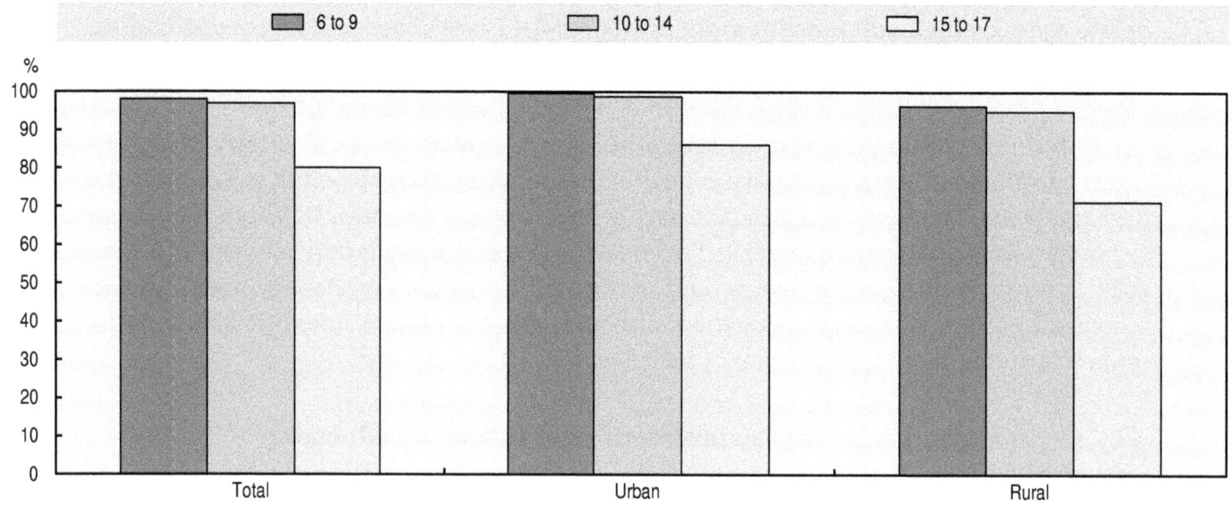

Source: Data provided by DGEEC on the basis of EPH (DGEEC, 2017b).

StatLink http://dx.doi.org/10.1787/888933749864

Education and skills can play a major role in sustaining the fall in inequality

Educational outcomes are very unequal between rural and urban areas and particularly low in indigenous areas. Gaps are especially large in pre-school, where gross enrolment rates were 17% higher in urban areas in 2015, and in middle school, where the gap between urban and rural areas was 41% (data provided by MEC, based on administrative records). The gaps are even higher in indigenous areas, where enrolment in lower secondary school was 22% in 2008 (compared to 57% in rural and 102% in urban areas) and enrolment in upper secondary school was 5% in the same year (MEC, 2014).

A remarkable feature of access to school in Paraguay is that gender equality prevails throughout the school system. Differences in enrolment rates between girls and boys in 2015 were 0.4% for pre-primary education, 3.3% (in favour of boys) for basic education and 4.5% (in favour of girls) for middle school (upper secondary education) according to data provided by MEC, based on administrative records.

The challenge of increasing quality in education

Paraguay faces a significant challenge to improve learning outcomes in primary and secondary education. The national education evaluation authority (*Sistema Nacional de Evaluación del Proceso Educativo*, SNEPE) monitors education quality with regular evaluations in grades 3, 6 and 9, corresponding to the end of each of the three cycles of basic education. Students are classified according to four levels of competency, with the highest level (level 4) corresponding to the expected proficiency and corresponding to the capacities established in the national curriculum. An allowance is made to measure those that score below the first level.[11] According to the most recent available results, 78% of grade 3 students scored at level 2 or below in mathematics proficiency. Similarly, 74% of children in grade 3 scored at level 2 or below in communication.

Figure 3.28. **Inequality in gross enrolment rates**

2015

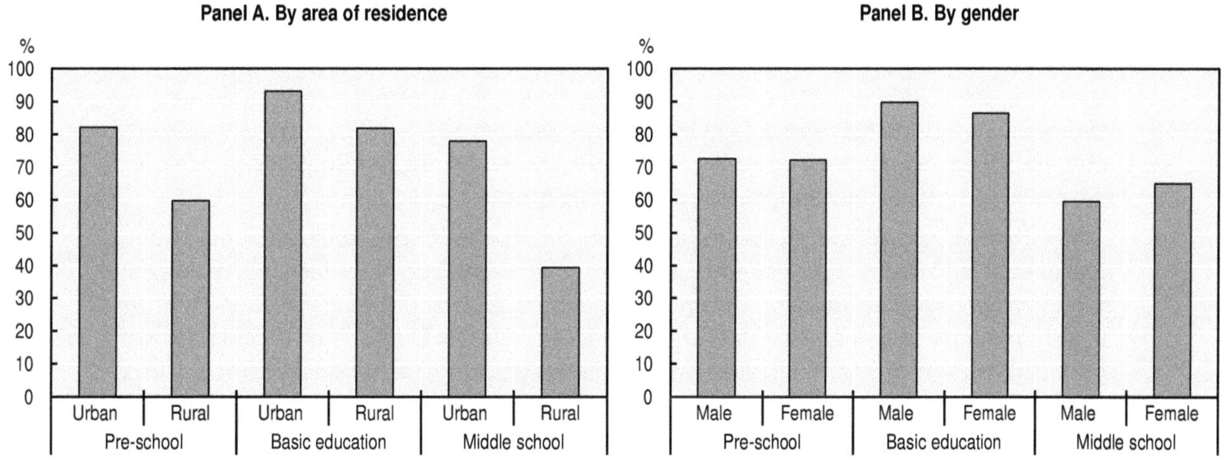

Source: Data provided by MEC on the basis of SIEC (Sistema de Información de Estadística Continua) information.

StatLink http://dx.doi.org/10.1787/888933749883

In internationally comparable evaluations, Paraguay scores well below comparator countries in terms of learning outcomes. In UNESCO's Third Regional Comparative and Explanatory Study (TERCE) (UNESCO, 2015), 83% of Paraguayan children in grade 3 scored at level 2 or lower in mathematics, and 77% scored in level 2 or lower in reading. TERCE follows a similar proficiency classification as the national SNEPE tests, and results are qualitatively similar. While TERCE is only available for Latin American countries, it is worth noting that the Latin American comparator countries in Figure 3.29 participate in the Programme for International Student Assessment (PISA). PISA average proficiency scores for these countries rank them in an almost identical order as their TERCE scores, with the highest, Chile, scoring 67 points below the OECD average (OECD, 2015a). Paraguay is part of PISA for Development (see Box 3.1) and the first results allowing a comparison of learning outcomes among 15 year olds will be available in 2018.

Figure 3.29. **Learning outcomes are behind those of regional comparators in Paraguay**

2013

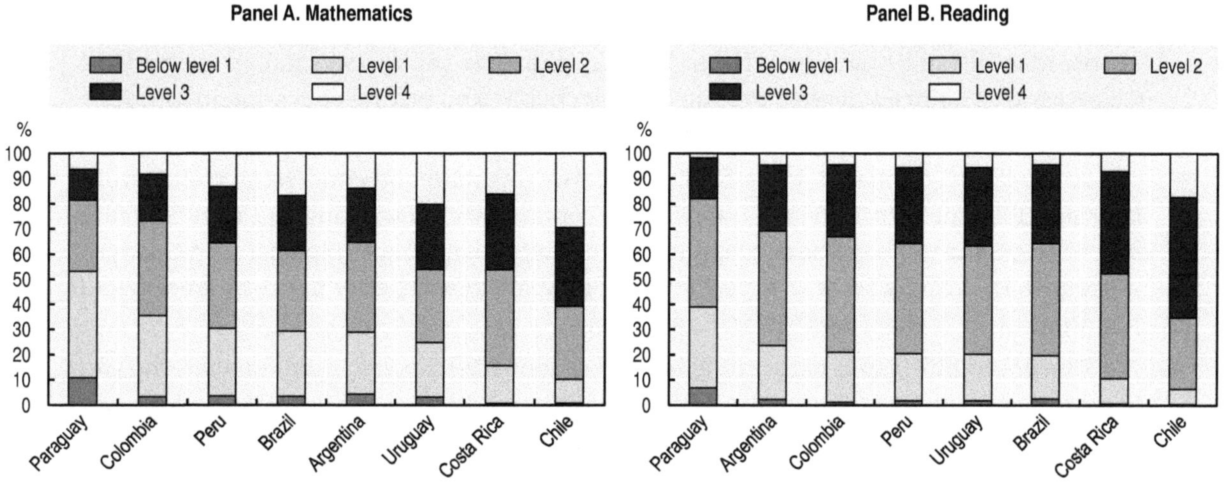

Source: TERCE, Latin American Laboratory for Assessment of the Quality of Education (LLECE) (UNESCO, 2015).

StatLink http://dx.doi.org/10.1787/888933749902

Box 3.1. **Paraguay and PISA for Development**

Paraguay is taking part in the OECD's PISA for Development project (PISA-D), which was designed to enable greater PISA participation by low and middle-income countries by extending the PISA test instruments to a wider range of performance levels, developing contextual questionnaires and data-collection instruments effectively to capture the diverse situations in low and middle-income countries, and establishing methods and approaches to include out-of-school young people in the assessments.

PISA-D builds capacity for managing and using the results of large-scale student learning assessment and using the results to support policy dialogue and decision making in participating countries and promotes peer-to-peer learning by bringing together countries already participating in PISA with PISA-D countries. The OECD and PISA-D countries will work collaboratively in the preparation and dissemination of a national report for each country, and in facilitating the resulting national policy dialogue. The in-school results will be published in December 2018 and the out-of-school results in December 2019.

Participating countries have each established a national centre and nominated a national project manager to ensure appropriate infrastructure and resources are in place to implement the assessment in accordance with the PISA technical standards. In Paraguay the national centre is located within the directorate for evaluation of educational quality (DECE), attached to the directorate-general for education planning. DECE is currently in the process of being incorporated into the national institute of educational assessment, which is in the process of being formed. The Paraguayan team has excelled in their implementation of the study, complying with every deadline and technical standard.

National assessments find that, at higher grades, there are fewer students at the lowest proficiency levels, but there are also fewer at the highest level. In mathematics 18% of students do not reach level 1 in grade 3, compared to 11% in grade 6 and 9% in grade 9 (MEC, SNEPE). However, by grade 9 as many as 52% of students in the cohort had left school in 2010, when the test was administered. The pattern can partly be explained by higher dropout rates among students struggling at school. However, the proportion of students achieving level 4 was also lower at higher grades, with only 2% in grade 9, compared to 9% in grade 3 in 2010.

Inequalities in learning outcomes are most pronounced between public and private establishments and to a lesser degree between rural and urban areas. As with enrolment rates, gender gaps in test performance are small. In mathematics, 78.2% of boys in grade 3 score at level 2 or below, compared to 77.7% of girls. The gap is also small in 9th grade at 0.6 percentage points. However, the gap between public and private education institutions is large, eight percentage points in grade 3, growing to 12 in 9th grade.

A significant difference in performance between urban and rural areas comes from language differences. In 2010 SNEPE applied the communication and language questionnaire in grades 3, 6 and 9, but it was only applied in both official languages (Spanish and Guaraní) in grade 6. The results show that performance in Spanish was better in urban areas while performance in Guaraní was better in rural areas.

The geographic gap is particularly large in secondary school. In mathematics, the gap in performance in grade 3 is small (0.8 percentage point difference in level 2 or below), but it is significant in grade 9 (almost five percentage points). Moreover, while on average 65% of urban students complete secondary school at the expected age only 36% of rural students do (World Bank, 2015).

Resources for education in Paraguay

Paraguay faces significant gaps in social infrastructure, including in education. A detailed analysis of gaps in school infrastructure carried out by the World Bank based on 2008 data found that a substantial proportion of schools, especially in urban areas, suffered from lack of space (Wodon, 2016). The same study found major differences between urban and rural schools in terms of basic amenities, with only half of rural schools having sanitation or toilets compared to 80% of urban schools. Wodon (2016) also noted that the fall in education expenditure left little space to fill this gap. As a response, Paraguay has significantly increased expenditure on education, and the MEC is implementing an updated prioritisation process to manage resources. Among other things, the process aims to encourage larger, better-equipped schools, including in rural areas.

The country has significantly increased public funding for education in the past decades. The crisis of the late 1990s and early 2000s coincided with a major fall in spending on public education. Education expenditure as a share of GDP has since recovered to 4.6%, a level that is comparable to the regional average and the average of benchmark countries, although it remains almost a percentage point below the OECD average.

Figure 3.30. **Government expenditure on education as a share of GDP**

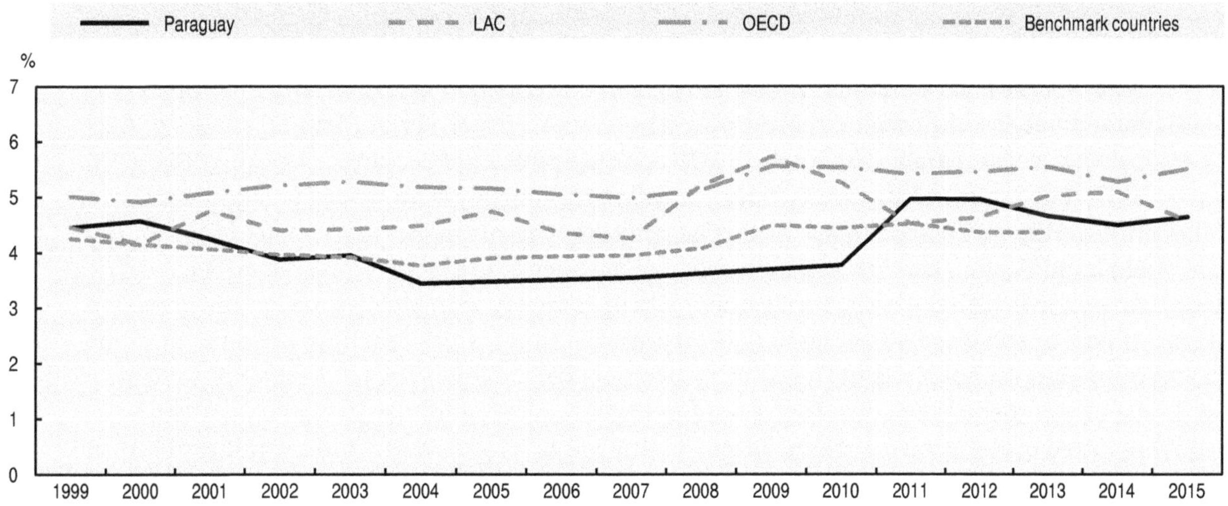

Note: Data for Paraguay for the years 2013, 2014, 2015 are preliminary.

Source: UIS/UNESCO and MEC, Paraguay, BCP for GDP data for Paraguay.

StatLink http://dx.doi.org/10.1787/888933749921

Not only has the amount of education spending changed, but so also has its composition, through the earmarking of part of the royalties obtained from the binational hydropower plant of Itaipú to education and supporting expenditure. Created in 2012, the *Fondo Nacional de Inversión Pública y de Desarrollo* (FONACIDE) is a budgetary fund that channels resources within a set of quotas established by law. Of the resources 30% are attributed to a fund for education and research (*Fondo para la Excelencia de la Educacion y la Investigación* [FEEI]) and 25% to local governments, which have to spend at least 50% of this transfer on education infrastructure and 30% on school meals programmes (Decree 9966/2012, Art. 13). If these two elements are compounded, FONACIDE therefore dedicates 50% of the resources it receives to education. In 2016 FONACIDE received USD 369 million

(PYG 2.1 trn). By comparison, the total investment budget for the Ministry of Education in 2015 was PYG 426 billion or USD 72 million.

Limited absorptive capacity hinders the potential impact of increases in education finance. Despite the significant sums earmarked, there are significant hurdles in the way of putting these resources to good use. In 2015, only a fraction of the funds had been transferred to the FEEI or municipalities (10% of transfers, or 5.4% of income had gone to the FEEI, 38% to local governments). In 2016, transfers were much closer to those mandated by law, with 26% going to municipal and departmental governments (including specific transfers for compensation mandated by law). However, the execution rates of these funds are low (Molinier, 2016). The FEEI only committed 30% of its allocation in 2015 and 28% in 2016 (Contraloría General de la República, 2016, 2017).

Expenditure per student is similar in primary and secondary education, but much higher than the benchmark countries in tertiary education. Moreover, while public expenditure in all other levels of education is progressive in Paraguay, public expenditure in tertiary education is regressive (in an absolute sense) (Giménez et al. 2017). The recovery in the share of public expenditure on education and the increase in real public expenditure in education during the 2010-15 period (48%) have allowed the country to attain levels comparable to those of benchmark countries in primary and secondary education. Paraguay stands out because of the amount of resources dedicated to tertiary education: it spends 55% of GDP per capita per student in tertiary education out of the public purse. This is particularly striking given that the increase in tertiary enrolment was largely realised in private institutions, where expenditure per student is, at 19% of GDP per capita, comparable to those in OECD countries from the benchmark group (CONACYT, 2016). Public expenditure on tertiary education in Paraguay is an order of magnitude above the level spent by benchmark countries, only comparable to Mexico. This pattern is partly explained by the fact that a significant share in expenditure by the Universidad Nacional de Asunción (UNA), the main public university in Paraguay, is in fact devoted to the provision of health services by the *Hospital de Clínicas*, the university's teaching hospital, and one of the largest hospitals in the country (Molinier, 2016). However, the budget of the entire faculty of medicine of the UNA is only 12.6% of total expenditure in tertiary education as reported by the Ministry of Education and Science. While this constitutes significant bias in the data reported in Figure 3.31, expenditure per student would still be much higher than in benchmark countries if it the whole of the faculty of medicine's budget were deducted from expenditure in tertiary education.

Paraguay has sufficient human resources in education but needs to increase the prevalence of qualifications to ensure quality. Figure 3.32 shows that pupil/teacher ratios for basic and secondary education are similar and in line with those of benchmark countries. Indeed, there was a significant increase in the number of centres for teacher training and the number of candidates trained in the first half of the 2000s. The oversupply of would-be teachers led to a moratorium in new entries to training cycles in 2006-13. On the other hand, given the relatively recent implementation of the framework for competitive entry into teaching, there remain gaps in teacher training (PREAL, 2012). Of all primary teachers 13.4% do not hold the appropriate qualification,[12] double the proportion of Colombian teachers. The figure for pre-primary is significantly higher, at 54%, which poses questions regarding the potential benefits of that cycle. A significant effort is therefore being put into on-the-job training for teachers.

Figure 3.31. **Expenditure on education per student as a share of GDP per capita, by level of education**

2015 or latest available

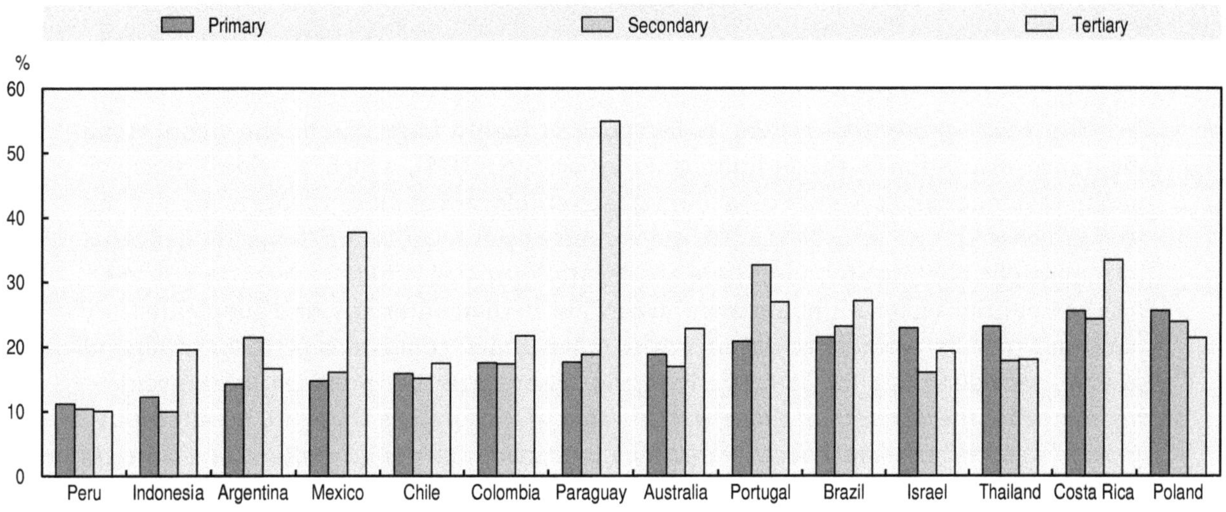

Source: MEC for Paraguay, UIS for other countries.

StatLink http://dx.doi.org/10.1787/888933749940

Figure 3.32. **Pupil/teacher ratio, by level of education**

2015 or latest available

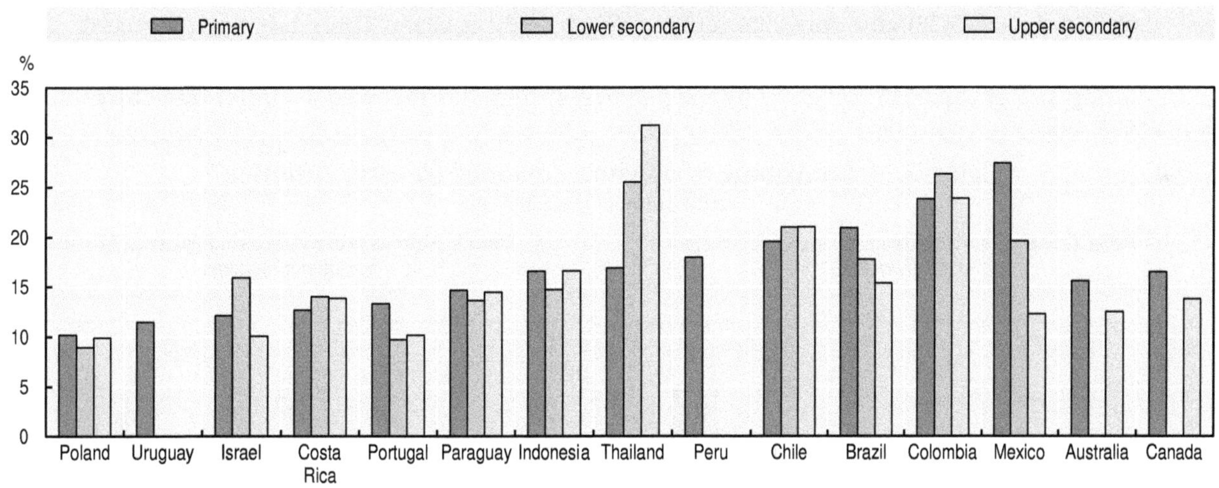

Source: UIS/UNESCO; MEC for Paraguay; *OECD Education at a glance 2016* (OECD, 2016).

StatLink http://dx.doi.org/10.1787/888933749959

The creation of a sizeable scholarship programme in 2015 for study abroad has the potential to contribute to human capital formation and the quality of education in the country. With the aim of improving higher education teacher training and enhancing the supply of qualified labour for science, technology and innovation in the country, the *Programa Nacional de Becas de Posgrados en el Exterior Don Carlos Antonio López* (BECAL) provides postgraduate scholarships for Paraguayans to study in top universities abroad in science and technology, selected areas for innovation and in education sciences. By March 2017, the programme had financed 790 scholarships, with a sizeable budget (20.6 million USD over the first two years, equivalent to 8% of total annual public expenditure in tertiary education in 2015) (FEEI, 2017). The internationalisation of students follows successful experiences from other countries, like Chile's *Becas Chile* Programme, or Kazakhstan's *Bolashak*, where similar programmes have transformed key areas of the private and public sectors through the accumulation of skills and the creation of transnational networks.

The social protection system is highly fragmented and limits the efficiency of social service delivery

The social protection system in Paraguay is highly fragmented. The main social insurance institution is the *Instituto de Prevision Social* (IPS), which provides pensions, health insurance and coverage of labour risks to employees of most private firms. Beyond workers covered primarily by the IPS, the various social security functions are delivered by a multiplicity of institutions. There are separate pension funds for public employees, for the financial sector, for municipal workers, for parliamentarians, and supplementary pension funds for workers at certain major state-owned companies (ANDE, Itaipú) and private pension funds for co-operatives and others. The IPS provides work accident insurance for the majority of those workers that are insured as there are no alternative providers. Social assistance is delivered by a multiplicity of public entities, and consists mostly of income support, as basic health coverage is universal, a function that is carried out by the Ministry of Health.

Social security coverage is low and fragmented

Social security coverage is low compared to the rest of Latin America despite recent improvements in coverage. Only 22% of the employed population contribute to a pension system (Figure 3.33) and only 29% report having medical cover. There has been a recent increase in coverage rates, with health raising from 22.7% to 28% between 2010 and 2015, and falling to 25.9% in 2016. Coverage by the pension system has followed a similar trajectory.

Figure 3.33. **Contributory pension coverage in Latin America**

2014 or latest available

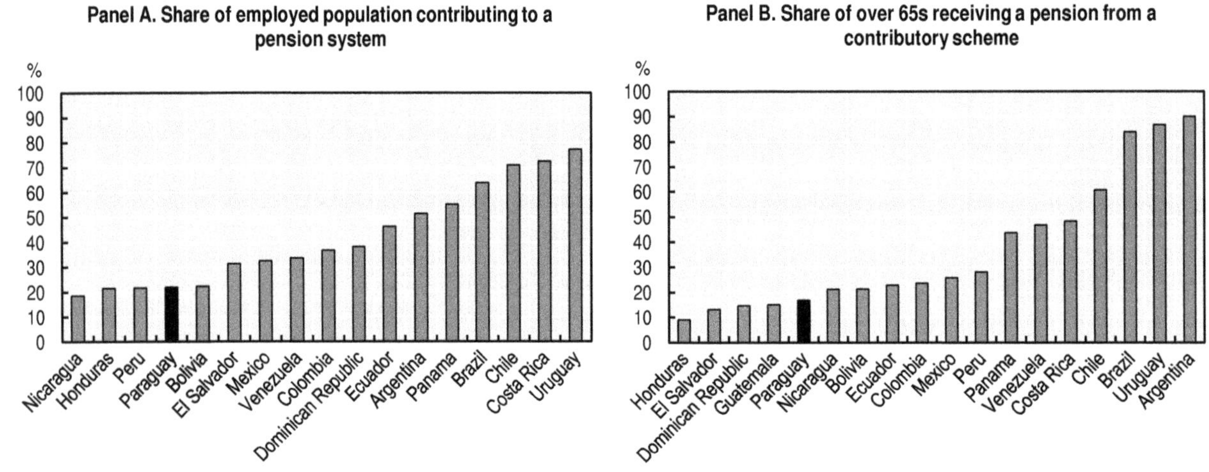

Source: IDB SIMS database, MTESS (2015) for Paraguay.

StatLink http://dx.doi.org/10.1787/888933749978

The low coverage reflects informality in the labour market but also institutional features of the design of the social protection system. Indeed, pension and health insurance coverage are voluntary for the self-employed and stay-at-home mothers, who, since 2013[13] can be affiliates of the pension branch of the IPS. The pension system was also opened to domestic workers, who previously could only pay into the health insurance component of the IPS. However, coverage in those groups is minimal: 363 own-account workers and employers according to the IPS,[14] and 22% of domestic workers according to IPS data. Beyond informality and the limitations with respect to independent workers, limitations also exist in the public sector, where so-called contract workers are not required to contribute to the pension system (and largely do not, which explains why only 80.7% of public employees are covered). Low coverage is also a reflection of lack of enforcement.

The pension system is a defined-benefit scheme, and the IPS pension (which covers dependent workers in the private sector) is very generous for those who receive a pension, although relatively rigid. The net replacement rates[15] calculated by the OECD pension model, place Paraguay as the country with the most generous pension system in Latin America. Indeed, the OECD pension model estimates replacement rates above 100 per cent, compared to the OECD average of 63% (for a full-career average earner, OECD, 2015b). This results from high gross replacement rates and the low coverage of the personal income tax. However, this generosity is only for the few. When the necessary contribution density to attain a minimal pension is taken into account, only 4.6% of the active population have sufficient density and only 12.6% are expected to have a pension in the future (Navarro and Ortiz, 2014). A large number of contributors, who through breaks in their careers or transitions between formal and informal work, will not reach the minimum number of annuities, are effectively subsidising a very generous system for the few that will ultimately receive pensions.

The multiplicity of regimes and pension schemes in Paraguay contributes to inequality in benefits. Different pension regimes have significantly different contribution rates and in some cases, like the multiple regimes under the *Caja Fiscal* which covers state employees, even when they have the same contribution rates, they have different retirement rules, minimum contributions and replacement rates. A framework is in place (Ley 3856, 2009) to allow would-be pensioners to claim pro-rated benefits when they have transited from one scheme to the other.

Figure 3.34. **Net pension replacement rates for average earners**

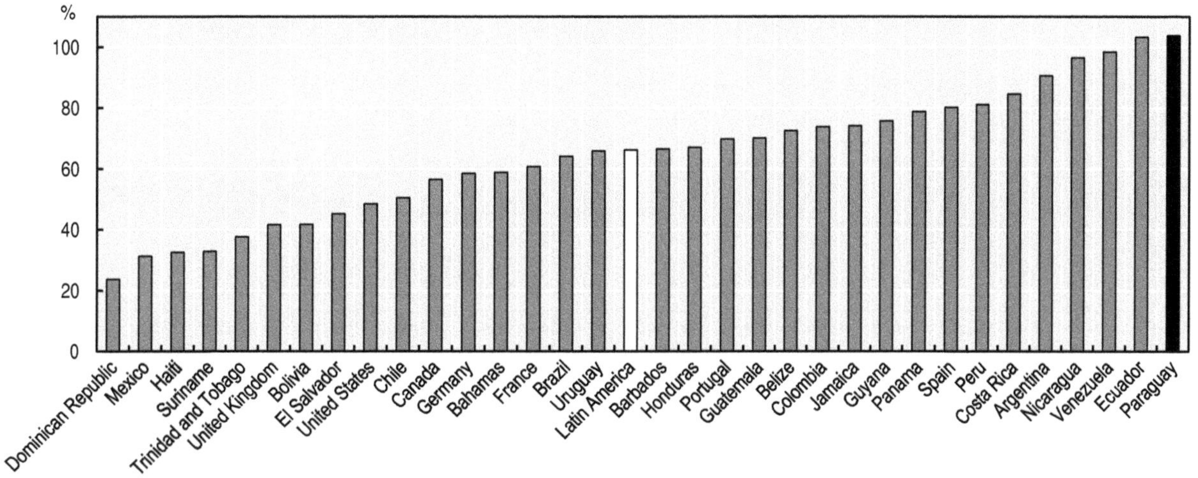

Note: The figure displays net replacement rates for male average earners.

Source: OECD/IDB/The World Bank (2014).

StatLink http://dx.doi.org/10.1787/888933749997

The multiplicity of regimes also poses financing problems. Not all regimes are equally sound financially. While the IPS has reserves to face short and medium-term liabilities, the *Caja Fiscal*, which covers state employees is estimated to face an implicit deficit of 40 to 50% of GDP in presented discounted value (Larraín, Viteri and Zucal, 2013). Some regimes have had to resort to emergency reform or recapitalisation to avoid becoming financially unsound. Another issue in financing is the use and placement of pension reserves. The sector is not regulated and funds can make risky investments, which if unsuccessful may jeopardise the scheme, and increase the potential hidden liability that the state has to face if future older citizens are left without a pension.

A fragmented health system and high out-of-pocket payments sustain inequalities

The health system is also fragmented between various providers of insurance and services. The system is mixed, with a public and a private subsector. The Ministry of Health and Social Welfare (*Ministerio de Salud y Bienestar Social*, MSPBS) administers the public component and provides services directly. The public health sector also includes the health services of the social security institute (IPS), the hospital of the national university of Asunción, the military and police health services and health services provision by the secretariat for disabled persons (*Secretaria Nacional por los Derechos Humanos de las Personas con Discapacidad* – SENADIS), the *Dirección de Beneficencia y Ayuda Social* (DIBEN, directorate for charity and social assistance, dependent on the presidency), local government, and by the health services of the firms managing the binational hydroelectric power plans. Employees in the private sector who are affiliated to the IPS also receive health services from the IPS. The private sector is constituted by private health insurance providers and private providers of, pre-paid plans and health services.

Figure 3.35. **Access to health services has improved while insurance coverage remains low**

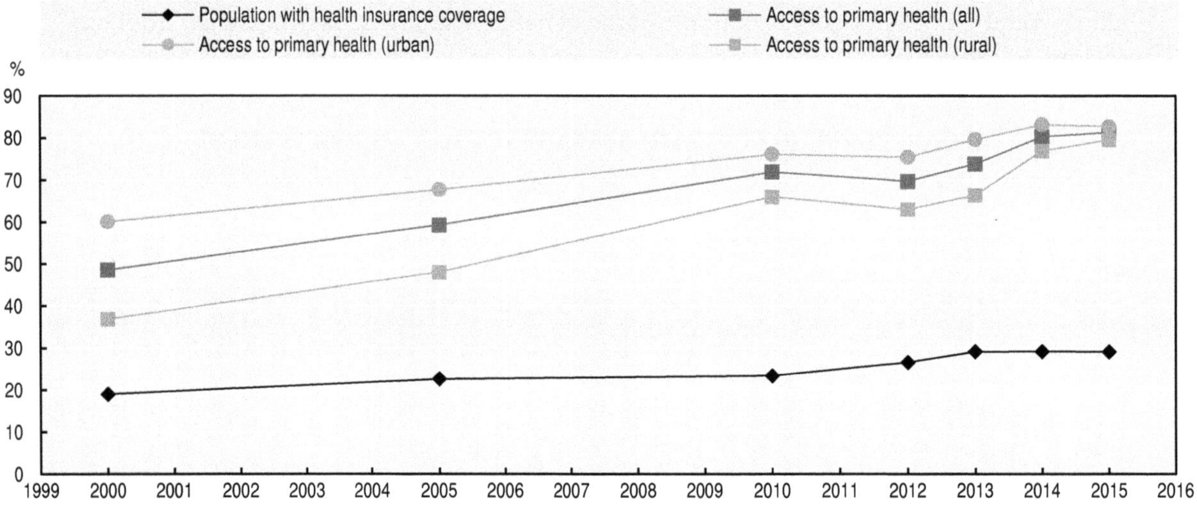

Note: Access to primary health services is approximated by the share of the population injured or sick that consulted a medical professional.

Source: Authors calculations based on EPH (DGEEC, 2017) and Benítez (2017).

StatLink http://dx.doi.org/10.1787/888933750016

Access has increased in recent years but given the high levels of informality and non-compliance, health insurance prevalence is low in Paraguay (29% for the whole country, only 14% in rural areas). Affordability is an important factor: about half of the uninsured

(1.7 million people) say they do not have health insurance because it is too expensive. It should be noted that since 2008 health services provided by the MSPBS network have been free. This was the culmination of a process started in 2000 with free attention to pregnant women and children under five, then extended progressively to other groups and to other services (including vaccines and essential medicines). The system has also been extended to include family health units (*unidades de salud de la familia*, USF) which are meant to respond to most health needs in a given territory. They are the basic means to provide health service in remote areas. Each USF comprises a doctor, nurse or obstetrician, nurse auxiliaries and community workers. There are currently about 800 USFs in the country. The social security institute covers 21% of the population (salaried workers in the private sector and of autonomous public entities, teachers and a minority of insured independent workers and domestic workers). Other insurers (public and private) cover 8% of the population. This leaves over 70% of the population who are only covered by the free services provided by the Ministry of Health (MSPBS).

The universality in basic health provision and the geographical extension of services seem adequate, although challenges remain, especially in terms of equal access. Progress in access to health services has been notable, especially in rural areas. While only 37% of rural dwellers felt they had access to a medical consultation in 2000, 76% of them had access in 2014 (Benítez, 2017). The increase in access to health has resulted mainly from closing the gap between rural and urban dwellers. According to survey data, only a minority of people who were sick or had an accident did not consult a health professional because of inaccessibility of service (only 2% of those not seeking attention, DGEEC, 2015). In spite of this increase in effective service, two key sources of inequality remain. First, the depth of coverage varies significantly across insurance and service providers, with the IPS covering more pathologies and treatments than many other insurance schemes. Both the IPS and the Ministry of Health have health establishments able to offer services covering a range of complexity across the country. The USFs are the main entry point to the country's health system, however, and only exist in the Ministry of Health's system. Second, mortality patterns suggest that certain areas are behind the national curve in the epidemiological transition. Indeed, deaths from communicable diseases have fallen significantly in the past 15 years, but remain a major cause of death in more isolated regions (especially Boquerón and Alto Paraguay) (Casalí and Velásquez, 2016).

Fragmentation can also lead to financing issues because of the lack of patient referral and costing agreements. In particular IPS and MSPBS provision is financed through separate channels but the broader coverage of the MSPBS facilities can lead IPS-insured patients to consult at other facilities. International experience shows that parallel systems can deliver results in terms of coverage but can also generate inefficiencies in staffing, equipment and financial flows. The Ministry of Health is currently implementing a model of integrated health networks to make advances in universal coverage while creating better links between providers at the local and national level.

Despite these advances, health is largely financed by households in Paraguay. Public expenditure in health has increased notably since the mid-2000s, reaching 4.2% of GDP in 2014, but households still finance a sizeable proportion of expenditure on health (Casalí and Velasquez, 2016). This is due in part to out-of-pocket payments, which the WHO estimated were as high as 49% in 2014, among the highest in the Latin American region. According to Giménez (2012), this is largely due (for about half of the out-of-pocket expenditure) to the cost of drugs, followed by studies and finally hospitalisation. Since the elimination of user fees in 2008, access to free drugs has reached an increasing proportion of the population (over 50% of those in the first three quintiles). However, Benitez (2017) finds that out-of-pocket payments for health services still represent 10% of income for the poorest quintile, as opposed to 4% for the richest quintile, thereby sustaining inequalities.

Fragmentation and the need for institutionalisation in social protection

Throughout the social protection system – income support, pensions and health – there is fragmentation and a disconnect between providers that can generate inefficiencies and adverse incentives. Indeed, with minimum contributions for pensions relatively difficult to meet, workers closer to retirement age are likely to forego formal employment altogether, since they have access to health services via the MSPBS and would not receive a pension from IPS if they contributed.

Institutional and operational responsibilities for social assistance overlap. Action in favour of the population in poverty is largely based around programmes, rather than being rights-based, except for health services. As a result, there are multiple agencies (SAS, STP, SENAVITAT, SNNA among them) with their own methods for identifying beneficiaries, including different proxy means tests. The *Secretaría Tecnica de Planificación* (STP) has recently prepared a targeting instrument (*Ficha social*) that is destined to encompass targeting processes for multiple programmes. This effort is part of the push for a co-ordinated poverty reduction programme under the umbrella programme *Sembrando Oportunidades*. However, certain programmes still use their legacy instruments (e.g. that used by the CCT programme Tekoporã). Systematic enrolment is the exception rather than the rule. While the social cabinet of the presidency holds an integrated social information system (SIIS) which covers 95 social programmes, it contains programme information, rather than a unified roster of beneficiaries. Legacy attributions sometimes seem to clash with mandates: for example, the *Secretaria de Accion social* (SAS), which manages the main conditional cash transfer programme (Tekoporã), also manages a programme aimed at facilitating access to public services by legalising the ownership of land (which it owns) in the favour of beneficiaries. At the same time, the knowledge and mandate for urban development and housing rests with the SENAVITAT. Co-ordination between agencies and ministries is perceived to have improved across government programmes. In the field of urban development, where interventions from a large number of agencies are needed, there is still need for a co-ordinated budget planning process that can contribute to optimising public expenditure in territories.

Co-ordination between institutions seems to work through *ad hoc* interfaces, but certain problems will require it to be institutionalised. In the field of poverty reduction, the national poverty reduction programme *Sembrando Oportunidades* establishes a number of mechanisms from targeting to intervention and monitoring to increase co-ordination and provide an integrated approach. In particular, addressing informality will require that better linkages are created between active labour market policies offered by the labour ministry and the national training system, and the social security and fiscal institutions. There has been progress in this respect, as the IPS can now share information with a view to enforcing declaration and payment obligations, which was prohibited by law in the past. Beyond enforcement functions, programme and policy design also require good institutional links to be effective.

Notes

1. Paraguay measures poverty on the basis of two absolute poverty lines: the extreme poverty line, defined on the basis of the cost of a food basket and the so-called "total" poverty line, which measures the cost of a basket including non-food items. Both lines are calculated separately for the Greater Asunción area, other urban areas and rural areas.
2. The programme also includes the management of centres acting as safe havens for children and social support.
3. Higgins et al. (2013) indicated that only 25% of the extreme poor received benefits via Tekoporã, a figure lower than the 39% for all the poor. Paraguay was an exception in the region in this respect, with every other country being able better to reach the extreme poor.
4. Paraguay also runs a quarterly labour force survey, the *Encuesta Continua de Empleo* (ECE). Data drawn from the EPH is preferred for international comparisons and for aggregate descriptions in this chapter because it is nationally representative, unlike ECE.
5. Field work for the EPH has been carried out at the end of the calendar year, while the agricultural year is July to June, which explains a misalignment of employment growth with annual GDP growth for the primary sector.
6. Official figures released by the National Statistical Agency (the *Direccion General de Estadística, Encuestas y Censos*, DGEEC) report labour force participation rates for all respondents to the employment module (aged 10 and above), and therefore report significantly lower labour force participation rates (62.6% for 2016).
7. These calculations are based on data from the Paraguayan Labour Force Survey (*Encuesta Continua de Empleo*, ECE) and cover urban areas only (see OECD/CAF/ECLAC, 2016 for details).
8. In Paraguay, the working age is 14 and above, and survey instruments capture employment data for those aged 10 and above. The age of 25 is taken to allow international comparison on adults who are deemed to have completed their education.
9. The gap between population projections for 2012 based on the 2002 census and population estimates based on the 2012 census were significant for school-age children: the five to nine cohort was found to be 6% smaller in the 2012 census than projected on the basis of the 2002 census, the ten to14 cohort was found to be 4% smaller. These gaps, however, explain only half the fall in net enrolment rates.
10. Data from the main household survey (the *Encuesta Permanente de Hogares*) had limited geographical coverage until 2015, but the excluded departments, Boquerón and Alto Paraguay, only represent 1% of the population, and hence do not explain this gap.
11. In mathematics, the first level in grade 3 involves recognising mathematical concepts, elements and basic calculations; in reading and communication the first level corresponds to comprehension of explicit relationships made in the text.
12. Data from UIS/UNESCO corresponding to 2012.
13. Ley 4933, in force since 2013.
14. Information collected during field mission, March 2017.
15. Net replacement rates measure a person's pension entitlement as a fraction of pre-retirement earnings (net of personal income taxes and social security contributions paid by workers and pensioners).

References

Alaimo, V. and W. Tapia (2014), "Perspectivas del mercado de trabajo y las pensiones en Paraguay" [Perspectives on the labour market and pensions in Paraguay], Nota técnica #772, Unidad de Mercados Laborales y Seguridad Social, Banco Interamericano de Desarrollo.

BCP (2017), Anexo Estadístico del Informe Económico [Statistical annex to the economic report], Banco Central del Paraguay, Asunción, *https://www.bcp.gov.py/anexo-estadistico-del-informe-economico-i365* (consulted August 2017).

Benítez, G. (2017), "Paraguay: distribución del Gasto en Salud y Gastos de Bolsillo" [Paraguay: distribution of health expenditure and out-of-pocket expenditure], CADEP, Observatorio Fiscal, June.

Casalí, P and M. Velásquez (2016), *Paraguay, Panorama de la protección social: diseño, cobertura y financiamiento* [Paraguay, panorama of social protection: design, coverage and financing], International Labour Organization, Santiago.

CEDLAS and the World Bank (2017), *Socio-Economic Database for Latin America and the Caribbean*, CEDLAS (Centre for Distributive, Labor and Social Issues in Latin America, Universidad Nacional de La Plata, Argentina) and the World Bank, *http://sedlac.econo.unlp.edu.ar/eng/*.

Cohen, D. and L. Leker (2014), "Health and Education: Another Look with the Proper Data", CEPR Discussion Paper No. DP9940, available at *https://ssrn.com/abstract=2444963*.

Cohen, D. and M. Soto (2007), "Growth and human capital: good data, good results", *Journal of Economic Growth*, Springer, Vol. 12(1), pages 51-76, March.

CONACYT (2016), *Estadísticas e indicadores de ciencia y tecnología de Paraguay 2014/15* [Statistics and indicators for science and technology in Paraguay 2014/15], Consejo Nacional de Ciencia y Tecnología (CONACYT), Asunción.

Contraloría General de la República (2017) *Informe sobre la rendición de cuentas de la ejecución de los programas y proyectos financiados con recursos del FONACIDE al 31 de diciembre de 2016* [Report on the execution of programmes and projects financed with FONACIDE resources to 31 December 2016], Comptroller-General of the Republic, Asunción, March.

Contraloría General de la República (2016), *Informe sobre la rendición de cuentas de la ejecución de los programas y proyectos financiados con recursos del FONACIDE al 31 de diciembre de 2015* [Report on the execution of programmes and projects financed with FONACIDE resources to 31 December 2015], Comptroller-General of the Republic, Asunción, March.

DGEEC (2017a), "DGEEC presentó nueva serie de pobreza y pobreza extrema" [DGEEC presents new series for poverty and extreme poverty], website of the Dirección General de Estadística, Encuesta y Censos, Paraguay, available at *www.dgeec.gov.py/news/DGEEC-PRESENTO-NUEVA-SERIE-DE-POBREZA-Y-POBREZA-EXTREMA.php*.

DGEEC (2017b), *Encuesta Permanente de Hogares* [Permanent Household Survey] (database), Dirección General de Estadística, Encuestas y Censos, Fernando de la Mora, *http://www.dgeec.gov.py/microdatos/index.php*, accessed August 2017.

DGEEC (2016), "Empleo informal: Encuesta Permanente de Hogares EPH 2010-2014" [Informal employment: Permanent Household Survey EPH 2010-2014], Dirección General de Estadística, Encuestas y Censos, Fernando de la Mora.

DGEEC (2015), *Principales Resultados. Encuesta Permanente de Hogares 2015* [Main results: Permanent Household Survey 2015], Dirección General de Estadística, Encuestas y Censos, *http://www.dgeec.gov.py/Publicaciones/Biblioteca/resultado%20eph2015/PUBLICACIONES%20EPH%202015%2008-05-17.pdf*.

ECLAC (2016), *Panorama Social de América Latina 2015 (Social Panorama of Latin America 2015)*, United Nations Economic Commission for Latin America and the Caribbean, Santiago.

Elías, R., G. Walder, and D. Sosa (2016), *Perfiles de la exclusión educativa en la República de Paraguay* [Profile of educational exclusión in the Republic of Paraguay], Investigación para el desarrollo and UNICEF, Asunción.

FEEI (2017), Informe de avance: Programa Nacional de Becas "Don Carlos Antonio López" [Progress Report: National Scholarship Programme Don Carlos Antonio López], Fondo para la Excelencia de la Educación y la Investigación, 31 March 2017.

Giménez, E. (2012), "Introducción al sector salud en Paraguay: Una aproximación conceptual y metodológica para el análisis sectorial" [Introduction to the health sector in Paraguay: a conceptual and methodological approach to sector analysis], Instituto Desarrollo, Asunción.

Giménez, L. et al (2017), "Paraguay: Análisis del Sistema fiscal y su impacto en la pobreza y la equidad" [Paraguay, Analysis of the fiscal system and its impact on poverty and equity], Documento de trabajo, Ministerio de Hacienda, Secretaría Técnica de Planificación del Desarrollo Económico y Social, CEQ Institute and the World Bank.

Higgins, S. et al. (2013), "Social spending, taxes and income distribution in Paraguay", CEQ Working Paper No. 11, CEQ Institute, Tulane University, *www.commitmentoequity.org/publications_files/Paraguay/CEQWPNo11%20Paraguay%20Nov%202013.pdf*.

ILO (2016), ILOSTAT (database), International Labour Organization, Geneva *http://www.ilo.org/ilostat/*.

ILO/DGEEC (2016), *Trabajo infantil y adolescente en el sector rural agrícola, pecuario, forestal y de pesca o piscicultura en Paraguay: Encuesta de Actividades de Niños, Niñas y Adolescentes* [Child and adolescent labour in the rural agricultural, livestock, forestry, fisheries and piscicultural sectors in Paraguay: Survey of activities of children and adolescents], International Labour Office and Dirección General de Estadística, Encuestas y Censos del Paraguay, Asunción.

Lachi, M. (2014), "La libertad sindical en el Paraguay, según resultados de las denuncias presentadas a los órganos contralores de la OIT (2003-2013)" [Freedom of association in Paraguay, according to the outcomes of complaints presented to monitoring bodies of the ILO (2003-2013)], Working Paper N. 23, Centro de Estudios y Educación Popular Germinal, Asunción.

Larraín, G., A. Viteri and I. Zucal (2013), "Análisis actuarial y de gobernanza de la Caja Fiscal y Caja Bancaria y apoyo a propuesta de ley de inversiones" [Actuarial and governance analysis of the *Caja Fiscal* and the *Caja Bancaria* and support to the investment bill], mimeo, cited in Alaimo and Tapia (2014).

MEC (2014), *Informe Nacional Paraguay Educación para Todos* [Paraguay national report: education for all], Ministerio de Educacion y Cultura, Paraguay, Asunción, Junio 2014.

MEC-SNEP (2013), Resultados de las evaluaciones: Area matemática [Results of evaluations: mathematics], Dirección General de Planificación Educativa, Dirección de Evaluación de la Calidad Educativa, Asunción, September 2013.

Molinier, L. (2016), "El derecho a la educación y el gasto público en Paraguay" [The right to education and public expenditure in Paraguay], Servicio Paz y Justicia, Asunción, October.

MTESS (2017), *Informe de Gestión y Rendición de Cuentas 2016* [Accountability and management report 2016], Ministry of Labour, Employment and Social Security of Paraguay, January 2017, Asunción.

MTESS (2015), *Boletín Estadístico de Seguridad Social 2015* [Social Security Statistical Bulletin 2015], Ministerio de Trabajo, Empleo y Seguridad Social, Asunción.

Navarro, B. and E.Ortiz (2014), "La reforma de pensiones de Paraguay" [Pension reform in Paraguay], Nota de política No. 13, Centro de Análisis y Difusión de la Economía Paraguaya, Asunción.

OECD (2016), *Education at a Glance 2016: OECD Indicators*, OECD Publishing, Paris, *http://dx.doi.org/10.1787/eag-2017-en*.

OECD (2015a), *PISA 2015 Results (Volume I): Excellence and Equity in Education*, OECD Publishing, Paris, *http://dx.doi.org/10.1787/9789264266490-en*

OECD (2015b), *Pensions at a Glance: OECD and G20 Indicators*, OECD Publishing, Paris, *http://dx.doi.org/10.1787/pension_glance-2015-en*.

OECD (2013a), *Recommendation of the Council on Gender Equality in Education, Employment and Entrepreneurship*, adopted on 29 May 2013 by the OECD Council at Ministerial Level, *https://www.oecd.org/gender/C-MIN(2013)5-ENG.pdf*.

OECD (2013b), *OECD Employment Outlook 2013*, OECD Publishing, Paris, *http://dx.doi.org/10.1787/empl_outlook-2013-en*.

OECD/CAF/ECLAC (2016), *Latin American Economic Outlook 2017: Youth, Skills and Entrepreneurship*, OECD Publishing, Paris, *http://dx.doi.org/10.1787/leo-2017-en*.

OECD/CIAT/IDB (2016), *Taxing Wages in Latin America and the Caribbean*, OECD Publishing, Paris, *http://dx.doi.org/10.1787/9789264262607-en*.

OECD/IDB/The World Bank (2014), *Pensions at a Glance: Latin America and the Caribbean*, OECD Publishing, Paris, *http://dx.doi.org/10.1787/pension_glance-2014-en*.

PREAL (2013), *El desafío es la equidad: Informe de progreso educativo. Paraguay* [The challenge is equity: Educational progress report. Paraguay], Programa de Promoción de la Reforma Educativa en América Latina y el Caribe and Instituto Desarrollo.

Ramirez, J. (n.d.), "Paraguay: inversión en protección social 2013-2014" [Paraguay: investment in social protection 2013-2014], document for the project "Debates y acciones para mejorar la calidad de la inversión social en Paraguay", CADEP, Asunción. *http://paraguaydebate.org.py/wp-content/uploads/2015/10/Gasto-social-version-web-21oct.pdf*.

Rossi, M. (2016), "Evaluación de Impacto del Programa Tekoporã" [Impact evaluation for the Tekoporã programme], Final report, Consultancy "Evaluación de Impacto de los programas Tekoporã y Abrazo", May 2016, available at *www.economia.gov.py/application/files/9514/7939/4429/Evaluacion_de_Impacto_del_Programa_Tekopora_07062016.pdf*.

SAS (2016), "Informe de Gestion Institucional" [Institutional annual report], Secretaría de Acción Social, Asunción, December.

SENAVITAT (2017), "Informe de Gestión Institucional: 20 000 viviendas", [Institutional anual report: 20 000 homes], Secretaría Nacional de la Vivienda y el Hábitat, July, Asunción.

SENAVITAT (2016), "Tercera Conferencia de las Naciones Unidas sobre la Vivienda y el Desarrollo Urbano Sostenible – Habitat III. Informe Nacional del Paraguay" [Paraguay National Report – Third UN conference on housing and sustainable urban development], Secretaría Nacional de la Vivienda y el Hábitat, Asunción.

SENAVITAT (2012), "PLANHAVI: Plan Nacional de Hábitat y Vivienda del Paraguay" [PLANHAVI: National habitat and housing plan], Secretaría Nacional de la Vivienda y el Hábitat, Asunción, available at *www.senavitat.gov.py/sitio/wp-content/uploads/2013/10/15.1-Planhavi1.pdf.*

SFP (2017), Data portal, *Secretaría de la Función Pública*, consulted July 2017, *http://datos.sfp.gov.py/visualizaciones/resumen.*

SNPP (2016), *Informe de Gestión Institucional. Servicio Nacional de Promoción Profesional* [Annual report: National service for professional promotion], Asunción.

UNESCO (2017), UIS.stat (database), United Nations Educational, Scientific and Cultural Organization, *http://data.uis.unesco.org/Index.aspx* (accessed September 2017).

UNESCO (2015), *Informe de resultados: Tercer Esudio Regional Comparativo y Explicativo (TERCE) (Third Regional Comparative and Explanatory Study)*, Laboratorio Latinoamericano de evaluación de la calidad de la educación, UNESCO, Santiago de Chile.

Wodon, Q. (2016), *School Infrastructure in Paraguay: Needs, Investments, and Costs*, World Bank Studies, the World Bank, Washington DC, doi: 10.1596/978-1-4648-0448-9.

World Bank (2017a), *World Development Indicators* (database), *https://data.worldbank.org* (consulted July 2017).

World Bank (2017b), *PovcalNet: an online analysis tool for global poverty monitoring* (database), World Bank, *http://iresearch.worldbank.org/PovcalNet/home.aspx* (consulted May 2017).

World Bank (2015), *Volatility and Inequality as Constraints to Shared Prosperity*, Paraguay Equity Assessment, World Bank, Washington DC.

Multi-dimensional Review of Paraguay
Volume 1. Initial Assessment

Chapter 4

Towards sustainable environment in Paraguay

Paraguay is endowed with vast natural wealth in terms of biodiversity, energy, water sources and fertile land. This chapter examines the country's performance in environmental outcomes as well as their impact on citizens' well-being. Paraguay performs well in several environmental indicators, given its clean energy mix, low air pollution, and low greenhouse gas and carbon emissions. However, Paraguay's territorial and development model is gradually increasing environmental pressure. Access to clean water, electricity and waste management are still not available for a large part of the population. Deforestation, explained by the current expansion of the agriculture and livestock sectors, remains one of the most urgent areas for environmental sustainability. Paraguay also faces challenges in land management and administration, which is linked to the concentration of land ownership and the rural-to-urban migratory flows. The chapter analyses the main constraints in Paraguay's institutional framework and the capabilities to address these challenges in the future.

Geography has bestowed on Paraguay one of the most biodiverse ecosystems in the world. With access to a large tropical forest and a vast number of water endowments, the country provides abundant resources for agriculture and livestock development. One of the cleanest energy mixes in the region, based on the use of hydropower, has allowed Paraguay to manage to keep the economy's carbon intensity at low levels and allowed the country to control air pollution. Total greenhouse emissions also remain relatively low. However, the current economic expansion, largely based on the use of land for agriculture and livestock development, has put increasing environmental pressure on the country. Deforestation remains one of the most critical issues in terms of environmental sustainability.

While costs are low by comparison with other countries, access to public services, including water, sanitation and waste management is still limited for a large part of the population, and regional disparities in the quality and distribution of these services persist. The rapid urbanisation process has increased pressure in Asunción and other cities, and shortages of water and its poor quality are major concerns for the authorities, particularly in urban areas. In rural areas, natural disaster prevention has gained importance after two recent episodes where agricultural production was affected.

To maintain the current economic momentum and guarantee that it benefits the entire population, Paraguay needs to incorporate the sustainable use of environmental resources and capabilities into its development agenda. There are considerable needs in terms of environmental protection that are not being met. The regulatory framework against deforestation is insufficient and is not being implemented, and more support to strengthen the institutional setting is needed, particularly at the local level. Waste management is another issue of concern, and is mostly based on landfilling as the primary disposal method. Improving land management will be fundamental to the implementation of a strategic plan for the environment.

The purpose of this chapter is threefold. First, it starts by assessing how well Paraguay is performing in terms of fundamental environmental outcomes, as well as their impact on citizens' well-being. Second, it aims to identify the capacity constraints (in particular, institutional and economic) that may be leading to areas of poor performance in some of these indicators. Third, the chapter establishes some linkages between the environmental assessment and the potential barriers to Paraguay's development agenda in the long term.

The move from the countryside: Recent trends

Urbanisation trends

Since the 1980s, Paraguay has experienced a high rate of urbanisation as a result of demographic trends and increasing migration from rural to urban areas. Asunción, the country's capital, and the departments of Central y Alto Paraná house the largest proportion of the country's urban population. Within these departments, most of the urban population is centralised in two areas: the metropolitan area of Asunción and the metropolitan area of

Ciudad del Este. The population's congregation around the capital, as in other countries in the region, is substantial. In 2012, when the latest census was carried out, the metropolitan area of Asuncion was home to 37% of the total national population (Figure 4.1). This overconcentration occurs in a limited area of 520 km^2, leading to environmental degradation and an inadequate supply of public services.

In terms of territorial population distribution, there are substantial differences among the country's urban centres. Approximately 20% of the country's urban population centres have only 1 000 to 2 000 inhabitants. This figure contrasts with the fact that a few cities – Asunción, Ciudad del Este, Luque, San Lorenzo and Capiatá – are home to large numbers of the population with over 200 000 individuals. Current disparities in the distribution of the population highlight the need for a more coherent territorial policy. The National Development Plan 2030 takes this challenge into consideration, and an assessment of the country's territorial policy is one of the current priorities of the government. Defining a model of occupation and organisation of the territory and for a land management policy with an adequate population density that facilitates the efficient provision of public services will have, as will be presented in the chapter, a considerable impact on the country's environmental performance.

In a context of high concentration in few densely populated areas, cities of a medium size could play an important role in redesigning Paraguay's territorial policy. The country's intermediate cities are composed of a group of diverse and dynamic towns with populations of between 15 000 and 60 000, located in the country's Eastern region. Paraguay's main intermediate cities include Caacupé, Carapeguá, Curuguaty, Filadelfia, Horqueta, Juan Eulogio Estigarriba, San Estanislao, San Juan Nepomuceno, San Ignacio, Santa Rita, Santa Rosa del Aguaray and Tomas Romero Pereira. Over the past decades, Paraguay's intermediate population centres have shown a slow, but steady, growth in population. This is partly due to the growing agricultural sector in these places and their key role in the production of some of the country's main commodities, in particular soybeans and meat. A better distribution of the population could allow for the decentralisation and more efficient provision of public services, while encouraging regional investment.

Figure 4.1. **Evolution of the rural and urban population in Paraguay**

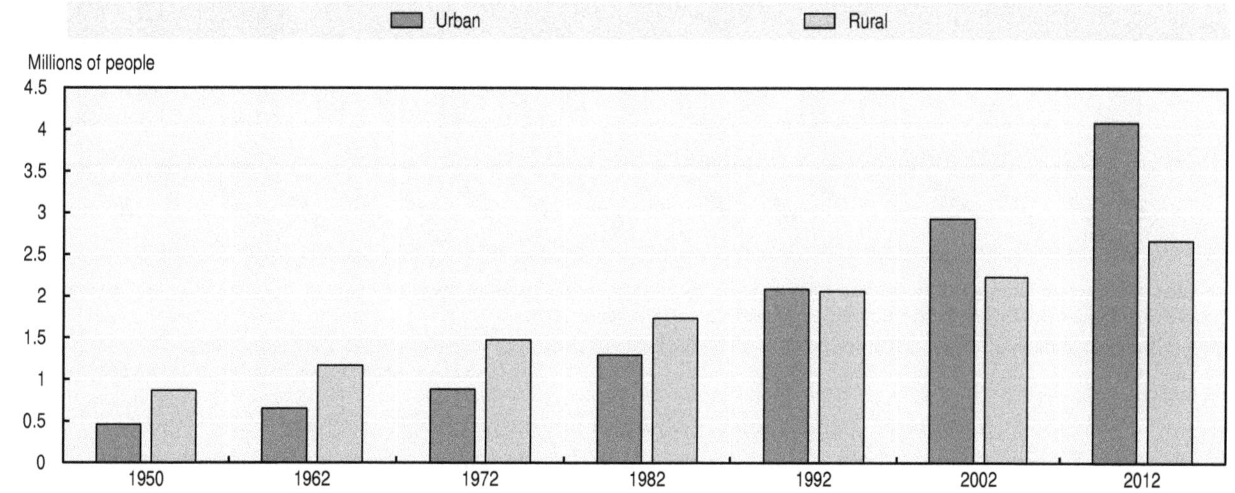

Source: Dirección General de Estadística, Encuestas y Censos, 2015.

StatLink http://dx.doi.org/10.1787/888933750035

Main environmental outcomes in Paraguay

Water access and quality

Paraguay has a large supply of fresh water, thanks to its geographical characteristics. The country is divided by the Paraguay River into two regions: the East, with a semitropical humid climate, and the Chaco region, an alluvial plain with semi-arid lands and high temperatures. Because of the natural features of this type of geography, the East has more than 800 rivers and streams and rich underground water resources that can be tapped for agriculture and domestic purposes. With a 3 170 000 km^2 area, the La Plata's drainage basin is the second largest in South America and home to several hydroelectric projects, among them Itaipú, the second largest in the world. Such a diverse ecosystem in the Eastern Region allows for a better settlement of the population (near main rivers and the La Plata basin).

Figure 4.2. **Access to freshwater and water withdrawals by department**

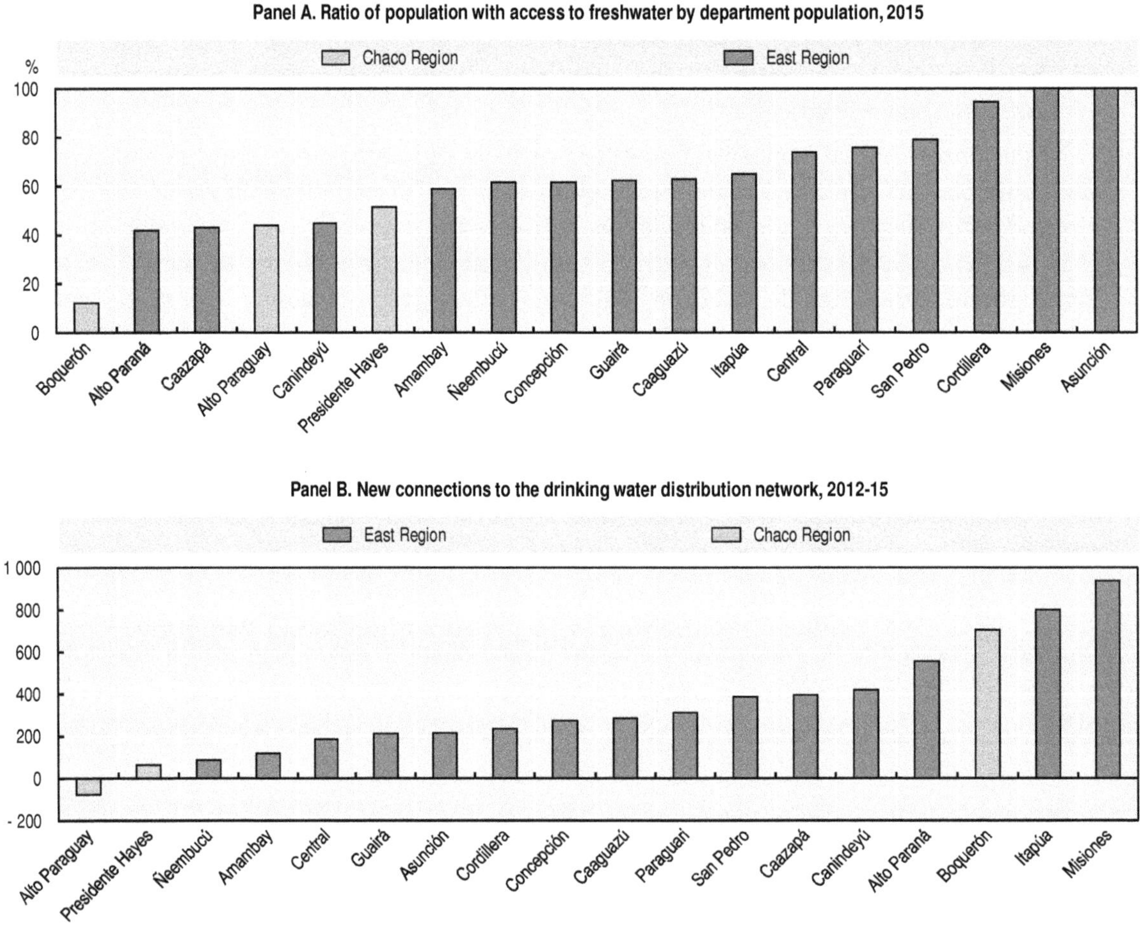

Note: Panel A. The population with access to freshwater is estimated on the basis of dwellings served. For Asunción and Misiones the estimates are higher than the estimated population and the ratio is set to 100%.

Source: Authors' calculations, based on Dirección General de Estadística, Encuestas y Censes (DGEEC), 2015 and 2012.

StatLink http://dx.doi.org/10.1787/888933750054

However, in spite of the abundance of water sources, the way they are distributed and treated poses problems. By 2015, nearly 75% of the Paraguayan population had access to water withdrawals, according to the National Regulatory Agency for Water, and 20% of that share was located in the main economic departments of the country. The Chaco region and the Northern departments are among the most deprived departments in the country in terms of access to water (Figure 4.2, Panel A). Departments near the La Plata basin, such as Alto Paraná or Caazapá also report low levels of access.

There has been progress in water infrastructure during the past few decades, but there is still much room for improvement. The Chaco region faces significant challenges in updating and improving water infrastructure. Surface water, such as that from rivers, is almost non-existent in this part of the country and water from beneath the ground is brackish. At the moment, communities in the region use elevated tanks that are fed by rainwater which is distributed to different public stand pipes using windmills and gravity. However, this system has proven to be inefficient because of the presence of animals and humans in the neighbourhood, and the lack of systematic maintenance (WWF, 2017c). In spite of public investment in upgrading the infrastructures for water supply and cleaning, challenges persist in this area. In 2012, Paraguay reported a 40% increase in improved water sources with respect to 1990 (World Bank, 2017). Nevertheless, only 0.6% of the total renewable water available in the country was fresh water. Water quality becomes a more worrying problem when account is taken of the elevated mortality rates in the country linked to it. Among the selected benchmark countries, Paraguay has the second highest mortality rate arising from exposure to unsafe water, sanitation and hygiene services, with an average of two people dying per 100 000 inhabitants annually (Figure 4.3).

Figure 4.3. **Mortality rate attributed to exposure to unsafe water, sanitation and hygiene (WASH) services**

Cases per 100 000 population, 2012

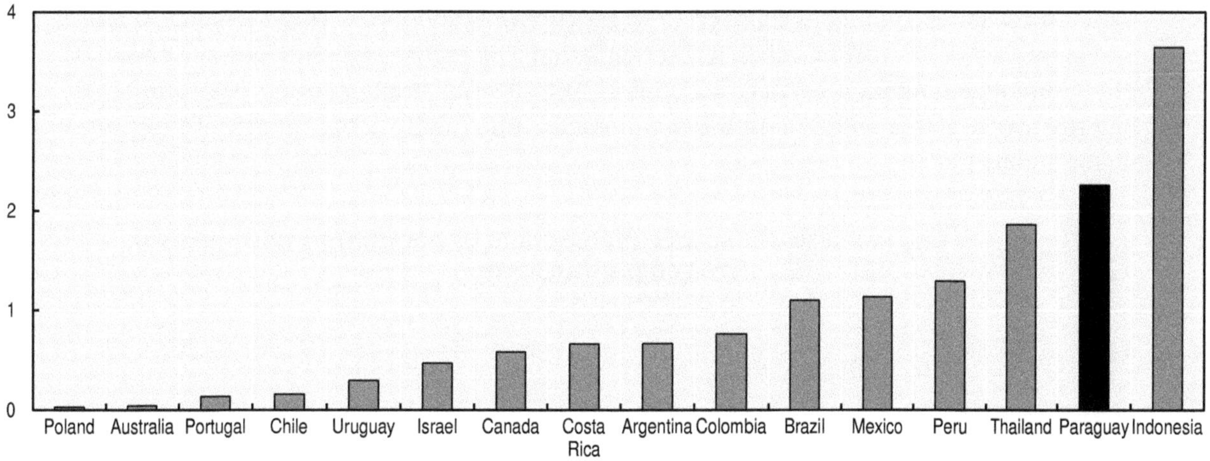

Source: World Health Organization (2017).

StatLink http://dx.doi.org/10.1787/888933750073

Sewerage infrastructure also constitutes a major challenge. In 2015, with a local coverage of around 11% in sanitary sewer networks and treatment for only 3% of the total population, Paraguay's sewerage system was considered, along with those of Haiti, Honduras and Guatemala, to be one of the most deficient in Latin America (ECLAC, 2016). The consequences for the well-being of the population are considerable, as access to sewerage promotes a healthy environment for each household and the community. Inadequate treatment can cause different diseases that can have a substantial impact, such as cholera or chronic diarrhoea (UNICEF/WHO, 2013). Among the benchmark countries, Paraguay has the highest post-neonatal rate of death caused by diarrhoea (13% in 2015, Figure 4.4), five percentage points above the LATAM average and at the same level as sub-Saharan countries such as Côte d'Ivoire and Liberia.

Figure 4.4. **Percentage post-neonatal deaths due to diarrhoea, 2015**

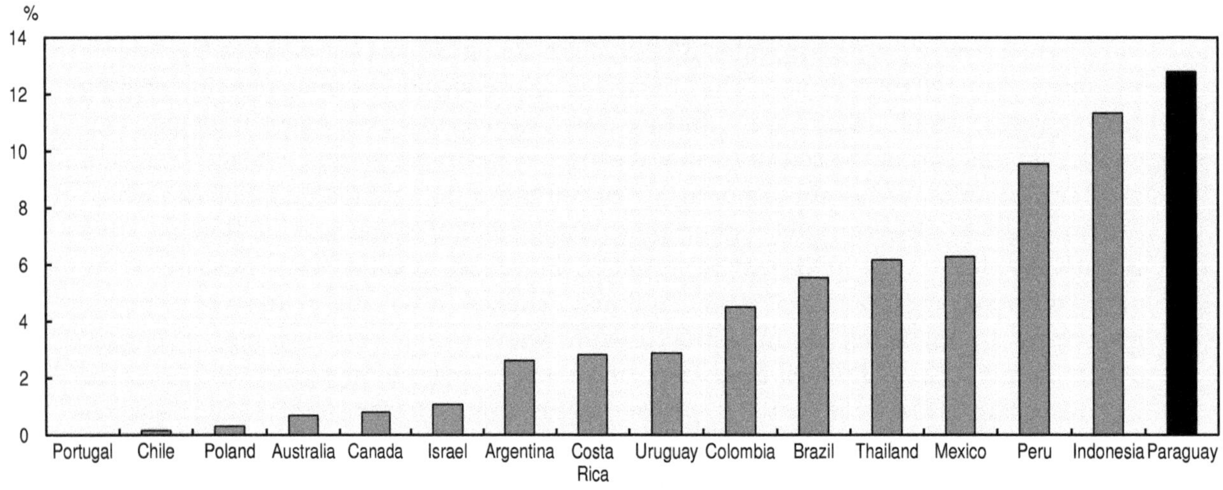

Source: World Health Organization (2015).

StatLink http://dx.doi.org/10.1787/888933750092

An inadequate sewerage network tends more to affect the rural population. Given the complexity of the water cycle, zones with low quality sewerage services, such as rural zones, could have contamination of potable water by sewage. As the use of water-processing and storage methods such as wells, septic tanks and latrines, does not guarantee a level of quality, agricultural zones are highly exposed to water contamination, that could expand to food and animals (ECLAC, 2016). Overall, water regulation in Paraguay lags. SENASA, the national environmental sanitation service, which is responsible for implementing environmental law relating to rivers and underground water, has little institutional capacity to regulate water quality.

Figure 4.5. **Improved water source (percentage of population with access), by geographic zone**

1994 vs. 2012

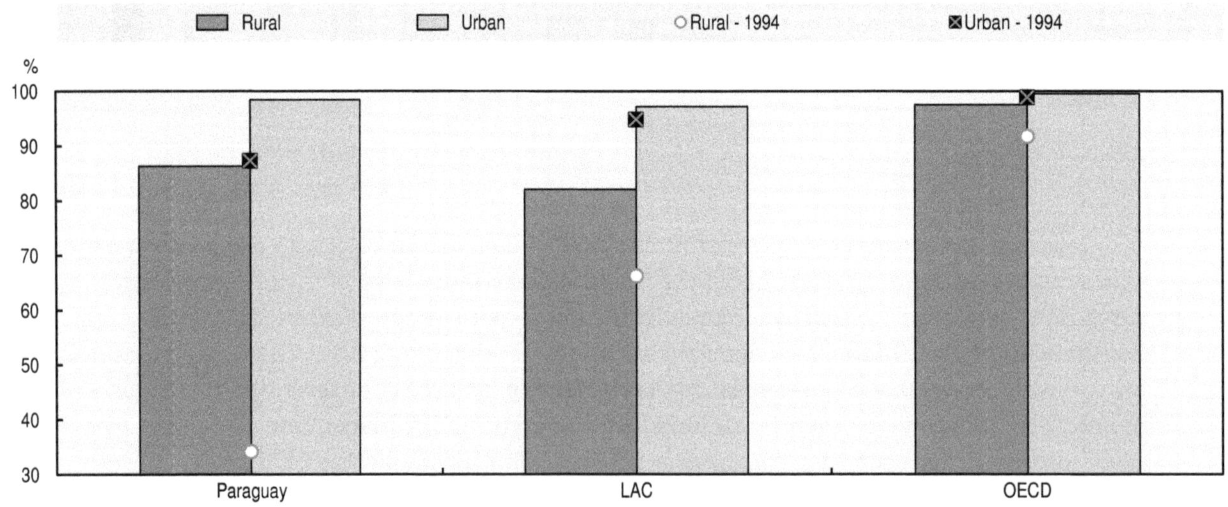

Source: World Development Indicators (World Bank, 2017) and DGEEC (2012).

StatLink http://dx.doi.org/10.1787/888933750111

Differences in access between rural and urban areas are particularly high in Paraguay, in comparison with Latin American countries and with OECD members (Figure 4.5). In comparison with Latin American countries, improvement of water sources in rural areas has been significant, but the gap between rural and urban areas is still similar. Contrary to OECD countries where both rural and urban areas improved, Paraguay still has a 22 percentage point gap in water source improvement. This difference is even more noticeable considering that Paraguay is a country based on agro-industry and livestock and fresh water in rural areas is essential to the production system. Of the total fresh water withdrawal, 79% is used in agriculture.[1]

Agricultural production in Paraguay can also be a cause of water contamination. The excessive use of nitrate fertilisers could be associated with the high level of metals within the water cycle (Willaarts et al., 2014). Countries based on agro-industry have used fertilisers to increase their productivity and make them more competitive in international markets. Globally, the consumption of fertilisers rose from 89 kilograms per hectare in 2002, to over 126 in 2013. Paraguay went from 66 kg in 2005 to 105 kg in 2014 (FAO, 2016). If this trend continues, water contamination caused by nitrates could limit the availability of domestic water and also contribute to the increase of biomass load within the water (a phenomenon also known as eutrophication) (ECLAC, 2016). Clear examples of the eutrophication effect are observed in the Ypacaraí Lake and the Pirayú streams. Samples taken from these bodies of water showed that the increase of micronuclei is mainly driven by the cytotoxic effect of fertilisers and pesticides that are released in bulk into rivers and streams (López Arias et al., 2013). This type of contamination has consequences not only for local communities, but could extend to other areas, given the nature of water to circulate[2] (ECLAC, 2016).

Figure 4.6. **Annual freshwater withdrawals, by sector (% of total freshwater withdrawal)**

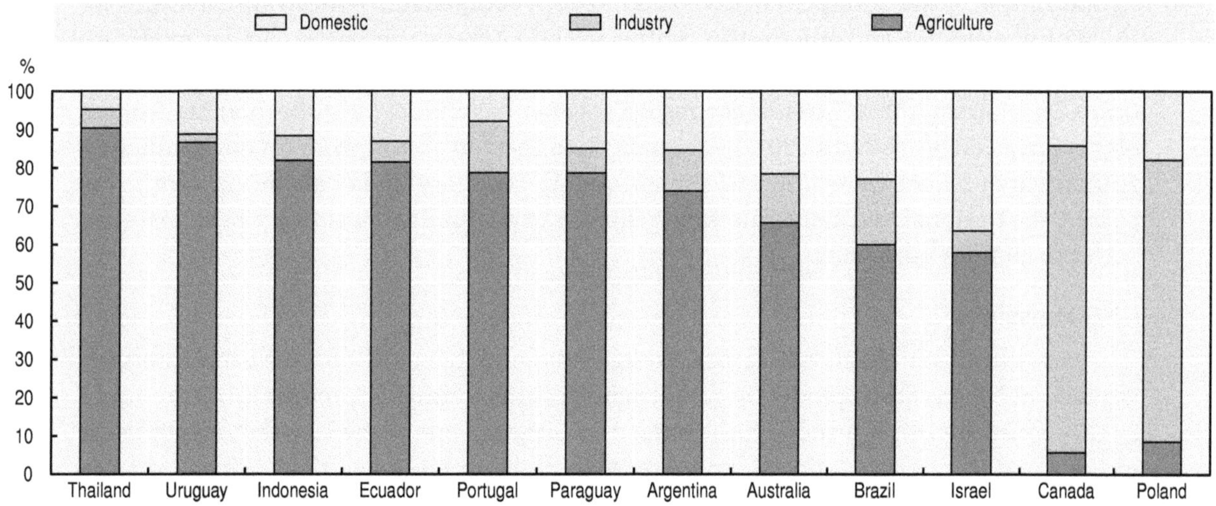

Source: DGEEC and World Development Indicators, World Bank (2017).

StatLink http://dx.doi.org/10.1787/888933750130

If untreated, an excessive increase in biomass in water could bring futures challenges for Paraguay. Sedimentation of the soil is a natural process, partially created geologically, but also by human activity in putting nitrates into water (Callisto et al., 2013). In much of the work associated with hydroelectric generation, the phenomenon of sediment accumulation is critical to the life of reservoirs and electro-mechanical equipment. In a country where all energy production is hydroelectric-based, water sedimentation is an issue for the future (World Bank, 2017). The eutrophication phenomenon together with the climate change effect, including the *El Niño* phenomenon (a period of warming of the sea in the Ecuador region), could represent a threat for Paraguay's energy security (ECLAC, 2016).

Air quality

Air pollution in urban areas is still not a major environmental concern in Paraguay, but pressure on air quality is growing. Available data suggest that total carbon monoxide (CO) emissions increased from 1 100 units in 1990 to 2 178 units by 2000, mainly explained by agriculture and changes in land use. By contrast, total nitrogen emissions have remained fairly stable over the same period, with a decrease from 110 to 87 units. Emissions of volatile organic compounds (VOCs) increased significantly, from five to 58 units over the 1990s. Other air pollutants such as sulphur oxides (SOx) remain low (0.16 units in 2000) and did not show any increases during the same period. The number of vehicles in use in Paraguay, a common source of gas emissions in emerging economies, increased (from 256 000 units in 2005 to 370 000 in 2014), but remains lower in per inhabitant terms than in OECD economies. In addition, the management of air quality regulation and monitoring is one of the areas under the responsibility of the Environmental Secretariat (SEAM). However, today, an effective air quality system monitoring emissions is lacking and data on air emissions are not available for all years and for the entire territory.

The exposure of the Paraguayan population to air pollution is relatively low when compared to other benchmark countries, and lower than in neighbours Argentina and Uruguay. Between 2005 and 2013, peak concentration of small particles (exposure to particulate matter [PM]2.5) decreased by nearly 40% (Figure 4.7). The share of the population exposed to more than than 10 micrograms/m^3, a standard level of air quality, also fell significantly over the same period, from 71% to 14%. A comparison of mean annual exposure to PM2.5 in Asunción and other urban centres in Latin America show the city has moderate levels of PM concentrations, comparable to those in Buenos Aires, Montevideo, San José or Quito. By contrast, other cities in the region (e.g. Rio de Janeiro, Lima, Bogotá) have much higher emission levels (WHO, 2011). Air quality has been an area of work for environmental authorities in recent years. In 2014, the air quality law ("Ley de la calidad del aire") was passed, the National Air Directorate was created, and air quality towers have been installed better to monitor air quality.

GHG emissions

Paraguay has a clean, low-carbon energy mix, mostly based on renewable energies. Production-based carbon productivity, a measure of gross domestic product (GDP) produced by CO_2 emissions, is high and only surpassed by Uruguay, one of the cleanest energy users in the world (Figure 4.8, Panel A). An increase in carbon productivity indicates that more GDP is being created per unit of carbon dioxide emitted, which in general is interpreted as beneficial for the environment. At the same time, the energy intensity of the economy (energy supply per unit of GDP, Figure 4.8, Panel B) is low and has remained fairly stable over the past decade. Work in the area of climate change has progressed, and is an important component of the National Development Plan.

Figure 4.7. **Mean population exposure to PM2.5**

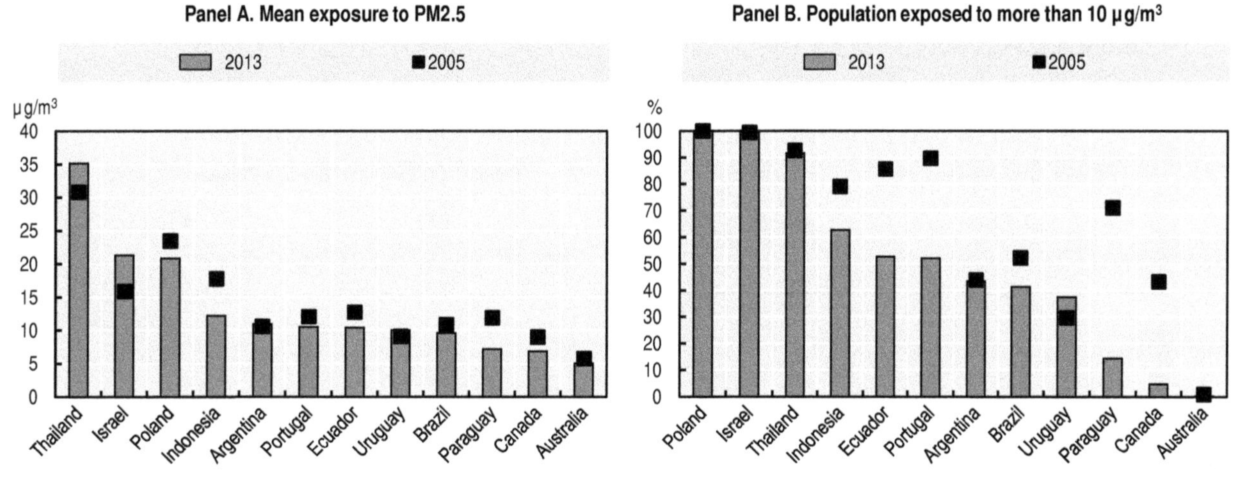

Note: Mean population exposure to fine particulate matter is calculated as the mean annual outdoor PM2.5 concentration weighted by population living in the area. It is the concentration level, expressed in micrograms per cubic meter (µg/m3), to which a typical resident is exposed throughout a year.

Source: Green Growth Indicators, OECD.

StatLink http://dx.doi.org/10.1787/888933750149

Figure 4.8. **CO_2 productivity and CO_2 intensity**

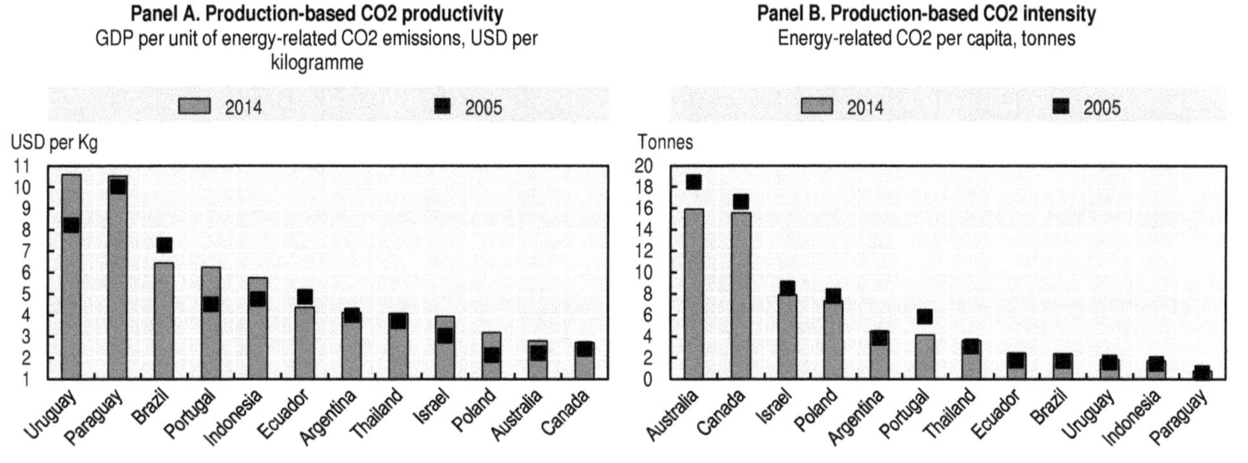

Note: CO_2 productivity defined as GDP generated per unit of CO_2 emitted through fuel consumption. Production-based CO_2 is the proportion of CO_2 emissions, total, per capita and per USD1 GDP (PPP).

Source: OECD (2017a), Green Growth Indicators.

StatLink http://dx.doi.org/10.1787/888933750168

In terms of greenhouse-related emissions, between 2005 and 2013 greenhouse gas emissions increased in Paraguay by 76%, when land-use change and forestry are included, but they remain low when compared to benchmark economies (Figure 4.9, Panels A and B). Most countries decreased their GHG emissions during the same period. The largest share of GHG emissions per capita in Paraguay comes from transport, which is much higher than in the benchmark countries (Figure 4.9, Panel C).

Energy

Paraguay has a considerable stock of primary energy. Given the country's strategic position in the La Plata basin and its environmentally diverse regions, Paraguay can count on an enormous variety of water, gas and natural resources capable of producing biomass.

Since 1970, the country has conducted major efforts to produce primary energies and, by 2011, Paraguay had increased its production volume six times compared with 40 years before (MOPC, 2011).

Figure 4.9. **Total greenhouse gas (GHG) emissions with and without land-use change and forestry (metric tonnes carbon dioxide equivalent - $MtCO_2e$)**

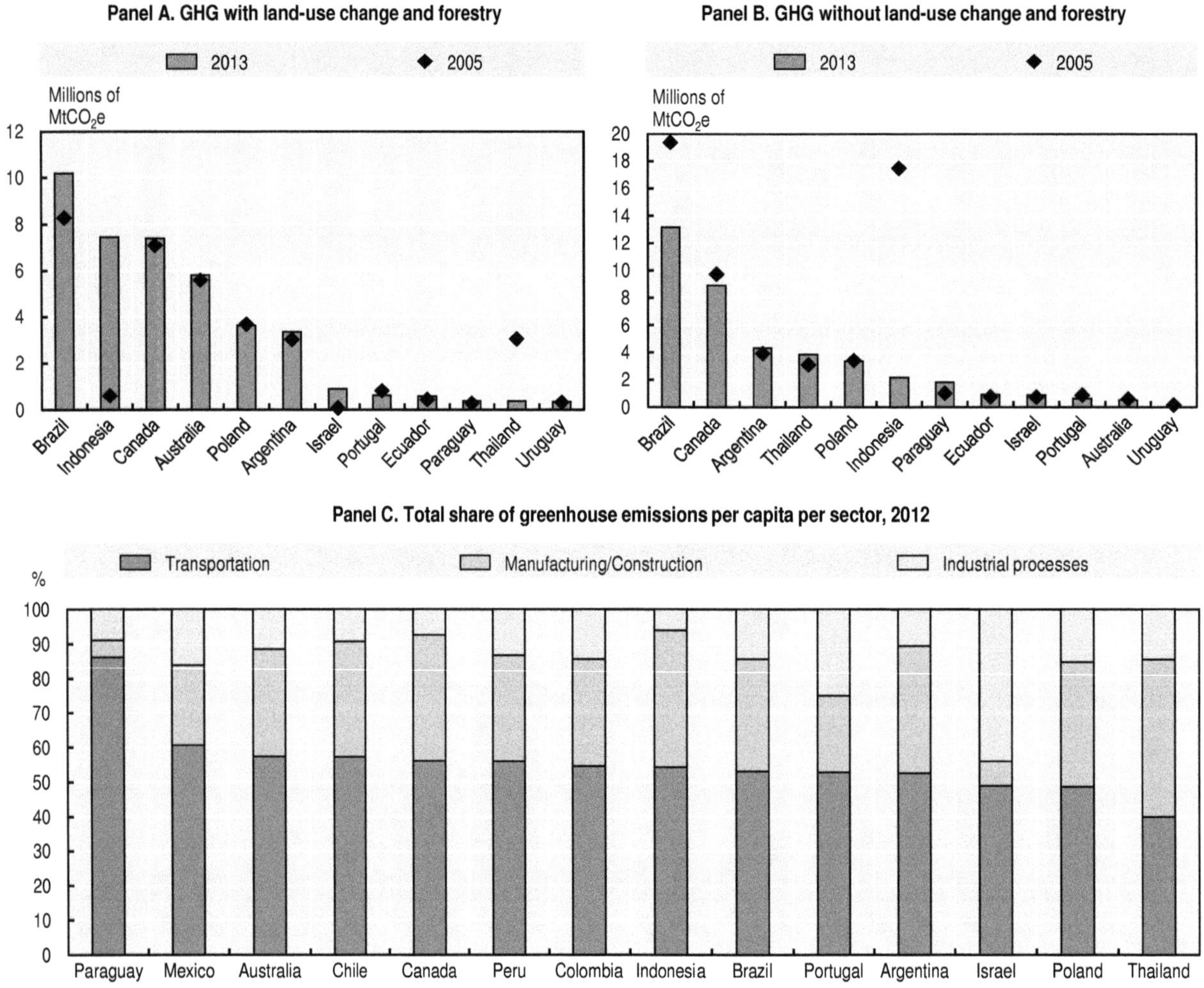

Source: CAIT Climate Data Explorer, FAOSTAT Emissions Database and OECD/IEA (2014).

StatLink http://dx.doi.org/10.1787/888933750187

The Paraguayan energy mix is mainly composed of renewable and local energy. Since 1960, after negotiations between the Brazilian and the Paraguayan governments, and the signing in 1973 of the Itaipú Treaty, the country has experienced an energy revolution. Producing more than 2.4 million megawatt hours (MWh) since its inauguration in 1984, the Itaipú binational dam is one of the biggest hydroelectric stations in the world. In 2015, hydro-energy accounted for 68% of the total primary energy production in the country. The other 32% came from biomass (24%) such as charcoal and wood, and other biomasses (8%), which include waste from forestry and cotton (DGEEC, 2015). The importance of the biomass component in Paraguay's energy matrix is reflected in the government plans to foster reforestation through the new energy policy and national reforestation plan.

With one of the cleanest energy productions in the world, the whole of Paraguay's electricity comes from renewable resources. The binational dams produce in total 70%

of their output for the Paraguayan market (MOPC, 2011), which is sufficient to satisfy the whole electricity demand in the country. The rest is exported to neighbouring countries (Figure 4.10). Paraguay is the only country among those selected as benchmark countries to have a 100% use of renewable energy in its total production of electricity. Also, as fixed costs decrease rapidly with production, electricity prices in Paraguay are among the cheapest in Latin-America. In 2011, one kilowatt hour (KWh) cost USD 0.06 in Paraguay, as opposed to a median price of USD 0.16 in the region (OLADE, 2017). However, Paraguay is a major consumer of polluting energy. Of total energy consumption only 29% is electricity. The rest of energy consumption breaks down into fuel (56%, mainly diesel with 38%), and biomass energy (16%) such as wood and charcoal (DGEEC, 2015). Almost all the demand for hydrocarbon fuels comes from the transportation sector (MOPC, 2011, see Figure 4.9, Panel C). This dependence on fuel is also linked to the fact that Paraguay's vehicle park increased by 165% from 2007 to 2015 (DNRA, 2017).

Figure 4.10. **Energy consumption and energy production in Paraguay by source, 2015**

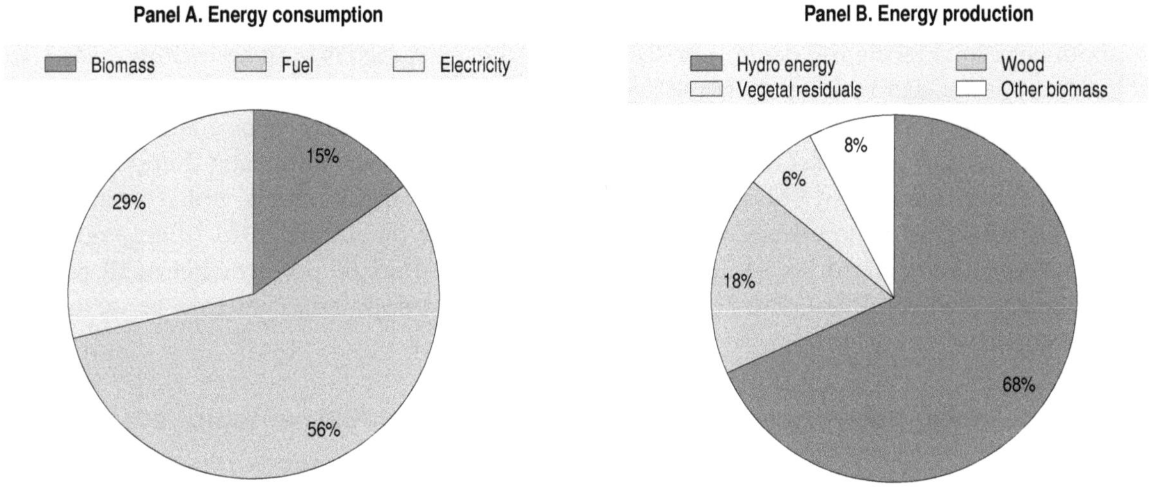

Source: Viceministerio de Minas y Energía (VMME), 2017.

StatLink http://dx.doi.org/10.1787/888933750206

Figure 4.11. **Renewable electricity, percentage of total electricity generation**

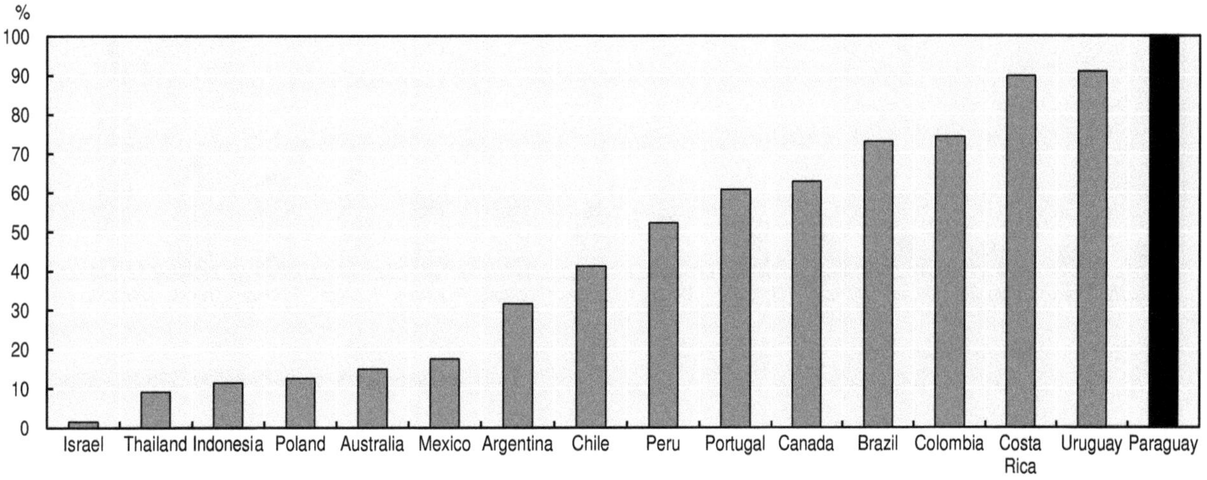

Source: OECD (2017a), Green Growth Indicators.

StatLink http://dx.doi.org/10.1787/888933750225

Biomass is still heavily used in Paraguay, especially in poor urban suburbs and rural areas. In 2015, wood represented 67% of the total share of biomass energy, with about 52% of rural households using it, mostly for cooking (DGEEC, 2015). In urban areas, biomass is also used for daily activities, including cooking and pottery. The high use of biomass products in these areas could be related to two main factors: on the one hand, the more limited access to electricity in rural zones, and on the other, the low energy intensity of Paraguay's productive sectors. Most people living in the countryside use wood to cook as a cultural habit or following the patterns of rural life (GNESD, 2015). However, even if around 98% of the rural population have access to electricity; the density of electrification lines differs among different geographic areas. The southern part of the country has most of electricity connections, giving the Chaco region just 10% of the total electric network (GNESD, 2015). In urban areas, hydroelectric energy is also not used because of high energy distribution costs.

Paraguay's low energy intensity can be explained by the nature of its productive sectors and by energy consumption trends. As already indicated, Paraguay's energy intensity (CO_2 emissions from fuel combustion per unit of GDP) is low by international comparison in both per capita terms and per unit of GDP (Figure 4.12). As Paraguay is an agriculture-based economy (the sector accounts for 26% of the country's GDP, [BCP, 2017]), its production sectors do not require the same intensity of energy use as the industry or manufacturing sectors. The agriculture sector makes little use of technological capital, and therefore the use of energies is limited. This explains Paraguay's energy intensity levels, which is similar to Peru's but lower than those of Argentina and Uruguay (Enerdata, 2015). Compared to some benchmark countries, Paraguay has the best environmental performance of all, and far better than countries with comparable land size and population, such as Israel and Costa Rica.

Figure 4.12. **Energy intensity, total primary energy supply (TPES) per capita, 2014 vs 2005**

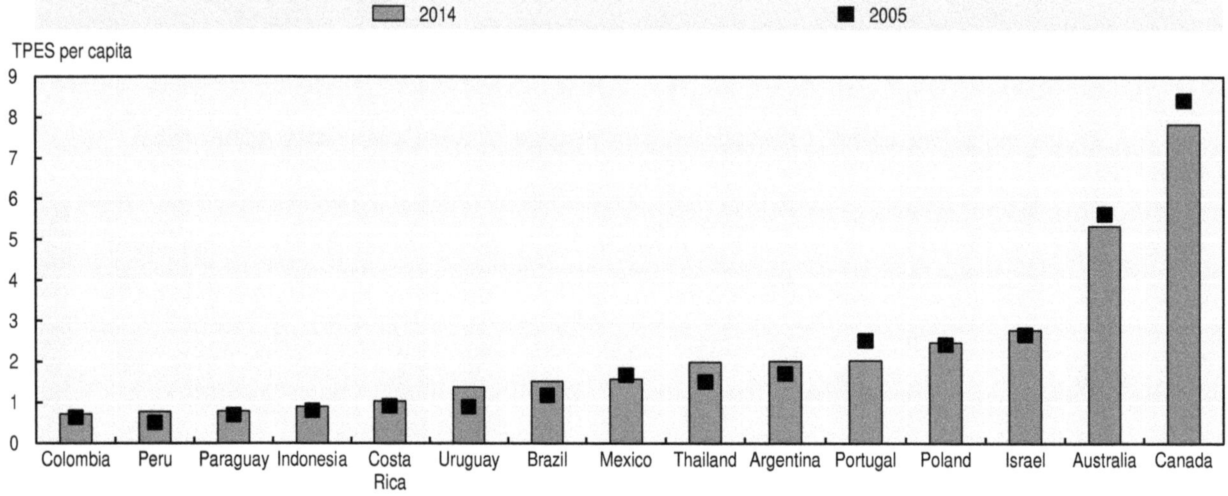

Source: OECD (2017a), Green Growth Indicators.

StatLink http://dx.doi.org/10.1787/888933750244

Despite the availability of spare capacity in electricity generation, an acceleration in growth will require further development in generation capacity to satisfy demand. In terms of electricity supply, Paraguay is likely to be able to export electricity well into the

21st century. Indeed, average production is expected to be around 67 000 GWh per year with the hydropower plants currently in operation, while demand was 13 018 GWh in 2013. A prospective exercise carried out as a basis for the country's energy policy (Fundación Bariloche, 2015) considers a *business-as-usual* (BAU) scenario with 3% growth in GDP and trend changes in energy intensity, and an *alternative* scenario with 5.2% growth in GDP and significant changes in the economy following the objectives of the National Development Plan. In the former, current installed capacity would be sufficient until 2040. In the latter alternative scenario, however, industrial energy consumption would outpace growth and the necessary capacity to respond to demand with reasonable margins would reach currently installed capacity in electricity generation by 2029. As a result, Paraguay has developed a National Energy Policy (adopted by Decree 6092/2016) which contemplates further development of hydroelectric energy alongside the development of other sources of energy as well as actions to improve energy efficiency, accelerate the replacement of other sources by electricity and improve electrical integration.

The Paraguayan government has acted to improve the regulatory framework in this area. In June 2015, the National Congress voted on a biofuel law (Law 5444/15 for the consumption promotion of absolute [99% pure] and alcohol-based fuel), decreeing that all fuels in the country should contain a minimum threshold of bio-fuel extracted from renewable and sustainable resources (VMME, 2017). The Ministry of Agriculture accompanies the implementation of the law with technical assistance in the production of sugar cane and corn for alcohol. To increase energy-generation capacity in some areas other than the two large hydroelectric projects of Itaipú and Yacyretá, the government has started to promote the construction of mini-hydroelectric plants. In 2015, the government, with the national council for the production and independent transportation of electric power, started approving the construction of ten small hydroelectric plants with an investment of USD 60 million for the first project.

With rapid environmental degradation and access to abundant clean hydropower energy, Paraguay could be at the forefront of environmental policy in the region, promoting renewable energy, building an energy-efficient technology, and improving energy utilisation in transport, among other areas. Paraguay enjoys low GHG and CO_2 emissions, thanks to clean electricity production from hydropower. However, only 29% of total energy consumption comes from this clean electricity, the bulk coming from fuel and biomass. Transport, which accounts for nearly 90% of Paraguay's GHG emissions, is one area where improvements could be introduced. The country could consider gradually increasing projects based on electricity-based systems (Sauer et al., 2015). This could include, for example, updating the bus fleet, one of the main sources of pollution in urban areas. A purchase of electric buses could not only reduce air emissions but also transport costs. Another approach consists in reducing biomass consumption, which represents a high share of Paraguay's total energy consumption (Blanco et al, 2017). The industrial sector is the main user of biomass, particularly in the areas of grains, cassava and starch production, as well as dairy production. Biomass consumption for household consumption is also high, particularly for cooking and heating purposes. Low wood costs partially explain the bias towards biomass consumption (Maennling and Todelano, 2013).

Conservation and biodiversity

Agriculture and the environment: Establishing the linkages

Paraguay is among the largest producers of soybeans and among the ten largest exporters of beef worldwide. By 2014, soybean and meat production constituted 25% of GDP and accounted for 65% of exports. In 2014, the country ranked as the sixth largest world producer and fourth largest exporter of soybeans.[3] Within Latin America, Paraguay is classified as third in soybean production levels, after Brazil and Argentina. The country's area for soybean and meat production has considerably extended in recent years. While the consolidation of the agriculture and livestock sector has driven the economy in recent years, it has also underlined the increasing pressure on natural resources. Yields in Paraguay are comparable to those of other countries in the world and, partly because of the use of direct seeding, the country has one of the highest production yields in the world (Figure 4.13). Over the last two decades, the area dedicated to soybean production has increased 5.7 times, while production increased ninefold (WWF, 2016). Indeed, yields of crops in Paraguay are comparable to those of benchmark countries, and have increased at equal rates. In the Eastern Region in particular, the area dedicated to soybean planting has increased considerably, almost tripling over the last 20 years. In the Western Region, the ranching industry has taken the lead and has increased its production area by 43%. The surface area of production of both soybeans and meat is expected to increase over the next few years, which puts considerable pressure on the conservation of forest areas.

Figure 4.13. **Yield of cereal crops by year**

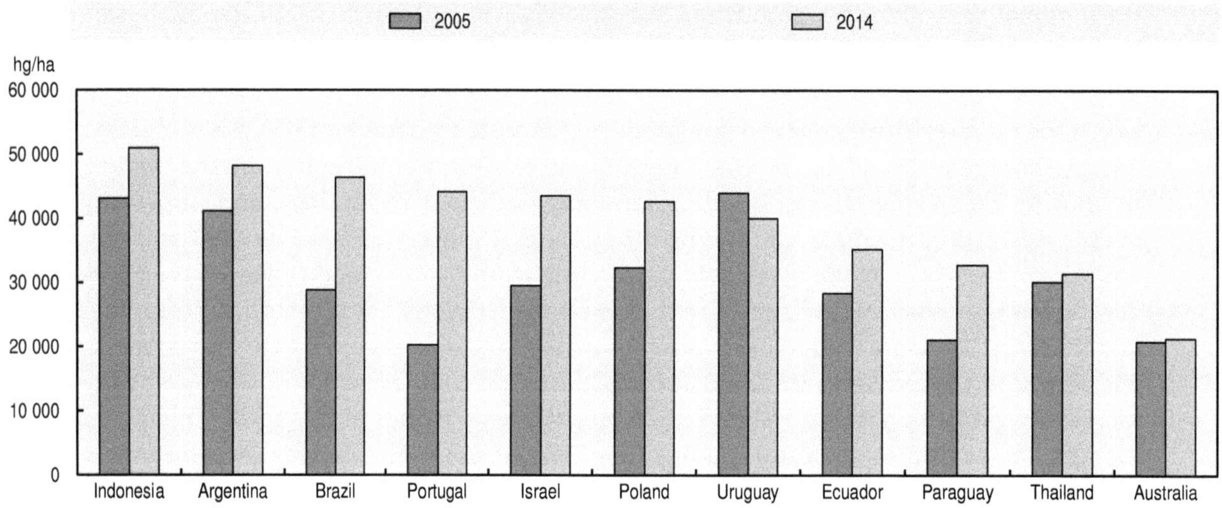

Source: Food and Agriculture Organization of the United Nations (FAO), 2017.

StatLink http://dx.doi.org/10.1787/888933750263

Deforestation in Paraguay has become an issue of growing concern for the authorities in recent years. Between 2005 and 2015, the drop in the percentage of forest land area in the country is estimated to have been over 17% (FAO, 2015). Other estimates, which include increasing levels of illegal deforestation, are more pessimistic. This figure is well beyond the rate observed in some of its regional peers, such as Brazil and Ecuador (Figure 4.15, Panel A). Moreover, the average annual deforestation rate was estimated at 1.39% in 2015 (Figure 4.15, Panel B). This represents the highest deforestation rate among the countries analysed (World Bank, 2017). The FAO's 2015 Global Forest Resources Assessment analyses the ongoing trends on forest preservation and highlights Paraguay as the country with the third greatest annual net loss of forest area between 2010 and 2015, surpassed only by Nigeria and Zimbabwe (FAO, 2016). Yet, Paraguay's use of land for agriculture remains within the average of the benchmark countries (Figure 4.15, Panel C). Important policy lessons could be drawn from the experience of other countries on a strategy to control deforestation (see Box 4.2).

Figure 4.14. **Losses in forest area and increases in soy production by region (in hectares)**

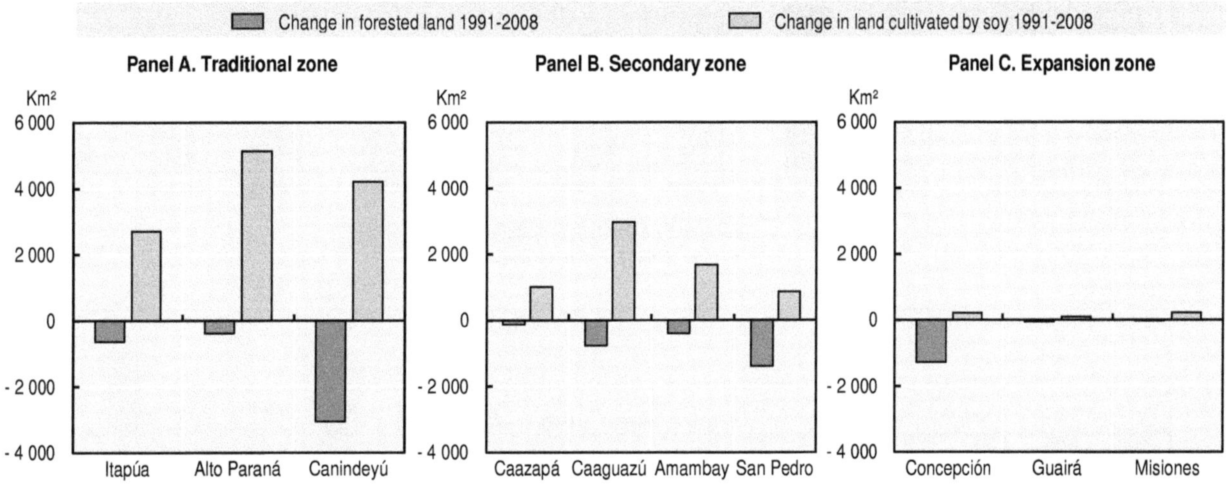

Note: Traditional zones include the departments of Itapúa, Alto Paraná and Canindeyú, which historically have had the largest amount of soybean production. Secondary zones include San Pedro, Caaguazú, Amambay and Caazapá, where soybean production exists but on a smaller scale. Expansion zones include Concepción, Guairá, and Misiones, where soybean production is gaining land surface area.

Source: WWF (2016) based on National Agriculture Census (CAN).

StatLink http://dx.doi.org/10.1787/888933750282

Deforestation processes in Paraguay have been relatively recent, starting during the late 20th century, first with intense logging of hardwood, and later conversion of forests to croplands or pasture. Nowadays, soybean cultivation (particularly in the Eastern Region), with around 3 million hectares devoted to its cultivation (WWF, 2014a), and to lesser extent cattle ranching, have been the main drivers of deforestation, as the global demand for commodities such as meat and soybeans continues to grow. Until 2003, the expansion of the soybean and cattle industry was accompanied by intense deforestation, reaching rates of approximately 300 000 hectares a year. In 2004, with the enactment of the "Zero Deforestation Law" (Law 2524/04), deforestation rates decreased significantly (see Box 4.1).

Cattle ranching and the meat industry in Paraguay

Together with the development of agriculture, Paraguay's meat industry is today one of the most dynamic sectors of the economy. In 2012, the country ranked as the world's ninth largest beef exporter, accounting for 3% of total beef exports. However, while the total number of cattle increased between 1991 and 2008, there was a simultaneous decrease in the number of farms in the industry. In the Eastern Region, the total area devoted to ranching fell by 2.7%. However, within zones there seems to be mixed evidence, with some departments increasing the total amount of land used for cattle ranching and others reducing it. In the Western Region, where ranching is predominant, there was an increase of approximately 40% in land devoted to this activity (WWF, 2014).

Figure 4.15. **Forest area and annual deforestation rates in Paraguay**

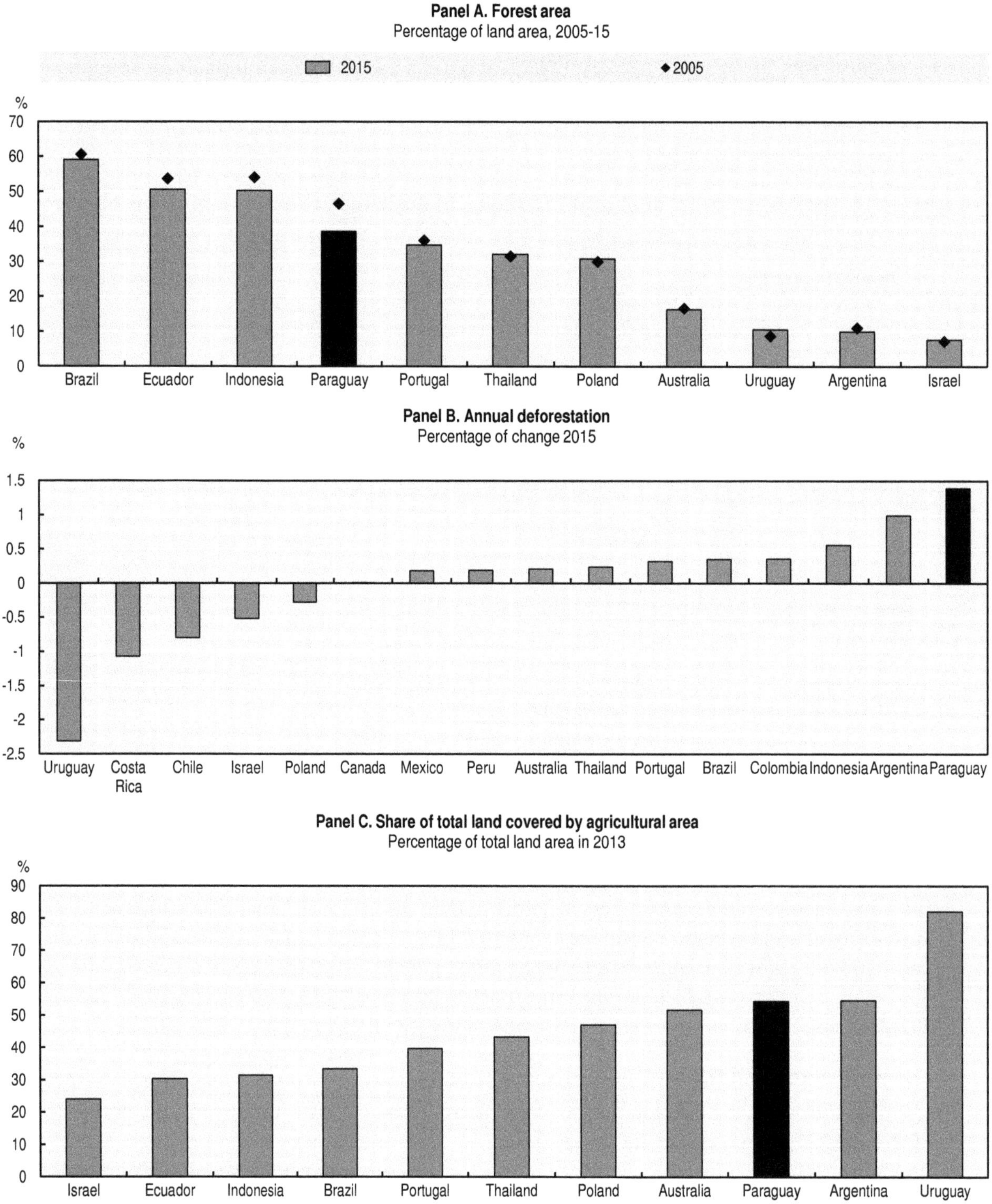

Source: World Bank (2017).

StatLink http://dx.doi.org/10.1787/888933750301

Box 4.1. **Paraguay's Zero Deforestation Law**

In 2004, Paraguay amended its policy on deforestation by approving in the senate a zero deforestation law in the Eastern Region of the country. The law established a temporary moratorium on native forest conversion to any other land use and is due to be in force until 2018. The law emphasises three aspects. First, it prohibits the transformation or conversion of lands with forest cover for agricultural use or the construction of human settlements. Second, it establishes the Secretariat of the Environment (SEAM) and the National Forestry Institute (INFONA) as the responsible parties for creating a baseline inventory of existing native forests. Third, it calls for an independent audit using geo-referenced technology to review land use plans.

The law has been credited with a significant slowdown in deforestation rates in Paraguay (close to 80% lower than the previous rate). Part of this achievement comes from a coalition and a platform for dialogue between the government, civil society representatives and the private sector.

Figure 4.16. **Land used for cattle ranching in Paraguay, by zones**

Areas in km^2

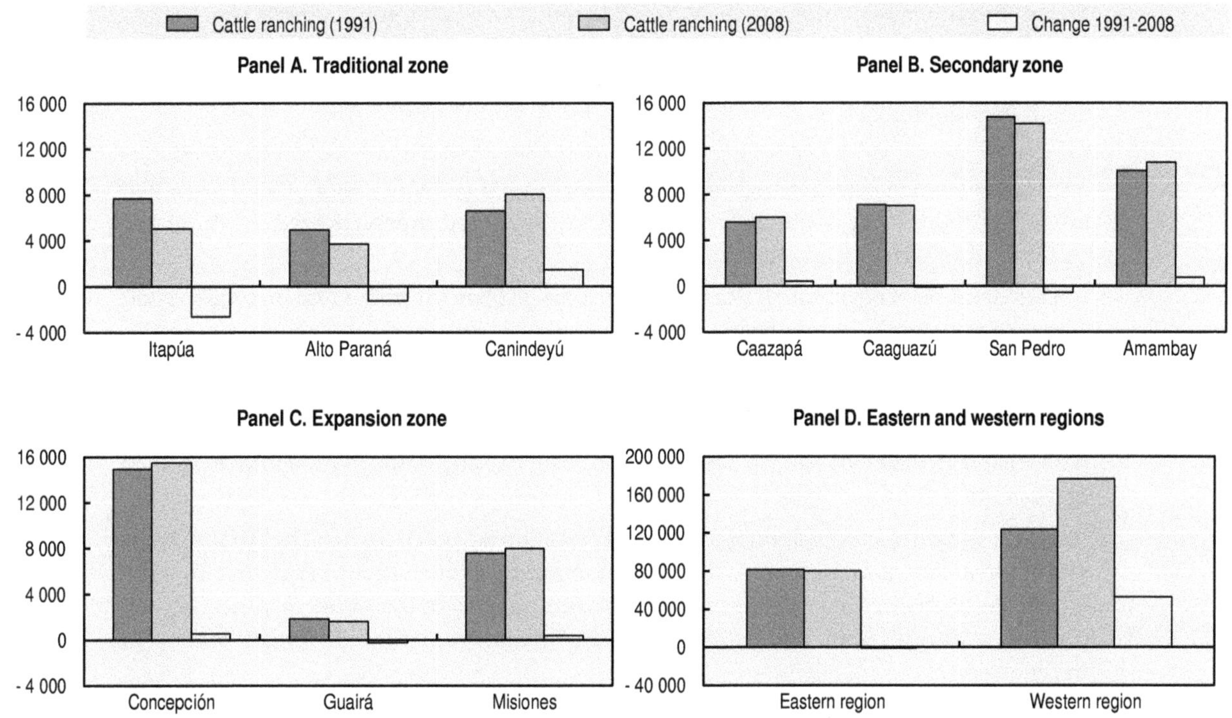

Note: Traditional zones include the departments of Itapúa, Alto Paraná and Canindeyú, which historically have had the largest amount of soybean production. Secondary zones include San Pedro, Caaguazú, Amambay and Caazapá, where soybean production exists but on a smaller scale. Expansion zones include Concepción, Guairá, and Misiones, where soybean production is gaining land surface area.

Source: WWF (2016) based on National Agriculture Census (CAN).

StatLink http://dx.doi.org/10.1787/888933750320

The change in the area devoted to ranching in the Eastern Region is partly accounted for by the expansion of soybean land surface. Nowadays, an increasing amount of soybean production is taking place in areas that had traditionally been used for ranching, as small livestock producers see the sale or rental of their land to soybean producers as a source of financing. Although, the volume of beef exports increased by over 294% between 2003 and 2014, the proportion of ranching in Paraguay's GDP remains at around 5%.

Box 4.2. **Reducing deforestation: The case of Brazil**

Between 2000 and 2013, Brazil managed to halt deforestation and reduce greenhouse gas emissions by over 40%, while increasing income per capita by approximately 30%. Moreover, in 2014, the annual deforestation rate in the Amazonia Legal region, comprising all nine states in the Amazon basin, was 75% below the average of the previous ten years. In view of this precedent, by 2020, Brazil is likely to overshoot its target of reducing deforestation in the region by 80% (OECD, 2015, OECD, 2016).

Brazil's progress is largely explained by the government's launching of an action plan for the prevention and control of deforestation in the Amazonia Legal (PPCDAm) in 2004. This initiative combined advanced monitoring systems, strengthened enforcement, credit restrictions, expansion of protected areas, and promotion of sustainable natural resource use. Additionally, the congress passed legislation such as the forest code, which requires landholders to set aside a share of their land for forest and soil conservation and restoration.

Determined implementation of the PPCDAm, together with wide support from civil society, the private sector, and the international community, led to significant policy changes that have resulted in a 75% decline in the annual deforestation rate of the Amazon. Some of these are highlighted below:

- Large increases in the number of protected areas. Since 2000, when Brazil established its national system of protected areas (SNUC), the number and surface of official protected areas has more than doubled. By March 2015, protected areas covered 17.2% of the country's terrestrial area and inland waters.
- Implementation of payment for ecosystem services (PES) programmes and income support schemes designed to compensate poor households in rural and forest communities for environmental conservation. Among these programs is Bolsa Verde, a federal programme providing payments for adoption of environmental practices and technical training to support beneficiaries in meeting their conservation commitments. It is seen as a potentially efficient way to curb deforestation, with low payments per hectare of avoided deforestation.
- Implementation of new technology and better monitoring practices have helped targeting and enforcement. Brazil is a world leader in monitoring deforestation via satellite imaging, which has been a crucial factor in reducing forest clearing in the Amazon. A nearly real-time monitoring system alerts authorities if deforestation and forest degradation occur in the region.
- Increased international development co-operation funds. Funding from international and bilateral co-operation has helped finance the PPCDA and other biodiversity-related programmes and has added implementation capacity to the government machine.
- Increased public investment in environmental-relevant infrastructure. In 2014, 15% of lending by the Brazilian Development Bank was environment-related. This, and other sources of funding and support, has contributed to Brazil's rank as the seventh largest investor in renewable energy

To make up for forest lost in the past, the country has made efforts to increase preservation areas and the amount of land with guaranteed protection status. In 2000 only 3% of forest area in Paraguay was classified as protected. In 2015 the protected area had increased by 162%. This increase was mostly concentrated in the Atlantic Forest. However, by 2015 the proportion of original forest area protected in Paraguay (below 5%) was still lower than in most benchmark countries (Figure 4.17). Another government initiative to address environmental concerns is embodied in the Law No. 3001-06a, which provides a compensation mechanism for environmental damage and serves as a complement to a previous law for the "rational management of forest lands", which had established that all rural landholders must preserve at least 25% of their property as forests (Box 4.3). The law's main objective is to promote conservation, protection, and recovery of the country's natural resources through a fair valuation and retribution of "environmental services".[4] It aims to achieve this through creating a market for environmental services certificates. The certificates must be purchased by all agents who are mandated by law to invest in environmental services, and may be traded in the international market for the payment of compensation associated with environmental damage, or used as compensation for local taxes. In this sense, the law establishes that all activities classified as having a high impact on the environment must include in their investment scheme compensation for environmental services through the purchase of environmental services certificates. The investment in environmental services of these projects must not be smaller than the 1% of the total cost of the project. However, in 2013, seven years after the law was established, an audit revealed that the Secretariat of the Environment (SEAM), the main authority in charge of the law's application, had been "irregular" in its performance in fulfilling its assigned "commitments, responsibilities, functions and attribution".

Figure 4.17. **Terrestrial protected areas (percentage of total land area)**

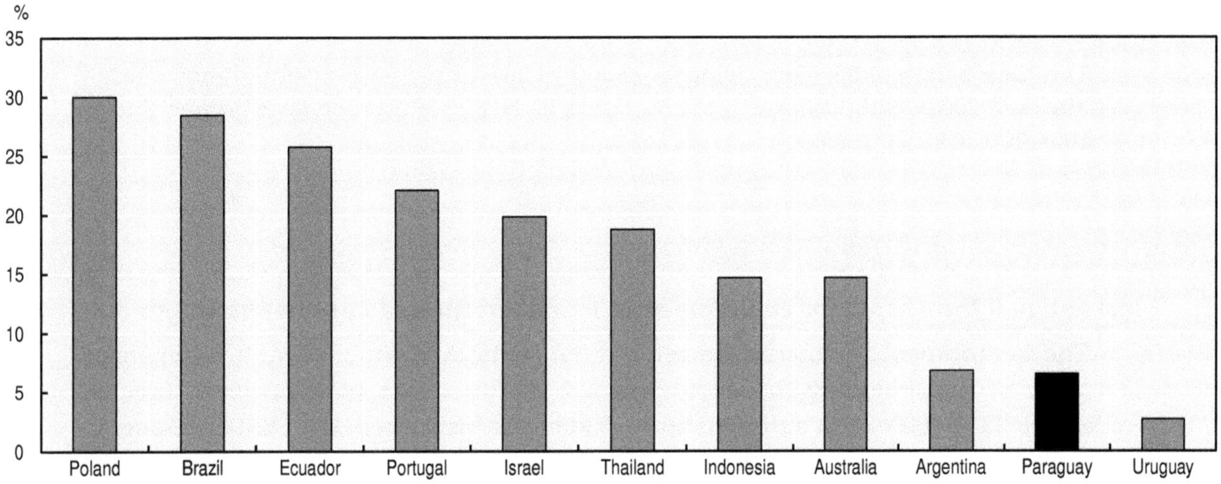

Source: World Development Indicators (2017).

StatLink http://dx.doi.org/10.1787/888933750339

Improving biodiversity outcomes

Paraguay has played host to a wide variety of wildlife in recent years, and biodiversity is at the core of the environmental concerns for the country. Located in the centre of La Plata basin, the environmental division of the country is the perfect habitat for 35 000 animal species. The Chaco region is especially important for these species. Comprising several habitats such as the savannahs and the thorn forest, this geographic zone has the biggest number of such wildlife (WWF, 2017b). However, there is a growing demand for agricultural products such as soya, beef and foods related to biofuels, and the number of companies exploiting this region is constantly growing, threating these unique habitats (WLT, 2017). The Chaco-Pantanal transition zone is under threat of being drained, polluted and even lost through the spread of agriculture.

Box 4.3. **Using payments for environmental services: The case of Costa Rica**

Costa Rica is a pioneer in the use of payments for environmental services. The country's compensation system aims to incentivise preservation and to remunerate agents for their provision of environmental services. Unlike in Paraguay, the system does not involve the use of certificates, but consists of simple direct payments managed though different programmes for a set of activities that are classified in the "environmental services" category. The initiative consists of four main programmes: i) the programme of recognition of environmental benefits consists of a direct payment to small and medium-scale producers for the use of "green or living" fences and terraces, and for soil condition improvement; ii) the basin management programme, managed by the Costa Rican Electricity Institute (ICE), provides electricity supplies and material to farmers who develop activities that ensure the sustainable use of natural, social and economic resources under an integrated and participatory approach; iii) the environmental services payment (PSA) programme provides financial recognition to farmers for environmental services which include a direct payment for the planting of individual trees, and an annual compensation per hectare of land earmarked for conservation or agroforestry, the programme being financed through the National Forestry Financing Fund (FONAFIFO) and implemented by the Ministry of Environment and Energy (MINAE); iv) the recognition of environmental benefits for organic production (RBAO), a direct payment to organic producers for a maximum period of three years.

The PSA is partly credited for helping the country achieve negative net deforestation rates in the early 2000s, after having one of the world's highest deforestation rates (Pagiola and Platais, 2016; OECD, 2017b).

Environmental capabilities in Paraguay

Institutional framework for environmental management and current challenges

The Environment Secretariat (Secretariat del Medio Ambiente – SEAM) is the entity in charge of implementing the environmental norms at the national level. Created under Law 1561/2000 as an autonomous and autarkic institution, the SEAM became an autonomous body from the Ministry of Agriculture. It is responsible for assessing the environmental impact on the national territory, assessing the effect of future crops, granting environmental licences and permits, managing wetlands and reinforcing the implementation of environment-related laws (such as climate change regulation). Not being a separate ministry, as is the case in other countries in the region, the secretariat faces today challenges in terms of visibility and resources. On the other hand, the INFONA (Instituto Forestal Nacional) is the enforcement authority of forestry law, responsible for managing forest areas and keeping control of the national forest reserves. Created under

Law 3464/2008 as an autonomous and autarkic institution, it is a decentralised entity with administrative autonomy that succeeded the Servicio Forestal Nacional (SFN), an agency under the Ministry of Agriculture. INFONA is also responsible for changes in land use.

The institutional framework for agriculture development faces challenges in terms of financing, institutional co-ordination and product prioritisation. There are considerable gaps in resources and productivity between the "dynamic" agro-business sector (concentrated in soy, wheat and meat) and the subsistence agriculture sector that occupies a large part of the rural population. For the latter, the Ministry of Agriculture is responsible for enhancing the competitiveness of small and medium-sized producers through technical assistance and direct support for investment. While the Ministry of Public Works is in charge of developing road infrastructure in rural areas, the Ministry of Agriculture provides assistance for facilitating business initiatives. On the financial side, budget implementation is limited and reflects high levels of inefficiency. Also, monitoring mechanisms for the management of agricultural resources are non-existent. There is not, for instance, a statistical office tracking information for the agriculture sector. Capacity-building among public servants is another area where the Ministry of Agriculture could develop further. On the institutional side, proposed legislation was recently submitted to parliament for improving the co-ordination mechanisms between the ministry and other agencies in the sector.

There are considerable needs in terms of environmental protection that are not being met. The secretariat lacks the staff (it only has 400 employees for the whole territory) and the institutional capacity to ensure its functions are carried out. In terms of budget, the secretariat also has limited resources to implement its mandate. Nearly 60% of resources come from fines and licences, and the remaining 40% from the central budget. Local authorities do not have the capacity to provide environmental protection. In spite of the need to decentralise environmental control activities, there are neither the capacity nor the resources within municipalities to take responsibility.

Initiatives on education have played a significant role in updating Paraguay's human capital stock in the farming sector. Together with direct support instruments towards subsistence agriculture, some efforts for improving capacity-building programmes in the agriculture and livestock sector are remarkable. The *Dirección de Educación agropecuaria* (farming and ranching) has been instrumental in developing new curricula and introducing innovations in the sector. However, a more global vision of the *escuelas agropecuarias* is still needed, that really addresses the provision of skilled labour in the sector and develops entrepreneurial capacity. Progress has been made in integrating higher education and universities into Paraguay's agriculture sector. Research by universities in the sector has increased, and the creation of several research centres such aseptic (Paraguayan Institute of Agricultural Technology), Centro de Ganaderos para Experimentación Agropecuaria (CEA), and Ibio (Instituto de Biotecnología Agrícola) (from the private sector), with the support of the national council of science and technology (CONACYT) have contributed to strengthening public and private research programmes in this sector. Still, research and innovation are concentrated on soy, wheat and livestock, and today few resources are devoted to other products where family agriculture could expand. The national directorate for agriculture has also been instrumental in supporting a new vision for agriculture schools, and integrating an entrepreneurship approach into secondary schooling.

Box 4.4. **Paraguay's multilateral agenda in agriculture**

Paraguay has engaged actively in the multilateral arena to adhere to different standards in the agriculture sector. In the area of sanitary and phytosanitary measures, a National Technical Committee was created in 2005 (6626/05 decree) to adopt WTO standards related to the sector. These are co-ordinated by mainly by SENAVE (for seeds and vegetables) and SENACSA (animal). Through MERCOSUR, Paraguay has also adhered to good practices for imports of pork, canines and felines. Paraguay has also made significant efforts to establish accreditation programmes for professions related to agriculture and livestock activities (e.g. veterinaries).

In relation to OECD, Paraguay has adhered to a number of Council recommendations on Trade and Agriculture. Some OECD recommendations have been adopted while others are currently under review.

Below a short description of the decisions where Paraguay currently participates:

C(2007)69. The OECD scheme for the Certification of Forest Reproductive Material. This scheme aims to encourage the production and use of forest tree seeds or plants that have been collected, processed, raised, labelled and distributed in a manner that ensures their "trueness to name". This material is intended for use in a variety of forestry functions, including timber production, soil protection and environmental criteria. *http://www.oecd.org/tad/code/forestreproductivematerial.htm*.

C(2006)95. Scheme for the application of international standards for fruits and vegetables. The scheme promotes international trade through the harmonisation of implementation and interpretation of marketing standards. *http://www.oecd.org/agriculture/fruit-vegetables/*.

C(2005)1. Decision of the Council revising the OECD standard codes for the Official testing of agricultural and forestry tractors. The decision aims to facilitate trade by enabling either an exporting or an importing country to accept with confidence the results of tests carried out in another country. *http://acts.oecd.org/Instruments/ShowInstrumentView.aspx?InstrumentID=217&Lang=en&Book=False*.

C(2000)146/FINAL. OECD schemes for the varietal certification of the control of seed moving in international trade.

Paraguay subscribes also to well-established recommendations of the OECD Council concerning the role of agriculture in the planning and management of peri-urban areas (C(1979)18/FINAL), the standardisation of packaging for the international transport of fresh or refrigerated fruit and vegetables (C(1976)124/FINAL) and the labelling and identification of fresh fruit and vegetables (C(1972)100/FINAL).

Waste management

The proportion of Paraguay's population with access to waste collection services is low when compared to other countries in the region. With a large number of people living in urban areas, waste collection and management have become major issues of responsibility for municipal administrations. Inappropriate waste management is associated with falling health outcomes and diseases including dengue fever, leptospirosis and breathing difficulties. The coverage of waste management services in Paraguay (57% of the population) is considerably lower than the regional average of 93% (PAHO/AIDIS/BID, 2010). In addition, close to 50% of solid waste final disposal sites are open-air dumps with all the sanitation and environmental risks that they represent, the remainder being considered controlled (PAHO/AIDIS/IDB, 2010).

Figure 4.18. **Waste collection coverage percentage, 2010**

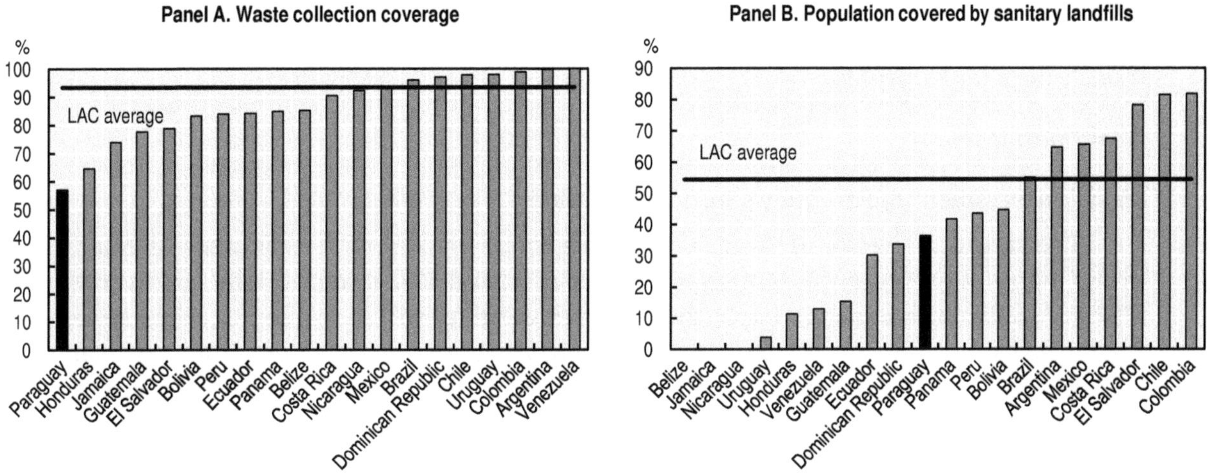

Source: PAHO/AIDIS/IBD (2010).

StatLink http://dx.doi.org/10.1787/888933750358

Resources devoted to waste management are low. In Paraguay, 56% of the services are municipal, 36% are private and 8% of municipalities have both municipal and private services. In 2010 only 19% of municipalities had a proper waste management plan, compared to 57% in Peru and Costa Rica or 74% in Uruguay and Argentina (PAHO/AIDIS/IDB, 2010). In addition, the level of human resources in municipalities dedicated to waste collection and management (3.1 employees per 10 000 inhabitants) in Paraguay is low, compared to countries such as Brazil (7.48), Uruguay (4.7) and the Latin American average (5.6). The number of collection vehicles for waste management in Paraguay (1.49 vehicles per 10 000 inhabitants) is also lower than the regional average (3.96 vehicles per 10 000 inhabitants). The average amount of solid urban waste (i.e. *residuos sólidos urbanos* or RSU) generated in Paraguay is around 1.2 kilogrammes a day, varying between 0.5 and 1.5 kg/person/day. Hospital-related waste is collected with other RSU with some exceptions (such as Asunción). Currently, there is no registry of sewerages, or other studies about the management of solid waste. Difficulties in waste management in Paraguay are associated with the increase of the informal economy and the lack of co-ordination in planning at the national, subnational and municipal levels. As in other countries in the region, Paraguay's urbanisation process will increase municipal waste generation, thus access to waste collection services will become increasingly important. Fewer than 40% of the population are covered by sanitary landfills, where waste is isolated until it is safe, whereas coverage in Colombia and Chile is above 80%.

There is no equivalent of an extended producer responsibility system, like the one that operates in most OECD countries. This system requires manufacturers of hazardous waste (pesticides, batteries, tyres, fluorescent lamps and electronic devices) to recover these products at the end of their useful life. Paraguay lacks a real recycling infrastructure to separate waste collection. Recycling remains a very limited activity.

Environmental taxes

The country has implemented some measures on environmental taxes. The environmental services law ("ley de servicios ambientales" 3001) aims to provide a tax exemption for land used for reforestation. It also includes environmental certificates to be deductible from income tax. In practice, the implementation of the law is pending and the regulation is still non-existent (enforcement of the law is poor). Costa Rica has implemented an interesting model of environmental services that could serve as benchmark for Paraguay.

Risk management

A risk assessment of Paraguay's agriculture sector

The agriculture sector in Paraguay accounts for nearly 20% of the country's GDP and more than 40% of its exports. Moreover, it employs around 40% of the working population. Taken together, these factors imply that risk and volatility within the sector might have major economic and social implications. Paraguay has not been exempt from external shocks, including climatic phenomena, that have seriously affected the performance of the agriculture sector. While commercial agriculture has been expanding in terms of both surface and production during the past decade, the average yield per hectare in family farming has decreased. The productivity gap between commercial and family agriculture projects has grown. In the agricultural production process, soy, maize and wheat play key roles, accounting, on average, for 56%, 18%, and 12% respectively of the planted area between 2009 and 2012. Commercial agriculture has gradually moved away from cotton and sesame, given the fall in international prices for these commodities in recent years. From an employment perspective, cassava, beans, white maize, cotton, sesame, fruits and vegetables, are also important as they constitute the main farming crops in family agriculture and key staples within households' consumption baskets. Organic sesame production has also gained traction recently thanks to demand from Japan, and there could be an opportunity to develop a competitive value chain in the sector.

Soy and livestock production in Paraguay entails a number of environmental and economic risks, which need to be considered. First, production risks associated with grain production are mostly agro-climatic risks and diseases. For soy, the main sources of risk are droughts, which in past years have reduced the average yield. For others, such as maize and wheat, excess rainfall and early frosts also threaten yields and quality. Second, market risks, and in particular volatility in export prices (resulting from changes in production, seasonal variations and weather events) are relevant for soybean and maize production. Third, logistic risks in Paraguay exist, given the country is landlocked, which could include uncertainty in the supply of river barges for transport to ocean ports, variations in transport costs through using barges at different periods, and uncertainty related to poor infrastructure in production areas. Livestock production also carries a number of risks, related to droughts, floods and frosts. Droughts negatively affect the birth rate of cattle, as well as their weight and expected meat output. Floods are directly linked to animal death, weight loss, and costs associated with renting pastures and transporting animals. Health-related risks exist as well, affecting cattle, sheep and goats. Today, Paraguay is one of the main meat exporters globally, and the country is certified as free from foot-and-mouth disease and classic swine flu by the World Organization of Animal Health. Finally, environmental risks in the country's livestock industry are related to land invasion and cattle rustling.

Box 4.5. Improving the management of volatility in agriculture production: Economic and environmental costs

At the macroeconomic level, fluctuations in Paraguay's business cycle have been closely linked to changes in agriculture production. Drops in agricultural production (both for the domestic and foreign markets) can entail growth slowdowns and reduce tax collection. On average, losses associated with production risks are estimated to be around 5.4% of agriculture GDP, which represents half a percentage point of annual economic growth. These numbers become larger when accounting for livestock losses and the impact on family agriculture.

The impact of agriculture fluctuations can go beyond the primary sector and affect other parts of the supply chain. Farmers linked to soy, maize and rice production are the most affected by drought-related drops in yields, as their production and income decrease, and their capacity to repay debt and invest is reduced. Other actors in the supply chain, including processing, distribution, and commercialisation can face losses associated with reductions in activity.

For livestock production, the most substantial impact is associated with drought. Droughts lead to reductions in pasture, which affect production costs and profitability. At the farmers' level, severe droughts may lead to unsustainable levels of debt because of high financing and transaction costs, and the absence of the kind of long-term financing that would allow them to recover from these shocks.

Overall, part of the variation in production and losses faced by farmers and other actors along the supply chain can be explained through unavoidable, non-mitigated risks. These risks could be addressed through adequate farming practices, infrastructure investments, and accurate and timely information. Higher investment in R&D and better access to affordable insurance could also limit the negative impacts of the described risks.

Land management and administration

Paraguay faces a significant challenge in land management and administration, which is linked to the significant rural-to-urban migratory flows. In rural areas, the possibility that land granted via land reform can be sold illegally to large farmers limits the impact of the action of the national institute for rural development INDERT, responsible for implementing land reform and for rural development. Land reform works through INDERT buying, parcelling and granting land in "colonies". However, it has limited capacity to overcome the obstacles posed by lack of previous topographic measures and disrupted registry histories. As a result, only a small fraction of colonies have received property titles, with INDERT focusing instead on granting certificates of entitlement to farmers. Some measures have been recently introduced to reduce irregularities in land transfer. To prevent beneficiaries of the agrarian reform from selling their rights, Law 4682 of 2012 was introduced, forbidding selling or buying lots or fractions.

Land ownership in Paraguay is highly concentrated and has become more so in recent years. Between 1991 and 2008, almost 23 000 productive units disappeared within an area of 400 000 ha, almost half the size of government purchases for land reform purposes. In urban areas, the capacity of local governments to carry out adequate urban planning is limited. A large majority of municipalities do not have land use plans. Indeed, the land register has limited coverage even in several urban areas. As a result, urban development is unorganised, and the capacity of municipalities to collect property taxes (which should be a sizeable share of revenue) is reduced. However, some efforts are being made by the Cadastre, in particular to reduce the *double titling* phenomenon in land ownership, whereby the same piece of land has several "owners". Currently, while the country is made up of 400 000 km^2 of land, nearly 500 000 km^2 are registered.

Many deficiencies in land management come from the different governance structures responsible for it. In this respect municipalities have a crucial role in the procedure of land registration. However, a regulatory body that guides and supervises the municipalities' activities in this process is lacking. As in the case of some urban areas, municipalities lack the human resources and capacity to implement ordinances regarding land use. The National Planning Secretariat has made efforts to assist local governments with the development of municipal sustainable development plans. As municipalities depend largely on central government transfers, they could be further encouraged to use part of these resources to develop local capacity. Furthermore, beyond the fiscal incentive for municipalities to improve land registration, which would allow them to increase tax revenues, a territorial perspective for updating the land register is required. At the national level, the absence of proper legislation for land use planning renders difficult the implementation of a national strategy for land management. In the global context of the implementation of the New Urban Agenda, Paraguay has an opportunity to implement a territorial agenda for the development of cities and municipalities, under the principles of sustainability, inclusion and resilience.

Tackling the deficiencies in land management could be an important driver in reducing territorial inequalities between urban and rural areas. Having access to land title, financing resources, technological innovation, education, and basic and productive infrastructure can reduce vulnerability and increase resilience in the light of agricultural risks (Arce and Arias, 2015, De Waroux et al. 2016). Most farmers in Paraguay lack definite land title, exacerbating existing differences in income, and access to public services (education, health, and infrastructure) and technical assistance. Not having collateral, a lack of land title also translates into a lower access to financial markets. Integrating land management in Paraguay's development agenda will be a crucial component for guaranteeing social, economic and environmental sustainability.

Notes

1. The Secretariat of the Environment (SEAM) highlights the presence of pesticides in waterways, together with high levels of lead, chromium and mercury. Recent studies also point to the existence of glyphosate in crops.
2. Pollution havens are a major concern in Paraguay and could explain the high levels of deforestation and pollution in the Chaco region.
3. Global consumption of soybeans has been driven by European markets and China. More than 90% of global production came from six countries: Brazil, United States, Argentina, China and Paraguay. The main destinations for Paraguay's soybean exports are Russia, Germany, Mexico and Spain.
4. Under this law, "environmental services" are defined as services dedicated to the management, preservation, and recovery of the ecosystem's functions that directly or indirectly benefit "populations".

References

Arce, C. and D. Arias (2015), "Paraguay agricultural sector risk assessment: Identification, prioritisation, strategy and action plan", *World Bank Group Report*, No. 93943-PY, World Bank Group, Washington, DC.

Banco Central de Paraguay (BCP) (2017), *Boletín de Cuentas Nacionales*, *https://www.bcp.gov.py/boletin-de-cuentas-nacionales-anuales-i370*.

Blanco, G. et al. (2017), "Energy transitions and emerging economies: A multi-criteria analysis of policy options for hydropower surplus utilization in Paraguay", *Energy Policy*, 2017, *http://www.sciencedirect.com/science/article/pii/S0301421517303579*.

CAIT Climate Data Explorer database, World Resources Institute, *http://cait.wri.org/*.

Callisto, M. et al. (2013), "Eutrophication of lakes" in *Eutrophication: Causes, Consequences and Control*, Springer Netherlands, Dordrecht.

De Waroux, Y. et al. (2016), "Land-use policies and corporate investments in agriculture in the Gran Chaco and Chiquitano", *Proceedings of the National Academy of Sciences*, Vol. 113, No. 15, pp. 4021-4026.

DGEEC (2015a), Principales resultados de la Encuesta Permanente de Hogares, 2015 [*National Directorate of Statistics, Surveys and Census. Main Results from the Permanent Household Survey, 2015*], *http://www.dgeec.gov.py/Publicaciones/Biblioteca/resultado%20eph2015/PUBLICACIONES%20EPH%202015%2008-05-17.pdf*

DGEEC (2015b), Proyección de la Población Nacional, Áreas Urbana y Rural por Sexo y Edad, 2000-2025. Revisión 2015.

DGEEC (2012), Principales Resultados de la Encuesta Permanente de Hogares, 2012 [*National Directorate of Statistics, Surveys and Census. Main Results from the Permanent Household Survey, 2012*], *http://www.dgeec.gov.py/Publicaciones/Biblioteca/EPH2012/principales_resultados_EPH2012.pdf*.

DNRA (2017), Dirección Nacional de Registro de Automotores. Informe Estadístico, Asunción, *http://www.pj.gov.py/contenido/155-direccion-del-registro-de-automotores/1479*.

ECLAC (2016), *Desafíos de la seguridad Hídrica en América Latina y el Caribe*, Serie Recursos Naturales e Infrastructura, Economic Commission for Latin America and the Caribbean, Santiago, Chile.

Enerdata (2015), *Indicators on agriculture and fishing* (presentation), Taller de trabajo del Proyecto BIEE/Mesoamérica, Base de Indicadores de Eficiencia Energética, Unidad de Planeación Minero Energética, Bogotá.

FAO (2017), *Food and Agriculture Statistics* (database), Food and Agriculture Organization of the United Nations, Rome.

FAO (2016), *Global Forest Resources Assessment 2015: How are the World's Forests Changing?*, Food and Agriculture Organization of the United Nations, Rome, *http://www.fao.org/3/a-i4793e.pdf*.

FAOSTAT Emissions Database, *http://www.fao.org/faostat/en/#home*.

Fundación Bariloche (2015), "Elaboración de la Prospectiva Energética de la República de Paraguay 2013-2040" *[Development of Energy Foresight for the Republic of Paraguay 2013-2040]*, Itaipú Binacional, Fundación Parque Tecnológico Itaipú and Universidad Corporativa Itaipú, Asunción, November 2015.

GNESD (2015), "Access to energy services in Latin America and Caribbean: Lessons learned from the Paraguay case study", *Country Report Paraguay*, Global Network on Energy for Sustainable Development, Copenhagen.

López Arias T. et al. (2013), "Diagnóstico Ecotoicológico y genotóxico de los afluentes del lago Ypacarai, mediante bioensayos con Dahpnia magna straus, Danio reriom Lactuca sativa L y Allium cepa L.", Universidad Nacional de Asunción, Facultad de Ciencias Exactas y Naturales, Asunción.

Maennling, N. and P. Toledano (2013), "Leveraging Paraguay's hydropower for sustainable economic development", Vale Columbia Center on Sustainable International Investment, New York.

MOPC (2011), *Situación de Energías Renovables en el Paraguay*, Ministerio de Obras Públicas y Comunicaciones, Asunción.

MOPC/VMME (2013), *Producción y Consumo de Biomasa Sólida en Paraguay*, Ministerio de Obras Públicas y Cominicaciones, Viceministerio de Minas y Energías, Asunción.

OECD (2017a), *Green Growth Indicators*, OECD Publishing, Paris, *http://dx.doi.org/10.1787/9789264268586-en*.

OECD (2017b), *Agricultural Policies in Costa Rica*, OECD Publishing, Paris, *http://dx.doi.org/10.1787/9789264269125-en*

OECD (2016), *Evaluation Insights: Forests and Sustainable Forest Management*, OECD Publishing, Paris, *https://www.oecd.org/dac/evaluation/Evaluation-Insights-Forests-Final.pdf*.

OECD (2015), *OECD Environmental Performance Reviews: Brazil 2015*, OECD Publishing, Paris, *http://dx.doi.org/10.1787/9789264240094-en*.

OECD/IEA (2017), *World Energy Outlook 2017*, Paris, *http://www.iea.org/bookshop/750-World_Energy_Outlook_2017*.

OLADE (2017), Boletín Informativo de la Organisación Latinoamericana de Energía (OLADE), Julio.

Pagiola, S. and G. Platais (2016), "Payments for environmental services", *Environment Strategy Notes*, No. 3, World Bank Group, Washington, DC.

PAHO/AIDIS/BID (2010), *Informe de la Evaluación Regional del Manejo de Residuos Sólidos Urbanos en América Latina y el Caribe 2010*, Pan American Health Organization, Inter-American Association of Sanitary and Environmental Engineering (AIDIS), and Inter-American Development Bank, Washington, DC.

Sauer, I.L. et al. (2015), "Bolivia and Paraguay: a beacon for sustainable electric mobility?" *Renewable Sustainable Energy Reviews* 51, pp 910–925, Elsevier, *http://www.sciencedirect.com/science/article/pii/S1364032115006103*.

UNICEF/WHO (2013), *Ending Preventable Child Deaths from Pneumonia and Diarrhoea by 2025*, World Health Organization/The United Nations Children's Fund, Paris.

Viceministerio de Minas y Energía (2017), Reseña energética. Dirección de Recursos Energéticos. *http://www.ssme.gov.py/vmme/index.php?option=com_content&view=article&id=1213&Itemid=598*.

WHO (2017), *World Health Statistics* (database), World Health Organization, Geneva.

WHO (2015), MCEE-WHO methods and data sources for child causes of death 2000-2015, World Health Organisation and Maternal Child Epidemiology Estimation, Geneva. *http://www.who.int/healthinfo/global_burden_disease/ChildCOD_method_2000_2015.pdf*.

WHO (2011), *Air Quality Guidelines, Target Values, Standards and Objectives*, World Health Organization, Geneva.

Willaarts et al. (2014), "Seguridad Hídrica y Alimentaria en América Latina y el Caribe: Implicaciones regionales y globales", Fundación Botín, Cantabria.

WLT (2017), Saving the Paraguayan Wilderness (website), World Land Trust, Suffolk, United Kingdom, *http://www.worldlandtrust.org/projects/paraguay*.

World Bank (2017), *World Development Indicators* (database), World Bank Group, Washington DC.

WWF (2017a), *State of the Atlantic Forest*, World Wildlife Fund, Puerto Iguazú, Argentina.

WWF (2017b), Southern South America: Bolivia, Paraguay, and Argentina (website), Word Wildlife Fund, *https://www.worldwildlife.org/ecoregions/nt0210*.

WWF (2017c), Guardianes del Acuífero (website), World Wildlife Fund, *http://www.wwf.org.py/que_hacemos/proyectos/campana_acuifero_patino*.

WWF (2016), *Social, Economic and Environmental Analysis of Soybean and Meat production in Paraguay*, World Wildlife Fund, Asunción.

WWF (2014), *The Growth of Soy: Impacts and Solutions*, World Wildlife Fund, Gland, Switzerland.

WWF (2011), *Making a Pact to Tackle Deforestation in Paraguay*, World Wildlife Fund, *http://internationaltreefoundation.org/wp-content/uploads/2011/04/Paraguay-FINAL-30-march-2011.pdf*.

Multi-dimensional Review of Paraguay
Volume 1. Initial Assessment

Chapter 5

Paving the way to sustainable development, peace, justice and strong institutions in Paraguay

Strong institutions are essential to creating wealth and maintaining peace, order and security. In turn, good governance is fundamental to the legitimacy of institutions and to delivering high-quality goods and services to people. This chapter investigates aspects associated with good governance. It starts by analysing features of the Paraguayan democracy and the rule of law. It then looks at the public-sector integrity framework and existing strategies to fight corruption, followed by an assessment of the strategies to promote openness, which include transparency, citizen participation and accountability. Later, it describes the co-ordination mechanisms between different government institutions and levels. Subsequently it looks at the satisfaction with public services by socio-economic groups and if these differences could signal the lack of a differentiated response towards vulnerable groups. It ends by arguing that a solid basis of high-quality official statistics is required to support policy making and enhance transparency in Paraguay.

Government capacity in Paraguay is comparatively limited

A government is made up of accumulated institutional memory, a trained bureaucracy and sufficient financial resources to fulfil its tasks. In turn, governments are responsible for guaranteeing the fundamental rights required to maintain social order and peace and for delivering goods and services to citizens. While these goods and services could be delivered through several channels (e.g. direct provision or outsourcing) governments are ultimately accountable to citizens for their provision. Governments are also expected to adhere to high ethical standards, take account of people's views and allocate public resources efficiently.

As Paraguay speeds up the pace of its economic and social development, the size and expectations of the middle class are expected to increase and consequently so are the number and complexity of tasks requiring government intervention. Compared to Latin American and Caribbean (LAC) and Organisation for Economic Co-operation and Development (OECD) countries Paraguay has a relatively small government. In 2015, government expenditures reached 25% of GDP in the country compared to 34% in LAC countries and 45% in OECD countries. Consistently, the proportion of public employment as a share of total employment is relatively low, at 9.8%, when compared to LAC (12%) and OECD (21%) averages. While in recent years both proportions have increased, government capacity remains fairly limited and that will challenge its ability to respond rapidly and effectively to rising citizens' expectations and demands (Figure 5.1). Strategically planning the right mix of skills for the civil service in the years to come would help the government not only to meet strategic objectives, but also increase efficiency, responsiveness and quality in service delivery.

Figure 5.1. **Paraguay's government capacity remains comparatively limited**

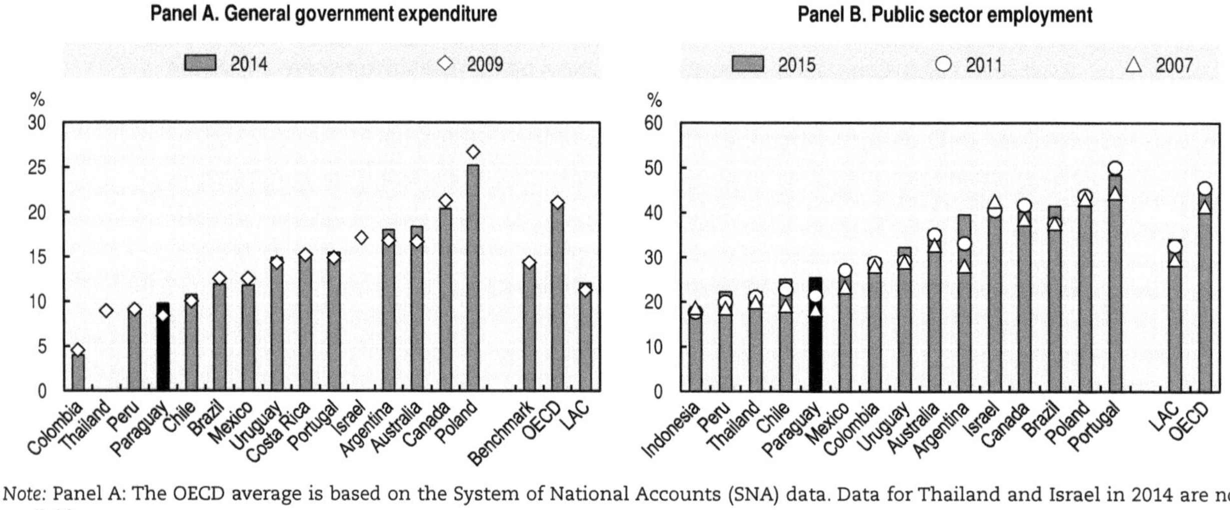

Note: Panel A: The OECD average is based on the System of National Accounts (SNA) data. Data for Thailand and Israel in 2014 are not available.

Source: Panel A: International Monetary Fund (2017), *World Economic Outlook* (database), *https://www.imf.org/external/pubs/ft/weo/2015/01/weodata/index.aspx*. Panel B: ILO (2017) ILOSTAT (database), *http://www.ilo.org/global/statistics-and-databases/lang--en/index.htm*.

StatLink http://dx.doi.org/10.1787/888933750377

Beyond the actual capacity of government, people's perception of government performance and integrity also matters. In particular, trust in government is one of the most important foundations upon which the legitimacy and sustainability of political systems are built. It influences government's ability to govern and enables it to act without resorting to coercion. High levels of trust are an efficient means of lowering transaction costs in any social, economic and political relationship (Fukuyama, 1995). While trust in government could be affected by a wide array of phenomena such as corruption scandals, government performance and approval of the incumbent government, consistently low levels of trust will impede the implementation of reform and lead to lower rates of compliance with rules and regulations (OECD 2013b). In 2016 only 28% of the Paraguayan population reported trusting the government, three percentage points lower than in 2006 (Figure 5.2). Maintaining and strengthening commitment to inclusiveness, transparency, responsiveness and efficiency on the part of government is required for increasing levels of institutional trust (OECD 2017a).

Figure 5.2. **Percentage of population reporting confidence in the national government**

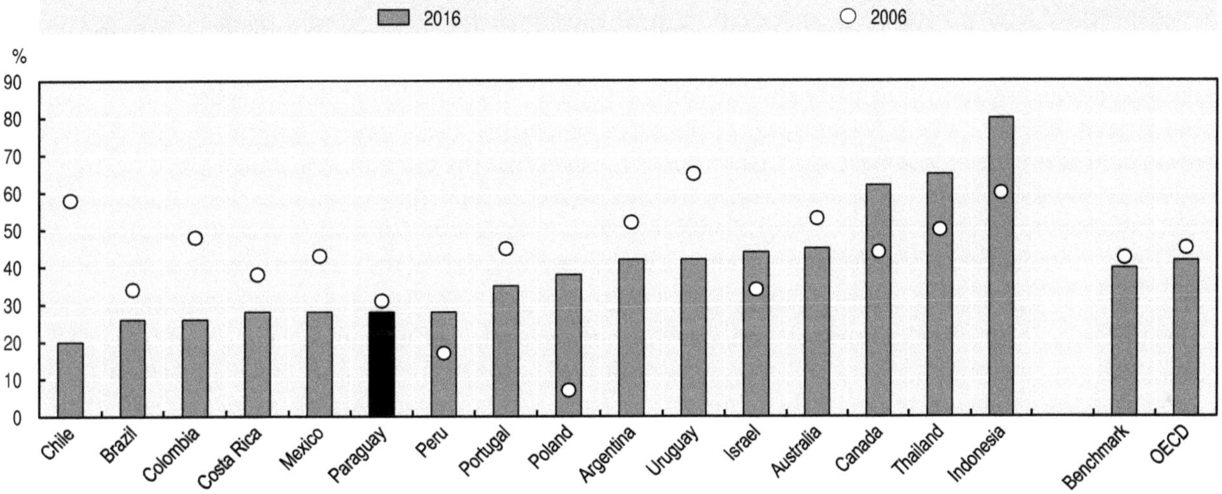

Source: Gallup (2017), Gallup World Poll (database).

StatLink http://dx.doi.org/10.1787/888933750396

Developing strong institutions is key for achieving sustainable development

The Paraguayan democracy is consolidating

Setting out its vision for Paraguay in 2030, the National Development Plan (NDP) envisages the country as a "democratic, supportive state, subsidiary, transparent and geared towards the provision of equal opportunities." The NDP also recognises the advances that have been made since the return of democracy in 1992 to protect fundamental rights and consolidate democratic institutions (NDP, pp. 37). Both the 1992 constitution and the 1996 electoral code include the set of rights and duties (e.g. voting, press freedom, freedom of expression, freedom of association, voting rights) traditionally associated with democracy. Yet the consolidation of democracy has been a convoluted process (Box 5.1), punctuated by attempts to overthrow the government in office, *coups d'état*, murders of political leaders, irregular and contested elections and political impeachments. As such Paraguay is considered to be in the consolidation phase of its democracy and some scholars have even categorised it as a low-quality democracy (Barreda and Bou, 2010).

Box 5.1. **Towards the consolidation of democracy, a convoluted process**

Between 1954 and 1989, Paraguay was a dictatorship led by General Alfredo Stroessner, with the state under the control of Stroessner's Colorado party and the armed forces (Abente Brun, 2011). In 1989, Stroessner was overthrown in a military coup led by General Andrés Rodriguez, who allied himself with the political opposition on an agenda to liberalise the economy and, crucially, to reform the 1967 constitution. In elections held shortly after the coup, the Colorado party (now headed by General Rodriguez) was elected to complete the 1988-1993 term. During this period, in 1991, the first municipal elections to appoint mayors *(intendentes)* took place. Compared to the earlier presidential elections where it obtained around 20% of votes, the Partido Liberal Radical Autentico (PLRA) won 34% of the vote consolidating its position as the main opposition force.

During 1991, elections of representatives to the constitutional assembly were called; the Colorado party obtained a significant majority of 55.1% of the vote. The constitutional assembly opted for a model of a weak executive and a strong parliament (Abente Brun, 2011). General Rodríguez exerted some pressure to include an article allowing his possible re-election; but ultimately, a clause was included in the constitution forbidding presidential re-election. Following the promulgation of the constitution in 1992 elections were called for 1993.

In the 1993 elections the Colorado party faced internal disputes to select its candidate between Juan Carlos Wasmosy (representative of the reformist wing of the party) and Luis María Argaña (representing more traditional sectors of the party and including several of Stroessner's traditional supporters). Following the internal election, where Wasmosy was selected as candidate, allegations of fraud were raised (several years later members of Wasmosy's campaign acknowledged that the election was actually won by Argaña). Subsequently, the national election was won by Wasmosy but once more the electoral process was disorganised and contested to the point where former US president Jimmy Carter who was invited to verify the process met the three candidates to obtain assurances that the problems faced during the election would not be repeated.

For the 1998 elections, the internal election of the Colorado party was again convoluted, General Lino Oviedo, who had led a failed *coup d'état* against President Wasmosy was selected as candidate but shortly after sent to jail by the military courts and his condemnation was ratified by the Supreme Court. From jail, General Oviedo supported the candidacy of Raúl Cubas Grau as president and Luis María Argaña as vice-president. With 54% of votes Cubas was elected president in 1998 and shortly after commuted Oviedo's sentence, starting a legal battle between the government and the Supreme Court. The murder of Vice-President Argaña created further instability leading to both Cubas and Oviedo leaving the country. Luis González Macchi, the president of the congress, was then appointed president; yet, according to the constitution it was necessary to call elections to replace the vice-president. Following the 1999 election Julio César Franco, from the opposition party PLRA, was elected vice-president, thereby eroding the legitimacy of González Macchi as head of the government, though he was able to finish his term.

In spite of the reorganisation of the political opposition the Colorado party maintained its hegemony and in 2003 Nicanor Duarte Frutos was elected president and ran a relatively stable government. However, in 2007 President Duarte began efforts to change the constitution to allow his re-election leading to massive popular demonstrations that forced the government to pull back on its efforts to institute re-election.

In 2008 former bishop Fernando Lugo, representing a coalition of opposition parties, was elected president breaking a hegemonic party regime that had lasted 61 years. However, in 2012, following a confrontation between peasants and the police, president Lugo was impeached by the parliament and replaced by vice-president Federico Franco to end his presidential period.

In 2013 new statutory elections took place and Horacio Cartes Jara from the Colorado Party was elected president. In turn, recent attempts to reform the constitution in favour of the possibility of the re-election of Cartes and Lugo resulted in violent demonstrations leading to the takeover of the parliament by demonstrators in March 2017.

Source: Authors.

A core characteristic of a solid democracy is the organisation of periodic elections that should be free and fair. In this context the OECD recognises the right of people to express their political voice as a fundamental component for enhancing well-being (OECD 2013a; OECD 2015). The analysis of data coming from a variety of sources sheds light on some key features of the Paraguayan democracy.

Figure 5.3 Panel A displays the turnout at presidential elections since the 1990s extracted from the Institute for Democracy and Electoral Assistance (IDEA) dataset. Elections took place in Paraguay even during the dictatorship; however, elections occurring under the Stroessner regime were fraudulent and opposition parties had neither guarantees of impartiality nor a real option of accessing power (Nickson, 2010). Consequently, voter turnout data in Paraguay are only considered reliable since the 1998 election when in addition to being conducted according to democratic rules the electoral lists were updated (Figure 5.3, Panel A). In the presidential election of 1998 the participation rate reached 80%, one of the highest for countries in the region over the period 1996-2000. Participation decreased for the subsequent two elections reaching its lowest point (60.3%) in 2008 and bouncing back to 68% in 2013 (though still below the level reached in 1998). Scholars have documented abstention in Paraguay as a phenomenon affecting mainly the young and rural populations (López, 2014).

Figure 5.3. **Voter turnout at national elections is stable but satisfaction with democracy remains at low levels**

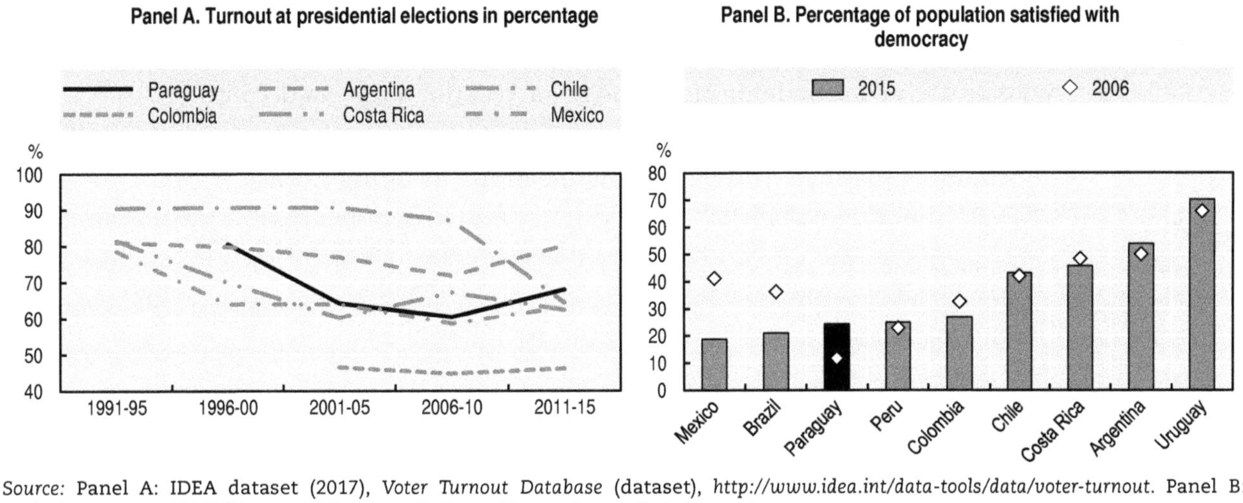

Source: Panel A: IDEA dataset (2017), *Voter Turnout Database* (dataset), *http://www.idea.int/data-tools/data/voter-turnout*. Panel B: Latinobarometro (2015), "Datos 2015", Banco de Datos (dataset), *www.latinobarometro.org*.

StatLink http://dx.doi.org/10.1787/888933750415

Compared to other countries in the region turnout at presidential elections is not particularly low in Paraguay. However, democracy goes beyond elections. Moreover, the meaningfulness of competitive elections depends on additional conditions such as their freedom and fairness, the existence of freedom of expression, reliability of the media, association rights, existence of opposition parties that are free to criticise, rights for minorities, and equal treatment by the justice system. Scholars have associated these components with a liberal conception of democracy.

According to Ferrín (2016), who has done an extensive analysis for European countries, a survey question about the satisfaction with democracy provides a reliable summary measure of respondents' assessments of how well the liberal[1] elements of democracy work. According to the latest available data from the Latinobarómetro, less than one quarter of Paraguayan citizens are satisfied with how democracy works in their country, the third lowest of LAC countries in the benchmark group (Figure 5.3, Panel B). Nevertheless, between 2006 and 2015, satisfaction with democracy increased by 12.6 percentage points in Paraguay, the largest increase in the benchmark LAC countries, thereby signalling a certain degree of resilience by democratic institutions in a period punctuated by several episodes of political instability (see Box 5.1).

Yet challenges still lie ahead for the consolidation of democratic institutions. When asked whether they agree with a number of statements about democracy, fewer than half of Paraguayans consider that democracy is preferable to any other form of government, the lowest in LAC countries of the benchmark group. More worrying is the fact that 37% of the population consider that in some circumstances an authoritarian government is preferable to a constitutional one, shedding light on the positive views of some sectors of the population about having an authoritarian government in office (see Figure 5.4, Panel A). In turn, less than 20% of the population consider elections to be honest a share that has declined since 2006 (see Figure 5.4, Panel B).

Unlike other countries in the southern cone (i.e. Argentina and Chile) where transition to democracy occurred in the framework of a breakdown of the population with the ruling elite and a democratic or military defeat of the armed forces, in Paraguay the process was led by the army itself and segments of the ruling elite remained in office. In other words, while elections represented the beginning of the transition in Paraguay (see Box 5.1) they were the end of it in Chile and Argentina (Juárez, 2015). Further promoting political participation and ensuring the effective application of democratic values such as the reliability and diversity of media and the consolidation and respect of opposition parties is essential for ensuring human rights as well as maintaining peace and social order in the years to come.

Figure 5.4. **Percentage of the population considering that an authoritarian government could be justified and perceiving elections as being honest**

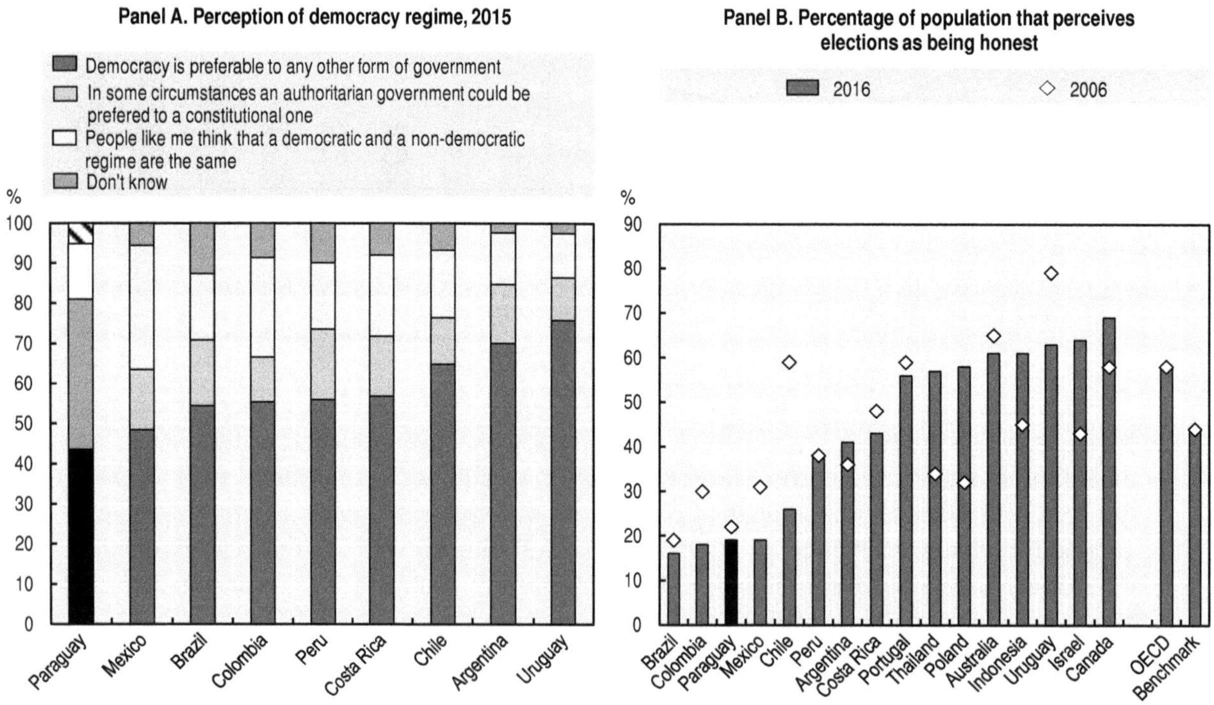

Source: Panel A: Latinobarometro (2015), "Datos 2015", Banco de Datos (dataset), *www.latinobarometro.org*. Panel B: Gallup (2017), Gallup World Poll (database).

StatLink http://dx.doi.org/10.1787/888933750434

Finally, while voting is certainly the most popular means through which individuals "control" the appointment of government officials, there are other ways that allow individuals to influence government officials, their political choices and the political system (Boarini and Díaz, 2015). Citizens can express their political voices by signing a petition, joining a political organisation or participating in a political rally or demonstration, among other activities. These activities are relevant as they can provide a corrective to public policy by revealing people's views and needs, maintain political vigilance among citizens, and improve the quality of a democracy (OECD, 2011). In this context, an important indicator of the propensity of people to engage in political activities other than voting is the share of the population that voiced their opinion to a public official. In 2016, only 8% of the Paraguayan population reported voicing their opinion to a public official over the last month, the lowest proportion within the benchmark group (Figure 5.5). Furthermore, following Chile (10 percentage points [pp]) Paraguay experienced the second largest decrease on this variable between 2016 and 2006 (8 pp.).

Figure 5.5. **Compared to the benchmark group, Paraguayan population that reported voicing their opinion to a public official is very low**

Percentage of the population who voiced their opinion to a public official

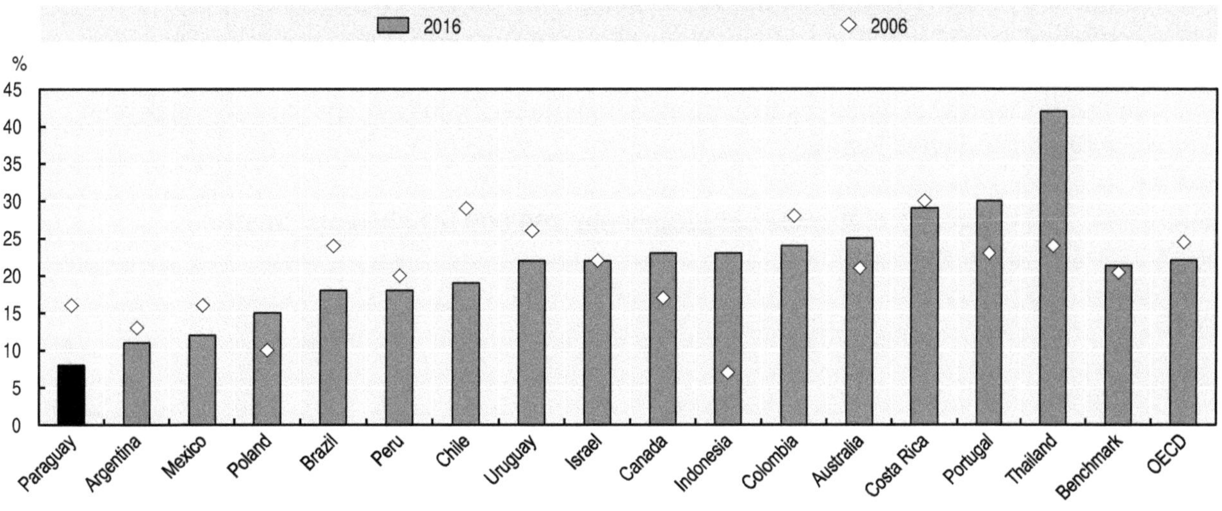

Source: Gallup (2017), Gallup World Poll (database).

StatLink http://dx.doi.org/10.1787/888933750453

Continuing to strengthen the justice system is crucial for ensuring the rule of law

To strengthen the independence of the judicial branch the 1992 constitution earmarked 3% of the national budget to finance the judiciary. As stated in the constitution, the application of justice is the responsibility of the Judicial Branch composed of the Supreme Court of Justice, the tribunals and the courts.[2] The Judicial Council (*Consejo Superior de la Magistratura*) is an independent body in charge of selecting and proposing candidates for positions in the justice system and providing specialised legal training in the judicial school. It is composed of representatives of the three branches of power, the legal practice and academia.[3]

The Supreme Court is the highest authority for the application of justice; it has nine members called ministers of the Supreme Court[4] (Ministros de la Corte Suprema) divided into three chambers: constitutional, commercial-civil and criminal. The core functions of the Supreme Court are: the supervision of all bodies of the judicial branch; to rule on conflicts of jurisdiction and competence between different courts; to issue its own rules and procedures; judge on the due instances as specified in the law; judge on *habeas corpus* without prejudice to the jurisdiction of other judges and courts; judge on unconstitutionality; act as a second instance court in the cases established by law; to preventively suspend judges who are judicially prosecuted until a final decision is reached; to supervise detention and imprisonment institutions; and to advise on the jurisdiction conflicts between the executive and the departments and between departments and municipalities.

Beyond its core functions of administering justice, the Paraguayan Supreme Court has a very large range of functions including: a) selecting court members, judges and fiscal agents from the candidates proposed by the Superior Council of the Judiciary; b) swearing in justices, prosecutors and any other relevant officials; c) appointing Supreme Court ministers that will become members of the Superior Council of the Judiciary; d) appointing the general superintendent of justice upon proposal from the superintendence; e) preparing the draft budget of the judicial branch, etc.

The justice system in Paraguay is confronted with several challenges in fulfilling its objectives of administering timely justice in a transparent and fair manner. For example, the country has a relatively low number of judges with only seven per 100 000 people when compared with 11 in the benchmark group and 18 in European Union countries (Figure 5.6) posing challenges to the efficient delivery of justice. Besides the relatively low number of judges is the array of functions that are to be undertaken by judges (specified above) beyond the administration of justice.

Figure 5.6. **Number of judges per 100 000 inhabitants, 2015**

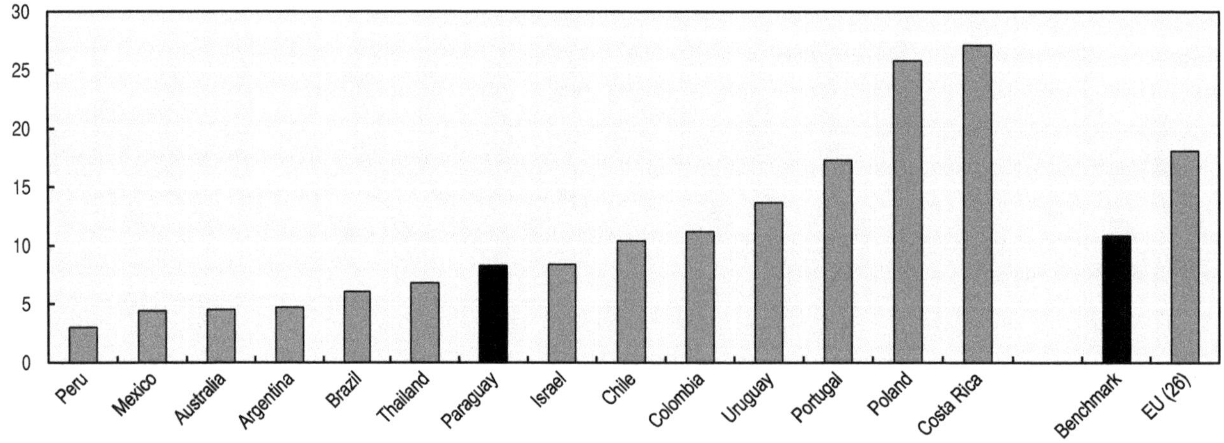

Notes: Data for Costa Rica are 2014. Data for Israel, Uruguay and Brazil are 2011. Data for Uruguay and Brazil were extracted from the Iberoamerican Summit of Justice Ministries (COMJIB). Data for Canada and Indonesia are not available. Professional judges or magistrates mean both full-time and part-time officials authorised to hear civil, criminal and other cases, including in appeal courts, and to make dispositions in a court of law.

Source: UNODOC (2017), Crime and Criminal Justice Statistics, *http://www.unodc.org/unodc/fr/data-and-analysis/statistics/crime.html*; CEPEJ (2017) for the EU (26) average.

StatLink http://dx.doi.org/10.1787/888933750472

According to the latest available evidence only 28% of the Paraguayan population trust the judiciary, a level that is substantially lower than for the benchmark group (42%) and the OECD (54%). In turn, when analysing the Paraguayan data by socio-economic characteristics, the results indicate that people living in urban areas (32%) trust the judicial system more than those living in rural areas (25%). Similarly, people who finished tertiary education (40%) tend to trust the judiciary more than those with lower education levels. A similar trend is found by income groups, where people belonging to the highest income quintiles reported higher levels of trust in the judiciary (Figure 5.7). The differences in trust levels across groups could stem from their capacity to overcome barriers to accessing justice; such barriers could be geographic (proximity), economic or cultural (e.g. the belief that the system is only for a privileged few). In spite of recent efforts to improve access to justice (Box 5.2) the system is still perceived as distant and responding only to the needs of a privileged few (ISSAT, 2015).

Figure 5.7. **People belonging to the highest income quintiles reported higher levels of trust in the judiciary**

Percentage of the population that reported trust in the judiciary, 2016

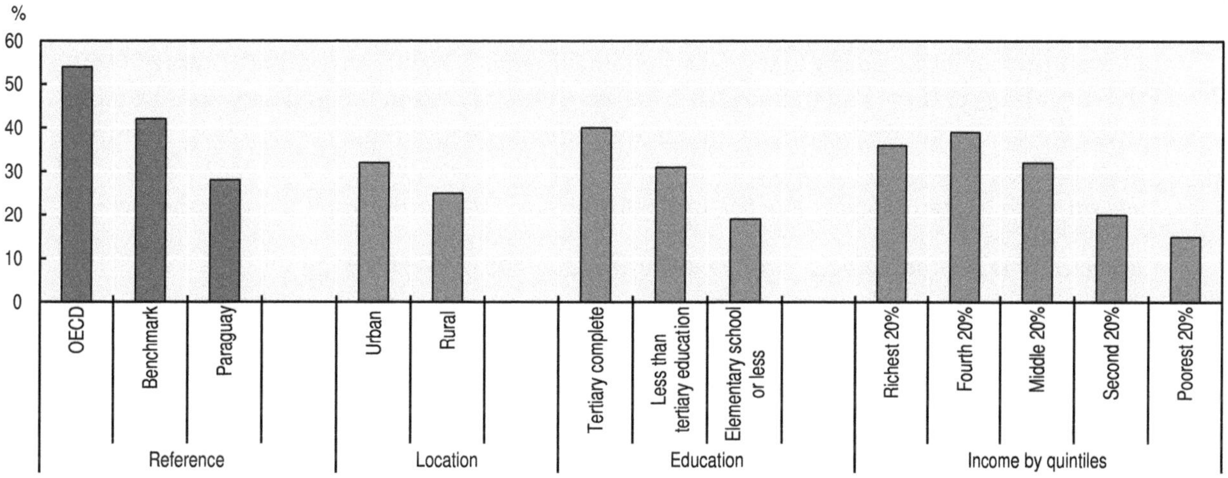

Source: Gallup (2017), Gallup World Poll (database).

StatLink http://dx.doi.org/10.1787/888933750491

Box 5.2. **The Houses of Justice (HoJ)**

Since 2015, Paraguay has recently begun to establish Houses of Justice (HoJ), based on the French institutions of the same name *(maisons de justice et du droit)*, which are designed to facilitate access to legal advice and services to vulnerable populations. To date, only one house (located in Concepción) is fully operational, but it is planned that more will be established in regions across the country. The Houses of Justice offer the following set of basic services: a) legal orientation and information; b) legal assistance; c) sponsoring or legal representation; d) derivation of judicial procedures to mediation instances; e) comprehensive care for women, children and other groups in a situation of vulnerability as well as co-ordination for the provision of health services. A set of additional services can also be provided by Houses of Justice on specific issues requiring legal assistance (e.g. identity problems, legalisation of land titles, neighbourhood conflicts, domestic violence, alimony and child support pensions, etc). The population targeted by HoJ are people in situation of vulnerability, with comprehensive attention for some specific groups (i.e. women, children, the disabled and members of the indigenous population) if required. In this context, judicial enablers (*facilitadores judiciales*), community leaders working to improve access to justice and belonging to a programme led by the judicial branch are considered key actors within the HoJ.

A final concern is the level of judicial independence in Paraguay. The 1992 constitution certainly improved the institutional design by assigning a fixed budget to the judicial branch; modifying the selection mechanism of judges and creating the SJC; increasing the period on the bench for ministers of the Supreme Court (from five years aligned with the presidential mandate to indefinite terms up to 75 years of age) and increasing the range of constitutional powers of the Supreme Court.

Yet, scholars still consider that Paraguayan judicial independence is deficient (Turner, 2010; Basabe-Serrano, 2015). Such a trend has been attributed to the pervasive influence of informal institutions prevalent during the dictatorship and deeply entrenched in the Paraguayan political and judicial systems (Basabe-Serrano, 2015). The mechanisms threatening judicial independence in Paraguay are co-optation (means used by politicians to appoint judges who will be attentive to their interests), clientelism (the exchange of court-based favours between judges and politicians) and judicial corruption (the use of public authority for the private benefit of court personnel). According to several scholars (Seligson, 1998; Vial, Orrego and Alcaraz, 2006) the prevalence of these patterns explains the low levels of trust in the judiciary and the fact that they have not increased following the institutional changes that came with the return of democracy. In general the universal application of the rule of law is challenged by a justice system with limited capacity and the tasks of which go beyond the application of the law.

Insecurity is comparatively high and more prevalent in border areas

Personal security concerns people's vulnerability to a wide range of threats as well as how safe they feel. According to Latinobarometer, when asked about the country's main problem in 2015, the leading answer reported by 24.5% of Paraguayans was crime and public security. Similarly, 50% of Paraguayans do not feel safe when walking alone at night, the highest level for LAC countries included in the benchmark group (see Figure 5.8, Panel A). However, the evidence is mixed. While still at the high end of the benchmark group, the homicide rate decreased from 15.9 per 100 000 people in 2006 to 8.8 in 2014 (Figure 5.8, Panel B). However, homicides rates vary across departments, ranging from 94.5 homicides per 100 000 people in Amambay to 2.4 in Cordillera (Figure 5.9).

Figure 5.8. **The homicide rate has decreased but insecurity perception remains high**

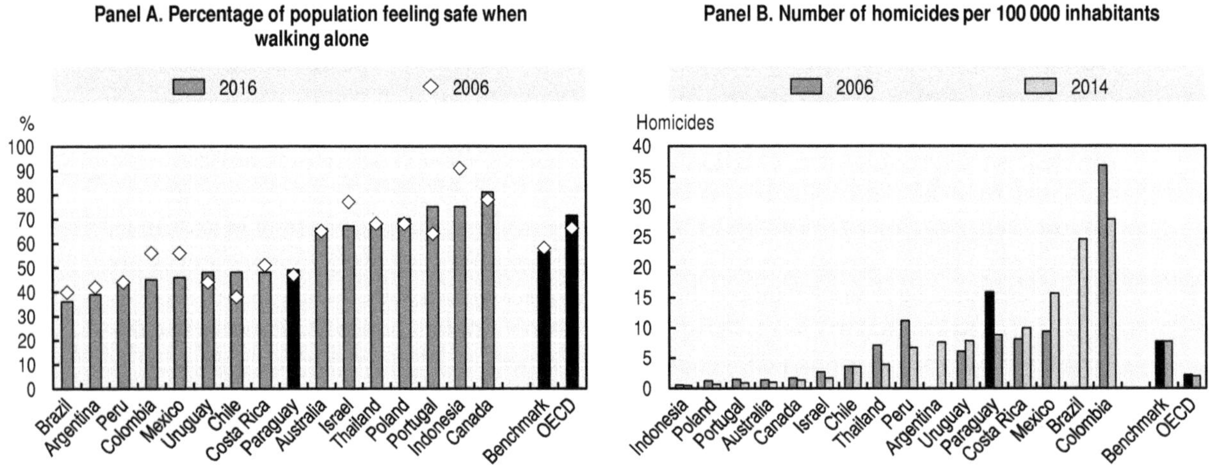

Note: Data for Canada are 2013. Data for Israel are 2012. Data for Indonesia are 2008.

Source: Panel A: Gallup (2017), Gallup World Poll (database). Panel B: World Bank (2017a), *World Development Indicators* (database), Washington DC, *http://data.worldbank.org*; OECD (2017b), health dataset, *https://data.oecd.org/health.htm*.

StatLink http://dx.doi.org/10.1787/888933750510

Figure 5.9. **The homicide rate shows a mixed picture**

Panel A. Homicide rate per 100 000 inhabitants by department, 2015

Panel B. Change in the homicide rate per department between 2014 and 2015

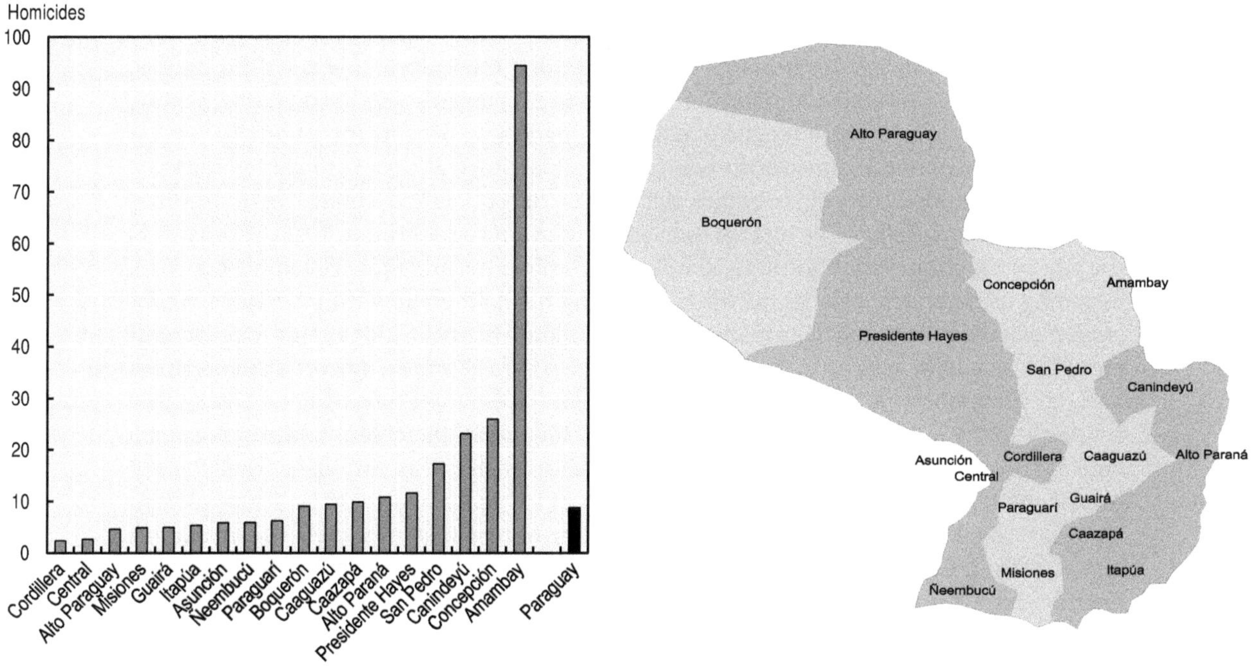

Note: Panel A: Data for Neembecú are 2014. Panel B: Departments in grey is where the rate increased, those in blue are those departments where the rate decreased.

Source: Observatorio Nacional de Seguridad y Convivencia Ciudadana (2017).

StatLink http://dx.doi.org/10.1787/888933750529

The departments with the highest homicide rates (Amambay, Concepción, Canindeyú and San Pedro) all border Brazil, or are close to the border with it (Figure 5.9). These departments are the area of operation of the Paraguayan People's Army (*Ejercito del Pueblo Paraguayo* or EPP) a guerrilla group operating since at least the early 1990s in Paraguay (Box 5.3). Furthermore, this border is notorious for being highly porous, with smuggling and illicit trade common and contributing to accentuating the institutional weakness. According to UNODC, in the region Paraguay is the largest producer of marijuana and accounts for around 15% of the global trade in this drug. Additionally, the absence of substantial air control mechanisms has made Paraguay a transit point for drug flights carrying cocaine from Bolivia and Peru (ISSAT, 2015).

Since 2013, the government has launched a large-scale operation (the "Plan Hendy") to fight smuggling by increasing controls. Additionally, in early 2014 a specialised anti-smuggling unit was established in the Public Prosecutors' Office operating mainly in Asunción and its metropolitan area. Despite such efforts smuggling is still prevalent and causes huge economic loss to the Paraguayan government. Drug traffickers, along with arms traffickers, counterfeiters, and money launderers, continue to take advantage of the country's weak law enforcement and porous borders to pursue criminal activities on Paraguayan territory. In conclusion, insecurity is comparatively high in Paraguay and more prevalent in border areas.

Box 5.3. **The Paraguayan People's Army (EPP)**

The *Ejercito del Pueblo Paraguayo* (EPP) (Paraguayan People's Army) is a rebel group operating since at least 1992 mainly in the Concepción and San Pedro departments but with some sporadic presence in the departments of Caaguazu and Canindeyú. It is a self-proclaimed Marxist group and its stated mission is to abolish the "bourgeois and liberal parliamentary system" and replace it with a regime of popular congresses. Since its inception the EPP has engaged in more than 100 armed actions including kidnappings, attacks on property, attacks on isolated police and military posts, bombs placed in media outlets and a branch of the attorney general's office as well as two attacks on electricity pylons (McDermott, 2015). Estimates of the size of the group vary from 30 to 50 full-time combatants and up to 200 members when including its extended logistics network, supplying the core group with food and a steady stream of intelligence. One of its main sources of funding has been kidnapping for economic motives. There have been up to 27 abductions linked to the EPP and on most occasions victims have been members of the Paraguayan ruling class. For example, one of EPP's best known actions was the kidnap and murder in 2004 of Cecilia Cubas, daughter of former president Raúl Cubas. Additionally, recent evidence also indicates that it is very likely that the EPP extorts money from marijuana growers in its area of influence and could be also exploiting its own crops (McDermott, 2015). The EPP is also connected with other rebel groups in the region, and it is documented that they have received training and advice from the Colombian guerrilla *Fuerzas armadas revolucionarias de Colombia* (FARC). Historically, the fight against the EPP was led by the police but following the arrival of President Cartes a decree was issued in 2013 allowing the military to be used for internal security followed by the establishment of a joint Task Force led by the army and reporting directly to the presidency, exacerbating rivalry between the police and the armed forces. Yet, the army lacks appropriate technology and has limited intelligence capacity which has resulted in relatively poor military results in the fight against the EPP. Furthermore, increased pressure to achieve results has resulted in accusations of human rights abuses and heavy-handed actions (McDermott, 2015).

Source: Authors.

Paraguay has advanced towards the development of a comprehensive and coherent integrity system, ensuring its effectiveness remains a big challenge

Corruption is commonly defined as the abuse of entrusted power for private gain (Transparency International, 2016b). Most corrupt practices take place at the interface between the private and the public sectors. More precisely, corruption affects decisions in the sense that efforts are placed into unproductive instead of productive activities. For example, corrupt public officials have incentives to create artificial bottlenecks and red tape to enable rent extraction which results in bureaucratic inefficiencies in the first place or they could prefer choosing contract modalities and projects where bribes are easier to obtain.

High levels of perceived corruption erode social capital and divert financial resources from investment in development and well-being and have been associated with diminishing trust in public institutions (OECD, 2013a; OECD, 2015). Furthermore, they discourage citizens from complying with their tax and other legal duties, thereby weakening the overall capacity of governments to implement public policies. While in the short run corruption may "grease the wheels of the government", in the long run it undermines economic growth, and intensifies environmental, social, and health problems (Holmberg, Rothstein and Nasiritousi, 2009; Djankov et al., 2009; Gupta, Davoodi and Alonso-Terme, 2002; Mauro, 1995).

Figure 5.10. **Perception and experience of corruption are high**

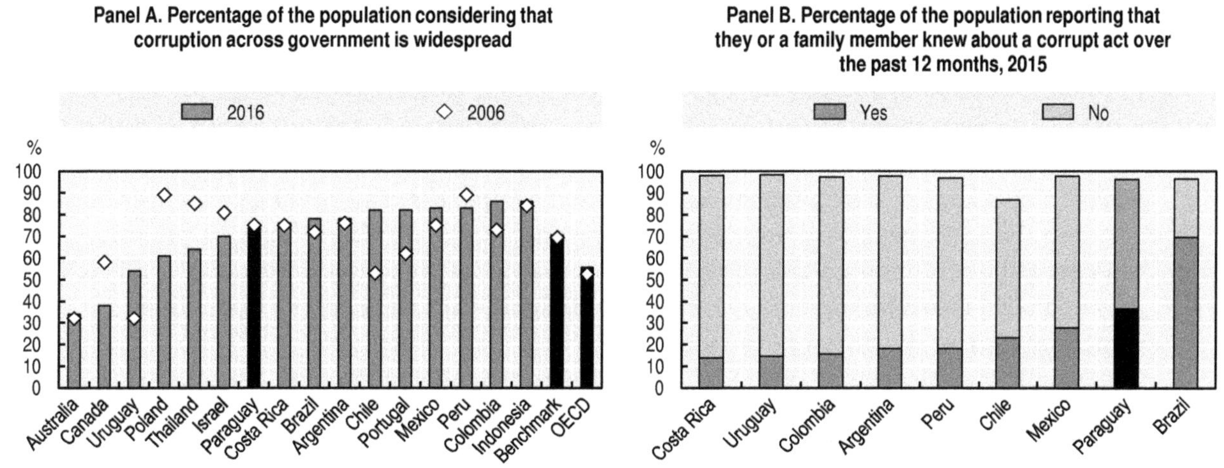

Source: Panel A: Gallup (2017), Gallup World Poll (database). Panel B: Latinobarometro (2015), "Datos 2015", Banco de Datos (dataset), *www.latinobarometro.org*.

StatLink http://dx.doi.org/10.1787/888933750548

According to the Gallup World Poll 74% of Paraguayans consider corruption to be widespread across government, a value that is slightly above the average of the benchmark group (71%). Furthermore, in the case of Paraguay, this figure has remained practically unchanged since 2006. According to Erlingsson and Cristinsson (2016) corruption perceptions could be framed by several factors such as information availability (e.g. a widely diffused scandal) ideological factors (e.g. overemphasising corruption perception if a government from the opposition is in office) and direct corruption experiences (e.g. paying a bribe). In the case of the latter, 37% of Paraguayans reported that they or a family member knew about corrupt behaviour occurring during the last 12 months,[5] after Brazil the second largest level for LAC countries of the benchmark group.

As part of its National Development Plan, the Paraguayan government has as a cross cutting objective to "reduce corruption by clarifying the rules, improving transparency and accountability mechanisms, increasing participation from beneficiaries and users in the scrutiny of the various programmes at the different levels of government". In this context several initiatives[6] have been taken as part of the National Plan for the Prevention of Corruption (NPPC) approved by decree 4900 of 2016 and in line with the provisions set forth by the United Nations Convention Against Corruption (UNCAC). The ultimate goal of the plan is to reduce structural or systemic weakness of public institutions, reduce opportunities for corruption, promote the correct use of public resources and boost trust in public institutions. The NPPC includes nine areas of emphasis[7] which translate into 58 concrete commitments involving several public institutions. According to the government 41 of those commitments have been fully met, 12 are in the process of being met, and five need to be redefined.

One of the core institutional pillars in the fight against corruption has been the recently created national anti-corruption agency (SENAC). SENAC was legally established in 2012 with the mission of leading the implementation of policies to increase transparency and fight against corruption in all institutions of the executive branch, as well as improving co-operation between public sector institutions and social actors to fight corruption. SENAC was allocated a budget enabling it to start operating only in 2014. With the goal of reaching citizens who want to submit complaints and access corruption data SENAC has established an anti-corruption website as a platform for denouncing alleged cases of corruption in the public administration and accessing corruption data. Complaints can be submitted anonymously or requesting encrypted protection of personal data.

SENAC has been successful in co-ordinating and ensuring that all institutions within the executive establish a unit for fighting corruption by providing guidelines for such a purpose and including a description of the functions to be undertaken by each of these units. In addition, it has contributed to raising awareness about public sector corruption and has become a key actor for channelling corruption complaints. Still, several challenges lie ahead in the battle against corruption, including ensuring that public managers prioritise the new anti-corruption units, improving co-ordination between the units and the office of the Public Prosecutor, and, finally, ensuring the political will to follow through on the complaints raised. As shown in the table below, only 4.1% of complaints submitted since 2013 resulted in the opening of an administrative investigation (Table 5.1).

Table 5.1. **Many complaints are submitted but few investigations are opened**

Number and percentage of administrative investigations opened

Year	Number of complaints submitted to SENAC	Number of complaints that resulted in the opening of an administrative investigation	Percentage of the complaints that resulted in the opening of an administrative investigation
2013	58	19	32.8
2014	52	5	9.6
2015	44	0	0
2016	697	11	1.6
Total	**851**	**35**	**4.1**

Source: SENAC, *http://www.denuncias.gov.py*.

Figure 5.11, Panel A shows that in 2015 slightly more than 70% of the Paraguayan population considered that little or no progress had been achieved in the fight against corruption over the previous two years. While it is still too early to judge the effectiveness of the anti-corruption policy, these results shed light on the importance of maintaining efforts for strengthening, and giving visibility to, the work of SENAC. Additionally, the National Transparency Team (*Equipo Nacional de Transparencia*) was recently created, as a collective effort bringing together SENAC with several institutions[8] for implementing plans to improve the relative position of Paraguay in the perception-based corruption measures; in particular the Corruption Perception Index generated by Transparency International. The National Transparency Team is working on a technical diagnosis on transparency and the creation of an inter-sectoral committee. By this measure, Paraguay ranks in the top third of most corrupt countries for which data are available (87 out of 176 countries or territories). Furthermore, with a score of 30/100, Paraguay is the country with the second lowest score for the benchmark group Figure 5.11, Panel B). The implementations of actions to lower the composite score should lead to a real change of instruments, processes, structures and, ultimately, behaviours rather than to a formalistic response that could influence some of the methodological foundations of the index.

Different public organisations face different operational risks and have different levels of tolerance to risk, given their visibility and political significance. Initiatives such as the National Transparency Team are useful as means of ensuring a whole-of-government approach to the overall goal of fighting corruption. Additionally, knowledge sharing and dialogue spaces are important for highlighting innovations and good practices in integrity management.

Figure 5.11. **Progress has been achieved but there is still a long way to go on the battle against corruption**

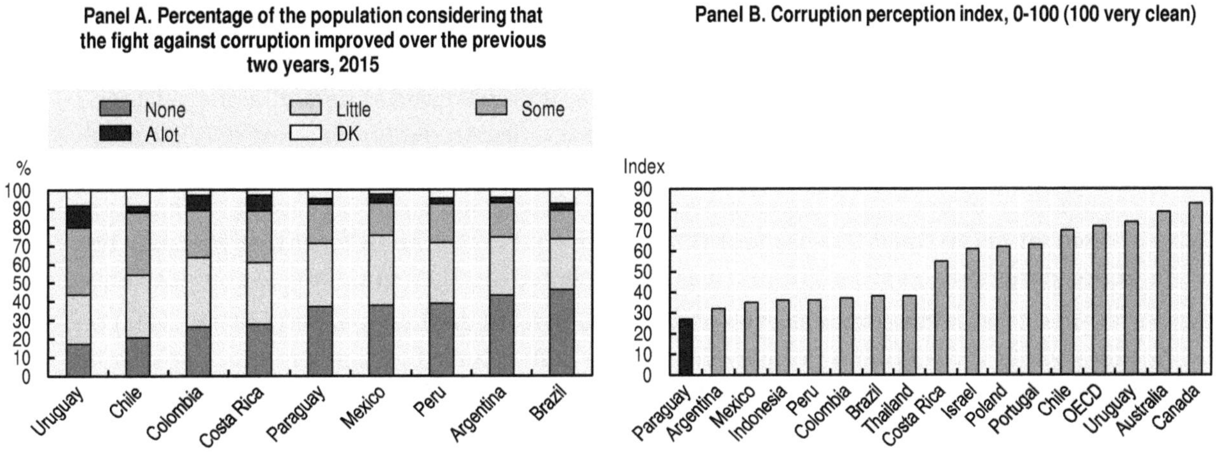

Source: Panel A: Latinobarometro (2015), "Datos 2015", Banco de Datos (dataset), *www.latinobarometro.org*. Panel B: Transparency International (2016a).

StatLink http://dx.doi.org/10.1787/888933750567

Another instance of corruption prevention is the network for transparency and anti-corruption co-ordinated by SENAC comprising more than 82 public agencies. As part of this network the Transparency and Anti-Corruption Units (UTA) within public institutions work with SENAC to monitor government priorities in matters of ethics, integrity, corruption, risk management, citizen participation, access to public information and accountability. In 2017, slightly more than half the institutions submitted their annual plans. The first monitoring process of each plan is expected for the last trimester of the year.

Finally, the role of SENAC is limited to undue behaviours associated mainly with receiving bribes and other forms of embezzlement (i.e. misappropriations or other diversions of property by a public official). But corruption is associated with a broader range of phenomena such as conflict of interest, revolving doors (e.g. movement of people into and out of key policy-making posts in the executive and legislative and regulatory agencies), lobbying and the financing of political campaigns: areas, in which regulation in Paraguay is weak or absent. Recently SENAC approved an accountability manual for public institutions dependent on the executive branch to be implemented by the UTAs. However, an integrated framework encompassing measures to fight the wide array of corrupt practices would be a key asset for further strengthening integrity in Paraguay.

An area where Paraguay has made strides in the fight against corruption is public procurement. In the first place the electronic procurement system, in existence since 2003, ensures that all information (e.g. legal framework; announcement of tenders; calendar of openings, etc.) is available online. Furthermore, since 2005 the Procurement Agency (DNCP) includes as part of its electronic procurement system a whistle-blowing function where anonymous complaints on possible corruption acts occurring during the public procurement process can be made. The identity of the whistle-blower is protected by a mechanism put in place within the system though no specific legal provision exists for this purpose.[9]

To fully reap the benefits of open government it is required to pro-actively support citizen engagement and the re-use of public information

The National Development Plan (NDP) recognises the Open Government Action Plans as the instruments that will pave the way towards a more open and transparent government. The general open government strategy in Paraguay was conceived as a stand-alone policy and not as part of other policy or strategy. The Technical Secretariat for Planning (STP), through the General Direction of Information for Development, was designated as the institution in charge of co-ordinating the open government strategy and since 2012 Paraguay has been a member of the Open Government Partnership (OGP).[10] In the OGP context Paraguay has adopted three action plans. The first was implemented in 2012 mentioning 15 commitments.

The first action plan was evaluated by the independent review mechanism (IRM) on the basis of three criteria: a) relevance to the OGP values; b) a moderate or substantial transformative impact and a substantive or complete level of compliance. According to the IRM from the 15 commitments initially assumed by Paraguay three complied with the criteria mentioned above: i) the development of an integrated system for administrative careers (SICCA) and a public employment web portal (*Paraguay Concursa*); ii) the implementation of an e-procurement system with an online catalogue; and iii) the exchange information system (SII), linking government institutions through an electronic application. While in general terms the plan was aimed at improving transparency and efficiency in public administration, ensuring access to information and the improvement of public services through the use of information technology and communications (ICT), most of the actions were effectively linked to the development of information systems and substantially less to mechanisms for civic participation and accountability.

To a large extent the first action plan could be considered a pilot exercise for implementing a whole- of-government approach to promote transparency, empower citizens, fight corruption and harness new technologies for strengthening governance. Additionally, it was also useful for disseminating the open government narrative and language across government institutions. However, the plan had a narrow scope (focused mainly on the use of ICT) and encountered a degree of resistance from government institutions that were expected to implement some of the commitments. The lack of incentives for institutions to co-operate and the lack of policy linkages produced a bottleneck to compliance with some of the commitments set out in the strategy and highlighted the need for a greater co-ordination effort to implement a whole-of-government Open Government Strategy.

Following the limited compliance with the first action plan, a special unit for co-ordination of all Open Government initiatives (*Dirección General de Gobierno Abierto*) was created within the Technical Secretariat for Planning (STP), and the government ratified its commitment to Open Government and Transparency. The action plan for the 2014-16 period was conceived through a participative approach involving 12 government institutions and nine civil society organisations. The second strategy set out nine commitments: five in the areas of transparency, two each in the fields of citizen participation and accountability.

One of the major achievements of the second action plan was the approval in September 2014 of law number 5.282 regarding the free access of citizens to information and government transparency. The law took effect in 2015 and guarantees "free citizen access to public information and governmental transparency" obliging state institutions to disclose information requested by citizens in respect of salaries, official travel, contracts and any information not designated as secret. The regulatory decree was signed in September 2015 and henceforth the law has been valid. The law's implementation is the responsibility of the Ministry of Justice.[11] In turn, SENAC has put in place a monitoring mechanism of compliance with disclosure obligations (e.g. active transparency) of executive branch institutions. Making public information available is a first crucial step for promoting transparency, integrity and increasing trust in public institutions. Achieving the benefits pursued by the law would require that citizens and civil society develop ownership and fully exercise their right to know about how public money is spent and many other aspects of public life. As stated in the third Open Government Action Plan (2016-18) the government could play a key role by leading actions to disseminate the law.

In addition, governmental transparency is framed by Law 5.189/2014 establishing the mandatory provision of information on the use of public resources, remuneration and other compensation received by civil servants. The Public Function Secretariat (SFP) is in charge of verifying compliance with this law. Public institutions not complying with the disclosure of information could be subject to fines as stipulated in the law. In 2014 more than 180 institutions were not complying with the disclosure of compensation information but by April 2017 only 28 institutions were considered as non-compliers. An important achievement of the law is the disclosure of compensation information by local governments. For the same reference period (April 2017) 224 out of the 250 municipalities were disclosing their compensation information.

Open data portals are important vehicles for disseminating public information. Paraguay has advanced in this regard by launching an online data portal (*www.datos.gov.py*) aimed at enabling open access to public data.[12] The country ranks fourth among Latin America countries with available information in the OECD Index on Open Government Data (Figure 5.12). The index assesses government efforts to implement open data in three areas: data availability on the national portal; data accessibility; and government's support to re-use stakeholder engagement on a score of 0 (lowest score) to 1 (best possible score).

Figure 5.12. **Promoting the re-usability of public data is an area where improvements could be made**

OURdata Index: Open, Useful, Reusable Government Data, 2015

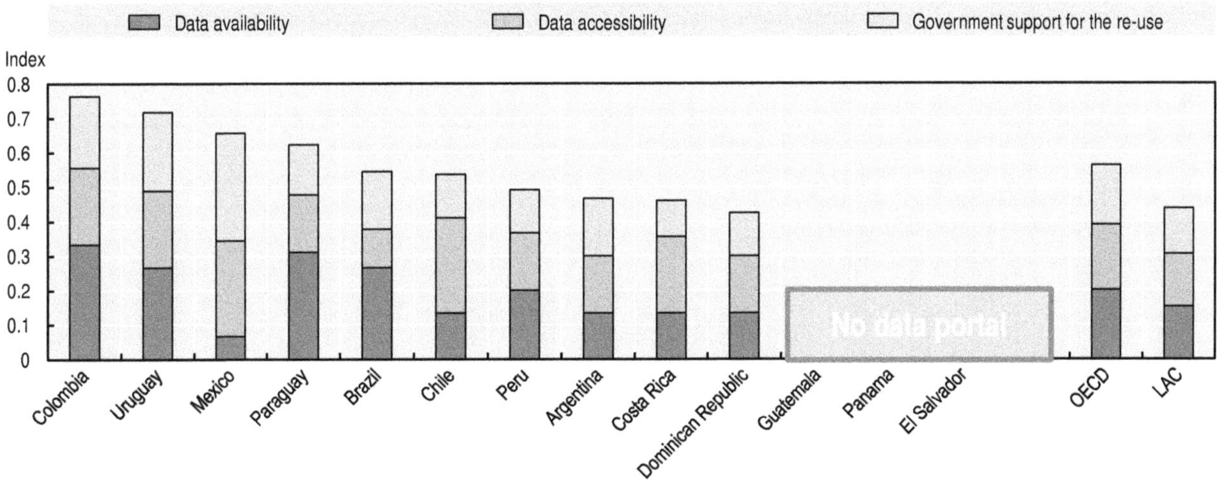

Source: OECD (2016).

StatLink http://dx.doi.org/10.1787/888933750586

The analysis of the subcomponents of the index sheds light on the aspects where improvement is required. While substantial efforts have been made to ensure the availability of public information further efforts could be made to guarantee its accessibility (e.g. user-friendly formats, tools that facilitate access to the information, notifications of updates, etc.) and support its reuse (e.g. increasing open data literacy through information sessions for citizens and businesses, making the release of data part of the performance indicator of organisations, etc). Considerable efforts have been made to enhance openness by making information available; however, challenges remain to tailor public information to citizens' needs and strengthen accountability mechanisms.

Much progress on other commitments has also been achieved. For example, through decree number 1732/2014, the National Team of Country Strategy (ENEP), which played a fundamental role in the definition of the National Development Plan has been given formal existence as an advisory and consultative body of the national government. Although not including the full spectrum of actors in Paraguayan society, ENEP's cross-sectoral long-term vision is of fundamental importance supporting inter-institutional dialogue and for setting a long-term vision for the country, especially for complex, multidimensional issues requiring whole-of-government responses.

However, the potential of the Centre of Government (CoG) as a co-ordinating body to deal with such multidimensional issues remains untapped with a continued over-reliance on bilateral communications among relevant government actors as the key decision mechanisms. On a scale of zero (very little co-ordination) to four (strong co-ordination), perception of co-ordination and collaboration between ministries and with the administration in Paraguay scores one (CEPII, 2012). This is significantly below OECD member countries, Latin American countries and the benchmark group. Such a poor performance could be explained by a lack of formal institutionalised channels to discuss relevant horizontal issues with a very strong role for the president as the last instance for decision making. Apart from the Open Government strategy itself there are few examples of cross-governmental policy co-ordination committees. Institutionalising mechanisms to ensure the co-ordination, monitoring and evaluation of complex policy initiatives is of the essence in maximising the results of cross-governmental initiatives.

Figure 5.13. **There is potential to improve co-ordination across government units**

Perception of co-ordination among public institutions, 2012, Index 0-4(strong co-ordination)

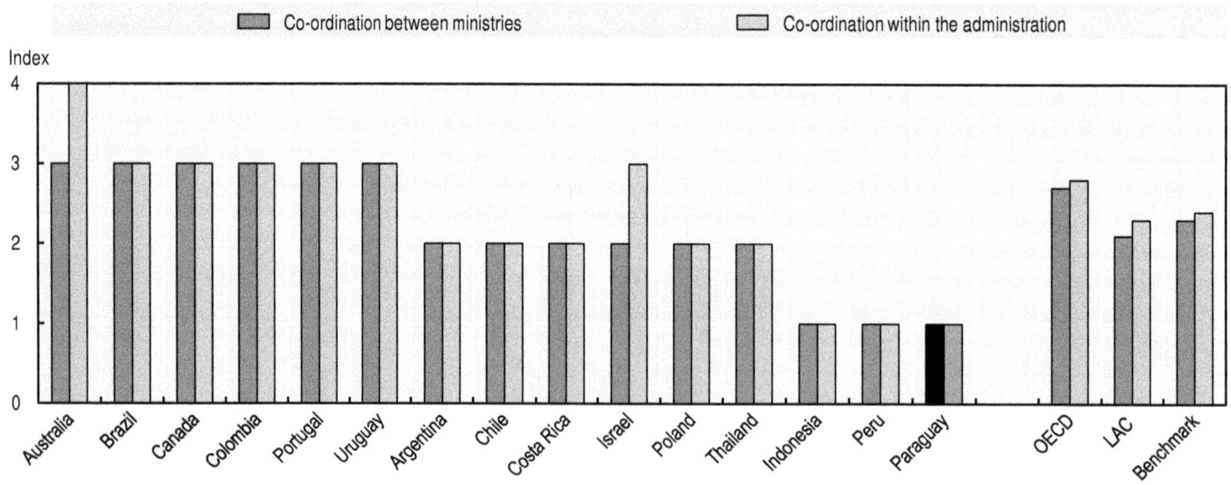

Note: The Institutional Profiles Database provides an original measure of countries' institutional characteristics through composite indicators built from perception data. The perception data were gathered through a survey completed by country/regional Economic Services (*Services économiques*) of the French Ministry for the Economy and Finance and the offices of the *Agence française de développement*.

Source: CEPII (2012), Institutional Profiles Database, *www.cepii.fr/institutions/EN/ipd.asp*.

StatLink http://dx.doi.org/10.1787/888933750605

Another area where objectives were set by the second OG action plan was the creation and/or strengthening of 50 municipal development councils. To date the target has been outperformed and more than 100 councils have been set up. Such councils are a space for collaboration between the government, the private sector and civil society in the municipality with the objective of developing and monitoring municipal development plans. The role of these councils is becoming increasingly relevant as the numbers and functions of municipalities have been increasing over time. While still relatively weak in terms of financial resources, municipalities have an important degree of autonomy for using some of their budgetary allocations (e.g. royalties from binational companies) and own-earned resources (e.g. a percentage of the revenue collected from property taxes: according to the law municipalities own 70% of the money collected from land and property taxes while the remaining 30% is split between the departments [15%] and a distribution fund [15%] for lower income municipalities). In addition to identifying local priorities the councils could play an important role for ensuring the articulation and effective co-ordination between national, departmental and local policies that would lead to a multiplier effect in the use of financial resources and therefore has the potential to maximise the effects of public policies.

The third OG action plan establishes ten commitments and 62 subcommitments for the period 2016-18. Some of the commitments build on previous actions to try to maximise their impact (e.g. access to information, open government data, etc.). However, for the first time, this action plan establishes commitments in specific policy areas such as health, education and environment that are framed by targets as stated in the Sustainable Development Goals. Complying with these commitments will require high levels of engagement by government institutions as well as co-ordination across the different agencies and bodies involved. An approach integrating and harmonising different strategies would help to maximise the effect of government actions.

Bringing people on board is essential for spreading out the benefits of development

As part of the cross-cutting lines of action put forward in the NDP, tackling inequality of opportunities is recognised as one of the basic challenges for Paraguay. In this context, the NDP acknowledges the importance of levelling the playing-field so that circumstances such as gender, place of birth, ethnicity and family context will not limit the opportunities available to individuals. The government has made several efforts to increase equality of opportunity, among them a 2016 law protecting women against violence and special provisions for the indigenous population in several public policies.

One of the mechanisms through which governments could influence the chances of succeeding in life is the provision of public services. Those services should meet the expectations of citizens, and citizens' experiences with front-line public services are expected to have a direct effect on their satisfaction with those services. In Paraguay, satisfaction with several public services is lower than both the OECD and benchmark country average, including the health-care system, the public transportation system, the quality of roads and infrastructure, and the city or area where people live (Figure 5.14, Panel A). However, the share of Paraguayans who are satisfied with the education system is slightly above the OECD average (69% of Paraguayans, compared with 67% in the OECD).

Satisfaction with some public services varies by geographical location (see Figure 5.14, Panel B). Satisfaction with health care, public transportation, and the quality of roads and highways is higher in urban than in rural areas. In turn, satisfaction with the city or area where people live is slightly higher in rural (63%) than urban areas (61%). Conversely, satisfaction with the education system is somewhat higher in urban (70%) than in rural areas (68%).

Figure 5.14. **Satisfaction with key services and the overall satisfaction with the city/area where people live**

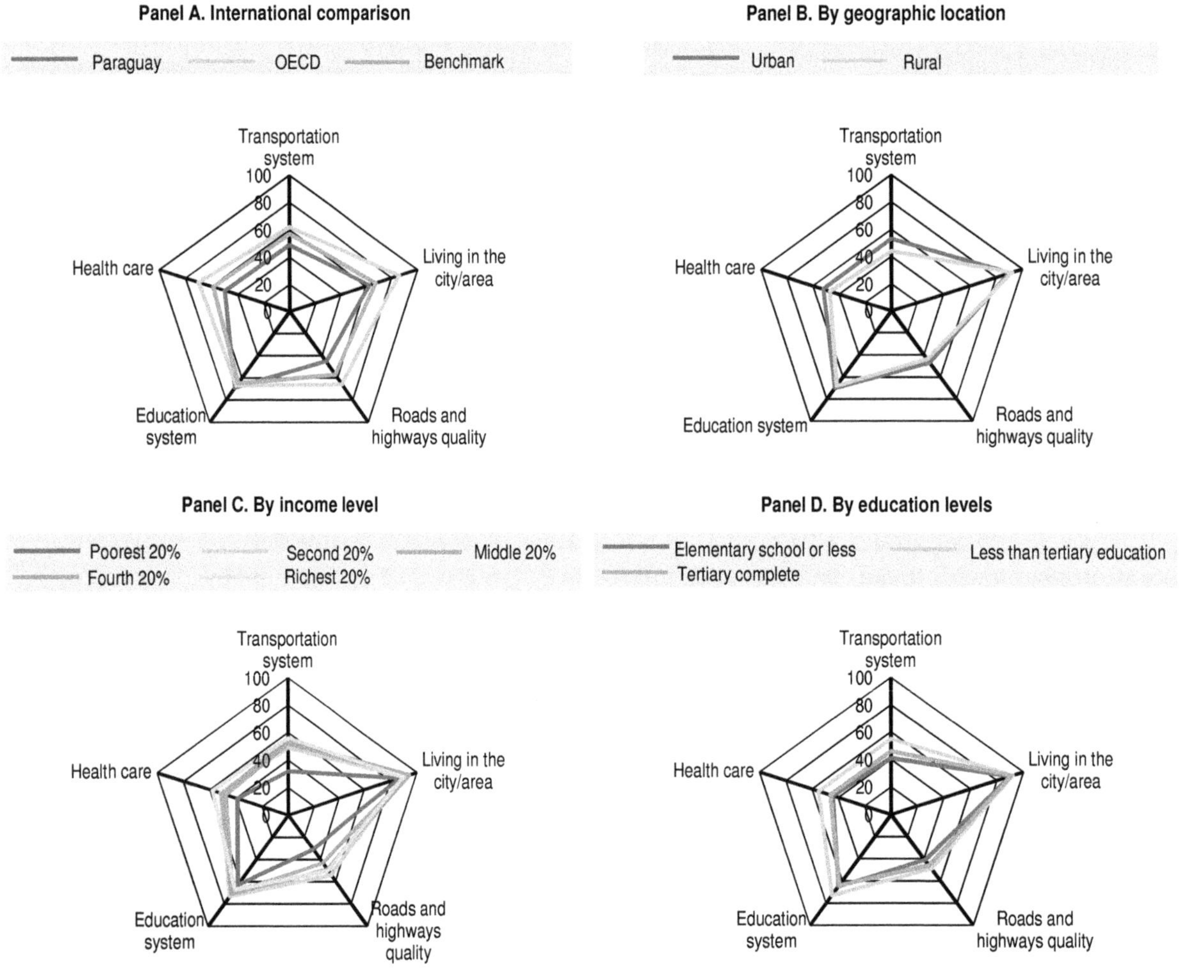

Note: The graphs show the percentage and breakdown by categories of people who answered "yes" to the following question. In the area or city where you live are you satisfied with the education system; in the area or city where you live are you satisfied with quality of health care; in the area or city where you live are you satisfied with the public transportation system; in the area or city where you live are you satisfied or dissatisfied with the roads and highways; are you satisfied with the city or area where you live.

Source: Gallup (2017), Gallup World Poll (database).

StatLink http://dx.doi.org/10.1787/888933750624

Satisfaction with some key public services tends to be higher by income levels (see Figure 5.14, Panel C). While 75% of the population belonging to the top income quintile report being satisfied with the area or city where they live, only 54% of the bottom income quintile say the same (a 24 percentage points difference). With the exception of the education system (four percentage points) the difference between the top and the bottom income quintiles is about 20 percentage points for all other services considered (i.e. health care, the public transportation system and the quality of roads and infrastructure).

In the case of satisfaction with key public sectors by education level the trend is less clear (see Figure 5.14, Panel D). With the exception of the education system, people with less than tertiary education report lower levels of satisfaction than those who have completed tertiary education. Nevertheless, in almost all cases (apart from overall satisfaction with the city or area where they live) those in the intermediary category (less than tertiary education) report the highest satisfaction with public services on average with scores above those of people who completed tertiary education. While these results appear to be counterintuitive, they could be explained by higher expectations from this segment of the population on the quality of services they should be receiving. A similar argument has been made by Boidi and Zechmeister (2015) to explain the decline over time in the satisfaction with health and education services in Paraguay. Overall, satisfaction with health care, public transportation and the quality of roads and highways in Paraguay is comparatively low. In turn, people in rural areas are less satisfied than those living in cities. Similarly, people in the highest income quintile reported, on average, higher satisfaction levels than people in the lowest one.

Improving overall satisfaction with key public services is a major challenge for Paraguay. Even more so in the cases of groups with fewer advantages (e.g. people located in rural areas and in the bottom income group) for whom a differentiated approach could be required. Satisfaction with public services could be influenced by several elements such as good timing in the provision of services, geographical proximity, consistency in provision, perceived quality, affordability and matching of special needs, among others. A comprehensive assessment of the factors underlying low satisfaction with services in Paraguay is required fully to explain these results and develop strategies for improvement.

More and better statistical evidence is required to inform the development of policies

To reap fully the benefits of reforms undertaken by the Paraguayan government a strong basis of high-quality evidence is required. In this context, the production of statistics is essential to monitoring progress and achieving development targets. Furthermore, statistics are crucial to providing an environment of evidence-based decision making and to holding governments accountable for their activities. The assessment and modernisation of the Paraguayan National Statistical System (NSS) could therefore constitute a major step in this direction. Currently, the production and dissemination of official statistics in Paraguay are shared among several entities of the NSS.

- **The Directorate General of Statistics, Surveys, and Censuses (DGEEC)**, through the Decree-Law 11.126 of 1942, reorganises and co-ordinates the statistical services of the Republic of Paraguay. Under this law, the DGEEC is the main statistical agency, which has the responsibility of co-ordinating and integrating all official statistical activities as well as ensuring consistency and harmonisation of statistical standards, concepts, definitions and adoption of classifications in some subjects and focuses mostly on the production of income, demographic and social basic statistics and indicators, mainly unemployment and poverty. The DGEEC is part of the presidency and under the responsibility of the Ministry of Economic Social Development and Technical Planning (STP). Decree 3087 of the law mentions the organic and functional autonomy of the DGEEC.
- **The Central Bank of Paraguay (BCP)** operates under the Law 489/1995, Charter of the Central Bank of Paraguay, which establishes the obligations of public and private entities to co-operate with the BCP for the preparation and publication of macroeconomic statistics. The law guarantees the statistical confidentiality of information provided to the BCP. This is an autonomous technical institution that has independence in its choice of data sources, methods, and data dissemination policies, within the limits of available resources. Processes and activities in the workplace ensure a culture that promotes institutional

integrity. The BCP has recently set up a transparency portal where people can ask for information and the BCP has the obligation to respond within a period of 15 days.[13]

- **The Ministry of Finance (MoF)**, under the Law 1.535/99 on financial administration, has the right to request information from various public institutions and establishes provisions related to the procedures for preparation of the government accounting system, the requirement of submitting reports, and the confidentiality of information. The Ministry of Finance produces government finance statistics (GFS) on an impartial basis, based on a culture of professional independence. While the terms and conditions for preparing and reporting budget execution data are known to the public, the terms and conditions under which GFS are compiled are not. In the MoF and BCP, rules provide clear guidelines on staff behaviour and administrative procedures, which are made known to the staff.
- **The Civil Status Registry**, through the Civil Status Registry's Office, is the organism in charge of recording the vital facts and vital acts of individuals during their lifetime, according to the law. The registry has more than 480 local offices located in zones where it is considered necessary. It is a dependency of the Ministry of Justice.
- Many **line ministries** are also responsible for statistical operations to generate indicators. Such is the case of the Ministry of Agriculture and Livestock, the Ministry of Education, the Ministry of Health, the Ministry of Environment, the Ministry of Justice, the Ministry of Labour and Social Security, and the Ministry of Public Works and Communications. Commonly data is collected by ministries through administrative records that are not harmonised between institutions. In many instances, the DGEEC is not always involved in these data collection activities and does not have a programme for reviewing the quality of administrative data.

Overall, the production of statistics for the period 2013-17 is by the National Strategy for the Development of Statistics (NSDS). Indeed, while the BCP is focused on macroeconomic statistics and the MoF on government finance statistics, the main data collection activity across the NSS is the permanent household survey, *Encuesta Permanente de Hogares* (EPH) at the national level conducted by the DGEEC. The survey focuses mainly on employment and income but also collects data on education, health, ownership of durable goods, ICT and in some years also migration patterns. In turn, the latest population census was conducted in 2012 though it achieved only 74.4% coverage and therefore could not be validated as representative of the Paraguayan population. DGEEC concluded that the indicators needed for the preparation of projections were consistent with their historical trends and therefore usable. Finally, the DGEEC also conducts one-off, or specific, surveys. For instance, it has carried out a survey on governance (2009), an economic census (2010), a survey on children and adolescents (2011), a survey on micro, small, medium sized and big enterprises (2015).

In respect of economic statistics the country has improved the production of economic aggregates, based on the System of National Accounts, 1993 (SNA,1993), by increasing coverage but is still struggling to provide up-to-date data, particularly for the quarterly national accounts. The same applies to the monthly index of economic activity. In the case of other indicators such as the consumer price Index (CPI) and tax statistics the coverage is also limited. More generally, many sectors are not well covered by data production in Paraguay, such as manufacturing and services[14] and there are no industrial production surveys.[15] In terms of monetary policy, there are no employment data with the necessary frequency required to inform the design of labour policies, although the DGEEC collects a quarterly labour force survey for Asunción and Central department.

While the methodologies used for the generation of statistics in Paraguay are broadly consistent with internationally accepted standards, guidelines, or best practices, Paraguay is not compliant[16] with IMF Special Data Dissemination Standard (SDDS) for the provision of economic and financial data to the public. Since March 2017, Paraguay is the second country in Latin America to implement the recommendations of the e-GDDS. Compliance with those standards is important in two different ways: on the one hand by enhancing the availability of relevant and comprehensive statistics required to underlie sound macroeconomic policies; on the other as guidance for countries having international credits or wanting to access multilateral funding mechanisms. At the regional level, Paraguay is a signatory to the regional Code of Good Practice in Statistics in Latin America and the Caribbean (CEA/ECLAC) which aims to improve the quality of statistical output and build trust in national statistical institutes and enhance the comparability of regional statistics.

Improving the generation of high quality statistics would require overcoming several bottlenecks currently faced by the statistical system. For a start, co-ordination[17] of the NSS by the DGEEC with the BCP, line ministries and other data producers could be strengthened. There is a need to update the statistics law to assign clearly responsibilities among data-producing agencies[18] and for co-ordinating them, and respond to the national and international challenges of official statistics (e.g. new data sources and non-governmental producers) Procedures for data-sharing and co-ordination within the MoF and between the MoF and other data-producing agencies could also be improved. In turn, Paraguay could benefit highly from a regular mechanism for enhancing intersectoral data consistency in the form of a statistical council[19] as a high-level forum including representatives from key stakeholders (e.g. suppliers, producers and users) for promoting and developing official statistical activity at the national level. Ensuring that the NSS has sufficient human and financial resources[20] is essential for moving ahead in the development of high quality statistics in Paraguay.

Another area where improvement is required is the consistency and coverage of official statistics. Some examples could illustrate these issues. In the case of the education sector similar data are produced by several producers. On the one hand, the Ministry of Education through the education management information system (EMIS) sponsored by UNESCO generates education indicators. On the other, the permanent household survey (*Encuesta Permanente de Hogares*) as well as multiple indicator cluster surveys (MICS) collected by DGEEC and several ministries of health collect similar information. In turn, the existence of different sources has resulted in misreporting. The second example, concerns the Ministry of Justice which oversees civil registration (UNICEF, 2016). In spite of the major progress achieved over the past years still 15% of births in Paraguay are still not registered, especially amongst the indigenous population. Involving the DGEEC in the development of data collection activities and methodologies could contribute to overcoming these challenges. Finally, a third area calling for further action is the timing of official statistics. For example, the quarterly national accounts and the monthly index of economic activities are often published with delays.

The updating of the statistical system through an appropriate legal framework, and its co-ordination could bring great benefits to Paraguay. The implementation of the Recommendation of the OECD Council on good statistical practice could assist the country in this endeavour. In addition to improving the evidence base for policy making and supporting efforts towards transparency it would also contribute to the reporting of the national and international agenda, especially the 2030 agenda and the Sustainable Development Goals (SDGs), an area where the DGEEC is expected to take a leading role but where it could require additional help.

Notes

1. A liberal conception of democracy is measured through questions as to whether: i) opposition parties are free to criticise the government; ii) elections are free and fair; iii) voters can discuss politics freely; iv) political parties provide a differentiated offer; v) governing parties are punished when they perform poorly; vi) governments explain their decisions to voters; vii) media are free to criticise the government; viii) rights of minority groups are protected; ix) the media provide reliable information to judge the government; and x) the courts treat everyone fairly.
2. The code of judicial organisation, law 871 of 1981 sets out the composition of the judicial branch and establishes that the administration of justice is the responsibility of: a) the Supreme Court of Justice; b) the Court of Accounts; c) the Courts of Appeal; c) the Courts of first instance; d) the civil and commercial courts and e) the Courts of Peace.
3. The Judicial Council is composed of a member of the Supreme Court of Justice appointed by it; a representative of the executive branch; a senator and deputy both nominated by their respective chambers of parliament; two members of the Lawyers School (*Colegio de Abogados*) appointed by their peers in direct election; a law professor of the National University (Public University) chosen by his/her peers and a law professor of the private universities with at least 20 years of experience; chosen by his/her peers.
4. Prior to the 1992 constitution the executive was in charge of appointing judges and magistrates of the different courts; clearly affecting their independence. The 1992 constitution determined that ministers of the Supreme Court would be appointed by the senate with approval from the executive from a group of three candidates prepared by the Superior Council of the Judiciary (SCJ). High levels of co-operation are required between the Supreme Court and the SCJ, such as collaborating to select a shortlist of candidates.
5. The question included in Latinobarometer is the following: ¿Ha sabido ud o algún pariente de algún acto de corrupción en los últimos 12 meses? (Have you or a relative known of an act of corruption in the last 12 months?).
6. Some of the initiatives for fighting corruption are the National Anti-Corruption Plan, the National Plan for Integrity, the Threshold Programme (Programa Umbral) phases I and II and other measures.
7. Among the many initiatives on this matter, internal control and integrity systems have been created (e.g. the Standard Model of Internal Control of Paraguayan Public Entities, MECIP), the executive branch ethics system and the inter-institutional anti-corruption network are being strengthened.
8. The institutions integrating the National Transparency Team are the Ministry of Finance, Ministry of Industry and Trade, Technical Secretariat of Planning, Ministry of Foreign Affairs, Ministry of Agriculture and Livestock, and the Ministry of Public Works and Communications, the Central Bank and the national customs office).
9. The OECD 2009 Anti-Bribery recommendation defines whistle-blower protection as the legal protection from discriminatory or disciplinary action for employees who disclose to the competent authorities in good faith and on reasonable grounds wrongdoing in the context of their workplace.
10. The Open Government Partnership is a multilateral initiative that aims to secure concrete commitments from governments to promote transparency, empower citizens, fight corruption, and harness new technologies to strengthen governance. In the spirit of multi-stakeholder collaboration, OGP is overseen by a steering committee including representatives of governments and civil society organisations. To become a member of the OGP, participating countries must endorse a high-level Open Government Declaration, deliver a country action plan developed with public consultation, and commit to independent reporting on their progress going forward. In total, 75 OGP participating countries and 15 subnational governments have made over 2 500 commitments to make their governments more open and accountable.
11. The ministry supervises the implementation of the law through the Public Information Access Office, which is in charge of a Unified Web Site for Public Information (Portal Unificado de Acceso a la Información Pública: *www.informacionpublica.gov.py*), the unique and centralised technological platform for access and management of the Public Information fulfilling the national legal requirements. This website has been in effect since 18 September 2015. To date, 5 522 requests for public information have been submitted. There are 117 public offices incorporated in the website; this represents 26.53% of the complete universe for public offices. Furthermore, the Ministry of Justice conducts training for public officers, students and citizens all over the country.
12. The Central Data Portal has been developed by the ICT ministry and is funded through international co-operation with USAID.

13. Yet, in some cases data requests cannot be supplied (e.g., data at the company level). Metadata posted on national websites are not easily available for most datasets, and the metadata posted on the IMF's Dissemination Standards Bulletin Board (DSBB) had not been updated since November 2004, despite significant changes made in the compilation and dissemination processes for most datasets during the past ten years.
14. The BCP elaborates the unit value indices of imports and exports, but they are not publicly available.
15. The BCP uses administrative records from the Ministry of Finance and volume information it can collect (oil, meat, non-metal industries, metal products (steel for construction, etc.).
16. Plans are currently under development in the BCP to be compliant with the IMF SDDS and the country is currently implementing the IMF's enhanced General Data Dissemination System (GDDS), a framework designed by the IMF to assist countries with relatively weak statistical capacity with an emphasis on data dissemination in the e-GDDS to support transparency, encourage statistical development, and help create strong synergies between data dissemination and surveillance.
17. Insufficient co-ordination of the NSS could lead to duplication of efforts and waste of resources. For example, in addition to the poverty surveys conducted by the DGEEC, other poverty surveys are also conducted and their results as criteria for participating at the conditional cash transfer program (Tekopora). Furthermore, it is common that line ministries and other agencies produce their own statistics with diverse methodologies and varying degree of consistency over time.
18. The current statistical legislation dates back to1942 and does not comply with the UN Fundamental Principles of Official Statistics. It states the need for this co-ordination but in practice it remains very limited. Moreover, the law mandates respondent participation in censuses and surveys but is not enforced A bill aiming to reinforce the leading and guiding role of DGEEC has been submitted to the parliament.
19. The current legal framework stipulates that a statistical council should be in place and indicates the institutions that take part in it; however, the institutional setting has not been updated and currently is not working. Poverty and population committees where methodological issues are discussed and changes on the main indicators are analysed meet regularly.
20. The lack of funding is one of the reasons of the partial implementation of the current NSDS (National Strategy for the Development of Statistics) as well as the delay in some data collection activities despite governmental efforts to support the production of statistics. Paraguay has relied on external support for conducting surveys and censuses. For example, the latest census in 2012 was 70% funded (USD 12.5 million) through a loan from the Inter-American Development Bank (IDB).

References

Abente Brun, D.(2011), "Después de la Dictadura", *Historia del Paraguay*, ed. Ignacio Telesca (After the Dictatorship, History of Paraguay), editorial Taurus, pp. 375-390, Asunción.

Barreda, M. and M. Bou (2010), "La calidad de la democracia paraguaya: un avance sobre caminos tortuosos" (The quality of Paraguayan democracy: progress on a winding road), *América Latina Hoy*, No 56, pp. 133-161, Ediciones Universidad de Salamanca, Salamanca.

Basabe-Serrano, S (2015), "Informal institutions and judicial independence in Paraguay, 1954-2011", *Law and Policy*, Vol. 37, No 4, University of Denver, Denver.

Boarini, R. and M. Díaz (2015), "Cast a ballot or protest in the street - Did our grandparents do more of both?: An age-period-cohort analysis in political participation", *OECD Statistics Working Papers*, 2015/02, OECD Publishing, Paris, *http://dx.doi.org/10.1787/5js636gn50jb-en*.

Boidi, M. and E. Zechmeister (2015), "Cultura y Política de la Democracia en Paraguay y en las Américas 2014: Gobernabilidad democrática a través de 10 años del Barometro de las Américas" (Culture and Politics of Democracy in Paraguay and the Americas 2014: Democratic governance through ten years of the America's Barometer), CIRD/LAPOP/Van Der Bilt University, Asunción.

CEPEJ, *http://www.coe.int/t/dghl/cooperation/cepej/evaluation/2016/STAT/default.asp*, accessed 30 May 2017.

CEPII (2012), Centre for Prospective Studies and International Information, *Institutional Profiles Database*, *www.cepii.fr/institutions/EN/ipd.asp*.

Cumbre Judicial Iberoamericana (2016), "Estructura y Competencia de Las Cortes y Tribunales Supremos de Justicia en Iberoamérica" (Structure and Competence of the Iberomerican Courts), Paraguay, Suprema Corte de Justicia de la Nación, México D.F.

Decree Law 11.126/1942, Decreto ley No. 11126, *Que reorganiza y coordina los servicios estadísticos de la República*, Gaceta Oficial, Asunción.

DGEEC (2013), *Estrategia Nacional de Desarrollo Estadístico, Plan Estadístico Nacional 2013-2017 (Preliminar)*, Asunción, *http://www.dgeec.gov.py/ende/LIBRO%20ENDE%20preliminar.pdf*.

Djankov, S. et al. (2009), "Disclosure by Politicians", *American Economic Journal: Applied Economics*, Vol. 2, pp. 179-209.

Erlingsson, G. and G. Kristinsson (2016), "Making Sense of Corruption Perceptions: Who to Ask (and About What?)", Working paper series 2016:13, The Quality of Government Institute (QoG), University of Gothenburg, Gothenburg.

Ferrín, M. (2016), "An empirical assessment of satisfaction with democracy", *How Europeans View Democracy*, Oxford University Press, Oxford.

Fukuyama, F. (1995), "Trust: the Social Virtues and the Creation of Prosperity", Free Press, New York.

Gallup World Poll, *http://www.gallup.com/products/170987/gallup-analytics.aspx* (accessed 30 May 2017).

GIZ (2013), "Building capacity in Paraguay's registration authority: Triangular Cooperation Peru – Paraguay – Germany", *https://www.giz.de/en/downloads/giz2013-en-building-capacity-registration-authority.pdf*, Bonn and Eschborn.

Gupta, S., H. Davoodi and R. Alonso-Terme (2002), "Does corruption affect income inequality and poverty?", *Economics of Governance*, Vol. 3, No. 1, pp. 23-45.

Holmberg, S., B. Rothstein and N. Nasiritousi (2009), "Quality of government: What you get", *Annual Review of Political Science*, Vol. 12, pp. 135-161. *http://www.annualreviews.org/doi/pdf/10.1146/annurev-polisci-100608-104510* (accessed 30 May 2017).

IDB (2011), News release: Paraguay will conduct a national population and housing census with IDB support, IDB publishing, Washington DC, *http://www.iadb.org/en/news/news-releases/2011-07-14/national-population-and-housing-census-in-paraguay,9453.html*.

IDEA dataset (2017), Voter Turnout Database (dataset), Institute for Democracy and Electoral Assistance, Stockholm *http://www.idea.int/data-tools/data/voter-turnout*, accessed 31 March 2017.

ILO (2017), ILOSTAT Database, *www.ilo.org/ilostat*, International Labour Organization, Geneva.

IMF (2017), *World Economic Outlook* (database), *https://www.imf.org/external/pubs/ft/weo/2015/01/weodata/index.aspx*.

IMF (2014), *Paraguay, Report on Observance of Standards and Codes*, IMF Publishing, Washington DC, *https://www.imf.org/external/pubs/ft/scr/2014/cr14248.pdf*.

ISSAT (2015), *Paraguay Country Profile*, *http://issat.dcaf.ch/fre,Geneva/Apprendre/La-bibliotheque-des-ressources/Fiche-des-profils-des-pays/Paraguay-Country-Profile*.

Juárez, J. (2005), "The Democratic Transition in Mexico and Latin America in the late 20th century", *Economía y Sociedad*, pp 99-116, Hidalgo, Mexico.

Latinobarometro, *http://www.latinobarometro.org/lat.jsp*, last accessed (May 30 2017).

Law 5.282/2014, *Ley No. 5282 De libre Acceso ciudadano a la información pública y transparencia gubernamental*, Gaceta Oficial, Asunción.

Law 5.189/2014, *Ley No. 5189 Que establece la obligatoriedad de la provisión de información en el uso de los recursos públicos sobre remuneraciones y otras retribuciones asignadas al servidor público de la República del Paraguay*, Gaceta Oficial, Asunción.

Law 1.535/1999, *Ley No. 1535 De Administración Financiera del Estado*, Gaceta Oficial, Asunción.

Law 489/1995, *Ley No. 489 Orgánica del Banco Central*, Gaceta Oficial, Asunción.

López, M. (2014), "Elecciones generales y votos en el Paraguay de 1989-2013. Develando Algunos Mitos" (*General elections and votes in Paraguay 1989-2013. Unveiling Some Myths*), Dialogo de Saberes, No. 40, pp. 159-182, Bogotá.

Mauro, P. (1995), "Corruption and growth", *The Quarterly Journal of Economics*, Vol. 110, No. 3, pp. 681-712.

McDermott, J. (2015), "The Paraguayan People's Army: A new rebel group or simple bandits?", Perspectivas 2/2015, Friedrich Ebert Siftung, Bogotá.

National Development Plan Paraguay 2030 (Plan Nacional de Desarrollo Paraguay 2030), *http://www.stp.gov.py/pnd/wp-content/uploads/2014/12/pnd2030.pdf*.

Nickson, A. (2011), "El Regimen de Stroessner (1954-1989)" (The Stroessner regime (1954-1989), History of Paraguay), *Historial del Paraguay*, editorial Taurus.

Observatorio Nacional de Seguridad y Convivencia (2017), Ministerio del Interior, *http://www.mdi.gov.py/index.php/seguridad-ciudadana/item/6207-observatorio-nacional-de-seguridad-y-convivencia-ciudadana-del-ministerio-cumple-5-a%C3%B1os-de-creaci%C3%B3n.*

OECD (2017a), *Trust and Public Policy How Better Governance Can Help Rebuild Public Trust*, OECD Publishing, Paris, *http://dx.doi.org/10.1787/9789264268920-en.*

OECD (2017b), health dataset, *https://data.oecd.org/health.htm*, OECD Publishing, Paris.

OECD (2016), *Government at a Glance: Latin America and the Caribbean 2017*, OECD Publishing, Paris, *http://dx.doi.org/10.1787/9789264265554-en.*

OECD (2015), *How's Life? 2015: Measuring Well-being*, OECD Publishing, Paris, *http://dx.doi.org/10.1787/how_life-2015-en.*

OECD (2013a), *How's Life? 2013: Measuring Well-being*, OECD Publishing, Paris, *http://dx.doi.org/10.1787/9789264201392-en.*

OECD (2013b), *Government at a Glance 2013*, OECD Publishing, Paris, *http://dx.doi.org/10.1787/gov_glance-2013-en.*

OECD (2011), *How's Life?: Measuring Well-being*, OECD Publishing, Paris, *http://dx.doi.org/10.1787/9789264121164-en.*

Seligson, M. (1998), "La cultura política en Paraguay: Lineamientos de estudios de valores democráticos para el año 1996" (The political culture in Paraguay: Guidelines of democratic values studies for 1996), *Transición y Valores Democráticos*, CIRD, Asunción.

System of National Accounts (1993), *https://unstats.un.org/unsd/nationalaccount/sna1993.asp*, accessed 30 May 2017, United Nations Statistics Division, New York.

Transparency International (2016a), *https://www.transparency.org/research/cpi/overview*, Berlin.

Transparency International (2016b), *https://www.transparency.org/what-is-corruption/*, accessed 30 May 2017, Berlin.

Turner, B. (2010), "Paraguay: Muchas novedades y poco cambio" (*Paraguay: Many novelties and little change*), revista de Ciencia Política No. 30, pp. 439-450.

UNICEF (2016), "Birth registration in Latin America and the Caribbean: Closing the gaps", Unicef publishing, New York.

UNODC, Crime and Criminal Justice Statistics, *http://www.unodc.org/unodc/fr/data-and-analysis/statistics/crime.html*, accessed 30 May 2017.

Vial, A., M. Orrego and L. Alcaraz (2006), "Cultura política y gobernabilidad 2006: crispación e incertidumbre, carencias y nuevos sueños (Political culture and governance 2006: tension and uncertainity, shortages and new dreams)", USAID and CIRD, Asunción.

World Bank (2017), *World Development Indicators* (database), Washington DC, *http://data.worldbank.org.*

Multi-dimensional Review of Paraguay
Volume 1. Initial Assessment

Chapter 6

Partnerships: Resourcing Paraguay's development agenda

This chapter describes how Paraguay's network of partnerships with external and domestic entities generates financing to support its development agenda. It examines public finances and the scope to increase the resources available for the public sector, focusing on the potential to improve the performance of Paraguay's public finance framework, including how to recalibrate expenditure towards areas that offer greater developmental returns, such as infrastructure, while maintaining fiscal sustainability. The chapter then examines the availability of resources for private-sector firms, through foreign direct investment (FDI) and financing from the domestic financial system, and the potential for a more effective domestic banking system. The focus throughout is on the resources that are, or could be, available for development activities, rather than how those financing flows have been used.

The statistical data for Israel are supplied by and under the responsibility of the relevant Israeli authorities. The use of such data by the OECD is without prejudice to the status of the Golan Heights, East Jerusalem and Israeli settlements in the West Bank under the terms of international law.

Sufficient flows of financing are needed to enable both the public and private sectors to drive national development. This chapter assesses the availability of financing flows that could support investment and other activities by both the public and private sectors. Financing for development activities can come from several different sources, both domestic and foreign. Given their nature, there can be a significant degree of substitutability between public and private sources of financing flows – for example, credit from the banking sector for the domestic private sector can also be absorbed by the public sector, or foreign direct investment (FDI) can be used to fund investment in public infrastructure. This chapter describes the financing flows for development activities that have been available to Paraguay in recent years, comparing these flows with the benchmark economies. It highlights areas where flows may be expanded or more effectively mobilised, in support of expanded development activities.The chapter also analyses the sustainability of different dimensions of these flows.

Development financing flows are those that are likely to be sustained into the longer term. This chapter focuses on those flows. Development financing should allow for the purchase of physical, productive assets, or those that are associated with ongoing and recurrent activities, such as remittances, or through all forms of taxation and other public revenues. It excludes financing flows that show a tendency to reverse, especially at shorter horizons, such as portfolio flows, or investments that are not for real assets with ongoing productive or developmental output, such as those in existing equities rather than new issues.

The remainder of this chapter is organised as it follows. First, it presents an overview of the country's financial flows available for development, considering both public and private financing sources. Second, it focuses on public resources, and in particular the structure of public revenues and expenditures in Paraguay compared to benchmark economies, as well as the fiscal balance that is sustainable into the medium term. Third, it analyses private financing and shows that the private sector is constrained by structural constraints within the domestic financial sector and limited mobilisation of FDI. It also shows the evolution of remittance flows, although these are relatively modest. Finally, it highlights where Paraguay might be able to expand the role of its private and public partnerships (PPPs) to support national development.

Paraguay's financial flows are low compared to those of benchmark economies and they are below those of OECD economies

International studies seek to highlight which flows and policies can contribute most to supporting financing for development. In support of implementation of the sustainable development goals (SDGs), the Addis Abba Action Agenda on Financing for Development describes the importance of a range of domestic and external sources of financing flows to enable development activities by both the public and private sectors. Other international organisations have sought to identify the policies that can improve their availability for emerging economies (World Bank, 2013; ECLAC, 2016a). Some flows are of the greatest importance for enabling development activities, and a policy agenda is required on how to maximise these flows and their effects, for example by improving tax administration, or by strengthening the linkages between FDI and domestic firms (Box 6.1). As a landlocked country, Paraguay faces particular challenges in structurally transforming its economy, harnessing benefits from international trade, and developing efficient transport and transit systems (United Nations, 2014). They should be considered in designing a financial strategy for Paraguay.

Box 6.1. **Financing flows for development activities**

Effective national development plans seek to mobilise the full range of resources available so as that the public and private sectors can invest and transform the structure of the economy and the well-being of the country's people. Development plans need estimates of the overall financial resources that the country can mobilise to realise its ambitions, and of how the country can make the most of these resources. This assessment is fundamental to the prioritisation of the development agenda, and is necessary to ensure that the development programme is sustainable.

The assessment focuses on the resources that could be available to support developmental investments and operations, rather than how they are used. As far as possible, this assessment should also account for the resources that are potentially available, rather than those that are, in practice, applied. Each of these flows is defined in terms of the size of the flow of resources, rather than the stock of resources that have already been provided. The main sources of financing support the investment and operations of private and of public actors respectively.

Resources for public sector development activities. A country's financing for development is generally dominated by the revenue mobilisation capacities of its public sector. Across most countries, including the benchmark economies, the public sector controls the most significant volumes of financing that can be allocated to development activities. Although the ratio of fiscal revenues to gross domestic product (GDP) remains low in emerging economies compared to OECD economies, fiscal revenues compared to private flows remain substantial, highlighting the need to increase private flows for development. The following comments describe broader trends that are illustrated in Figure 6.1.

1. The mobilisation of domestic resources through taxes and other forms of public revenue. The effectiveness, efficiency and progressiveness of the tax system are essential for successful domestic resource mobilisation. Most of each country's development financing flows are mobilised through the national budget. In the case of Latin America, taxes and social security contributions are close to 23% of GDP (OECD/ECLAC/CIAT/IDB, 2017). The scale of this financing is determined by the revenues that a country is able to raise from its own resources, less budgeted expenditure that is already earmarked and cannot be reallocated towards other developmental activities. In the short to medium term, non-discretionary expenditures are usually limited to payroll and interest expenditures, given that debt contracts and public-sector employment contracts cannot be adjusted in the short term. This concept of nationally mobilised revenues less non-discretionary expenditure can be termed "fiscal space". As the horizon becomes longer-term, all the budget is effectively discretionary and can be reallocated.

2. Improving the efficiency and effectiveness of spending, and so expanding budgetary resources available for development. This may include reallocating spending to support national development objectives, by cutting poorly targeted or distortionary subsidies, or increasing expenditure efficiency by improving public procurement and public finance management systems.

The difference between own-source revenues and non-discretionary expenditure generates the concept of the "fiscal space" that may be available for the public sector to finance development objectives. In practice, this observation reflects the narrow definition of non-discretionary expenditure. In addition to payroll and

Box 6.1. **Financing flows for development activities** *(cont.)*

interest payments, many countries (especially those with larger public sectors) may have components of expenditure that may not be readily reallocated; for example, countries may have significant transfers or other social payments, or they may fund activities that in other contexts are provided by the private sector. It may not be feasible to adjust these payments, especially while improving development outcomes.

3. Sustainable debt financing of the public-sector deficit. A prudent approach may be to maintain a sustainable level of public debt linked to the factors that can be used to service that debt (e.g. GDP, government revenues or exports). The sustainability of deficit financing will be linked with debt sustainability assessments.

4. Official development assistance (ODA), defined broadly to account for all forms of concessional flows, which can be used for certain development investments and over which the recipient government exerts only a degree of influence. Across the benchmark economies, ODA flows are a trivial source of financing for development by the public sector. The limited role of ODA financing is evident even when using a relatively broad definition, that includes the value of the concessionality of concessional lending. This metric does not record the quality or efficiency with which those financing flows are used. The modest volumes of ODA are likely to have significant benefits for development, given the associated processes intended to ensure that they are allocated to high-impact development activities.

Financing the contribution of private sector investments and operations to national development:

5. Domestic private sector investments, which are generally financed through the domestic banking system. These investments by businesses, especially small and medium-sized enterprises (SMEs), may be using credit borrowed by households, so it is important to include credit to all the private sector. Domestic credit flows make differing contributions to financing lending, largely linked to the state of the domestic banking system. In some countries, the amount of domestic plus non-resident lending to the private sector is declining as a share of GDP. This means that the banking system is reducing the amount of financing available for development activities by the private sector, and is generally observed in countries that had earlier experienced credit booms that turned out to be unsustainable.

In some countries, there is a large gap between the amount of financing actually provided to the private sector and the amount that would be expected given the level of financial depth. Proxies for credit to the private sector include income levels and the share of deposits in the domestic banking system. Among the benchmark economies, some have domestic financial systems that generate far greater levels of financing to the private sector than might be expected. This measure gives an approximation estimate on the funds that could be available if the financial sector were operating effectively. Thus, this can represent a measure of the amount of financing that could potentially be provided, relative to current conditions.

The contribution of the change in stock market capitalisation also varies significantly across countries, which is unlikely to reflect contributions to the financing available for the private sector. Changes in stock market capitalisation reflect also changes in the value of the companies that are listed. These changes can mean little in terms of the amount of financing that these companies are able to access, and it is not clear that this indicator alone is an effective indicator of the mobilisation of financing for productive private investments.

6. Foreign direct investment (FDI) can encourage investment in new, innovative or more efficient production modes and in the process can raise the productivity of domestic actors, depending on the business and regulatory environments. These flows do not include portfolio or offshore bank credits, given that the latter flows tend to be short-term and subject to rapid reversals. Higher-income countries are more likely to observe negative net foreign direct investment (FDI) inflows, while lower-income countries observe the opposite. The negative net inflows of FDI may reflect the maturity of earlier direct investments, for example as the owners of the investments repatriate the dividends generated by them. It also reflects a lack of new investment opportunities. In contrast, emerging markets may offer greater scope for new investment opportunities, while existing reinvestments in existing investments may continue.

Box 6.1. **Financing flows for development activities** *(cont.)*

7. Migrants' remittances generally contribute mainly to domestic consumption and household investment. A key factor for these transfers is their transaction costs. In some benchmark economies, net remittances are negative, reflecting the size of immigrants in these countries' labour markets and the salaries that these immigrants repatriate to their native countries. Apart from the poorest of the benchmark economies, even where net remittances are positive, their amount is modest.

8. Philanthropy and international partnerships usually work for the provision of global public goods or strive to address cross-cutting development issues. The values of these flows are likely to be less substantial for individual countries, and may be subsumed within ODA.

The distinction between public and private flows can be somewhat artificial, given that countries are increasingly blending the two. For example, countries may be using private FDI to fund public infrastructure projects through the structure of public-private partnerships (PPPs). The overall assessment must account for such blending.

Sources: Based on United Nations (2015), and authors' analysis of data from IMF (2017a), IMF (2017b); IMF (2016a), World Bank (2017) and World Bank (2016a).

Paraguay's financing flows available for development are low among the comparison countries and remain below OECD benchmark countries (Figure 6.1). On the public side, the available fiscal space (public revenues less committed expenditures) is small. Thanks to the implementation of the Fiscal Responsibility Law (FRL), Paraguay's public deficit remains one the lowest among benchmark countries and in the Latin American region. The FRL establishes a ceiling of 1.5% of GDP (or 1% average over a three-year period) on the government's fiscal deficit, limits any increase in annual expenditures to 4% in real terms and provides that wage increases in the public sector must be in line with increases in the minimum wage. When implemented in 2015, parliament increased the expenditures beyond those proposed by the central government, but excluded expenditures in infrastructure financed by international bond issuances from the calculation of the fiscal deficit for the purposes of the FRL (MH, 2016). In this sense, the low levels of deficit contemplated in the law could be challenging for increasing public investment (see Chapter 2).

The small fiscal space may be explained by both the low level of tax revenues (see following section) and the high level of non-discretionary expenditure[1] (51% of the total). It is worth noting that steps to reduce non-discretionary expenses are well under way. Measures to limit public wage growth, a hiring freeze and the reallocation of existing resources within the public sector to improve performance and productivity are being implemented to assure compliance with the Fiscal Responsibility Law's targets.

For the private sector, net FDI inflows generate a smaller flow of financing than in many other benchmark economies. Indeed, the ratio of FDI to GDP in Paraguay (close to 1%) is considerably lower than for the rest of benchmark countries. Both the public and private sectors make modest use of debt financing (Figure 6.1). For the public sector this reflects efforts to maintain debt sustainability while for the private sector this may reflect a more cautious lending position, possibly linked to the country's recent financial history. These trends are broadly consistent with the patterns observed across countries described in Box 6.1. However, it is noticeable that credit to the private sector (2.6%) is higher than in other benchmark countries. Remittance flows in Paraguay (2% of GDP) are higher than in most countries in the comparison group, although these figures do not subtract outward remittance flows. In all the total financing capacity from private sources in Paraguay (close to 6% of GDP) is relatively low when compared to other countries.

Figure 6.1. **Paraguay's overall financing flows available for development are low**

% of GDP, 2013-15 average

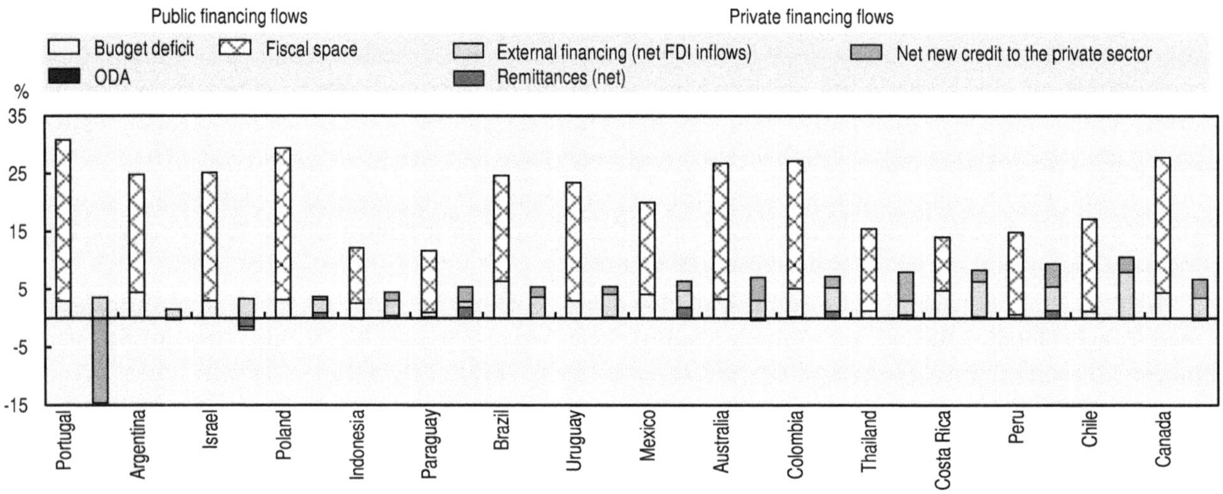

Note: "Fiscal space" is defined here as the amount of revenue a country mobilises itself, excluding grants, less non-discretionary expenditure, which is defined here to include interest payments and salary expenditure. The fiscal deficit is a proxy of the change in the public debt and is presented for general government whenever available inclusive of social security, and ODA refers to Official Development Assistance.

Source: Sources: OECD/ECLAC/CIAT/IDB (2017), OECD (2016b), World Bank (2017) [WDI], IMF 2017a [GFS]; IMF 2016a, 2016b [A4 Paraguay], World Bank 2016a [GFinDevtData].

StatLink http://dx.doi.org/10.1787/888933750643

Public financing flows suggest there is room to improve the level and composition of the taxation system

Total public revenues in Paraguay, are low in comparison with benchmark countries and given Paraguay's GDP per capita. This is partly explained by the lower tax rates of Paraguay compared to other economies. The largest share of public financing for development comes from fiscal space (see Box 6.1 for the definition of fiscal space employed), reflecting a solid public revenue base, although with high non-discretionary expenditures. Indeed, non-discretionary expenditure in Paraguay represents almost half of total revenues (Figure 6.2). ODA inflows are greater in Paraguay than for other countries in the region. Salaries and grants alone accounted for 12.1% of GDP in 2015 and 11.2% in 2016. The fiscal framework appears sustainable, although current infrastructure needs could create risks around the future sustainability of public debt.

Paraguay's fiscal space overall is relatively low in comparison with benchmark countries. But its mix is unusual in some respects. Public revenues are unusually reliant on non-tax revenues, which have contributed to offsetting fiscal budget imbalances in recent years. Non-tax revenues are the compensations and royalties that Paraguay receives from the Itaipú and Yacyreta hydroelectric plants. Royalties from these binational hydroelectric plants have averaged 2.9% of GDP since 2000 (OECD/ECLAC/CIAT/IDB, 2017; see Chapter 2). While a renegotiation of the Yacyretá treaty is pending approval, a clause from the Itaipú Treaty, which ends in 2023, could allow Paraguay to sell energy at market prices, which would represent a significant increase in revenues.

Figure 6.2. **Paraguay's financing flows for the public sector available for development are low**

% of GDP, 2013-15 average

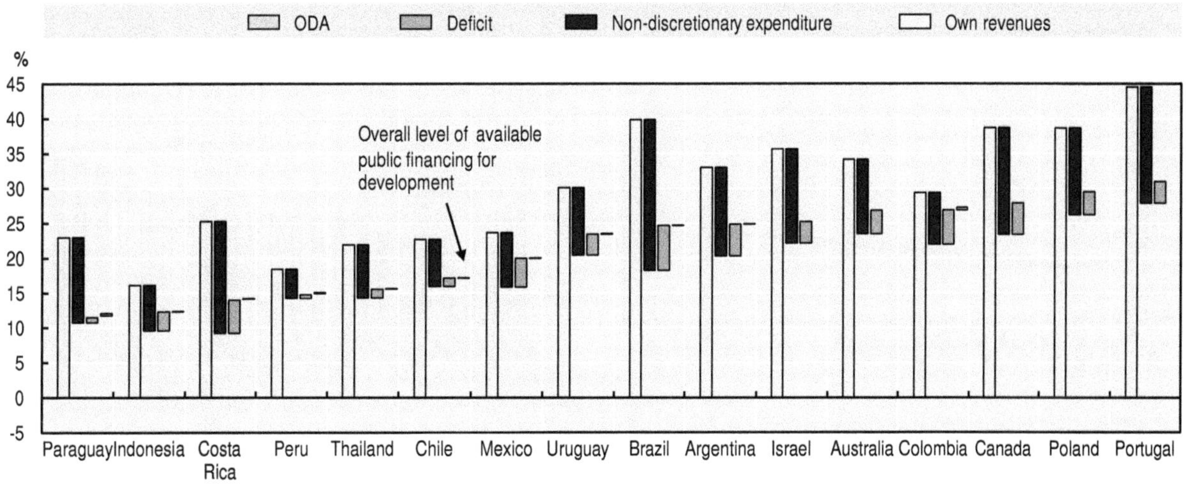

Note: Each bar represents the positive or negative contribution of each type of financing for public sector development activities. The total amount of financing for public development activities is the sum of tax and non-tax revenues raised by the public sector, less the non-discretionary expenditure, plus the fiscal deficit (a proxy of the change in the public debt, defined for general government inclusive of social security when available) and plus the Official Development Assistance (ODA).

Source: OECD/ECLAC/CIAT/IDB (2017), OECD (2016b), World Bank (2017), IMF (2017a); IMF (2016a), IMF (2016b), World Bank (2016).

StatLink http://dx.doi.org/10.1787/888933750662

Tax collection is low and efforts to fight evasion could be strengthened

Total tax revenues, as a share of GDP, continue to be low and concentrated in indirect taxes. Since 2000 tax revenues in Paraguay have increased by 5.4 percentage points of GDP, a rate higher than the growth of 4.9% of GDP in Latin America during the same period. Despite recent improvements, tax-to-GDP ratios continue to be low, 17.9% of GDP in 2015, relative to Latin America and OECD averages of 22.8% and 34.3% respectively (Figure 6.3). Paraguay's main sources of total revenues are taxes on the consumption of goods and services (mainly value added tax [VAT], excise taxes and taxes on foreign trade), and social security contributions. These groups of taxes and contributions represent 83% of total tax revenues, a proportion that is 18 and 24 percentage points higher than in Latin America and OECD economies respectively (Figure 6.4). In the context of trade deceleration, the increase in tax revenues has been driven by taxes on domestic activity which have compensated falls in taxes on foreign trade (including VAT levied on imports). While the latter fell from 6.5% of GDP in 2011 to 5% of GDP in 2016, revenues from all taxes on domestic activity increased from 6.0% of GDP to 7.5% in 2016 and social security contributions increased from 3.8% of GDP to 4.6% in 2016.

Total tax revenues rely on VAT (56% of total tax revenue) while the personal income tax (PIT) is, in its current form, an administrative aid to foster formalisation and VAT compliance. VAT is the main tax collected and the tax that has shown significant growth. In 2000 it accounted for 43% of total taxes, increasing to 50% of total tax revenue in 2016. Several reforms to VAT help explain this increase. In 2014 VAT was expanded and levied on the agricultural sector, although at a lower rate of 5%, with the possibility of setting differentiated rates between 5% and 10% (Law 5061/13), which might raise control difficulties for the tax administration, as these need to differentiate amongst distinct goods, altering the normal value chain, to apply the appropriate rate.

Figure 6.3. **Despite a recent increase, tax revenues are still low**

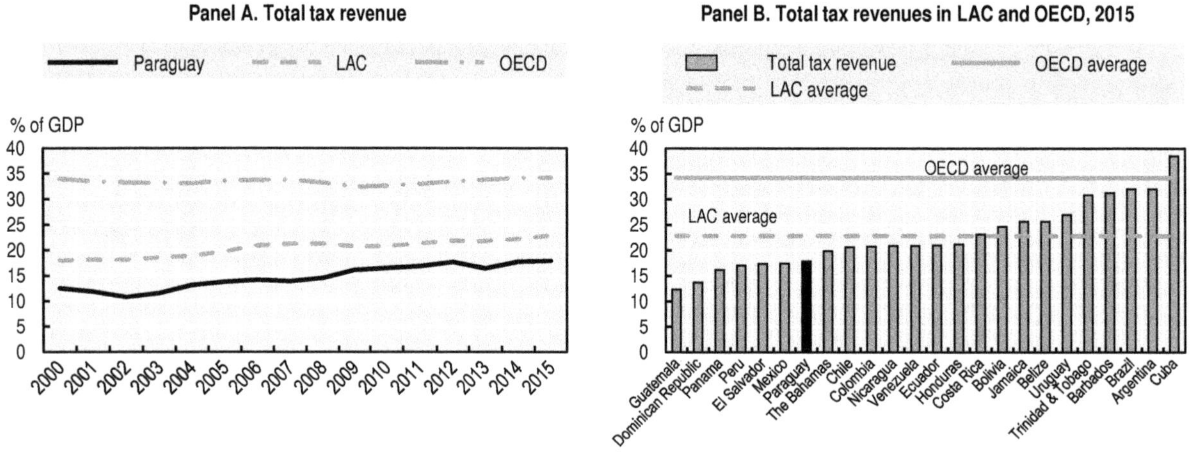

Source: (OECD/ECLAC/CIAT/IDB (2017), *OECD Revenue Statistics in Latin America and the Caribbean.*

StatLink http://dx.doi.org/10.1787/888933750681

Figure 6.4. **Paraguay's main sources of total revenues are taxes on the consumption of goods and services**

Share of total revenue and Percentage of GDP (in parentheses) by main group of taxes in 2015

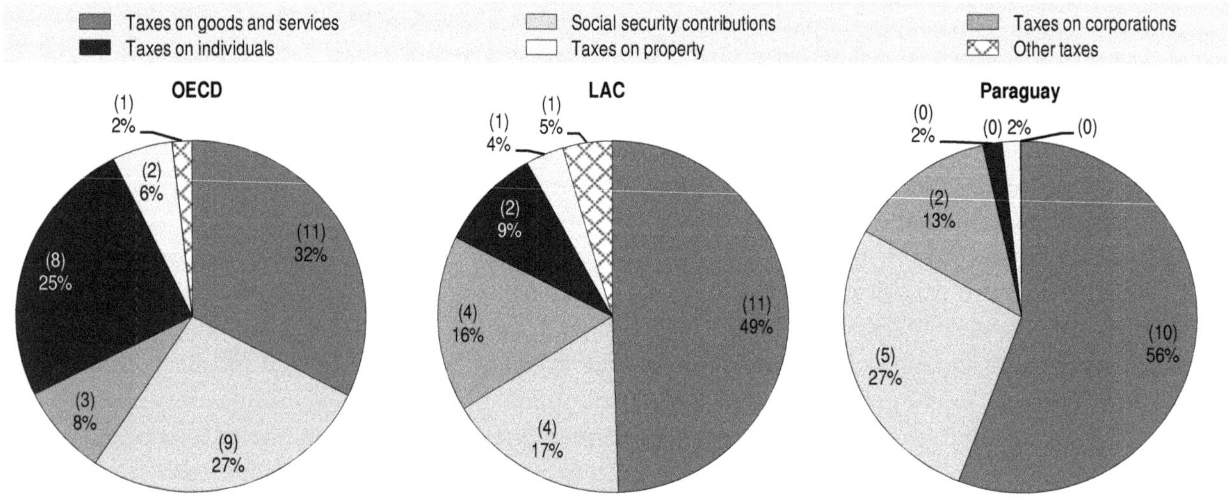

Source: OECD/ECLAC/CIAT/IDB (2017), *Revenue Statistics in Latin America and the Caribbean.*

StatLink http://dx.doi.org/10.1787/888933750700

Personal income tax, which dates from a law enacted in 2004 and was finally enforced in 2012, raises little revenue (1.1% of tax revenues in 2016) and serves mainly the purpose of encouraging formalisation by allowing numerous deductions on all kinds of invoiced expenditures. The contribution of the PIT to total tax revenues is lower than in benchmark countries (Figure 6.5). Furthermore, the high levels of lower threshold for the PIT schedule ensure that a great proportion of the population is exempt from any liability. This threshold was set at the equivalent of 120 annual minimum wages in 2012 and is set gradually to decrease until it reaches the equivalent of 36 annual minimum wages by 2019 (8% tax rate for 36-120 annual minimum wages, 10% tax for income higher than 120 annual minimum wages) (OECD/IDB/The World Bank, 2014). Some measures to limit deductions have been established (Decree No. 6560/16), improving the revenue-raising prospects of the tax in the long-run.

Figure 6.5. **The personal income tax ratio to total tax revenues is lower in Paraguay than in benchmark countries**

% of GDP, 2015

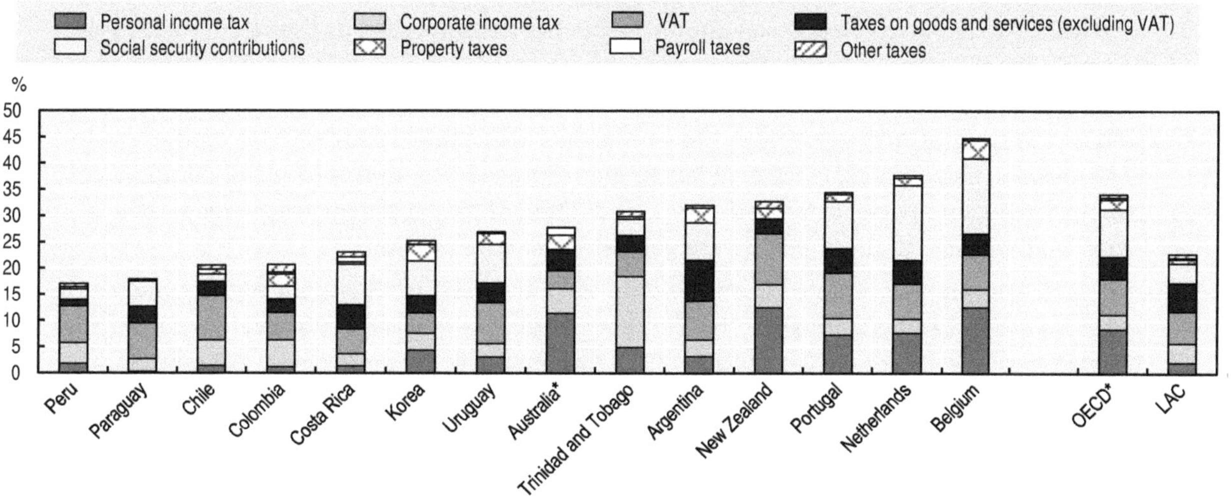

Note: Data for OECD economies are for 2014.

Source: OECD/ECLAC/CIAT/IDB (2017), *Revenue Statistics in Latin America and the Caribbean* and OECD (2016b), *Revenue Statistics 2016.*

StatLink http://dx.doi.org/10.1787/888933750719

The potential of the personal income tax has yet to be realised. In its current state it is inefficient as it increases administrative costs while raising few tax revenues. Paraguay's tax wedge, the difference between labour costs and an average worker's take-home pay, is 20.9% of labour costs. The tax wedge is comprised of the personal income tax and mandatory social security contributions paid by employee and employer. Paraguay's total tax wedge is lower than the Latin America and OECD averages of 21.7% and 35.9% of labour costs respectively. The tax wedge difference with OECD economies is entirely explained by the personal income tax, which is not levied at the average wage level or at the highest levels of income deciles (OECD/IDB/CIAT, 2016). The sum of standard allowances and exempted amounts provided by the current tax code is 1.95 times higher for individuals in the 10th income decile, effectively voiding the PIT's capacity to raise revenue (Barreix, Benítez and Pecho, 2017).

Improving other sources of tax revenues is critical to ensuring an adequate supply of funds for capital expenditures. The recent introduction of the tax on profits from agricultural activities in 2014 (*Impuesto a las Rentas de las Actividades Agropecuarias*, IRAGRO) yielded 0.2% of GDP in additional revenues by 2015. However, other sources of revenues have diminished. Taxes on foreign trade and excise taxes have declined by 0.4% and 0.2% of GDP during the last five years, in part because of a slowdown in the re-export trade, the zero tariffs within Mercosur as well as other trade agreements. The tax on profits from commercial, industrial or services activities (*Impuesto sobre la Renta Comercial, Industrial o de Servicios*, IRACIS) remained steady at 2.4% of GDP during this period.

Non-tax revenues have contributed to offsetting the fiscal budget imbalances. Non-tax revenues are the compensations and royalties that Paraguay receives from the Itaipú and Yacyreta hydroelectric plants (OECD/ECLAC/CIAT/IDB, 2017). Royalties and compensation payments from these binational hydroelectric plants have averaged 2.9% of GDP since 2000. However, these non-tax revenues decreased from around 26% of public revenues in 2001 to 11% in 2016. Furthermore, these sources of funds are susceptible to shifts in electricity production and demand, given Argentina and Brazil's economic volatility, and are projected to decrease in the medium term because of higher energy consumption in Paraguay. This underlines the need to improve revenue collection as sources based on tax revenues tend to be more stable over time.

Efforts to broaden the tax base should be further accompanied by the strengthening of the tax administration. Recent efforts to broaden the tax base through the enforcement of a personal income tax, extending VAT to agricultural products and co-operative associations, and the levying of new agricultural tax on profits from this sector will be ineffective if institutional frameworks, legal mechanisms and procedures to improve tax compliance and enforcement are not improved. The introduction of taxpayer registries, organisational improvements and audit strategies are good steps to curb evasion.

VAT evasion was reduced from 36.7% in 2012 to 30.9% in 2014, still higher than the evasion rate in Latin America (25.9%) (Giménez et al., 2017). Paraguay's revenue authority (*Subsecretaría de Estado de Tributación*, SET) has made good progress in strengthening institutional frameworks, administrative capacity, introducing taxpayer registries, control measures, and dismantling tax evasion schemes, but further improvements are needed. The SET authorities have emphasised the challenges and constraints that undermine tax compliance such as understaffing and unsatisfactory training of current staff (around 1 000 SET officials and 700 000 tax payers). Budget constraints also limit hiring additional staff, thus requiring the use of technology to make procedures more efficient, for instance exploring the option of exerting better control through electronic invoicing. Additional steps include legislation to increase the chances of an audit and sanctions given that the current probability and cost of being detected are low (SET, 2016). Nevertheless, the enforcement and efficiency of the law might be undermined by long legal procedures and the judicial system's lack of enforcement capacity. Paraguay's recent commitment to the Global Forum on Transparency and Exchange of Information for Tax Purposes in the fight against tax avoidance and its membership of the Inclusive Framework on Base Erosion and Profit Shifting (BEPS) are welcome. The latter provides governments with the tools to ensure that profits are taxed where economic activities are performed and where value is created. These tools also give businesses greater certainty about the application of international tax rules and standardising compliance requirements.

Tax expenditures are mainly concentrated in VAT and exemptions granted within the corporate income tax. Total tax expenditures were estimated around 1.92% of GDP in 2014, and most of the foregone revenue is concentrated in the VAT regime (1.36% of GDP). The VAT regime foregoes revenue by exempting fuels, private education and health services. Losses also arise from taxing goods and services in the basic consumer basket of goods and medicines at a lower rate (5%). The corporate income tax losses are less than 10% of the collection of the tax, exonerations are of smaller magnitude and it has a broad base but still amounts to 0.22% of GDP. In the case of personal income tax, the main factors behind tax expenditure are incomes that are not yet included in the tax base given the law's implementation schedule (0.13% of GDP). Exemptions from customs tariffs represent the remaining 0.2% of GDP (CIAT/SET/GIZ, 2015).

As in the case with other countries in the region, reducing compliance burdens in Paraguay can increase tax effort and public financing space, without imposing significant additional costs for payers. The tax system could be simplified, for example, by reducing the number of payments or streamlining administrative processes. Paraguay has made significant efforts in this direction (see Chapter 2). Simplifying compliance may increase collection, by reducing the scope for non-compliance and by encouraging greater declarations. Lower compliance costs may also contribute to reducing the size of the informal sector. Reducing compliance costs and strengthening collection could contribute to raising tax revenues and would bring tax receipts to the growth-supporting "tipping point", and can create the additional resources needed for increasing investment in Paraguay.

Limited non-discretionary public expenditures suggest that reallocating spending could improve developmental outcomes. Public expenditure allocations in Paraguay suggest there is a reduced scope for resources to be reallocated towards development priorities. Of total expenditure of between 16% and 18% of GDP over the past five years, the ratio of current expenditure to investment in 2016 has remained unbalanced, reaching 85% to 15% in 2016 (OFIP/CADEP, 2017). Salaries and wages still represent a high proportion of current expenditure (50% in 2016), even if it decreased slightly when comparing to previous years, whereas social security contributions have remained constant, in relative terms, in the expenditure structure. This share of GDP allocated to non-discretionary public expenditure is low relative to the other benchmark economies, even if capital expenditure and investment increased faster than current expenditure (20% against 3.2%) between 2015 and 2016.

Private financing flows are still low, but start to consolidate in the form of external investment and a sound financial sector

Overall, private financing equivalent to 5.5% of GDP for activities that were potentially developmental was available over 2013-15, compared with 11.8% of GDP for the public sector (highlighted above). These flows were generated by FDI (1.1%), remittances (1.6%) and the contribution of the domestic financial sector (2.6%).

Although FDI inflows dominate the financing available for private sector activities, they remain low when compared to other benchmark countries. FDI inflows averaged close to 1% of GDP over 2013-15 (WDI, 2017). External financing is therefore lower than for other comparison countries, whereas remittances contributed to a non-negligible share of private financing flows. Compared to benchmark economies, Paraguay exhibited relatively low private flows in the period 2013-15 (Figure 6.6).

Figure 6.6. **Compared to benchmark economies, Paraguay exhibited relatively low private flows**

Private sector financing flows, % of GDP, average 2013-15

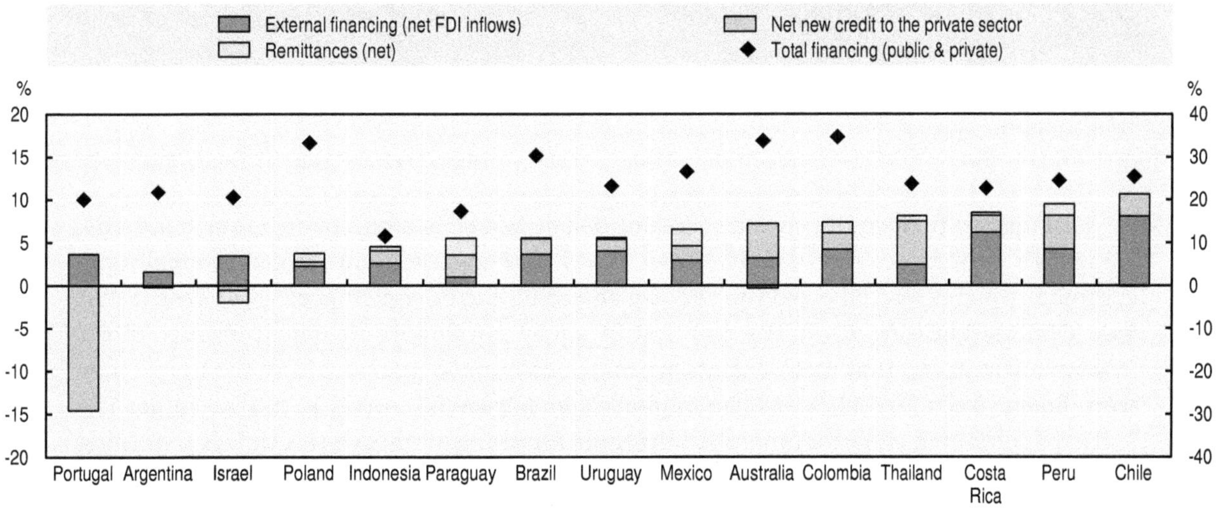

Source: World Bank (2017) [WDI], IMF 2017a [GFS]; IMF 2016a, IMF 2016b [A4 Par], World Bank 2016a [GFinDevtData].

StatLink http://dx.doi.org/10.1787/888933750738

Foreign direct investment inflows are growing, but could finance larger-scale activities

Paraguay was in 2015 the country with the second lowest share of FDI inflows as a proportion of GDP in the region, accounting for only 1.16% of GDP (WDI, 2017; Figure 6.7, Panel A). Being a small open economy, this is a modest share when compared to other small economies in the region such as Costa Rica or Panama. Moreover, Paraguay's foreign direct investments represent only 0.2% of the Latin America's total FDI. However, the overall trend of FDI inflows over the past five years is positive. Net FDI inflows to Paraguay averaged close to 1.8% of GDP over the period 2010-15, an improvement when compared to previous periods. FDI in Paraguay is centred on a number of sector-strategic hubs and usually associated with the employment of skilled labour. Most of the projects are concentrated in the east of the country. Although traditionally low, FDI in Paraguay has gained some prominence in recent years, as a result of the government's strategy for improving the investment framework, which has been successful in tapping international investment directed towards specific industries. Triggering factors to attract investment to Paraguay are the country's access to natural resources, low labour costs in comparison to its neighbours and the extremely favourable tax structure. Such sectors as the automotive, agro-business and telecommunications have received major investments recently and, in the near future, inward FDI should continue to be favoured by developing infrastructure projects.

Figure 6.7. **Paraguay has a low share of FDI inflows but can finance its deficit through FDI**

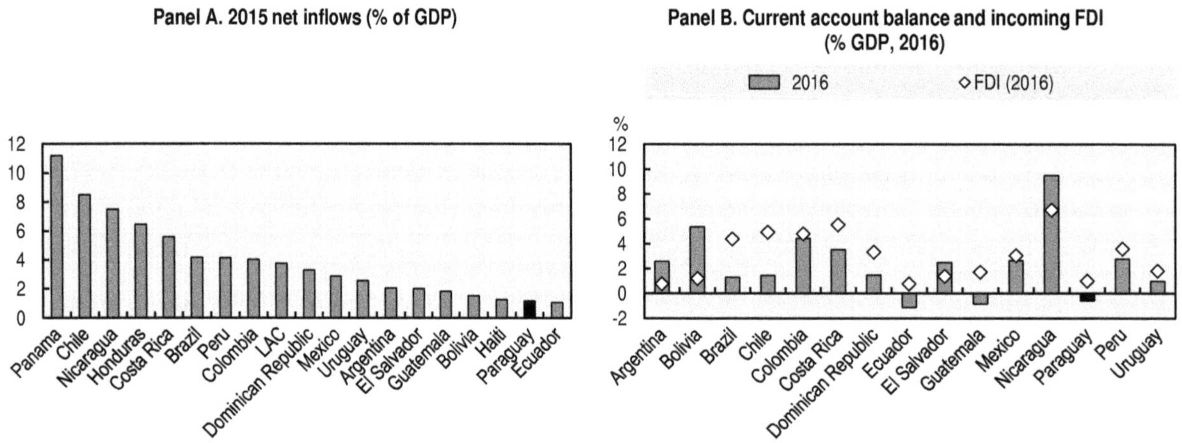

Source: Panel A: IMF and World Development Indicators (2017). Panel B: OECD/ECLAC/CAF (2018), *Latin American Economic Outlook 2018: Rethinking Institutions for Development*.

StatLink http://dx.doi.org/10.1787/888933750757

FDI inflows finance the current account deficit, which is small by regional standards. Paraguay's current account deficit, below 2% of GDP in 2015, has remained small; low commodity prices have allowed the country and other net energy importers, to keep it that way (OECD/ECLAC/CAF, 2016). The fact that Paraguay can finance its deficit through direct investment suggests that these deficits are more sustainable than would be the case if they were financed through shorter-term capital flows (Figure 6.7, Panel B). Still, a larger FDI participation would allow for more than the mere financing of the external deficit, becoming a sustainable financing source in areas such as infrastructure.

Paraguay's FDI stock has grown at a rapid pace, while the origin of foreign investment has shifted considerably over the past decade. Over the period 2003-15, the average growth of Paraguay's FDI stock was 15.1%. Overall, Latin American and the Caribbean have been losing ground as recipients of FDI, which accounts for 3.3% of the region's GDP (ECLAC, 2016b). Paraguay has not been the exception, and the country experienced significant contraction in FDI stocks after the 2008 financial crisis, following the recovery of the U.S. and other industrialised economies. Estimated FDI stock contraction in 2015 was of 18%. It is possible that these falls might be due to the cyclical nature of FDI, as in the preceding year net FDI flows had increased by 63% (BCP, 2017b). Together with the volatility of FDI inflows, the composition of investment by country has also changed (Figure 6.8). While in 2003, inward FDI in Paraguay came predominantly from the United States, a different pattern can be observed during the past decade: while the United States and Brazil remain the country's largest foreign investors, the US participation in Paraguay's FDI fell from 38% in 2003 to 27% in 2015, while Brazil's share rose from 11% to 19%. In addition, European economies such as Spain and the Netherlands have been gradually increasing their share of investment, accounting respectively for 9% and 5% of the country's FDI stock in 2015. Overall, the diversification of FDI sources for Paraguay signals a positive development towards the consolidation of an investment strategy.

Figure 6.8. **Together with the volatility of FDI inflows, the composition of investment by country has also changed**

Stock of FDI by years and country of origin

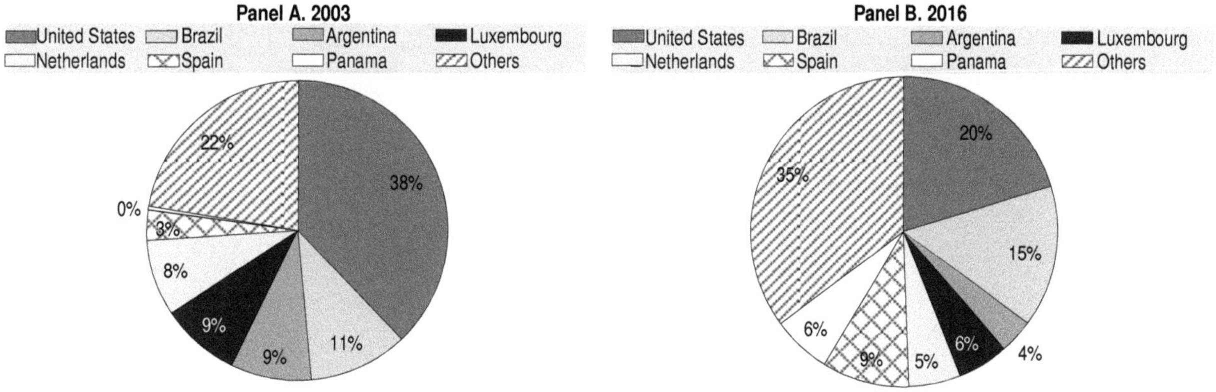

Source: Central Bank of Paraguay (BCP) (2017).

StatLink http://dx.doi.org/10.1787/888933750776

In terms of FDI stock distribution, the tertiary sector has consistently been the largest recipient in relative terms, although the secondary sector has been increasing its share in recent years (Figure 6.9, Panel A). Within the primary sector, which includes primary products and manufacturing of primary goods, oil processing accounted for more than 50% of foreign investment in 2015, followed by beverages and tobacco (15%) and livestock (12%,) (Figure 6.9, Panel B). Noticeably, only 11% of the investment stock in the primary sector is destined for agriculture. In the secondary sector, which includes non-agricultural processing and industries, more than 50% of the investment is accounted for by the chemical production industry (56%), followed by paper (12%) and textiles (11%). As for the tertiary sector, which involves services, they have been concentrated in financial intermediation (56%), communications (12%) and retail (4%).

Figure 6.9. **The tertiary sector has consistently been the largest recipient of FDI**

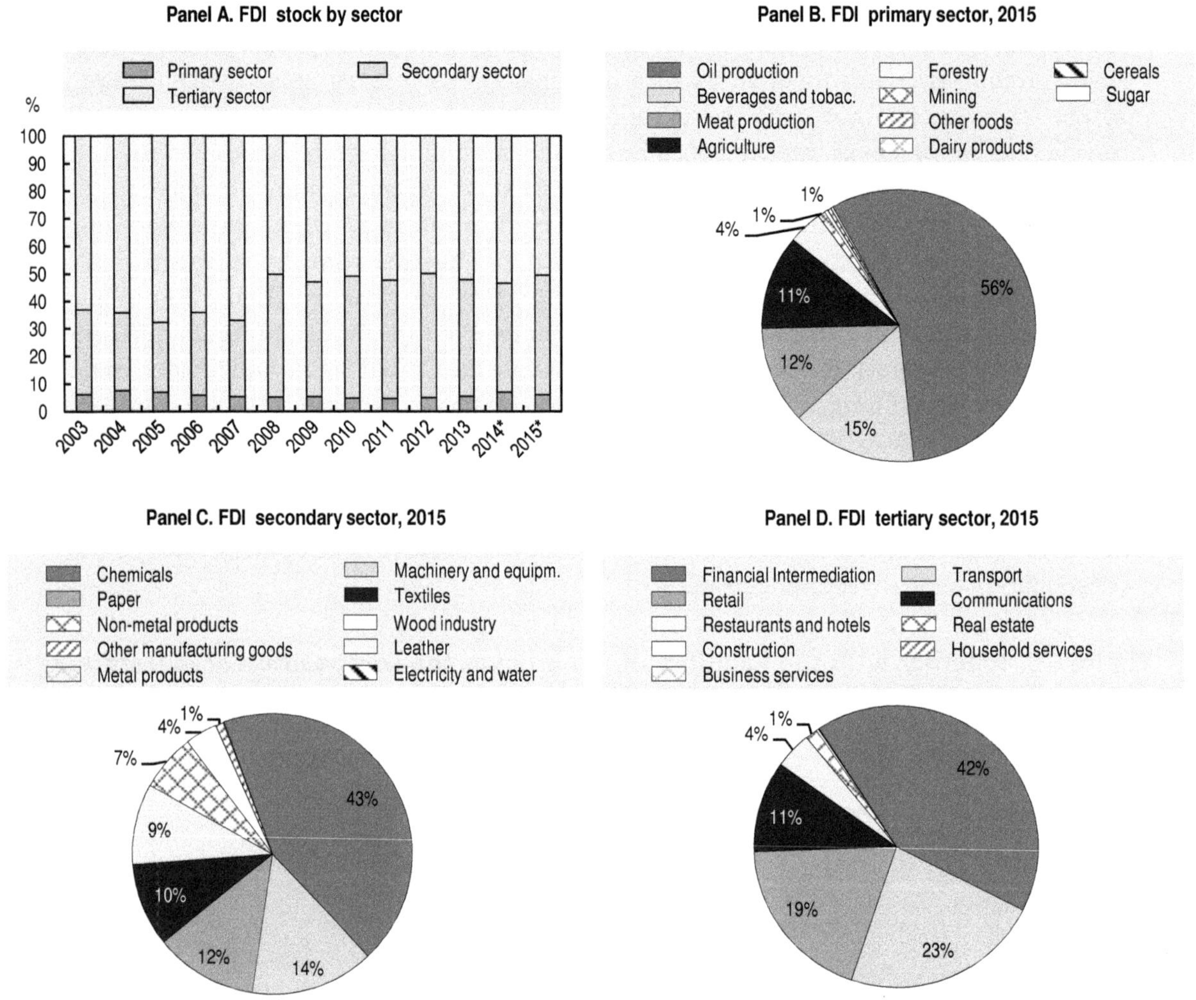

Source: BCP (2017b).

StatLink http://dx.doi.org/10.1787/888933750795

The structure of foreign investment in Paraguay suggests it could be improved in the future. Net FDI inflows in Paraguay have seen an increasing role for reinvested earnings, and a fall in intercompany loans and capital contributions (Figure 6.10). In some countries, the absence of a pool of incoming investments could underline the existence of a risk for external solvency. Indeed, Paraguay's current structure of direct investment inflows suggests that a greater repatriation of profits could shift net direct investment inflows to negative, generating challenges for financing other development activities and Paraguay's overall external accounts. A comparison with other countries in the region such as Chile, Colombia and Brazil, indicates a lower proportion of reinvested earnings in FDI, with a high share for equity capital and intercompany loans. Rebalancing the components of Paraguay's FDI structure, by bringing new projects for investment and depending less on established projects, could be part of the medium-term government strategy for investment attraction.

In Paraguay, FDI adds little value in terms of job creation

While the efforts for attracting investment to Paraguay are remarkable, the effect of these efforts on employment creation is still modest. Indeed, the industries with the highest levels of job creation in 2015 received relatively small amounts of foreign investment, as were the cases of the industries of business services, electronic components and food and tobacco. A notable exception is the case of the automotive sector, where employment creation continues to be substantial. On the other hand, firms with the highest levels of foreign investment (warehousing and storage, real estate and renewable energy) seemed to have had little value added in terms of job creation (Figure 6.11). A second stage of Paraguay's investment strategy could be to insist in incorporating employment creation as one of the priorities for investment attraction.

Figure 6.10. **Net FDI inflows in Paraguay have seen an increasing role for reinvested earnings**

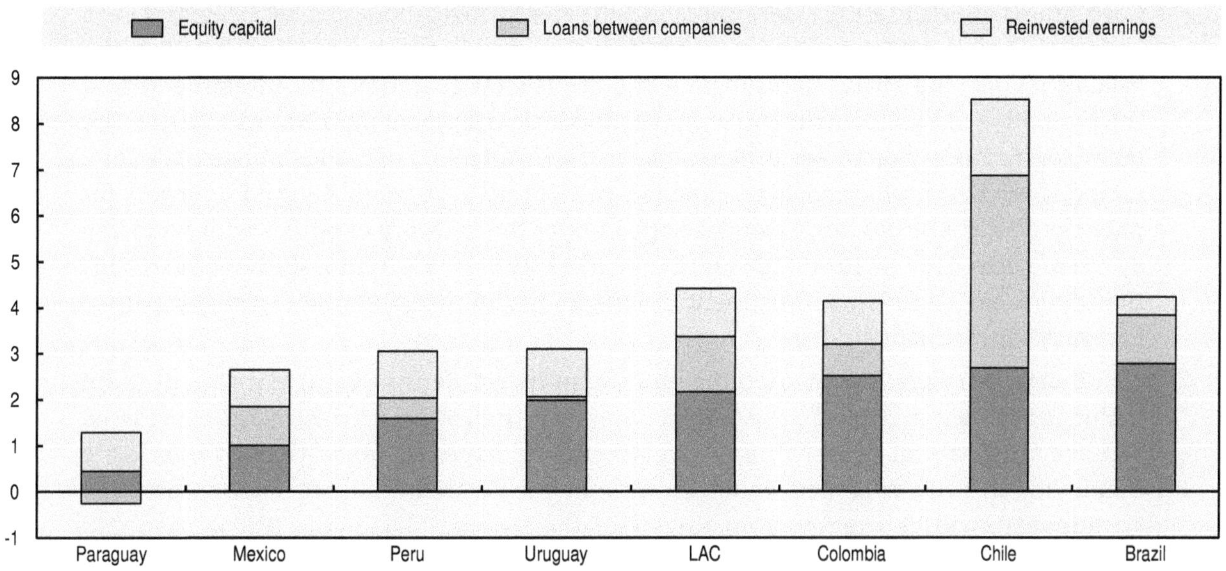

Source: OECD calculations based on ECLAC (2016b) and GDP estimates from IMF (2016b).

StatLink http://dx.doi.org/10.1787/888933750814

Figure 6.11. **Firms with the highest levels of foreign investment seems to have had little value added in terms of job creation in 2015**

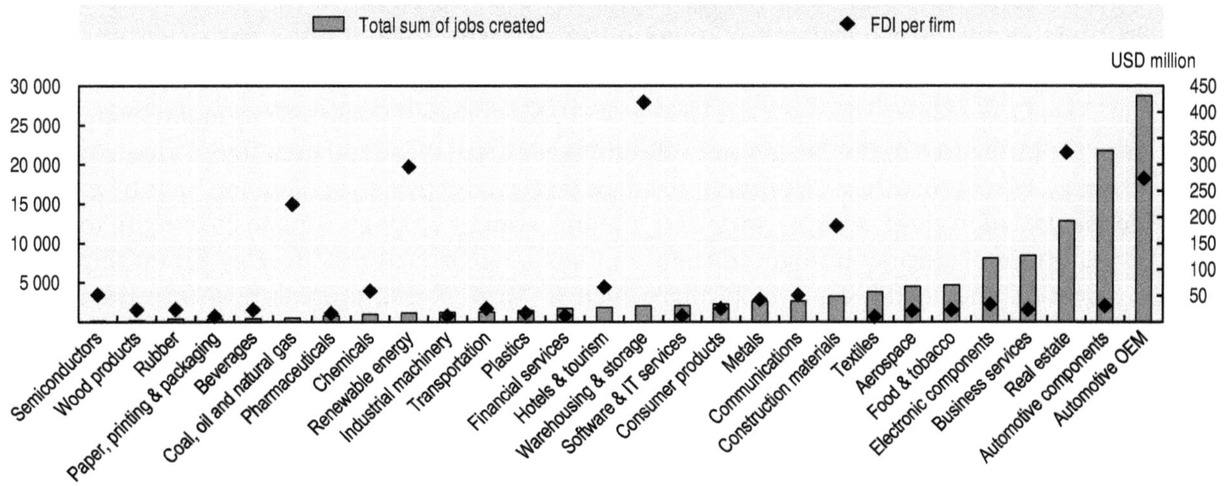

Note: Data for companies investing in Paraguay between January 2003 and March 2017.

Source: FDI Markets, 2017. OECD calculations.

StatLink http://dx.doi.org/10.1787/888933750833

Paraguay has made significant efforts to consolidate an investment promotion strategy

The recent increase in FDI flows has been partially driven by Paraguay's efforts to create an attractive regulatory framework for foreign investment. The current investment framework draws on Paraguay's comparative advantages, based on a competitive tax regime, a young labour force, low labour costs, low-cost clean electricity, a strategic location relative to other countries in the region. Having a simplified tax regime, together with some of the benefits provided by the Mercosur agreement, has created further incentives for countries such as Brazil and Argentina to increase their share of investment in the country. Government efforts to attract investment include special regulations and fiscal regimes such as the tax incentive scheme for national and foreign capital investment (Law No. 60/90), the *maquila* regime, the *zonas francas* regime and the law on guarantees for investments and the promotion of employment and socio-economic development (Law No. 5.542/2015). The latter, for instance, guarantees to beneficiaries the invariability of the income tax rate for a period of ten years, which could be extended to 15 or up to 20 years. A legal framework for public procurement has also been developed under the category of tender with financing by the provider (Law N° 5074/2013) and by the PPP Law (Law 5102/2013, see Chapter 2). This framework has stimulated investment of foreign capital and constitutes a major part of Paraguay's investment strategy.

Today, there are few restrictions on foreign investment in Paraguay. One of them includes acquisition of land close to the border (less than 50 km). Investments considered to have "high social content" (e.g. investments in deprived areas that will generate employment, provide added value for primary industries and are environmentally sustainable), will be exempt from the 5% of the income tax for the distribution and remittance of profits. Another important advantage for Paraguay is the generalised system of preferences Plus (SGP +), through which it can export around 6 500 products with zero tariff. Paraguay is the only Mercosur country with this status. Still, greater efforts are required to transform these benefits into more investment in high-productivity sectors. Investment regimes could also consider potential effects on the domestic industry over the long term, as competition between domestic and foreign industries has increased in some sectors (e.g. construction, metal-working), with foreign firms outperforming Paraguayan ones.

Measures to attract investment, diversify production and boost trade integration are being implemented by the Paraguayan authorities as part of their structural transformation strategy. Efforts to attract investment to encourage productive diversification have been concentrated in three main sectors: first, the investment strategy aims to contribute to transforming Paraguay into an efficient and sustainable food producer by promoting innovation and added value in primary sectors. To this end, programmes to attract investments for the insertion of Paraguay into new value chains (for instance, supporting rice production for the Arab market and chicken production directed at the Chinese market) and to add value to specific niche-products (e.g. organic food, craft beer, manioc flour) are being implemented. Second, the strategy aims to transform Paraguay into a factory for the region, through the use of different investment attraction instruments; the number of maquiladoras has increased significantly (from 46 firms in 2013 to 126 in 2016). The sectors with greatest dynamism are automotive parts, plastics, textiles, and footwear. Third, Paraguay's investment strategy is also embedded in the infrastructure development plan, in particular to transform the Hidrovía Paraná-Paraguay into a 24 hours route. The Ministry of Industry and Commerce (MIC) envisages the potential creation of clusters around these investments. In addition, with the support of the Inter-American Development Bank (IDB) and the Red de Exportaciones e Inversiones (*REDIEX*), the internationalisation of Paraguayan companies has been promoted through funds to support the development of exporting companies in strategic sectors (food, manufacturing, logistics). Although not a central part of it, Paraguay's strategy has focused on the development of the industrial sector, although the services sector, highly linked to agricultural production, has received some support, with more than 5 000 jobs created in the Asunción area (DGEEC, 2016).

The financial system should be further developed and become more inclusive

Paraguay's financial system is still being developed, becoming slightly more concentrated and with a lower foreign participation. It is currently composed of 17 commercial banks, including a public bank (Banco Nacional de Fomento), ten financial institutions, 89 co-operatives, 41 institutional investors, and 35 other institutions. Commercial banks in Paraguay hold the largest proportion of assets followed by savings and credit co-operatives. In December 2015 commercial banks accounted for about 73% of total assets, while credit and savings co-operatives accounted for 8% and institutional investors (e.g. insurance companies, the *Instituto de Previsión Social* and pension funds) represented about 15%. In the last decades there has been a decrease in the number of foreign-owned institutions in the banking system. Of the total assets held by banks, about 52% are held by banks that are majority locally owned, followed by 38% held by banks that are majority foreign owned, 5.7% from banks under state ownership (*Banco Nacional de Fomento*) and 3.8% in branches of foreign banks (BCP, 2016).

The country has a dual financial supervisory system. The Superintendence of Banks is the regulatory agency that oversees commercial banks, financial institutions, exchange bureaux and other deposit institutions. Co-operatives are regulated and supervised by the National Co-operative Institute (INCOOP). INCOOP enforcement power should be strengthened and supervision must be risk-based. There is deposit insurance for banks and financial institutions but not yet for members of credit co-operatives. Efforts to introduce legislation to establish a guarantees fund are in progress. In respect of financial regulation, the OECD *General Guidance on a Policy Framework for Effective and Efficient Financial Regulation* and the *High-Level Principles on Financial Consumer Protection* set out principles that should be considered. Some of these principles suggest that financial regulation should warrant a precautionary approach, be oriented to risks, seek to align incentives of participants with policy objectives, and ensure that all identified market failures and needs are properly addressed (OECD, 2010). In addition, financial consumer protection should be an integral part of the legal framework, regulation should reflect the characteristics of financial products, be responsive to new products, and providers of financial services providers should be appropriately regulated and supervised. In this direction, the Central bank is working on two projects, one for publishing financial costs and another to strengthen consumer protection norms for financial institutions.

Paraguay's capital markets are embryonic but could gain ground as a financing source. The country's stock exchange has seen a considerable growth in recent years, particularly in the corporate bond market. Financial institutions and private individuals are increasingly trading fixed-income securities, and for the first time in 2016 the secondary bond market surpassed the primary market (52% vs 48% of the total market). About 60% of securities are issued in guaraní (PYG) and the remaining 40% in dollars. The equity market remains less developed. The regulatory framework for the securities market, under the responsibility of the Comisión Nacional de Valores, is developing. In terms of integration, since 2017, the Comisión Nacional de Valores is an associate member of the International Organization of Securities Commissions (IOSCO), and some regional agreements have been signed by Asunción's stock exchange, such as with Montevideo's Stock Exchange.

The financial system is relatively solid when compared to benchmark countries. Banks are well capitalised, with sufficient access to sources of deposit financing and are highly profitable (Figure 6.14). The minimum requirements of capital adequacy are fulfilled with a ratio of regulatory capital to risk-weighted assets of around 18% in 2016 while the ratio for Latin America is around 15% and the minimum required is 12%. Most of the financial system funding comes from internal sources such as deposits. Customer deposits to total loans account for 94% which is high, although lower than the average in the region. In terms of liquidity in the banking system to meet cash demand, the liquid assets to total assets ratio has decreased slightly in recent years. Profitability indicators, measuring the efficiency of the financial system in Paraguay regarding the use of assets and capital are amongst the highest, compared to the regional average, and other benchmark countries (Figure 6.12, Panel C). However, both the return on assets (ROA) and the return on equity (ROE) have declined in recent years. Likewise, while the ratio of non-interest expenses to total gross income is low compared to other benchmark countries, it has increased considerably in recent years, rising from 24.5% in 2012 to 38% by 2016.

Although the number of banks has been reduced in the last decades, Paraguay's banking sector concentration level is not excessive and still competitive. A standard measure of bank concentration (the Herfindahl-Hirschman index), estimated with the assets of commercial banks and financial institutions results in 1 020.6 by June 2016, indicating a low level of concentration (1 500 to 2 500 indicates moderate concentration, higher than 2 500 indicates a high level of concentration) (BCP, 2016). Research for the 2000-12 period indicates a certain level of competition in the banking sector given that banks are willing to reduce margins by increasing market share; for each increase of 1 percentage point in the market share, the effective interest rate margin decreases by 0.0326 percentage points. However, there is little variation among banking providers and Paraguay remains a high-priced and high-profit market. New incentives and measures to encourage competition in the sector could help to reduce such interest rate margins.

Paraguay's interest rate spreads (16%) continue to be among the highest in the region (7%) and in comparison to the benchmark countries. Spreads increased at the beginning of the 2000s as a result of banking crises but as a result of regulation reforms margins followed a downward trend after that. However, they remain consistently high relative to other countries (Figure 6.13). Margins reflect risk-taking, regulatory costs and operating costs, among other factors. Failure to access complete information on customers increases credit risk, requiring higher-rate margins. Improving the quality and availability of credit information would promote financial deepening and inclusion by helping to reduce credit risk premiums and hence, spreads.

Figure 6.12. **Paraguay's financial system is relatively solid**

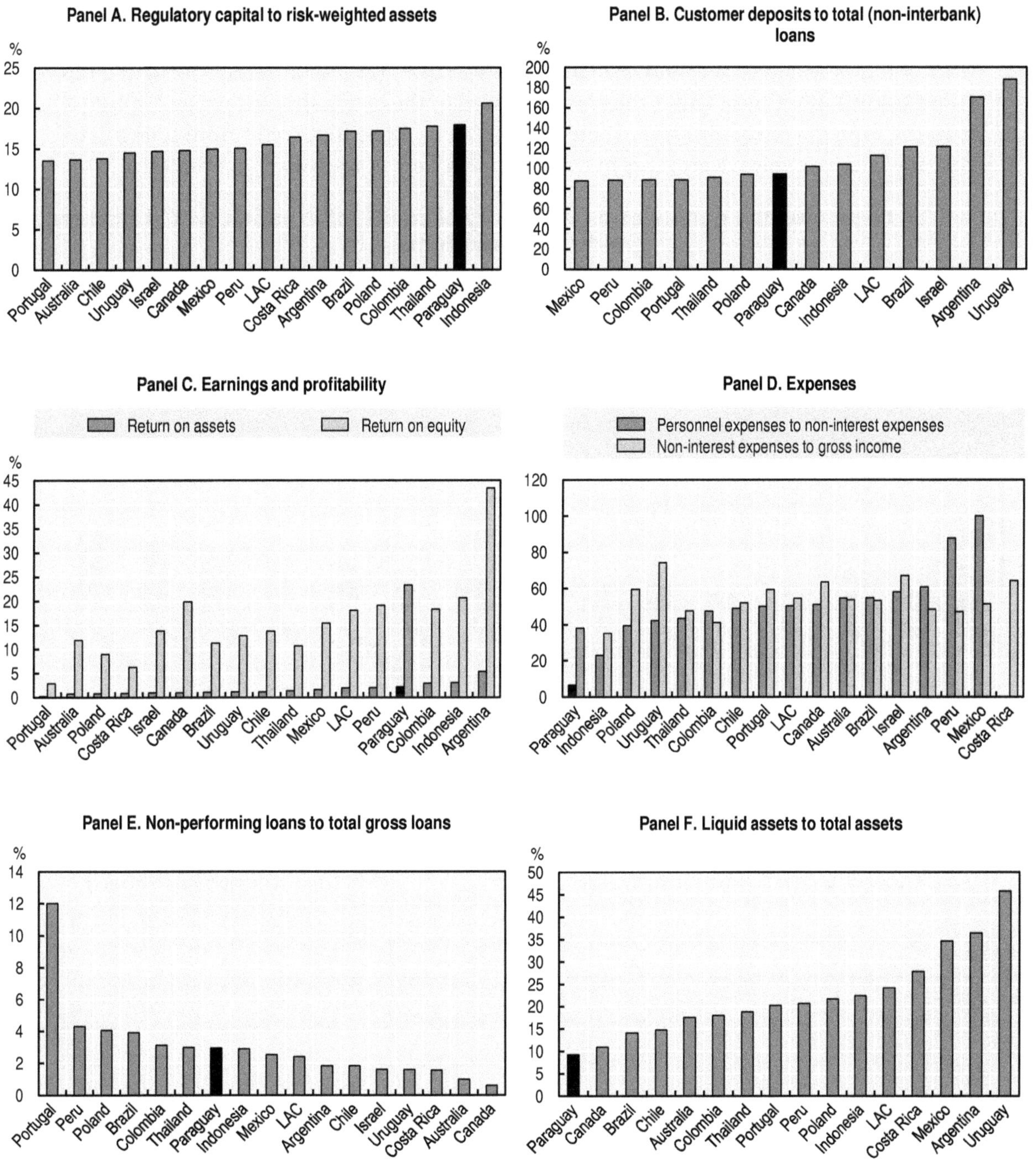

Source: International Monetary Fund (IMF), Financial Soundness Indicators Database (IMF, 2017a).

StatLink http://dx.doi.org/10.1787/888933750852

Credit growth has accelerated in recent years. Expansion of banking credit has been substantial (around 26% average growth over 2005-15 relative to 8% average growth over 1994-2004) and present in all economic sectors during the last years reflecting mostly macroeconomic fundamentals and the deepening and stability of the banking system. After peaking in 2015, credit growth has moderated as economic activity has slowed and financial conditions have become less favourable. The share of banking credit to private sector relative to GDP rose from about 11% in 2005 to 43% by 2015 on average (Figure 6.14, Panel A). The economic sectors that got the largest share of credit from commercial banks (by June 2016) were agriculture (22.8%), wholesale commerce (15.7%), and consumption (14.2%). Financial institutions provide a larger share of loans to consumption (25.3%) rather than to agriculture (16.5%) (BCP, 2016). Almost half of the credit provided by the national development bank (BNF) is in the form of consumer loans. There are also some signs that credit from unregulated non-traditional lenders is growing, but this remains a small fraction of credit (IMF, 2017c).

Figure 6.13. **Improving the quality and availability of credit information would help reduce credit risk premiums**

Interest rate spread (lending rate minus deposit rate)

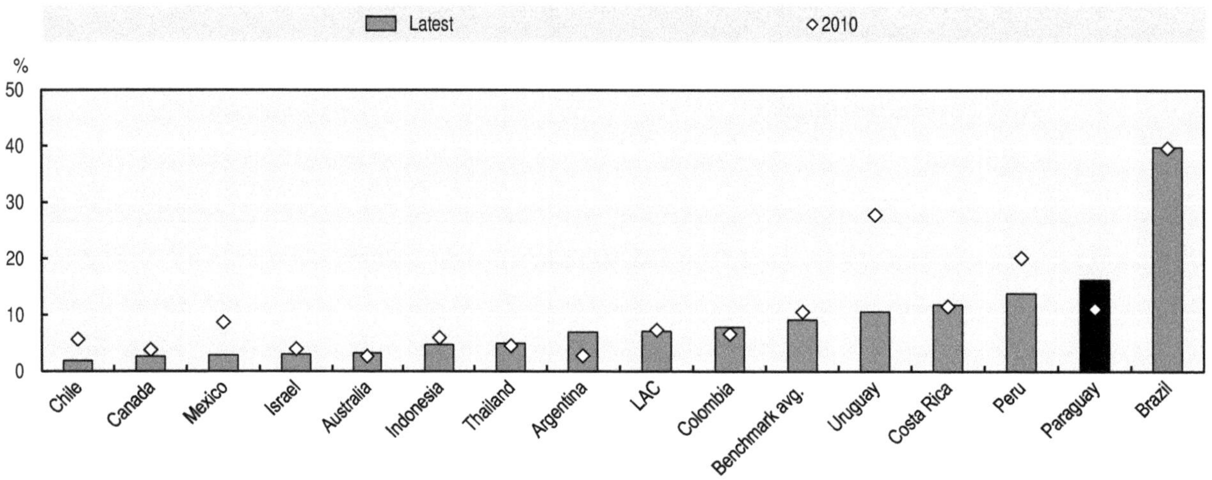

Note: Benchmark average does not include Portugal and Poland.

Source: World Bank, World Development Indicators database.

StatLink http://dx.doi.org/10.1787/888933750871

Figure 6.14. **Credit quality has been deteriorating in certain sectors and attention should be in monitoring non-performing loans**

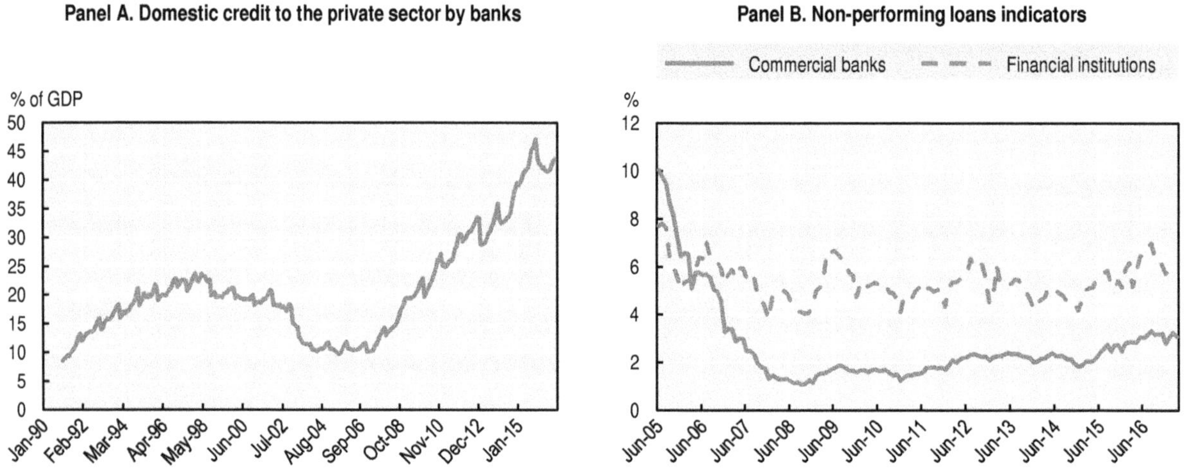

Source: Central Bank of Paraguay (BCP).

StatLink http://dx.doi.org/10.1787/888933750890

Credit quality has been deteriorating in certain sectors and attention should be concentrated on monitoring non-performing loans. The ratio of non-performing loans to total gross loans of commercial banks increased in recent years from around 1.2% at the end of 2010, to around 2.8% by the end of 2016 (BCP, 2017), a little higher than the Latin America average but lower than in countries such as Brazil or Peru. This increase in non-performing loans is observed as well in financial institutions (5.7% by end of 2016) and savings and credit co-operatives (10.1% by June 2016) (Figure 6.14, Panel B). Another indicator of credit quality deterioration is the increase in renewed, refinanced, restructured (RRR) loans as a proportion of total loans from 14.4% in June 2015 to 18.6% in June 2016, reflecting a weaker economic context as well as a decline in the international price of commodities and exports that affected the repayment capacity of producers. Authorities responded with transitional measures to support the agricultural sector through the renegotiation of credits (BCP, 2016).

The provision of long-term financing in Paraguay is hampered by a shortage of long-term deposits. The largest share of deposits (50%) is kept in cheque accounts, 16% in on-demand deposits, 0.3% in term savings and 34% in certificates of savings deposits. Likewise, the survey on the credit situation carried out by the Central Bank shows that one of the main reasons that make it difficult to grant long-term loans is the scarcity of long-term deposits (45%), followed by the lack of guarantees (21%), other activities with higher profitability, and shortage of long-term projects (BCP, 2017a). This phenomenon has been partially tackled through the role of public financial institutions, like AFD, that provide today credit lines for long-term financing, mainly for housing and SMEs.

Dollarization of the economy has decreased in the last decades but the level of dollarization is still high and has recently increased. In all 47.6% of credits are denominated in dollars and 48% of deposits. The agricultural sector tends to take credit in dollars (86.1% of total credits) as well as the exports sector (74.2% of total credits). On the other hand, families tend to take credits in guaranís (95.1% of total credits) for consumption. Credit granted in dollars to agents that do not generate foreign exchange amounted to 12% of the portfolio of banks and financial institutions in dollars by June 2016 (BCP, 2016).

In spite of the rapid growth in credit, financial inclusion is still very low and unequal in the country. Comparable data from 2011 show that the percentage of adults with an account at a financial institution in Paraguay is around 22%, much lower than in other Latin American and benchmark countries (Figure 6.15). Financial access in the country is unequal given that rural areas, lower-income households and small and medium-sized enterprises still do not have access to loans or other financial services. For instance, only 5.2% of the poorest 40% adults have an account in a financial institution compared to 33% for the richest 60%. Results from the 2013 Financial Inclusion Survey showed that five out of every ten adults in Paraguay are financially excluded (Gobierno Nacional, 2014) and only 29% adults have an account in a formal financial institution (the LAC average was 39% in 2011). Co-operatives play a key role in providing formal banking services as they had approximately 58% of all formal accounts in the country (EIF, 2014). Likewise, 19% of adults have an account in a co-operative, 12% in a bank and 2% in other institutions. In terms of coverage, 33%, or 73, of the country's 224 districts did not have any presence of banks through branches, bank agents or automated teller machines (ATMs) (BIRF/Banco Mundial, 2014). Surprisingly, few adults give as a primary reason why they do not have a bank account that financial institutions are too far away. Interestingly, 28% of adults used mobile money services and 10% say they will use it within six months (EIF, 2014). Over the past three years, access to information technologies, such as the *terminales de punto de venta* (points of sale –POS), is contributing to reduce the financing gap in rural areas.

Figure 6.15. **Despite the rapid growth in credit, financial inclusion is still very low and unequal in the country**

Account at a financial institution (% age 15+)

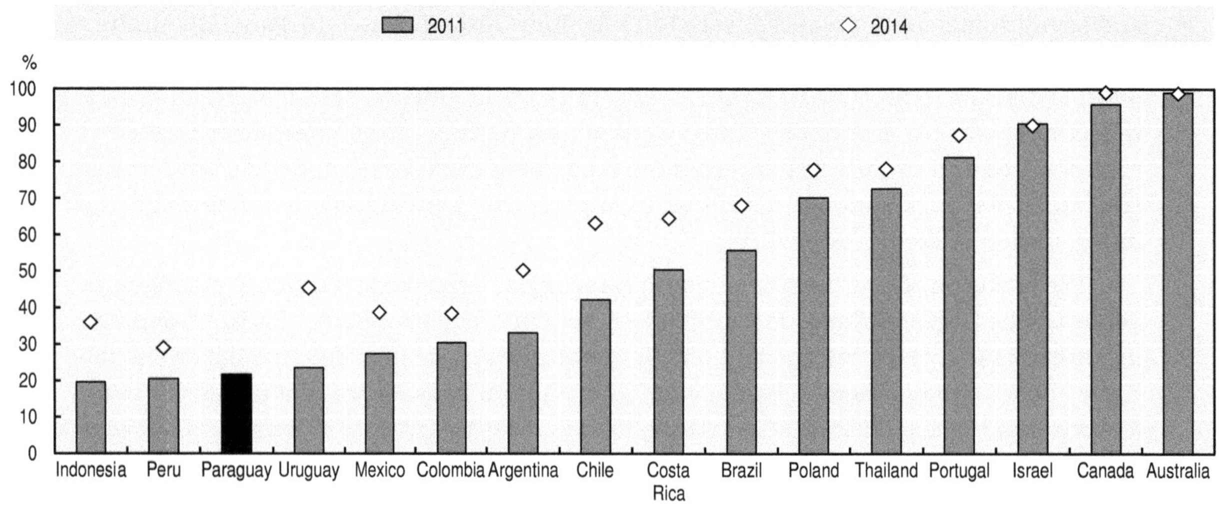

Source: World Bank, World Development Indicators Database.

StatLink http://dx.doi.org/10.1787/888933750909

Access to formal credit is still limited. In all, 34% of adults claim to have applied for a loan in the last year; 22% through a formal financial institution (13% at a co-operative and 8% at a commercial bank). Only 7% of adults reported having borrowed money to start a business. Among those who own a business, only 18% borrowed from a co-operative, 9% from banks, and 5% from a credit house. Likewise, loans to micro and small enterprises are still insufficient. Only 27% of all micro and small enterprises (formal and informal) took out loans and only 16% of agricultural microenterprises (formal and informal) borrowed. Products available in the market are not necessarily designed to meet the needs of these firms while furthermore micro-enterprises tend to be informal and often lack the necessary documentation. Co-operatives offer loans to 70% of urban microenterprises taking loans and 27% of agricultural microenterprises (EIF, 2014).

Lowering the costs and documentation requirements for opening accounts and obtaining loans while ensuring a correct risk assessment would significantly contribute to facilitating financial access. The lack of money and of the documentation required seem to be the main barriers to financial inclusion in Paraguay; 51% of individuals without bank accounts reported the lack of money as the main reason for not having an account, followed by lack of documentation (24% of individuals). Lack of documentation is an important constraint for those who are unemployed or informal, affecting informal small and medium enterprises in the same way.

Government efforts to boost financial access continue but much more needs to be done. The government launched a Financial Inclusion National Strategy in 2014 aiming to achieve the financial inclusion of 100% of households by 2030 (Gobierno Nacional, 2014). A survey of financial capacity is being implemented to underlie this strategy. In this context, several regulatory changes have been introduced, such as a new regulation on electronic payments as well as basic savings accounts and usage of accounts for wage payments. In addition, the Ministry of Industry and Commerce, together with the Industrial Paraguayan Union and Itaipú Binational, signed in 2015 an agreement to support microenterprises by providing financial resources (USD 200 000 to be provided as seed capital) and technical guidance for young entrepreneurs (Itaipú, 2015). Likewise, the World Bank's International Finance Corporation (IFC) will provide a USD 90 million loan to Banco Itaú Paraguay SA to expand SME access to finance. In terms of financial literacy, the government launched a campaign "*Más vale saber. Educación de Bolsillo*" ("Better to know: education in the pocket!") with the objective of providing information to the public about the proper use of financial tools as well as the rights and obligations of the financial sector. This campaign is much in line with the OECD *Good Practices on Financial Education and Awareness Relating to Credit* which represents a useful guide for governments seeking to develop financial education and awareness of credit programmes. Within the education system, the subject of "economic and financial education" has been introduced in the last year of high school. Reference material for this subject has been created and 190 000 teachers have been trained in using it. A "guide for the financial education of young people and adults" has been created, and is used by agencies for training. The guide focuses specifically on vulnerable populations. Further measures to enable individuals to know where to look for information, take informed decisions, develop skills of financial planning, etc. would enhance social and economic growth when complemented by prudential regulation and consumer protection (OECD, 2005).

The role of development banks should be strengthened

Strengthening the role of public financial institutions is crucial to boosting access to formal credit, mainly for SMEs and small agricultural producers, as Paraguay lags behind other countries in the region. For this purpose, public institutions must develop new financial products specifically designed for those that cannot access credit from private institutions. There are a few public financial institutions in Paraguay specialised in different segments: *Agencia Financiera de Desarrollo* (AFD), *Banco Nacional de Fomento* (BNF), *Crédito Agrícola de Habilitación, Fondo Ganadero* and *Secretaría Nacional de la Vivienda y el Hábitat*.

The *Agencia Financiera de Desarollo* (AFD) founded in 2005 is the only "second tier, or second floor" public bank (this is, one that, instead of lending directly to firms, grants credit indirectly through another bank) that provides credit to complement the funding structure of first floor entities to enable the execution of medium and long-term development programmes, with funds coming from loans with a state guarantee, donations, budget allocations, bonds issuance and its own capital (Law 2640, 2005). AFD is the only channel through which public sector loans are made to intermediary financial institutions. Some of the products provided by AFD are focused on housing, micro, small and medium enterprises, education, livestock, agriculture and infrastructure equipment, etc. AFD has met and exceeded its annual goals in terms of approved credits, increasing the amount from USD 86 million in 2015 to USD 244 million by 2016. The share of credits with terms of three or more years increased as well, from 23% in 2010 to 43% by 2016. Most of the credit provided is channelled to the housing sector (about 31%) followed by services (20%), SMEs (17%), agriculture and livestock sector (12%) (AFD, 2015). Despite these improvements, its contribution to financing SMEs has been small. Funds provided through MICREDITO and PROPYME programmes reached 1.7% and 5.4% of funds approved by June 2014 (BIRF/Banco Mundial, 2014).

The role of *Banco Nacional de Fomento* (BNF) to facilitate financial inclusion should be strengthened. The main function of BNF is the financial inclusion of those that cannot access funding sources through other institutions as well as promoting and financing projects to promote agriculture, livestock, forestry, industry and commerce. The BNF was created in 1961, experiencing several losses in the past because of inefficient management practices.

However, organic and functional restructuring started in 2003, enabling its gradual recovery. It is a medium-sized institution in the market with around 5% of the financial market assets. It has more than 50 branches and offers a range of savings and credit products; it also processes the payment of salaries to public employees as well as benefits to beneficiaries of social programmes. In this sense and to facilitate financial inclusion, BNF should take advantage of the extensive presence of its geographical network, the large number of branches and ATMs and its extension to rural areas (MH/BID, 2010). On the other hand, the BNF is still less efficient than private banks; it maintains an excessively high liquidity ratio (76% while private banks' average ratio is 47%); and its personnel and administrative costs are high (3.4% of personnel expenses versus deposits compared to 2.2% in private sector banks; administrative costs are 6.3% of deposits in the BNF compared to 4.9% in private sector banks) (BIRF/Banco Mundial, 2014). The recent reform to the Charter of the National Development Bank is intended to tackle previous inefficiencies, improve corporate governance and give the bank a more prominent role in providing financial support.

Development banks in Paraguay, mainly AFD and BNF, have been increasing their role in providing credit. However, relative to other countries in the region, their loan portfolio is still low (Figure 6.16). To strengthen their lending capacity and coverage, development banks should address several challenges. Innovative financial products specifically designed for different segments of the market should be developed while a minimum profitability should be guaranteed. Transparency and good practices of corporate governance would also prove important to ensure efficient management of financial resources. A strong and clear regulation that allows banks to finance subnational and municipal projects is also required. All of this should be accompanied by measures that incentivise financial intermediaries to reach targeted sectors (ALIDE, 2015) and by appropriate regulations that allow smaller cooperatives and financial institutions to operate with AFD funds and allow for greater channelling of financial resources (BIRF/Banco Mundial, 2014). Expanding the use of information technologies to speed up the process for granting loans through the two development banks could also be improved.

Figure 6.16. **Development banks in Paraguay have been increasing their role in providing credit but their loan portfolio is still low**

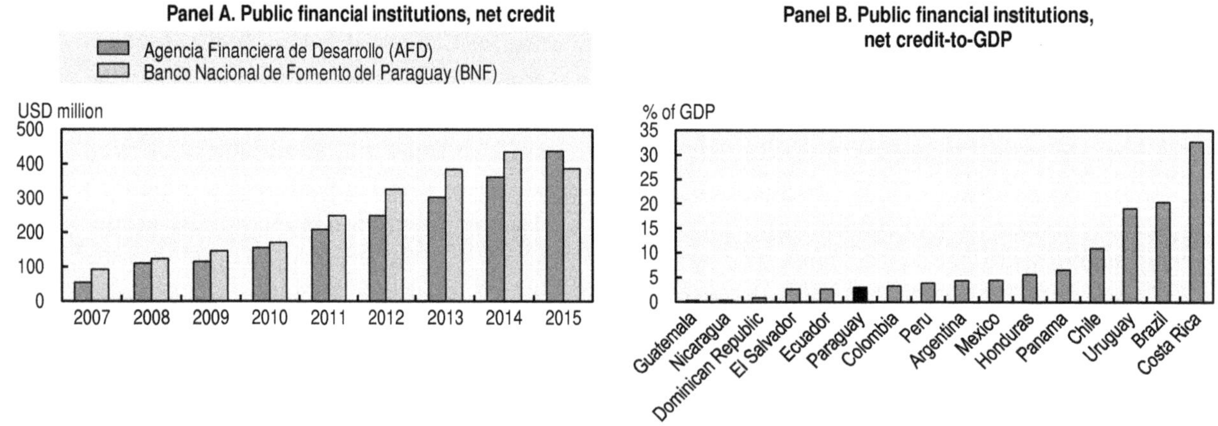

Note: Panel B is based on institutions under public ownership regime.

Source: Panel A: Asociación Latinoamericana de Instituciones Financieras para el Desarrollo (ALIDE). Panel B: Author's calculations with data from ALIDE and World Bank, World Development Indicators.

StatLink http://dx.doi.org/10.1787/888933750928

Note

1. Payroll and interest payments are considered non-discretionary in this chapter (see Box 6.1).

References

AFD (2015), Resultados y Desafíos de la Banca de Segundo Piso en Paraguay, Presentation for the International Seminar "Banca de Segundo Piso y su Contribución al Desarrollo", *https://www.afd.gov.py/userfiles/file/TEMA%205%20AFD%20JOSE%20MACIEL%20.pdf.*

ALIDE (2015), Banca de Desarrollo, estrategias, sostenibilidad y relación con políticas públicas, Presentation for the Seminar "Banca de Segundo Piso y su Contribución al Desarrollo", *https://www.afd.gov.py/userfiles/file/TEMA%202%20Romy%20CALDERON%20AFD%20paraguay%20agosto%202015%20pptx.pdf.*

Barreix, A., J. Benítez and M. Pecho (2017), "Revisiting personal income tax in Latin America: Evolution and impact", *OECD Development Centre Working Papers*, No. 338, OECD Publishing, Paris, *http://dx.doi.org/10.1787/16d42b4a-en.*

BCP (2017a), Encuesta sobre la Situación General del Crédito al Primer trimestre del 2017, Banco Central de Paraguay, *https://www.bcp.gov.py/encuesta-sobre-la-situacion-general-del-credito-al-primer-trimestre-del-2017-n795.*

BCP (2017b) "Estadísticas de Inversión Extranjera Directa en Paraguay"[*Foreign Direct Investment statistics for Paraguay*], Banco Central de Paraguay, *https://www.bcp.gov.py/userfiles/files/Anexo_IED_4_Trim_2016%281%29.xls.*

BCP (2016), Informe de Estabilidad Financiera, Banco Central de Paraguay.

BIRF/Banco Mundial (2014), Evaluación del lado de la oferta de la inclusión financiera en Paraguay, Banco Internacional de Reconstrucción y Fomento / Banco Mundial, Washington, D.C.

CIAT-SET-GIZ (2015), Estimación de los Gastos Tributarios en la República del Paraguay 2013 – 2016.

DGEEC (2016), *Encuesta Continua de Empleo*, Secretaría Técnica de Planificación, Dirección General de Estadísticas, Encuestas y Censos, Asunción.

ECLAC (2016a), *Economic Survey of Latin America and the Caribbean 2016: The 2030 Agenda for Sustainable Development and the challenges of financing for development*, Economic Commission for Latin America and the Caribbean, Santiago, Chile.

ECLAC (2016b), Foreign Direct Investment in Latin America and the Caribbean. Economic Commission for Latin America and the Caribbean Santiago. *http://www.cepal.org/en/publications/type/foreign-direct-investment-latin-america-and-caribbean.*

EIF (2014), Encuesta sobre Inclusión Financiera. Resultados finales., Ministerio de Hacienda de Paraguay, Asunción. *http://www.hacienda.gov.py/web-hacienda/archivo.php?a=8e8e9197a29ba19ca05c9d9f929ba08e5c9d9193a05c5f5d5e615ca49c9f98969b944d949f9ca29d4d5d635d615e615b9d91938e02d.*

FDI Markets Database (2017), Cross-border investment monitor. *https://www.fdimarkets.com/.*

Giménez, L. et al. (2017). *Paraguay: Análisis del Sistema Fiscal y su Impacto en la Pobreza y la Equidad.* Ministerio de Hacienda de Paraguay, Secretaría Técnica de Planificación del Desarrollo Económico y Social, Gobierno Nacional, CEQ Institute Tulane University, Banco Mundial.

Gobierno Nacional (2014), Plan Nacional de Desarrollo Paraguay 2030, Gobierno Nacional de Paraguay, Asunción. *http://www.stp.gov.py/pnd/wp-content/uploads/2014/12/pnd2030.pdf.*

IMF (International Monetary Fund) (2017a), *Government Financial Statistics* (database), (accessed 6 February 2017).

IMF (2017b), *World Economic Outlook*, (database), April 2017 edition, IMF, Washington, DC.

IMF (2017c), "Paraguay, 2017 Article IV Consultation", *IMF Country Report*, No. 17/233, International Monetary Fund, Washington, DC.

IMF (2016a), *World Economic Outlook* (database), October 2016 edition, IMF, Washington, DC.

IMF (2016b), "Paraguay, 2016 Article IV Consultation", *IMF Country Report*, No. 16/11, International Monetary Fund, Washington, DC.

Itaipú (2015), Itaipú apoya a las MIPYMES, Itaipú Binacional., *https://www.itaipu.gov.py/es/sala-de-prensa/noticia/itaipu-apoya-las-mipymes.*

Law 2640, 2. (2005), Ley No. 2640 "Que crea la Agencia Financiera de Desarrollo", República de Paraguay, *https://www.afd.gov.py/userfiles/file/Ley%20N%202640%20Que%20Crea%20la%20Agencia%20Financiera%20de%20Desarrollo(1).pdf.*

Law 5061, (2013), Ley 5061/13, "Que modifica disposiciones de la Ley N° 125/91 y dispone otras medidas de carácter tributario", República de Paraguay.

MH (2016), Offering Memorandum for Paraguay, March 2016. Ministerio de Hacienda de Paraguay, Asunción, *http://www.hacienda.gov.py/bonos/archivos_bonos/documentos/2-%20Final_Offering_Memorandum_%202016.pdf.*

MH/BID (2010), Paraguay: Banca Pública de Desarollo, Ministerio de Hacienda, Seminario de Promoción, Ministerio de Hacienda / Banco Interamericano de Desarrollo *http://www.hacienda.gov.py/web-hacienda/pub009.pdf.*

OECD (2016b), *Revenue Statistics 2016*, OECD Publishing. DOI: *http://dx.doi.org/10.1787/10.1787/rev_stats-2016-en-fr.*

OECD (2010), "Policy Framework for Effective and Efficient Financial Regulation", OECD Publishing. *https://www.oecd.org/finance/financial-markets/44362818.pdf.*

OECD (2005), Recommendation on Principles and Good Practices for Financial Education and Awareness., Recommendation of the Council. OECD Publishing, *http://www.oecd.org/finance/financial-education/35108560.pdf.*

OECD/ECLAC/CAF (2018), *Latin American Economic Outlook 2018: Rethinking Institutions for Development*, OECD Publishing, *http://dx.doi.org/10.1787/leo-2018-en.*

OECD/ECLAC/CAF (2016), *Latin American Economic Outlook 2017: Youth, Skills and Entrepreneurship*, OECD Publishing, Paris. *http://dx.doi.org/10.1787/leo-2017-en.*

OECD/ECLAC/CIAT/IDB (2017), *Revenue Statistics in Latin America and the Caribbean 2017*, OECD Publishing, Paris, *http://dx.doi.org/10.1787/rev_lat_car-2017-en-fr*

OECD/IDB/CIAT (2016), *Taxing Wages in Latin America and the Caribbean*, OECD Publishing, Paris, *http://dx.doi.org/10.1787/9789264262607-en.*

OECD/IDB/The World Bank (2014), *Pensions at a Glance: Latin America and the Caribbean*, OECD Publishing, Paris, *http://dx.doi.org/10.1787/pension--_glance-2014-en.*

OFIF/CADEP (2017), Monitoreo Fiscal de las Cuentas Públicas. Centro de Análisis y Difusión de la Economía Paraguaya, CADEP Piribebuy 1058, Asunción - Paraguay.

SET (2016), Resolución General No. 63 sobre emisión virtual de comprobantes. Subsecretaría de Estado de Tributación. Ministerio de Hacienda. Asunción.

United Nations (2015), *Addis Ababa Action Agenda of the Third International Conference on Financing for Development*, General Assembly resolution 69/313 of 27 July 2015, United Nations, New York.

United Nations (2014), Second United Nations Conference on Landlocked Developing Countries. Vienna Programme of Action for Landlocked Developing Countries for the Decade 2014-2024.

World Bank (2017), *World Development Indicators* (database), Washington, DC, *http://data.worldbank.org* (accessed 1 April 2017).

World Bank (2016a), *Global Financial Development Database (GFDD)*, World Bank, Washington, DC, *www.worldbank.org/en/publication/gfdr/data/global-financial-development-database.*

World Bank (2016b), *Doing Business 2017: Equal Opportunity for All*, World Bank, Washington, DC, *www.doingbusiness.org/~/media/WBG/DoingBusiness/Documents/Annual-Reports/English/DB17-Report.pdf.*

World Bank (2016c), *Migration and Remittances Factbook 2016, Third Edition*, World Bank,Washington, DC, *https://openknowledge.worldbank.org/bitstream/handle/10986/23743/9781464803192.pdf?sequence=3&isAllowed=y.*

World Bank (2015), *Global Financial Development Report 2015/2016: Long-Term Finance*, World Bank, Washington, DC, doi:10.1596/978-1-4648-0472-4.

World Bank (2013), "Financing for development post 2015", World Bank, Washington, DC, *http://documents.worldbank.org/curated/en/206701468158366611/Financing-for-development-post-2015.*

ORGANISATION FOR ECONOMIC CO-OPERATION AND DEVELOPMENT

The OECD is a unique forum where governments work together to address the economic, social and environmental challenges of globalisation. The OECD is also at the forefront of efforts to understand and to help governments respond to new developments and concerns, such as corporate governance, the information economy and the challenges of an ageing population. The Organisation provides a setting where governments can compare policy experiences, seek answers to common problems, identify good practice and work to co-ordinate domestic and international policies.

The OECD member countries are: Australia, Austria, Belgium, Canada, Chile, the Czech Republic, Denmark, Estonia, Finland, France, Germany, Greece, Hungary, Iceland, Ireland, Israel, Italy, Japan, Korea, Latvia, Luxembourg, Mexico, the Netherlands, New Zealand, Norway, Poland, Portugal, the Slovak Republic, Slovenia, Spain, Sweden, Switzerland, Turkey, the United Kingdom and the United States. The European Union takes part in the work of the OECD.

OECD Publishing disseminates widely the results of the Organisation's statistics gathering and research on economic, social and environmental issues, as well as the conventions, guidelines and standards agreed by its members.

OECD DEVELOPMENT CENTRE

The OECD Development Centre was established in 1962 as an independent platform for knowledge sharing and policy dialogue between OECD member countries and developing economies, allowing these countries to interact on an equal footing. Today, 27 OECD countries and 25 non-OECD countries are members of the Centre. The Centre draws attention to emerging systemic issues likely to have an impact on global development and more specific development challenges faced by today's developing and emerging economies. It uses evidence-based analysis and strategic partnerships to help countries formulate innovative policy solutions to the global challenges of development.

For more information on the Centre and its members, please see *www.oecd.org/dev*.

OECD PUBLISHING, 2, rue André-Pascal, 75775 PARIS CEDEX 16
(41 2018 20 1 P1) ISBN 978-92-64-30189-4 – 2018

www.ingramcontent.com/pod-product-compliance
Ingram Content Group UK Ltd.
Pitfield, Milton Keynes, MK11 3LW, UK
UKHW051500290926
15471UKWH00008B/1328

9 789264 301894